D1250830

SHORT STORY INDEX

Supplement 1955-1958

SHORT STORY INDEX

Supplement 1955-1958

AN INDEX TO 6,392 STORIES IN 376 COLLECTIONS

Compiled by

ESTELLE A. FIDELL
ESTHER V. FLORY

NEW YORK
THE H. W. WILSON COMPANY
1960

Published 1960
Printed in the U.S.A.

Library of Congress Card No. (53-8991)

Contents

Directions for Use

Part 1 of this Index is in dictionary form with author, title, and subject entries in one alphabet. Part 2 is a list of the collections indexed. Part 3 is a directory of publishers. The following directions apply to Part 1.

Author Entry. This entry gives the full name of the author, years of birth and death, whenever ascertainable, title of the story, author and title of the collection or collections in which the story is found. It may be recognized by the boldface type, *not* in capital letters.

Sample entry:

> **Bowen, Elizabeth,** 1899-
> Queer heart
> McClennen, J. comp. Masters and mas-
> terpieces of the short story

This means that the short story by Elizabeth Bowen, "Queer heart" appears in the collection entitled "Masters and masterpieces of the short story" compiled by J. McClennen. For fuller information about "Masters and masterpieces of the short story" consult the "List of Collections Indexed" under McClennen, Joshua.

Title Entry. This entry is used primarily to identify the author under whose name the full information will be given. Only the first word of each title entry is in boldface type.

Sample entry:

> **Queer** heart. Bowen, E.

Subject Entry. All stories in this Index dealing in whole or in part with a particular subject are listed under that subject. Such entries are in capital letters, in boldface type.

Sample entry:

> **SISTERS**
> Bowen, E. Queer heart

In some collections all the stories may deal with the same subject. In such cases the entry under that subject indicates the editor or author and title of the collection, followed by the number of stories. (The individual stories are also listed under that subject).

Sample entry:

> **BRAZIL**
> Reid, L. My Lady Happiness, and other
> short stories; 12 stories

The phrase "12 stories" identifies this type of entry.

SHORT STORY INDEX

Supplement 1955-1958

PART I

Author, title, subject index to short stories

A1 at Lord's. Johnston, R. T.

A. V. Laider. Beerbohm, Sir M.

ABANDONED CHILDREN. See Foundlings; Orphans

ABANDONED SHIPS. See Ships, Abandoned

ABDICATION OF KINGS. See Kings and rulers

ABDUCTION. See Disappearances; Kidnapping

Abdul Hadi's rifle. Smilansky, M.

Abdullah, Achmed, 1881-1945
Ambassador of poker
Lewis, J. D. ed. Dealer's choice

Abdullah, Mena Kashmiri
Grandfather tiger
Stivens, D. comp. Coast to coast

Abel Sanchez. Unamuno y Jugo, M. de

Abernathy, Robert, 1924-
Axolotl
Best science-fiction stories and novels: 1955
Grandma's lie soap
Merril, J. ed. SF: '57
Heirs apparent
Best science-fiction stories and novels: 1955
Magazine of fantasy and science fiction. Best from Fantasy and science fiction; 4th ser.
Junior
Merril, J. ed. S-F: ['56]
Peril of the blue world
Gallant, J. ed. Stories of scientific imagination

Abide with me. Van Doren, M.

ABILENE. See Kansas—Abilene

Able Baker. Whitehill, J.

ABNORMAL CHILDREN. See Children, Abnormal and backward

ABOLITION OF SLAVERY. See Slavery

Abortive mission. Bahr, J.

About, Edmond François Valentin, 1828-1885
Strange will
Costain, T. B. and Beecroft, J. eds. Stories to remember

About Geneva. Gallant, M.

Above the bright blue sky. Andrade, M.

Abramowitz, Shalom Jacob, 1836-1917
A nap, prayers, and strawberries
Schwarz, L. W. ed. Feast of Leviathan

Absalom, my son. Warner, S. T.

ABSENT-MINDEDNESS
Marchi, E. de. Missing letters
Thurber, J. Secret life of Walter Mitty

ABSOLUTION. See Forgiveness

Academic style. Macauley, R.

The **academicians.** Whitehill, J.

Accessory. Sandoz, M. Y.

Accident. Farrell, J. T.

The **accident.** Leafley, R.

Accident at the Inn. Coates, R. M.

ACCIDENT INSURANCE. See Insurance, Accident

ACCIDENTAL SHOOTING. See Hunting—Accidents

ACCIDENTS
Angell, R. In an early winter
Angoff, C. Curly
Bates, H. E. Summer in Salandar
Boyle, K. Maiden, maiden
Dee, B. The revolt of machines
Greene, G. Basement room
Hopkinson, H. T. Mountain madness
Lefley, R. The accident
Lowry, R. J. C. The bridge
Major, R. H. Climbing against death
Maupassant, G. de. Costly outing
Miller, E. M. Christmas present
Warner, S. T. Under new management
Wilson, A. Sad fall
See also Aeronautics—Accidents; Automobiles—Accidents; Drowning; Hunting—Accidents; etc.

ACCIDENTS, MINE. See Mine accidents

ACCOMPLICES
Pincherle, A. The caretaker

According to the law and the evidence. Polk, W. T.

The **accountant.** Sheckley, R.

ACCOUNTANTS
Curley, D. William Sanders and the dream of the future
Gallico, P. W. Lost hour
Lessing, D. M. The witness
Maupassant, G. de. Little walk
O'Hara, J. Public career of Mr Seymour Harrisburg
Pritchett, V. S. Chestnut tree
Sheckley, R. The accountant

Accursed bread. Maupassant, G. de

The **accursed** huntsman. Garrett, G.

AFRICAN TRIBES. See Africa—Native races; also names of individual tribes

After. Maupassant, G. de

After all I did for Israel. Levin, M.

After all these years. Gilbert, M. F.

After cornhusking. Ward, L. L.

After death. Maupassant, G. de

After Holbein. Wharton, E. N. J.

AFTER LIFE. See Future life

After the battle. Babel', I. E.

After the fair. Thomas, D.

After the show. Wilson, A.

After the storm. Hemingway, E.

After the sun has risen. Farrell, J. T.

After twenty years. Porter, W. S.

Afternoon of a faun. Ferber, E.

Afternoon of an author. Fitzgerald, F. S. K.

An **afternoon** with the appliances. Gold, H.

Agamemnon's career. Hale, L. P.

AGE. See Middle age; Old age

Age of miracles. Post, W. D.

Age of prophecy. St Clair, M.

Age of reason. Shaw, I.

AGED. See Old age

Agee, James, 1909-
The waiting
   Best American short stories, 1958

Agent of Vega. Schmitz, J. H.

AGENTS, LITERARY. See Literary agents

AGENTS, THEATRICAL
Babel', I. E. Di Grasso
Kober, A. Don't let no cracked-pot lay his fishhooks on your chronium
Kober, A. Even the averitch incomepoop's got a little egg nest put away
Kober, A. Good-bye to palship
Kober, A. A highly remockable chimpaneze with a head chuck-fulla grain matter
Kober, A. I wouldn't be your partner if you came beggin' me on your two bent knees
Kober, A. I'm not gonna cowtail to that bubble-headed bastid, if it's the last thing I do!
Kober, A. A red-faced chief who's just come offa the Indian reservoir

Agnon, Samuel Joseph, 1888-
In a Jerusalem cafe
   Frank, M. Z. ed. Sound the great trumpet
The minyan
   Frank, M. Z. ed. Sound the great trumpet
Story of tthe kerchief of my mother
   Kobler, F. ed. Her children call her blessed
Tehilla
   Tehilla, and other Israeli tales

Agostino. Pincherle, A.

Agree—or die. King, R.

An **agreement.** Harss, L.

AGRICULTURE. See Farm life

Ah love! Ah me! Steele, M.

Ah, the university. Collier, J.

Ahimaaz Ben Paltiel, 1017-1060?
Emperor Basil and Rabbi Shephatiah
   Schwarz, L. W. ed. Feast of Leviathan

Ahmed, Ali. See Ali, Ahmed

Aichinger, Ilse, 1921-
The advertisement
   Aichinger, I. Bound man, and other stories
Angel in the night
   Aichinger, I. Bound man, and other stories
Bound man
   Aichinger, I. Bound man, and other stories
Ghosts on the lake
   Aichinger, I. Bound man, and other stories
Moon story
   Aichinger, I. Bound man, and other stories
Opened order
   Aichinger, I. Bound man, and other stories
Private tutor
   Aichinger, I. Bound man, and other stories
Speech under the gallows
   Aichinger, I. Bound man, and other stories
Story in a mirror
   Aichinger, I. Bound man, and other stories
Window entertainment
   Aichinger, I. Bound man, and other stories

Aiken, Conrad Potter, 1889-
Silent snow, secret snow
   Thurston, J. A. ed. Reading modern short stories
Your obituary, well written
   Baudin, M. ed. Contemporary short stories v 1

AIR BASES, MILITARY
Frank, P. Christmas bogey
Lowry, R. J. C. Blaze beyond the town

AIR LINES
Miller, E. M. Mister Wister wins a war

Hostesses
Cory, E. Hero's children

AIR PILOTS
Asimov, I. Ideas die hard
Bahr, J. Abortive mission
Bahr, J. "Raidin' Maiden"
Bates, H. E. Sergeant Carmichael
Bell, J. N. I'm coming in
Blanton, L. D. Long night
Bradbury, R. Icarus Montgolfier Wright
Byrd, J. J. Cool one
Byrd, J. J. Copilot in doubt
Connell, E. S. Yellow raft
Elam, R. M. First man into space
Ellison, R. Flying home
Harris, J. B. Dumb Martian
Harvey, F. L. Flame-out
Harvey, F. L. Frightened pilot
Harvey, F. L. Murder in the sky
Harvey, F. L. Runaway bomber
Harvey, F. L. Stand by to bail out!

Alex, Frank, 1926-
Rats
American vanguard, 1956
ALEXANDER, THE GREAT, B.C. 356-
323
Blassingame, W. Horse that crossed the
world
Alexander, David
Coffee and—
Mystery Writers of America, inc. Crime
for two
Man who went to Taltavul's
Mystery Writers of America, inc. Big
time mysteries
Queen, E. pseud. ed. Ellery Queen's
awards: 11th ser.
Scarecrow
Mystery Writers of America, inc. For
tomorrow we die
Alexander, Sidney, 1912-
White boat
Hall, J. B. and Langland, J. T. eds.
Short story
Alexander. Maupassant, G. de
Alford, Howard
The shorn lamb
Orr, E. and Hammett, E. A. eds.
Delta Decameron
ALGERIA
Camus, A. The stranger
Maupassant, G. de. Allouma
Algren, Nelson, 1909-
Beasts of the wild
Best American short stories, 1957
So help me
Ribalow, H. U. ed. Treasury of Ameri-
can Jewish stories
ALHAMBRA
Irving, W. Legend of the Arabian astrol-
oger
Ali, Ahmed, 1908-
Before death
New Directions 15
Ali the Terrible Turk. Kersh, G.
Alibi Ike. Lardner, R. W.
Alicia. Sansom, W.
Alicky's watch. Urquhart, F.
Alien corn. Maugham, W. S.
Alkaline dust ain't snow. Adams, A.
All American. Lowry, R. J. C.
All for a pinch of snuff. Peretz, I. L.
All Gold Canyon. London, J.
All over. Maupassant, G. de
All summer in a day. Bradbury, R.
All that is necessary. Lofts, N. R.
All the brothers were bad. Drago, H. S.
All the dead pilots. Faulkner, W.
All the petals of all the roses in the world.
Clayton, J. B.
"All the sweet buttermilk. . ." MacDonagh,
D.
All the time in the world. Clarke, A. C.
All the way home. Armstrong, C.
All the world's tears. Aldiss, B. W.
All the young men. La Farge, O.
All through the night. Evans, M.

Allan, Glenn, 1901-
Boysi
Langford, W. F. ed. Book of better
stories
ALLEGORIES
Campbell, W. E. M. First sunset
Ferber, E. No room at the Inn
Franko, I. I. Tale about prosperity
Gide, A. P. G. Theseus
Kafka, F. Hunger artist
Lawrence, D. H. Man who loved islands
Peretz, I. L. The pious cat
Reid, L. Miss Glory
Simak, C. D. The answers
Tamási, A. Flashes in the night
Tamási, A. Old man December
Tolstoĭ, L. N. Graf. Skazka
Wilde, O. Happy Prince
Allen, E. Lee, 1926-
Red ink dilemma
Oberfirst, R. ed. 1955 anthology of best
original short-shorts
Allen, Hervey, 1889-1949
Boy turns turtle
Humphreville, F. T. ed. In other days
Allen, Merritt Parmelee, 1892-1954
Message for General Washington
Fenner, P. R. ed. Heroes, heroes, heroes
The Mudhen, V. S.
Furman, A. L. ed. Teen-age humorous
stories
Sound effects
Furman, A. L. ed. Teen-age humorous
stories
Allen, Steve, 1921-
The award
Allen, S. Girls on the 10th floor, and
other stories
The Blood of the Lamb
Allen, S. Girls on the 10th floor, and
other stories
The cats
Allen, S. Fourteen for tonight
Dialogue
Allen, S. Girls on the 10th floor, and
other stories
Gadarene swine
Allen, S. Fourteen for tonight
Girls on the tenth floor
Allen, S. Girls on the 10th floor, and
other stories
Hello again, darling
Allen, S. Girls on the 10th floor, and
other stories
House in Bel Air
Allen, S. Girls on the 10th floor, and
other stories
Houston incident
Allen, S. Fourteen for tonight
"I hope I'm not intruding"
Allen, S. Fourteen for tonight
If people would only think
Allen, S. Girls on the 10th floor, and
other stories
The interview
Allen, S. Fourteen for tonight
Joe Shulman is dead
Allen, S. Girls on the 10th floor, and
other stories
The judgment
Allen, S. Fourteen for tonight

AMBITION
Anderson, S. The egg
Campbell, W. E. M. Shop in St Louis, Missouri
Ellin, S. Best of everything
Gellhorn, M. E. For richer for poorer
O'Flaherty, L. Two lovely beasts
Pérez de Ayala, R. Prometheus

Ambler, Eric, 1909-
Journey into fear
    Haycraft, H. and Beecroft, J. eds. Treasury of great mysteries

Ambulance dogs. Colette, S. G.

Ambuscade. Faulkner, W.

Amelia. Seidenberg, E. S.

AMERICAN INDIANS. See Indians of North America; Indians of South America; also names of individual Indian tribes, e.g., Cheyenne Indians; Dakota Indians; etc.

AMERICAN SOLDIERS. See Soldiers, American

Americanisation of Shadrach Cohen. Block, R. E.

AMERICANS ABROAD
Shaw, I. Then we were three
    See also Americans in Africa; Americans in Asia; Americans in Europe; etc.

AMERICANS IN AFRICA
Gordimer, N. Horn of plenty

AMERICANS IN ASIA
Lederer, W. J. and Burdick, E. L. Ambassador and the working press
Lederer, W. J. and Burdick, E. L. Bent backs of Chang 'Dong
Lederer, W. J. and Burdick, E. L. Captain Boning, USN
Lederer, W. J. and Burdick, E. L. Employment opportunities abroad
Lederer, W. J. and Burdick, E. L. Everybody loves Joe Bing
Lederer, W. J. and Burdick, E. L. Everyone has ears
Lederer, W. J. and Burdick, E. L. Girl who got recruited
Lederer, W. J. and Burdick, E. L. Lucky, Lucky Lou #1
Lederer, W. J. and Burdick, E. L. Lucky, Lucky Lou #2
Lederer, W. J. and Burdick, E. L. Senator Sir
Lederer, W. J. and Burdick, E. L. Six-foot swami from Savannah
Lederer, W. J. and Burdick, E. L. The sum of tiny things
Lederer, W. J. and Burdick, E. L. Ugly American; 20 stories
Lederer, W. J. and Burdick, E. L. The ugly American and the ugly Sarkhanese

AMERICANS IN AUSTRIA
Gallant, M. Autumn day
Gallant, M. Poor Franzi

AMERICANS IN BURMA
Lederer, W. J. and Burdick, E. L. Nine friends
Lederer, W. J. and Burdick, E. L. What would you do if you were president?

AMERICANS IN CAMBODIA
Lederer, W. J. and Burdick, E. L. How to buy an American junior grade

AMERICANS IN CHINA
Whitehill, J. Cymbal makers

AMERICANS IN EGYPT
Stegner, W. E. City of the living

AMERICANS IN ENGLAND
Brandon, W. Brief enchantment
Crawford, C. Silver spoons
Household, G. The Greeks had no word for it
Household, G. Treasure hunt
James, H. International episode
Macauley, R. Guide to the Muniment Room
Montague, M. P. England to America
Rinehart, M. R. Tish marches on

AMERICANS IN EUROPE
Fitzgerald, F. S. K. One trip abroad
Kentfield, C. Innocence descending
Kubly, H. Paradiso
Shaw, I. Then we were three
Wharton, E. N. J. Souls belated

AMERICANS IN FRANCE
Boyle, K. Hilaire and the Maréchal Pétard
Boyle, K. Keep your pity
Boyle, K. Major engagement in Paris
Caryl, J. For every person in Paris there is a tree
Farrell, J. T. Dream of love
Farrell, J. T. Edna's husband
Farrell, J. T. French girls are vicious
Farrell, J. T. I want to meet a French girl
Farrell, J. T. Scrambled eggs and toast
Ferber, E. Light touch
Gallant, M. The picnic
Garrett, G. Don't take no for an answer
Haber, R. M. Journey to Milan
Hershman, M. Proposal perilous
Hill, P. Ben
Murphy, D. Camp in the meadow
Raphaelson, S. Last day in Paris
Rinehart, M. R. Salvage
Shaw, I. In the French style
Shaw, I. Tip on a dead jockey
Stafford, J. Maggie Meriwether's rich experience
Steele, M. Wanton troopers
Vidal, G. Pages from an abandoned journal
Wharton, E. N. J. Last asset

AMERICANS IN GERMANY
Boyle, K. Carnival of fear
Campbell, W. E. M. Personal letter
Innerst, I. Brother's ring
Macauley, R. End of pity
Macauley, R. Nest of gentlefolk
Stafford, J. My blithe, sad bird
Taper, B. Inge
Wolfe, T. Dark in the forest, strange as time

AMERICANS IN ICELAND
Anderson, P. Man who came early

AMERICANS IN INDIA
Henley, G. Private means
White, R. Devil of his own

AMERICANS IN IRELAND
O'Faoláin, S. Silence of the valley

AMERICANS IN ITALY
Balchin, N. Patience
Calisher, H. What a thing, to keep a wolf in a cage!
Ehrenfreund, N. Woman and child
Farrell, J. T. A baptism in Italy
Gellhorn, M. E. For better for worse
Glanville, B. The hero
James, H. Madonna of the future
Kubly, H. Divine ecstasy
Kubly, H. Mrs Gordon and the blind masseur
Malamud, B. Behold the key
Malamud, B. Lady of the lake
Miller, A. Monte Saint Angelo
Moretti, U. Dinner for the philosopher
Rudd, H. Devil's Plain
Wharton, E. N. J. Roman fever

AMERICANS IN JAPAN
Macauley, R. The mind is its own place
Sneider, V. J. Child of the regiment

AMERICANS IN KOREA
Sneider, V. J. Even the leopard

AMERICANS IN MEXICO
Bahr, J. Mexican interlude
Beaumont, C. Tears of the Madonna
Eastlake, W. Unhappy hunting grounds
Ferber, E. They brought their women
Graves, J. Green fly
Kerouac, J. Billowy trip in the world
Liberman, M. M. Big Buick to the pyramids
Sylvester, W. Death of Francisco
Williams, T. Night of the Iguana
Woolrich, C. Moon of Montezuma

AMERICANS IN MONTE CARLO
Stegner, W. E. Impasse

AMERICANS IN PARIS. See Americans in France

AMERICANS IN PUERTO RICO
Combs, P. Man on the beach

AMERICANS IN RUSSIA
Maugham, W. S. Mr Harrington's washing

AMERICANS IN SAMOA. See Americans in the South Sea Islands

AMERICANS IN SICILY
Kubly, H. For sentimental reasons
Kubly, H. The guest

AMERICANS IN SPAIN
Bellow, S. Gonzaga manuscripts

AMERICANS IN SWITZERLAND
Shaw, I. Voyage out, voyage home

AMERICANS IN THE PHILIPPINE ISLANDS
Lederer, W. J. and Burdick, E. L. Ragtime Kid

AMERICANS IN THE SOUTH SEA ISLANDS
Osbourne, L. The renegade

AMERICANS IN TIBET
Evarts, H. G. Horse for the colonel
Hilton, J. Lost horizon

AMERICANS IN VIETNAM
Lederer, W. J. and Burdick, E. L. The iron of war
Lederer, W. J. and Burdick, E. L. Lessons of war
Lederer, W. J. and Burdick, E. L. The ugly American

Amis, **Kingsley,** 1922-
My enemy's enemy
Winter's tales, 1

AMISH MENNONITES. See Mennonites

AMNESIA
Macgregor, J. M. Mind alone
Stewart, J. I. M. The ribbon

Amok. Zweig, S.

Among friends. Balchin, N.

Among the corn-rows. Garland, H.

Among the dahlias. Sansom, W.

Among those present. Robinson, L.

AMPUTATION
Maupassant, G. de. At sea

AMPUTATIONS OF LEG
Adams, A. Good for two drinks
Sørensen, V. Child's play

AMPUTEES. See Cripples

Amundson, **Grace**
Man of parts
Good housekeeping (Periodical) Editor's choice

AMUSEMENT PARKS
Bettis, B. B. Apollo
Rhine, R. Wilbur in the amusement park

Amy Foster. Conrad, J.

Anatomy lesson. Connell, E. S.

Anatomy lesson. Hardesty, R.

The **ancestor.** Lovecraft, H. P. and Derleth, A. W.

ANCESTRY. See Heredity

And a spoonful of grief to taste. Thomas, G.

And already lost. . . Armstrong, C.

And I am the attorney for the plaintiff. Kober, A.

". . .**And** my fear is great. . ." Waldo, E. H.

And now the news. . . Waldo, E. H.

And potato chips tomorrow. Moretti, U.

And the moon rose on Yellowhammer. De Eds, J.

And there are things for tears. Yellen, S.

And thou beside me. Reynolds, M.

"**And** what part of Europe do you come from?" Rowlands, L.

And what's your hobby? Schleyen, M.

ANDALUSIA. See Spain—Andalusia

Andalusian shawl. Morante, E.

Andersen, **Hans Christian,** 1805-1875
Emperor's new clothes
Rosenblum, M. ed. Stories from many lands
Fir tree
Jarrell, R. ed. Anchor book of stories
Lohan, R. ed. Christmas tales for reading aloud
Happy family
Laughton, C. ed. Tell me a story
Last dream of the old oak tree
Lohan, R. ed. Christmas tales for reading aloud
Little match girl
Lohan, R. ed. Christmas tales for reading aloud

Andersen, Hans C.—*Continued*
The nightingale
    Laughton, C. ed. Tell me a story
What the old man does is always right
    Costain, T. B. and Beecroft, J. eds.
    Stories to remember

Anderson, Ethel
Question of habit
    Stivens, D. comp. Coast to coast

Anderson, Poul, 1926-
The barbarian
    Magazine of fantasy and science fiction.
    Best from Fantasy and science fiction;
    6th ser.
Call me Joe
    Best science-fiction stories and novels;
    9th ser.
The immortal game
    Magazine of fantasy and science fiction.
    Best from Fantasy and science fiction;
    4th ser.
Journey's end
    Magazine of fantasy and science fiction.
    Best from Fantasy and science fiction;
    7th ser.
Man who came early
    Magazine of fantasy and science fiction.
    Best from Fantasy and science fiction;
    6th ser.
Un-man
    Greenberg, M. ed. All about the future

Anderson, Poul, 1926- and Dickson, Gordon R.
Adventure of the misplaced hound
    Anderson, P. and Dickson, G. R. Earthman's burden
Don Jones
    Anderson, P. and Dickson, G. R. Earthman's burden
In Hoka Signo Vinces
    Anderson, P. and Dickson, G. R. Earthman's burden
Sheriff of Canyon Gulch
    Anderson, P. and Dickson, G. R. Earthman's burden
Tiddlywink warriors
    Anderson, P. and Dickson, G. R. Earthman's burden
Yo ho Hoka!
    Anderson, P. and Dickson, G. R. Earthman's burden

Anderson, Sherwood, 1876-1941
Brother death
    Havighurst, W. ed. Masters of the modern short story
The egg
    Thurston, J. A. ed. Reading modern short stories
Nice girl
    Baudin, M. ed. Contemporary short stories v2
Seeds
    Thurston, J. A. ed. Reading modern short stories
Strength of God
    Laughton, C. ed. Tell me a story
The teacher
    Laughton, C. ed. Tell me a story

Andrade, Mona
Above the bright blue sky
    Winter's tales, 4

Andreev, Leonid Nikolaevich, 1871-1919
Seven who were hanged
    Hamalian, L. and Volpe, E. L. eds. Ten modern short novels

Andreyev, Leonid. See Andreev, Leonid Nikolaevich

ANDROIDS. See Automata

The **angel** and the sailor. Kentfield, C.

Angel at the grave. Wharton, E. N. J.

Angel from Julesburg. Fox, N. A.

Angel in the alcove. Williams, T.

Angel in the night. Aichinger, I.

Angel Levine. Malamud, B.

Angell, Roger, 1920-
In an early winter
    Best American short stories, 1956
Tennis
    Schwed, P. and Wind, H. W. eds. Great stories from the world of sport

ANGELS
Aichinger, I. Angel in the night
Chavez, A. Fiddler and the angelito
Malamud, B. Angel Levine
Pangborn, E. Angel's egg
Tazewell, C. Uninvited
Tolstoĭ, L. N. Graf. What men live by

Angel's egg. Pangborn, E.

ANGER
Enright, E. The bookkeepers
Schleyen, M. Sandy's angry day

Angioletti, Giovanni Battista, 1896-
Poor ghost
    Slonim, M. L. ed. Modern Italian short stories

An **angler** comes to life. Smith, E. W.

ANGLING. See Fishing

Angoff, Charles, 1902-
Alte Bobbe
    Ribalow, H. U. ed. Treasury of American Jewish stories
Artist and his wife
    Angoff, C. Something about my father, and other people
Aunt, Faigge
    Angoff, C. Something about my father, and other people
Avrom Moshe
    Angoff, C. Something about my father, and other people
Barnet Rosenberg
    Angoff, C. Something about my father, and other people
Benny
    Angoff, C. Something about my father, and other people
Beryl der Croomer
    Angoff, C. Something about my father, and other people
Big Jim Gordon
    Angoff, C. Something about my father, and other people
Broken warmth
    Angoff, C. Something about my father, and other people
Charlotte
    Angoff, C. Something about my father, and other people
Chatzkel
    Angoff, C. Something about my father, and other people

Annixter, Paul, pseud.—*Continued*
Devil of the woods
    Annixter, P. pseud. Devil of the woods
Dingo
    Annixter, P. pseud. Hunting horn, and
        other dog stories
The dog
    Annixter, P. pseud. Hunting horn, and
        other dog stories
Flounder, flounder in the sea
    Annixter, P. pseud. Devil of the woods
Gun dog
    Annixter, P. pseud. Hunting horn, and
        other dog stories
The heathen
    Annixter, P. pseud. Hunting horn, and
        other dog stories
His man
    Annixter, P. pseud. Hunting horn, and
        other dog stories
Horns of plenty
    Annixter, P. pseud. Devil of the woods
Hunting horn
    Annixter, P. pseud. Hunting horn, and
        other dog stories
Injun Devil
    Annixter, P. pseud. Devil of the woods
Keepers of the river dam
    Annixter, P. pseud. Devil of the woods
Krag of the K-9's
    Annixter, P. pseud. Hunting horn, and
        other dog stories
Monarch of the lagoons
    Annixter, P. pseud. Devil of the woods
Odyssey of Old Specs
    Annixter, P. pseud. Devil of the woods
Old Jasper and the fox teller
    Annixter, P. pseud. Hunting horn, and
        other dog stories
Red Knight
    Annixter, P. pseud. Hunting horn, and
        other dog stories
Search for the Fire Bird
    Annixter, P. pseud. Devil of the woods
Secret place
    Annixter, P. pseud. Devil of the woods
Seekonk, the tale of a sea gull
    Annixter, P. pseud. Devil of the woods
Stronger force
    Annixter, P. pseud. Hunting horn, and
        other dog stories
Tiger hound
    Annixter, P. pseud. Hunting horn, and
        other dog stories
Trumpeter of the air lanes
    Annixter, P. pseud. Devil of the woods
Annunzio, Gabriele d' 1863-1938
The wake
    Slonim, M. L. ed. Modern Italian short
        stories
Anomaly of the empty man. White,
    W. A. P.
Anonymous fame. Brown, W.
Another man like Johnny. Boorstein, R. S.
Answer. Brown, F.
The **answer.** Wylie, P.
The **answers.** Simak, C. D.
ANTARCTIC REGIONS
    Block, I. The bottom
        See also Arctic regions; Lapland

The **Anthem.** Gerchunoff, A.
ANTHRAX
    Easton, R. O. Death in October
ANTHROPOLOGISTS
    La Farge, O. Resting place
    Yellen, S. The mystic presences
ANTIPATHIES. See Prejudices and an-
    tipathies
ANTIQUE DEALERS
    Mankowitz, W. Blottik monopoly
    Mankowitz, W. Eight years in the mak-
        ing
ANTISEMITISM. See Jews
Antonov, Sergey
    The destroyer
        Loaf sugar, and other Soviet stories
ANTS
    Pohl, F. Let the ants try
Anty Bligh. Masefield, J.
ANXIETY. See Fear
Anything box. Henderson, Z.
APACHE INDIANS
    Austin, M. A. Van N. Stewed beans
    Faulkner, W. The waifs
    Horgan, P. Water in the wilderness
    Kastle, H. D. The enemies
    La Farge, O. Happy Indian laughter
APARTMENT HOUSES
    Aichinger, I. Window entertainment
    Enright, E. Tree of heaven
    Warner, S. T. Winter in the air
The **ape.** Pritchett, V. S.
APES
    Pritchett, V. S. The ape
Apollo. Bettis, B. B.
APOTHECARIES. See Pharmacists
APPARATUS, ELECTRICAL. See Elec-
    tric apparatus and appliances
APPARENT DEATH. See Death, Ap-
    parent
An **apparition.** Sandoz, M. Y.
APPARITIONS. See Ghosts; Hallucina-
    tions and illusions
APPENDECTOMY. See Appendicitis
APPENDICITIS
    Brown, J. The way I feel
Apperley, Charles James, 1778-1843
    The chase
        Welcome, J. and Orchard, V. eds. Best
            hunting stories
Appet, Nelson, 1910-
    The prophet
        Ribalow, H. U. ed. Treasury of Ameri-
            can Jewish stories
APPETITE
    Pincherle, A. Appetite
Apple tree. Bowen, E.
APPLE TREES
    Clayton, J. B. White circle
        See also Orchards
Applegate, Frank Guy, 1882-1932
    Indian divorce
        Schaefer, J. W. ed. Out West
    Tricks in all trades
        Schaefer, J. W. ed. Out West

ARIZONA—*Continued*

    Frontier and pioneer life
      See Frontier and pioneer life—Arizona

Arkhip. Tolstoĭ, A. N. Graf

ARM, ARTIFICIAL. See Artificial limbs

ARMED FORCES. See Soldiers; also subdivision Army under various countries, e.g., Great Britain. Army; United States. Army; etc.

ARMED FORCES DAY
    Lowry, R. J. C. All American

Armel, Camille
    The piano
      World prize stories; 2d ser.

Armenian writers. Saroyan, W.

ARMENIANS IN THE UNITED STATES
    Housepian, M. How Levon Dai was surrendered to the Edemuses
    Saroyan, W. Armenian writers
    Saroyan, W. Failure of friends
    Saroyan, W. Shepherd's daughter

Armistice in Venice. Marceau, F.

Armstrong, Charlotte, 1905-
    The albatross
      Armstrong, C. The albatross
    All the way home
      Armstrong, C. The albatross
    And already lost
      Queen, E. pseud. ed. Ellery Queen's awards: 12th ser.
    The enemy
      Armstrong, C. The albatross
    Evening hour
      Armstrong, C. The albatross
    Hedge between
      Armstrong, C. The albatross
    Laugh it off
      Armstrong, C. The albatross
    Miss Murphy
      Armstrong, C. The albatross
    Ride with the executioner
      Armstrong, C. The albatross
    Ten points for Mr Polkinghorn
      Armstrong, C. The albatross
    What would you have done?
      Armstrong, C. The albatross
      Queen, E. pseud. Ellery Queen's awards: 10th ser.

ARMY AIR FORCES. See United States. Air Forces

ARMY DAY. See Armed Forces Day

ARMY LIFE. See Soldiers; also subdivision Army under various countries, e.g. Great Britain. Army; United States. Army; etc.

Army of little ears. Child, C. B.

Around the dear ruin. Berriault, G.

Arr, Stephen, pseud. See Rynas, Stephen A.

Arrest. Harss, L.

Arrogant shoat. Campbell, W. E. M.

Arrow of God. Charteris, L.

ARSON
    Blake, A. McLeod's ordeal
    Faulkner, W. Barn burning
    Lesiņš, K. String of beads

ARSONISTS. See Arson

ART, CHRISTIAN. See Christian art and symbolism

ART COLLECTORS
    Derleth, A. W. Something in wood
    Kubly, H. Horseback
    Stewart, J. I. M. The heritage portrait

ART CRITICS
    Beliavsky, P. and Raspevin, A. M-Yes!
      See also Critics

ART DEALERS
    Carr, J. D. Incautious burglar
    Gordimer, N. Art dealers
    Huxley, A. L. The portrait

ART GALLERIES AND MUSEUMS
    Nagai, T. In a small art gallery
    Wilson, A. Realpolitik

ART OBJECTS
    Maupassant, G. de. Bric-a-brac
    Vincenz, M. Untold story

    Collectors
      See Art collectors

ART SCHOOLS
    Connell, E. S. Anatomy lesson
    Macauley, R. Academic style
    Steele, M. Wanton troopers
    Whitehill, J. The academicians

ART TREASURES IN WAR. See World War, 1939-1945—Art and the war

The **artful** Mr Glencannon. Gilpatric, G.

Arthur in Avalon. Balchin, N.

ARTHUR, KING
    Malory, Sir T. Sword in the stone

Arthur, Robert
    The glass bridge
      Mystery Writers of America, inc. A choice of murders
    Hard case
      Mystery Writers of America, inc. Big time mysteries
    Satan and Sam Shay
      Davenport, B. ed. Deals with the devil
    Sixty grand missing
      Mystery Writers of America, inc. Crime for two

Artie Bell. Lowry, R. J. C.

Artifact. Oliver, C.

An **artifice.** Maupassant, G. de

ARTIFICIAL LIMBS
    Davies, R. Benefit concert

Artificial nigger. O'Connor, F.

Artist and his wife. Angoff, C.

Artist at work. Camus, A.

ARTIST LIFE
    Camus, A. Artist at work
    Coppée, F. Christmas lovers
    Farrell, J. T. Edna's husband
    Garrett, G. The seacoast of Bohemia
    Hill, P. Ben
    Macauley, R. Academic style
    Moretti, U. And potato chips tomorrow
    Moretti, U. Anita had to be paid
    Moretti, U. Dinner for the philosopher
    Moretti, U. Find Lorenza
    Moretti, U. He should never have become a painter

ARTIST LIFE—*Continued*
Moretti, U. I couldn't leave them loose on the street
Moretti, U. Inge loved mystery
Moretti, U. The philosopher has an idea
Moretti, U. Rene's walk was too good
Moretti, U. A studio with sparrows on the clothesline
Moretti, U. Two weeks of talk
Moretti, U. Wanted: one hideous secretary
Moretti, U. We wanted Carmelo's statue
Moretti, U. Where's Francesca?
Porter, W. S. Last leaf
Artistic career of Corky. Wodehouse, P. G.

ARTISTS
Gerstäcker, F. W. C. Germelshausen
Mankowitz, W. Life in art
O'Flaherty, L. Child of God
Treat, L. Justice magnifique
Warner, S. T. Hee-haw!
Williams, T. Angel in the alcove
    See also Architects; Illustrators; Painters; Sculptors

ARTISTS' MODELS
Connell, E. S. Anatomy lesson
James, H. Real thing
Maupassant, G. de. Artist's wife
Artist's wife. Maupassant, G. de

ARTS AND CRAFTS
Samuel, E. H. Saffron rug

ARUNTA TRIBE. See Aranda tribe

As best he can. Household, G.

As I was going up the stair. Chester, A.

As it was and as it will be: a Christmas tale. Ready, W. B.

As Joe said. . . Sutherland, H.

As ye sow—. Fisher, D. F. C.

Asa rule. Williams, J.

Asaph. Stockton, F. R.

ASCENSIONS, BALLOON. See Balloon ascensions

Asch, Shalom, 1880-1957
Duty to live
    Schwarz, L. W. ed. Feast of Leviathan
Yechiel's Sabbath mother
    Kobler, F. ed. Her children call her blessed

Asch, Sholem. See Asch, Shalom

Ashbaugh, Dick
The case of the missing sources
    Saturday evening post (Periodical) Saturday evening post Carnival of humor
Day before summer
    Seventeen (Periodical) Seventeen's stories

Ashes. Mosenson, Y.

Ashton, Winifred
Dearly beloved of Benjamin Cobb
    Hudson, D. ed. Modern English short stories; 2d ser.
King waits
    Costain, T. B. and Beecroft, J. eds. More stories to remember

ASIANS IN THE UNITED STATES
Orr, E. Home again for Mr. Muff

Asimov, Isaac, 1920-
Brazen locked room
    Davenport, B. ed. Deals with the devil
Dead past
    Asimov, I. Earth is room enough
Dreaming is a private thing
    Asimov, I. Earth is room enough
    Merril, J. ed. S-F: ['56]
Dust of death
    Mystery Writers of America, inc. Big time mysteries
Each an explorer
    Merril, J. ed. SF: '57
Franchise
    Asimov, I. Earth is room enough
Fun they had
    Asimov, I. Earth is room enough
Gimmicks three
    Asimov, I. Earth is room enough
Ideas die hard
    Galaxy science fiction magazine. Third Galaxy reader
Immortal bard
    Asimov, I. Earth is room enough
Jokester
    Asimov, I. Earth is room enough
Kid stuff
    Asimov, I. Earth is room enough
Last trump
    Asimov, I. Earth is room enough
Let's get together
    Merril, J. ed. S-F: '58
Little lost robot
    Montgomery, R. B. ed. Best SF two
Living space
    Asimov, I. Earth is room enough
A loint of paw
    Magazine of fantasy and science fiction. Best from fantasy and science fiction; 7th ser.
The message
    Asimov, I. Earth is room enough
Satisfaction guaranteed
    Asimov, I. Earth is room enough
Singing bell
    Magazine of fantasy and science fiction. Best from Fantasy and science fiction; 5th ser.
Someday
    Asimov, I. Earth is room enough
Watery place
    Asimov, I. Earth is room enough

Asinari, Ronald J. 1930-
Convent of St Theresa
    New voices 2: American writing today

Ask a foolish question. Sheckley, R.

Ask me another. Gruber, F.

The assassin. Maupassant, G. de

ASSASSINATION
Samuel, E. H. Blind spot

ASSEMBLY-LINE METHODS
Swados, H. B. Joe, the vanishing American

ASSES AND MULES
Babcock, H. Feudin' and fussin'
Barker, S. O. Macho
Clayton, J. B. White against winter dawn
Coburn, W. Orneriest three
Daudet, A. Pope's mule
Faulkner, W. Mule in the yard

AUTOMATA—*Continued*
Sandoz, M. Y. Love-letter
Sheckley, R. The battle
Simak, C. D. How-2
AUTOMOBILE ACCIDENTS. See Automobiles—Accidents
AUTOMOBILE DRIVERS
Gaby, A. Fifty-two miles to terror
Holman, M. Power of suggestion
Schweitzer, G. Hit and run
Winterton, P. The man who wasn't scared
See also Hit-and-run drivers
AUTOMOBILE INDUSTRY AND TRADE
Swados, H. B. Joe, the vanishing American
AUTOMOBILE INDUSTRY WORKERS
Swados, H. Back in the saddle again
Swados, H. Day the singer fell
Swados, H. Fawn, with a bit of green
Swados, H. Joe, the vanishing American
Swados, H. Just one of the boys
Swados, H. On the line
Swados, H. One for the road
Swados, H. Present for the boy
AUTOMOBILE RACES
Rinehart, M. R. Mind over motor
AUTOMOBILES
Aramilev, I. Berendey
Balchin, N. The enthusiast
Byrd, J. J. Reluctant cop
Finney, J. Second chance
Johnson, W. R. Simmie, do something
McNeil, S. Old enough to drive
Sire, J. and Sire, G. Cherry-colored bomb
Tekeyan, C. Mac loved Mr Kelly
Ward, L. L. Bicycle built for two
Warner, S. T. Idenborough
Ziller, E. Journey to Brentwood

Accidents
Allen, S. The strangers
Bates, H. E. Death of a huntsman
Boyle, K. Your body is a jewel box
Bradbury, R. The crowd
Hawkins, J. and Hawkins, W. Cop without a badge
Howland, R. Magic night
Nemerov, H. Delayed hearing
O'Connor, E. A good man is hard to find
Sansom, W. Death in the Sunday city
Shaw, I. Dry rock
Wade, B. and Miller B. Bad time of day
Waldo, E. H. Twink
Wallace, F. L. Driving lesson

Racing
See Automobile races

Repairing
Saroyan, W. Idea in the back of my brother's head

Service stations
Farrell, J. T. Accident
Farrell, J. T. Fate of a hero
Autres temps. . . Wharton, E. N. J.
Autumn afternoon. Farrell, J. T.
Autumn day. Gallant, M.
Autumn fable. Coates, R. M.
Autumn salon. Colette, S. G.

Available data on the Worp Reaction. Miller, L.
Avalanche. Coombs, C. I.
AVALANCHES
Annixter, P. pseud. Horns of plenty
Coombs, C. I. Avalanche
AVARICE
Clemens, S. L. Man that corrupted Hadleyburg
Dreiser, T. Phantom gold
Tolstoĭ, L. N. Graf. How much land does a man need?
The **avenger.** Maupassant, G. de
AVERAGE
Coates, R. M. The law
Averchenco, Arcadii. See Averchenko, Arkadiĭ Timofeevich
Averchenko, Arkadiĭ Timofeevich, 1881-1925
Young man who flew past
Hall, J. B. and Langland, J. T. eds. Short story
AVIATION. See Aeronautics
AVIATORS. See Air pilots
AVIGNON. See France—Avignon
Avnieri, Uri, 1923-
The prisoner
Schwarz, L. W. ed. Feast of Leviathan
Avrom Moshe. Angoff, C.
Awake and sing. Sargent, E. N.
Awakening. Babel', I. E.
The **awakening.** Clarke, A. C.
The **awakening.** Corkery, D.
The **awakening.** Hutchison, B.
The **awakening.** Maupassant, G. de
The **award.** Allen, S.
AWARDS. See Rewards (prizes, etc.)
Away from it all. Morton, C. W.
Away to moonlight. Niland, D.
Awkward age. Carmichael, D.
Axe on Slumber Lake. Smith, E. W.
Axel's adieu. Olson, A. D.
Axolotl. Abernathy, R.
Ayala, Francisco, 1906-
The bewitched
Flores, A. ed. Great Spanish stories
Ayala, Ramón Pérez de. See Pérez de Ayala, Ramón
Ayers, James W.
Tongue of freedom
Oberfirst, R. ed. Anthology of best short-short stories v6
Aymé, Marcel, 1902-
Across Paris
Aymé, M. Across Paris, and other stories
Dermuche
Aymé, M. Across Paris, and other stories
The dwarf
Aymé, M. Across Paris, and other stories
Grace
Thurston, J. A. ed. Reading modern short stories
Same as: State of grace

Ballard, Willis Todhunter, 1903-
Builder of murderer's bar
Western Writers of America. Branded
West

BALLET
Angoff, C. Mother and I see Anna Pav-
lova
Jackson, D. V. S. Night filled with music
O'Faoláin, S. Old master

BALLOON ASCENSIONS
Edmonds, W. D. Cadmus Henry, balloon
observer

BALLOONS
Bellah, J. W. The secret of the seven
days

The ballroom. Sansom, W.

BALLS (PARTIES) See Parties

Baltenbach, Lawrence J. 1915-
Parson's dilemma
Oberfirst, R. ed. Anthology of best
short-short stories, v6

Balzac, Honoré de, 1799-1850
La Grande Bretêche
Costain, T. B. and Beecroft, J. eds.
Stories to remember

The bambino. Lowry, R. J. C.

BANDITS. See Brigands and robbers

BANDS (MUSIC)
Cassill, R. V. Biggest band

Bang-bang you're dead. Spark, M.

Bang on the head. Cookeson, T. V.

Bang the drum slowly. Harris, M.

BANGKOK. See Thailand—Bangkok

Banjo string. Reed, L.

Bank holiday, Corle, E.

BANK ROBBERS
Annixter, P. pseud. Choirboy
Blackburn, T. W. Pelado
DeRosso, H. A. Back track
Doyle, Sir A. C. Red-headed League
Faulkner, W. Home
Foster, B. Thief by choice
O'Rourke, F. Reaction
Spears, R. S. Sheriff's educated son

BANKERS
Bahr, J. Old banker Evan
Balchin, N. Arthur in Avalon
Cather, W. S. Tommy, the unsentimental
Coates, R. M. Rendezvous
Lesiņš, K. Lover's letter
O'Hara, J. Other women's households
Waldo, E. H. Microcosmic god
See also Banks and banking; Capi-
talists and financiers

Banks, Raymond, E. 1918-
Christmas trombone
Best science-fiction stories and novels:
1955
Littlest people
Best science-fiction stories and novels:
1955
The short ones
Magazine of fantasy and science fiction.
Best from Fantasy and science fic-
tion; 5th ser.

BANKS, COIN. See Coin banks

BANKS AND BANKING
Garland, H. "Good fellow's" wife
Joyce, J. A painful case
Leacock, S. My financial career

Bannack doctor. Fox, N. A.

Banquet of crow. Parker, D. R.

BAPTISM
Farrell, J. T. A baptism in Italy

A baptism. Guareschi, G.

A baptism in Italy. Farrell, J. T.

Barash, Asher, 1890-
Hai's well
Frank, M. Z. ed. Sound the great
trumpet
In Marburg
Tehilla, and other Israeli tales
Speed the plough
Schwarz, L. W. ed. Feast of Leviathan

The barbarian. Anderson, P.

BARBARIANS. See Man, Prehistoric;
Man, Primitive

BARBARITIES. See War

Barber of Broadway. McGeehan, W. O.

BARBERS
Caldwell, E. Vick Shore and the good
of the game
Glen, E. Dark pearl
Lardner, R. W. Haircut
Pincherle, A. Silly old fool
Pincherle, A. The strawberry mark
Pritchett, V. S. You make your own life
Robinson, A. Farlow express
Sansom, W. Impatience
See also Hairdressing

Barber's tale of his fifth brother. Arabian
nights

Barbudo, Antonio Sánchez
In the trenches
Flores, A. ed. Great Spanish stories

Barclay, Sylvia G.
The bubble
Oberfirst, R. ed. Anthology of best
short-short stories v5

BARDS. See Poets

Bare land. Wallenius, K. M.

Bargain in bodies. Schere, M.

A bargain's a bargain. Hilborn, N. C.

Barhash. Smilansky, M.

Baring-Gould, Sabine, 1834-1924
Tom a' Tuddlams
Fremantle, A. J. ed. Christmas is here

Bar-Joseph, Joshua, 1912-
Fettered Messiah
Frank, M. Z. ed. Sound the great
trumpet

Barker, A. L. 1919-
Mr Minnenick
Hudson, D. ed. Modern English short
stories; 2d ser.

Barker, Dudley
Trip to Paris
World prize stories; 2d ser.

Barker, Elliott
My dogs had what it takes
Western Writers of America. Hound
dogs and others

Barker, Shirley
Fog on Pemble Green
Queen, E. pseud. Ellery Queen's awards:
10th ser.
Barker, Squire Omar, 1894-
Macho
Western Writers of America. Wild
horse roundup
Pup and the bad man
Western Writers of America. Hound
dogs and others
Trail fever
Western Writers of America. Branded
West
The **barker.** Bahr, J.
Barmecide feast. Arabian nights
Barn burning. Faulkner, W.
Barn cuts off the view. Ferber, E.
Barnard, Leslie Gordon, 1890-
Four men and a box
Nelson, G. E. ed. Cavalcade of the
North
Barnet Rosenberg. Angoff, C.
Barney's Maggie. Macken, W.
BARNS AND STABLES
Ferber, E. Barn cuts off the view
Garland, H. Uncle Ethan Ripley
Rawlings, C. A. Young man on his own
Barnsley, Alan Gabriel
Bravery
Winter's tales, 2
BARONS. See Aristocracy
Baron's two francs. Coppée, F.
Barred door. Rhodes, E. M.
Barrel of fun. Jones, J.
Barrett, B. L.
Family tree
Short story, 1
Filial regard
Short story, 1
Troops of lovely children
Short story, 1
Victim of a lust
Short story, 1
Barrow Street. Sherman, R.
Barry, Jerome, 1894-
Double talk
Mystery Writers of America, inc. Big
time mysteries
Ice storm
Mystery Writers of America, inc. For
love or money
Inside stuff
Mystery Writers of America, inc. Crime
for two
Teen-age tales, bk 4
BARS. See Hotels, taverns, etc.
Bars of the cage. Balchin, N.
BARTENDERS
Allen, S. Girls on the tenth floor
Curley, D. A spring
Herbert, F. H. Husband trouble
Bartholomew, Cecilia
Seventeen
Stowe, A. comp. When boy dates girl
Bartimeus, pseud. See Ritchie, Louis Anselm
da Costa

Bartleby the scrivener. Melville, H.
Bartlett, Paul
Fronds of corn
New voices 2: American writing today
BASEBALL
Baer, A. Crambury Tiger
Broun, H. C. Last signal
Caldwell, E. Vick Shore and the good of
the game
Cheever, J. National pastime
Farrell, J. T. They ain't the men they
used to be
Gallico, P. W. The world of Babe Ruth
Graves, L. The pig-bristle slugger
Harris, M. Bang the drum slowly
Heuman, W. Rookie of the year
Heuman, W. Brooklyns lose
Johnson, N. Rollicking God
Johnson, O. M. Humming bird
Karner, E. F. One big error
Kaylin, W. Blaze of glory
Lardner, R. W. Alibi Ike
Lardner, R. W. Harmony
Lardner, R. W. Horseshoes
Lardner, R. W. Hurry Kane
Lardner, R. W. My roomy
Lowry, R. J. C. Little baseball world
McGiffin, L. Mr Kensington's finest hour
O'Hara, J. Bread alone
Olgin, J. Bazooka arm
Olgin, J. Hit and run
Olgin, J. Strike-out king
Olgin, J. Surprise attack
Payne, D. B. Better a tortoise
Schleyen, M. Bad one
Stanton, W. Dodger fan
Thurber, J. You could look it up
West, J. Public-address system
Wodehouse, P. G. Pitcher and the pluto-
crat

Basement room. Greene, G.

BASIL I, BYZANTINE EMPEROR, 813?-
886
Ahimaaz Ben Paltiel. Emperor Basil and
Rabbi Shephatiah

Basil and Cleopatra. Fitzgerald, F. S. K.

Basket bantam. Evans, E.

BASKETBALL
Ducovny, A. M. I am the athlete, the
chosen
Evans, E. Basket bantam
Hughes, V. J. Swede
Oldham, A. Zealots of Cranston Tech
Olgin, J. Dribbling fool
Olgin, J. Fraser brothers
Olgin, J. Point crazy
Olgin, J. Rebound man
Schleyen, M. Sandy's angry day
Stoutenburg, A. Score!
Worthington, J. Court revenge
Worthington, J. Nets are for fish

Basquerie. Kelly, E. M.

BASQUES
Craven, M. Susana and the shepherd
Fisher, D. F. C. Gold from Argentina
Fisher, D. F. C. Saint of the Old Semi-
nary
Kelly, E. M. Basquerie

Bass viol. Peretz, I. L.

Beaumont, Charles—*Continued*

Free dirt
Beaumont, C. The hunger, and other stories

The hunger
Beaumont, C. The hunger, and other stories

Infernal bouillabaisse
Beaumont, C. The hunger, and other stories

Last night the rain
Beaumont, C. The hunger, and other stories

Miss Gentilbelle
Beaumont, C. The hunger, and other stories

The murderers
Beaumont, C. The hunger, and other stories

Nursery rhyme
Beaumont, C. The hunger, and other stories

Open house
Beaumont, C. The hunger, and other stories

Point of honor
Beaumont, C. The hunger, and other stories

Tears of the Madonna
Beaumont, C. The hunger, and other stories

The train
Beaumont, C. The hunger, and other stories

Vanishing American
Beaumont, C. The hunger, and other stories
Magazine of fantasy and science fiction. Best from Fantasy and science fiction; 5th ser.
See also Oliver, C. jt. auth.

Beauquey, Michel
In the other's shoes
World prize stories; 2d ser.

Beautiful pattern. Ruhen, O.

Beautiful rebel. Jones, P.

BEAUTY. See Esthetics

BEAUTY, PERSONAL
Aichinger, I. Moon story
Mansfield, K. Revelations
Sandoz, M. Y. Grandmama Gladys

Beauty and beast. Sansom, W.

BEAUTY CONTESTS
Aichinger, I. Moon story
Sansom, W. Contest of ladies

Beauty is truth. Guest, A.

Beauty of holiness. O'Donovan, J.

BEAUTY SHOPS
Glen, E. Dark pearl
Welty, E. Petrified man

BEAVERS
Annixter, P. pseud. Keepers of the river dam

Bécquer, Gustavo Adolfo, 1836-1870
Master Pérez the organist
Flores, A. ed. Great Spanish stories

The **bed.** Maupassant, G. de

Bed no. 29. Maupassant, G. de

BEDOUINS
Samuel, E. H. Popularity
Shami, Y. Hamamah

The **bedquilt.** Fisher, D. F. C.

BEDS
Collins, W. Terribly strange bed

BEDUINS. See Bedouins

Beep. Blish, J.

Beer, Thomas, 1889-1940
Biography
Baudin, M. ed. Contemporary short stories v3
Tact
Laughton, C. ed. Tell me a story

Beerbohm, Sir Max, 1872-1956
A. V. Laider
Costain, T. B. and Beecroft, J. eds. Stories to remember
Enoch Soames
Davenport, B. ed. Deals with the devil
P.C.X. 36
Posselt, E. ed. A merry, merry Christmas book

BEES
Johnson, W. R. Simmie, do something
Lehmann, R. Dream of winter
Maeterlinck, M. Foundation of the city
MacMahon, B. King of the bees

BEETLES
Poe, E. A. Gold bug

Before the flood. Samuel, E. H.

Before the grand jury. Stuart, J.

BEGGARS
Faulkner, W. Mirrors of Chartres Street
Kubly, H. Mice
Maupassant, G. de. Father Judas
O'Flaherty, L. The beggars
Rea, D. Piededifico
Singer, I. B. By the light of memorial candles
Walpole, Sir H. Silver mask
See also Tramps

The **beggars.** O'Flaherty, L.

BEGGING. See Beggars

The **beginning.** Peel, D.

Behind the brick wall. Dery, T.

Behind the news. Finney, J.

Behind the white brick. Burnett, F. H.

Behold the key. Malamud, B.

Beigel, Uli, 1935-
The balancing man
Beigel, U. Victoria at night, and other stories

First alarm
Beigel, U. Victoria at night, and other stories

The game
Beigel, U. Victoria at night, and other stories

Green and yellow grasses
Beigel, U. Victoria at night, and other stories

Letterboxes ought to be yellow
Beigel, U. Victoria at night, and other stories

The merger
Beigel, U. Victoria at night, and other stories

Beigel, Uli—*Continued*
Mirror days
　Beigel, U. Victoria at night, and other stories
The mourners
　Beigel, U. Victoria at night, and other stories
Poor in spirit
　Beigel, U. Victoria at night, and other stories
The snapshots
　Beigel, U. Victoria at night, and other stories
Sparrows
　Beigel, U. Victoria at night, and other stories
Victoria at night
　Beigel, U. Victoria at night, and other stories
World without a sun
　Beigel, U. Victoria at night, and other stories

Beith, John Hay, 1876-
Pip's first cricket match
　Buckeridge, A. comp. In and out of school

Bek. Lesinš, K.

Beldon, A. A.
Road to the shore
　Kemp, P. K. ed. Hundred years of sea stories

Bel-Gazou and Buck. Colette, S. G.

Beliavsky, P. and Raspevin, A.
M-yes!
　Loaf sugar, and other Soviet stories

BELIEF AND DOUBT. See Faith

Bell, Joseph N.
I'm coming in
　Saturday evening post (Periodical) Saturday evening post stories, 1956

Bell, Josephine, pseud. See Ball, Doris Bell (Collier)

"Bell." Maupassant, G. de

Bell of charity. Kentfield, C.

BELL-RINGERS. See Bells and bell-ringers

Bell that sang again. Chavez, A.

Bell Wethers. Phelan, J.

Bellah, James Warner, 1899-
First blood at Harper's Ferry
　Saturday evening post (Periodical) The Post Reader of Civil War stories
How Stonewall came back
　Saturday evening post (Periodical) The Post Reader of Civil War stories
The secret of the seven days
　Saturday evening post (Periodical) The Post Reader of Civil War stories

Bellflower. Maupassant, G. de

Bellow, Saul, 1915-
Father-to-be
　Bellow, S. Seize the day
The Gonzaga manuscripts
　Bellow, S. Seize the day
　Prize stories, 1956: the O. Henry awards
Looking for Mr Green
　Bellow, S. Seize the day
Seize the day
　Bellow, S. Seize the day

BELLS AND BELL-RINGERS
Asimov, I. Singing bell
Chavez, A. Bell that sang again
Klimo, J. Ships bell
MacMahon, B. Sound of the bell

Bemelmans, Ludwig, 1898-
Dear General, what a surprise
　Lewis, J. D. ed. Great stories about show business
Inside, outside
　Burnett, W. ed. This is my best humor

Ben. Boyle, K.

Ben. Hill, P.

Benchley, Nathaniel, 1915-
Encounter on a train
　Oberfirst, R. ed. Anthology of best short-short stories, v6

Benchley, Robert Charles, 1889-1945
Christmas spectacle
　Posselt, E. ed. A merry, merry Christmas book
Ladies wild
　Lewis, J. D. ed. Dealer's choice
Love in Hollywood
　Lewis, J. D. ed. Great stories about show business

Bendine, Lu. See Bendine, Lucille Francis

Bendine, Lucille Francis, 1933-
Tender touch
　American vanguard, 1956

Beneath the saddle. Carter, R. G.

Benefit concert. Davies, R.

Benefits of American life. Farrell, J. T.

Benét, Stephen Vincent, 1898-1943
By the waters of Babylon
　Costain, T. B. and Beecroft, J. eds. Stories to remember
The Devil and Daniel Webster
　Davenport, B. ed. Deals with the devil
　First-prize stories, 1919-1957
　McClennen, J. comp. Masters and masterpieces of the short story
　Sterner, L. G. ed. Favorite short stories
The die-hard
　Saturday evening post (Periodical) The Post Reader of Civil War stories
Doc Mellhorn and the pearly gates
　Blaustein, P. M. and Blaustein, A. P. eds. Doctors' choice
End to dreams
　First-prize stories, 1919-1957
Freedom's a hard-bought thing
　First-prize stories, 1919-1957
Jacob and the Indians
　McClennen, J. comp. Masters and masterpieces of the short story
Judgment in the mountains
　Fenton, C. A. ed. Best short stories of World War II
King of the Cats
　Baudin, M. ed. Contemporary short stories v 1
Too early spring
　McClennen, J. comp. Masters and masterpieces of the short story

BENEVOLENCE. See Charity

Bennett, Arnold, 1867-1931
Outside and inside
　Lewis, J. D. ed. Great stories about show business

Between the skunk and the locket. Mc-
Kune, J. W.

Between the thunder and the sun. Oliver,
C.

BEVERLY HILLS. See California—Beverly Hills

The bewitched. Ayala, F.

The bewitched eggshell. Carmer, C. L.

Beyond the desert. Rhodes, E. M.

Beyond the shadow of a dream. Rice, C.

Bialik, Hayyim Nahman, 1873-1934
Legend of three and four
Schwarz, L. W. ed. Feast of Leviathan

Bible. Old Testament
David and Bathsheba
Laughton, C. ed. Tell me a story
David and Goliath
Laughton, C. ed. Tell me a story
Fiery furnace
Laughton, C. ed. Tell me a story
Garden of Eden
Laughton, C. ed. Tell me a story
Noah
Laughton, C. ed. Tell me a story
Romance of Esther
Schwarz, L. W. ed. Feast of Leviathan
Story of Jacob and Esau
Sterner, L. ed. Favorite short stories

Bible. Old Testament. Apocrypha
Destruction of Bel
Schwarz, L. W. ed. Feast of Leviathan

Bible. Old Testament. Jonah
Book of Jonah
Jarrell, R. ed. Anchor book of stories

Bible. New Testament
Pool of Siloam
Laughton, C. ed. Tell me a story
Story of the Good Samaritan
Sterner, L. G. ed. Favorite short stories
Story of the Prodigal Son
Sterner, L. G. ed. Favorite short stories
Same as: Prodigal Son

Bible. New Testament. Luke
Gospel according to St Luke
Lohan, R. ed. Christmas tales for read-
ing aloud

Bible. New Testament. Matthew
Gospel according to Matthew
Lohan, R. ed. Christmas tales for read-
ing aloud

BIBLE STORIES. See Biblical stories

Bibleback's Christmas beef. Adams, A.

BIBLICAL STORIES
Bible. Old Testament. David and Bath-
sheba
Bible. Old Testament. David and Goliath
Bible. Old Testament. Fiery furnace
Bible. Old Testament. Garden of Eden
Bible. Old Testament. Noah
Bible. Old Testament. Romance of Esther
Bible. Old Testament. Story of Jacob and
Esau
Bible. Old Testament. Apocrypha. De-
struction of Bel
Bible. Old Testament. Jonah. Book of
Jonah
Bible. New Testament. Pool of Siloam

Bible. New Testament. Story of the Good
Samaritan

Bible. New Testament. Story of the Prodigal Son

Bicycle built for two. Ward, L. L.

BICYCLES AND TRICYCLES
Saroyan, W. Rescue of the perishing
See also Cycling

BICYCLING. See Cycling

Bierce, Ambrose, 1842-1914?
The man and the snake
Aymar, B. ed. Treasury of snake lore

Big Aunty, collector. Allison, R. M.

Big Bertha. O'Donovan, J.

Big bird-watcher. Yorck, R. L.

Big Black and the bully. Patten, L. B.

Big, black, good man. Wright, R.

Big blonde. Parker, D. R.

Big Buick to the pyramids. Liberman, M. M.

The big ferryman. O'Connor, P.

Big givers. Samuel, E. H.

Big gun. Millholland, R.

Big Jim Gordon. Angoff, C.

Big kiss-off. Benson, B.

Big sleep. Chandler, R.

Big splash. Harmon, M.

The big stick. Sansom, W.

Big Tex. Folinsbee, P.

Big Tom plays monte. Adams, A.

The big trek. Leiber, F.

Big wheel. Todd, R.

BIGAMY
Fearing, K. Three wives too many
Maugham, W. S. Round dozen

Bigger than life. Weinberg, E.

Biggest band. Cassill, R. V.

Biggle, Lloyd
The tunesmith
Best science-fiction stories and novels;
9th ser.

Bilenchi, Romano, 1909-
The drought
Strachan, W. J. ed. Modern Italian sto-
ries

Bill, Edward E. 1887-
The rose
Oberfirst, R. ed. 1955 anthology of best
original short-shorts

The bill. Malamud, B.

Bill McGee's brother. Saroyan, W.

Bill sells a "bill of goods." McMullen, J. A.

Billabillian. O'Brian, P.

BILLIARDS
Sansom, W. Game of billiards
Tolstoĭ, L. N. Graf. Recollections of a
billiard-marker

Billowy trip in the world. Kerouac, J.

Bill's eyes. Campbell, W. E. M.

Bill's little girl. Gale, Z.

Billy and Hans. Stillman, W. J.

Billy Budd, foretopman. Melville, H.

Billy Bunter's booby-trap. Richards, F.

Bingham, Robert K. 1925-
Unpopular passenger
Jennings, F. G. and Calitri, C. J. eds.
Stories
Prize stories, 1955: the O. Henry awards
Bin Gorion, Micha Joseph, 1865-1920
Akiba story
Schwarz, L. W. ed. Feast of Leviathan
Golem of Prague
Schwarz, L. W. ed. Feast of Leviathan
Tales of demons and dervishes
Schwarz, L. W. ed. Feast of Leviathan
Biography. Beer, T.
Biography. Zistel, E.
Biography of a puppy. Terhune, A. P.
Biologist and his son. Fisher, D. F. C.
Bird, Dorothy Maywood
Skiing in a nutshell
Furman, A. L. ed. Everygirls sports
stories
Bird, Will Richard, 1891-
Movies come to Gull Point
Nelson, G. E. ed. Cavalcade of the
North
When a boy's a man
Swayze, B. ed. Short story magic
BIRD DOGS
Annixter, P. pseud. Gun dog
Annixter, P. pseud. Red Knight
Babcock, H. Deacon's grandpa
Babcock, H. Feudin' and fussin'
Babcock, H. Great day in the morning!
Babcock, H. Miss Priss
Babcock, H. Son of a bishop
Babcock, H. Tramp was a specialist
BIRD HUNTERS
Annixter, P. pseud. Gun dog
Babcock, H. Cousin Quesenberry Butts
and the boiled owl
La Farge, O. Thick on the bay
Bird in the bush. Rhodes, E. M.
Bird man. Stuart, D.
Bird-neck. Stuart, J.
Bird of paradise. Coleman, W. L.
Bird of the air. Gay, F.
Bird song. Goss, J. M.
Bird spotters. Streeter, E.
Bird watcher. Strong, L. A. G.
BIRD WATCHERS
Streeter, E. Bird spotters
Birdie Keller. Lochridge, B. H.
BIRDS
Annixter, P. pseud. Search for the Fire
Bird
Annixter, P. pseud. Seekonk, the tale of a
sea gull
Du Maurier, D. The birds
Francis of Assisi, Saint. Little flowers of
St Francis
Stuart, D. Bird man
See also names of particular birds:
e.g. Eagles; Cormorants; Parrots; etc.

Migration
Annixter, P. pseud. Trumpeter of the air
lines
The birds. Du Maurier, D.

Birds can't count. Clingerman, M.
Birds' Christmas carol. Wiggin, K. D. S.
Birth. O'Flaherty, L.
BIRTH CONTROL
Knight, D. World without children
BIRTH OF CHILDREN. See Childbirth
Birthday gift. Chute, B. J.
Birthday gift. Osgood, L.
BIRTHDAY GIFTS. See Gifts
BIRTHDAY PARTIES. See Birthdays
BIRTHDAYS
Beaumont, C. Vanishing American
Chute, B. J. Birthday gift
Hyman, M. Hundredth centennial
Lewin, I. Ring for Kathy's birthday
Lofts, N. R. Heaven in your hand
Schweitzer, G. Tomboy
Stanton, W. Last present
The birthmark. Heggen, T.
The birthplace. James, H.
Bishop, Leonard, 1922-
Chase the crippled dream
New voices 2: American writing today
The bishop. Chekhov, A. P.
BISHOPS
Chekhov, A. P. The bishop
Shaw, G. B. Miraculous revenge
Tolstoi, L. N. Graf. Three hermits
BISHOPS, CATHOLIC
Powers, J. F. Zeal
A bit of young life. Gordimer, N.
Bit off the map. Wilson, A.
The bitch. Colette, S. G.
Bitter farce. Schwartz, D.
Bitter honeymoon. Pincherle, A.
Bixby, Jerome, 1923-
One way street
Best science-fiction stories and novels:
1955
Bizarre affair of the seven nudes. Levin,
R. J.
Bjørnson, Bjørnstjerne, 1832-1910
The father
Jennings, F. G. and Calitri, C. J. eds.
Stories
Rosenblum, M. ed. Stories from many
lands
Sterner, L. G. ed. Favorite short stories
Blabbermouth. Waldo, E. H.
Black and white and gray. Summers, H.
Black beach. Carr, A. F.
Black boy. Boyle, K.
Black Christ of Adlerwald. Lofts, N. R.
Black colossus. Howard, R. E.
Black country. Beaumont, C.
Black ewe. Chavez, A.
Black kid. Pirandello, L.
Black kitten. Carr, A. H. Z.
Black Madonna. Lessing, D. M.
Black magic. O'Donovan, J.
Black mare. O'Flaherty, L.
Black mare. Sheehy, E.

BLACK MARKETS
Aymé, M. Across Paris
Chandler, D. 12 flights up
Black outlaw. Payne, S.
Black pits of Luna. Heinlein, R. A.
Black-purple in the corn. Ward, L. L.
Black Satin. Hankins, J. W.
Black spider. Lindeen, A.
Black-waxy near Waxahachie. Adams, A.
Blackberry winter. Warren, R. P.
The **blackbird**. O'Flaherty, L.
BLACKBIRDS
O'Flaherty, L. The blackbird
Blackburn, Alexander, 1929-
Golden river
American vanguard, 1956
Blackburn, Thomas Wakefield
Buckskin pensioner
Western Writers of America. Wild streets
Pelado
Western Writers of America. Branded West
Blackburn, Tom W. See Blackburn, Thomas Wakefield
Blackford, Charles Minor, 1898?-
Longer way
Everygirls adventure stories
Shadows on the reef
Furman, A. L. ed. Everygirls sports stories
Blackjack bargainer. Porter, W. S.
BLACKMAIL
Doyle, Sir A. C. Adventure of Charles Augustus Milverton
O'Flaherty, L. Red petticoat
Blackwood, Algernon, 1869-1951
Dream trespass
Langford, W. F. ed. Book of better stories
Empty house
Blackwood, A. In the realm of terror
Haunted island
Blackwood, A. In the realm of terror
Man whom the trees loved
Blackwood, A. In the realm of terror
Psychical invasion
Blackwood, A. In the realm of terror
Smith: an episode in a lodginghouse
Blackwood, A. In the realm of terror
Strange adventures of a private secretary in New York
Blackwood, A. In the realm of terror
The wendigo
Blackwood, A. In the realm of terror
The willows
Blackwood, A. In the realm of terror
With intent to steal
Ridler, A. B. comp. Best ghost stories
Blair, Clay, 1925-
Capture of the Swordray
Saturday evening post (Periodical) Saturday evening post stories, 1957
Blake, Andrea
McLeod's ordeal
Oberfirst, R. ed. Anthology of best short-short stories v5

Blake, L. J.
Those green trousers
Stivens, D. comp. Coast to coast
Blakiston, Noel
Facts of life
Pudney, J. ed. Pick of today's short stories, 9
Mrs Webster
Winter's tales, 3
Blancpain, Marc
Professor Darine
Lehmann, J. ed. Modern French stories
Blank page. Blixen, K.
The **blanket**. Dell, F.
BLANKETS
Brod, M. Story of a blanket
Blanton, Lowell D.
Long night
Prize stories, 1958: the O. Henry awards
Blasco Ibañez, Vicente, 1867-1928
El Gallardo
Schwed, P. and Wind, H. W. eds. Great stories from the world of sport
Blassingame, Wyatt, 1909-
Copenhagen and the Iron Duke
Blassingame, W. His kingdom for a horse
Gray Arab of Winston Churchill
Blassingame, W. His kingdom for a horse
Horse that crossed the world
Blassingame, W. His kingdom for a horse
Horse that saved a million lives
Blassingame, W. His kingdom for a horse
Horses of Joan of Arc
Blassingame, W. His kingdom for a horse
How Rienzi's name was changed to Winchester
Blassingame, W. His kingdom for a horse
Justin Morgan
Blassingame, W. His kingdom for a horse
Man's courage
Best American short stories, 1957
Prize stories 1957: the O. Henry awards
Stonewall Jackson and Old Sorrel
Blassingame, W. His kingdom for a horse
Strange fate of El Morzillo
Blassingame, W. His kingdom for a horse
Trojan horse
Blassingame, W. His kingdom for a horse
Truxton against Greyhound
Blassingame, W. His kingdom for a horse
Warrior and the First World War
Blassingame, W. His kingdom for a horse
Blasted pine. Annixter, P. pseud.
Blaze beyond the town. Lowry, R. J. C.
Blaze Face. Holmes, L. P.

Blaze of glory. Kaylin, W.

The Blessington method. Ellin, S.

BLIND

Adams, S. H. Such as walk in darkness

Byrne, D. Tale of my Aunt Jenepher's wooing

Campbell, W. E. M. Bill's eyes

Christensen, B. My eyes no longer hear

Faulkner, W. Episode

Gide, A. P. G. Pastoral symphony

Ingalls, C. J. Night is your friend

Maupassant, G. de. Blind man

Reid, L. A lifetime

Blind man. Maupassant, G. de

Blind man's hood. Carr, J. D.

Blind journey. Block, A. R.

Blind spot. Samuel, E. H.

Blinded. Staples, W.

BLINDNESS. See Blind

Blinker was a good dog. Lampman, B. H.

Blish, James

Battle of the unborn
Conklin, G. ed. Science-fiction adventures in mutation

Beep
Norton, A. M. ed. Space police

The box
Conklin, G. ed. Strange adventures in science fiction

Case of conscience
Montgomery, R. B. ed. Best SF

Bliss. Mansfield, K.

Blixen, Karen, 1885-

Babette's feast
Blixen, K. Anecdotes of destiny

Blank page
Blixen, K. Last tales

Caryatids, an unfinished tale
Blixen, K. Last tales

Cardinal's first tale
Blixen, K. Last tales

Cardinal's third tale
Blixen, K. Last tales

The cloak
Blixen, K. Last tales

Converse at night in Copenhagen
Blixen, K. Last tales

Copenhagen season
Blixen, K. Last tales

Country tale
Blixen, K. Last tales

The diver
Blixen, K. Anecdotes of destiny

Echoes
Blixen, K. Last tales

Immortal story
Blixen, K. Anecdotes of destiny

Night walk
Blixen, K. Last tales

Of hidden thoughts and of heaven
Blixen, K. Last tales

The ring
Blixen, K. Anecdotes of destiny

Sorrow-Acre
Jarrell, R. ed. Anchor book of stories

Tales of two old gentlemen
Blixen, K. Last tales

Tempests
Blixen, K. Anecdotes of destiny

BLIZZARDS. See Snow storms; Storms

Bloch, Robert, 1914-

Dig that crazy grave!
Queen, E. pseud. ed. Ellery Queen's awards: 12th ser.

I do not love thee, Doctor Fell
Best science-fiction stories and novels: 1956

Sock finish
Queen, E. pseud. ed. Ellery Queen's 13th annual

Blochman, Lawrence Goldtree, 1900-

Aldine folio murders
Cooke, D. C. ed. My best murder story

Dog that wouldn't talk
Mystery Writers of America, inc. For love or money

The girl with the burgundy lips
Mystery Writers of America, inc. A choice of murders

Red wine
Mystery Writers of America, inc. For tomorrow we' die

Swami of Northbank
Mystery Writers of America, inc. Crime for two

Block, Anita Rowe

Blind journey
Block, A. R. Love is a four letter word

Father image
Block, A. R. Love is a four letter word

Gee! Miss Marshall
Block, A. R. Love is a four letter word

Genesis
Block, A. R. Love is a four letter word

Love is a four letter word
Block, A. R. Love is a four letter word

Man among men
Block, A. R. Love is a four letter word

One day in April
Block, A. R. Love is a four letter word

One moment of truth
Block, A. R. Love is a four letter word

One of the boys
Block, A. R. Love is a four letter word

Perfect day
Block, A. R. Love is a four letter word

Sabbatical
Block, A. R. Love is a four letter word

Something borrowed—something blue
Block, A. R. Love is a four letter word

Something old—something new
Block, A. R. Love is a four letter word

Sunday morning
Block, A. R. Love is a four letter word

This boy, Jim Stephens
Block, A. R. Love is a four letter word

Whipping boy
Block, A. R. Love is a four letter word

Block, Arthur H. 1928-

Next time, stay home!
American vanguard, 1956

Block, Irvin, 1917-

The bottom
Fenner, P. R. ed. Heroes, heroes, heroes

Block, Libbie

What son tells everything?
Good housekeeping (Periodical) Editor's choice

Block, Rudolph Edgar, 1870-1940

Americanisation of Shadrach Cohen
Ribalow, H. U. ed. Treasury of American Jewish stories

Bound for Rio Grande. Dingle, A. E.

Bound man. Aichinger, I.

Bounty killers. Frazee, S.

Bourla, Yehuda, 1886-
At a glance
Frank, M. Z. ed. Sound the great
trumpet

Bowen, Elizabeth, 1899-
Apple tree
Ridler, A. B. comp. Best ghost stories
Her table spread
Jarrell, R. ed. Anchor book of stories
Ivy gripped the steps
Davin, D. M. ed. English short stories
of today, 2d ser.
Joining Charles
Thurston, J. A. ed. Reading modern
short stories
Maria
Hudson, D. ed. Modern English short
stories; 2d ser.
Queer heart
McClennen, J. comp. Masters and
masterpieces of the short story
Thurston, J. A. ed. Reading modern
short stories
Summer night
O'Donovan, M. ed. Modern Irish short
stories

Bowen, Robert Owen, 1920-
Matter of price
Best American short stories, 1955

Bowles, Paul Frederic, 1911-
Frozen fields
Best American short stories, 1958

BOWLING
Knapp, S. E. Fair play

Bowman, Blake Gilpin
Grease on her nose
Furman, A. L. ed. Everygirls sports
stories

Bowman, James K.
El patron
Miller, N. ed. New campus writing,
no. 2

Bowman's glory. Martyr, W.

The **bowmen.** Machen, A.

The **box.** Blish, J.

The **box.** Sneider, V. J.

BOXERS. See Boxing

BOXING
Cohen, O. R. Last blow
Doyle, Sir A. C. Croxley master
Farrell, J. T. Fall of Machine Gun Mc-
Gurk
Gallico, P. W. Thicker than water
Gault, W. C. Million dollar gesture
Hemingway, E. Fifty grand
Hendry, J. F. The disinherited
Kubly, H. Horseback
Lardner, R. W. Champion
Llewellyn, R. Now hear the cattle
London, J. Piece of steak
Lowry, R. J. C. Blood wedding in Chi-
cago
McGeehan, W. O. Barber of Broadway
Marquand, J. P. Simon pure
Schulberg, B. W. Session in Stillman's
gym

Symons, J. Eight minutes to kill
Vrettos, T. My name is Legion
Williams, T. One arm
Witwer, H. C. Leather pushers
See also Fighting, Hand-to-hand

The **boy.** Borgese, G. A.

Boy and the badger. Seton, E. T.

The **boy** and the brace. Macken, W.

Boy babies. Samuel, E. H.

Boy bad-man. Scott, W. R.

Boy-friend-in-law. Groszmann, L.

Boy in the back seat. Erdman, L. G.

Boy prophet. Fleg, E.

BOY SCOUTS
Chute, B. J. Three in a stew
Distler, A. J. Set her down

Boy turns turtle. Allen, H.

Boy with the big tongue. Green, H. G.

Boyhood. Farrell, J. T.

Boyle, Kay, 1903-
Ben
Boyle, K. Thirty stories
Black boy
Boyle, K. Thirty stories
Canals of Mars
Boyle, K. Thirty stories
Carnival of fear
Saturday evening post (Periodical) Sat-
urday evening post stories, 1954
Count Lothar's heart
Boyle, K. Thirty stories
Defeat
Boyle, K. Thirty stories
First-prize stories, 1919-1957
Diplomat's wife
Boyle, K. Thirty stories
Effigy of war
Boyle, K. Thirty stories
Episode in the life of an ancestor
Boyle, K. Thirty stories
Friend of the family
Boyle, K. Thirty stories
Herring piece
Boyle, K. Thirty stories
Hilaire and the Maréchal Pétard
Boyle, K. Thirty stories
How Bridie's girl was won
Boyle, K. Thirty stories
Keep your pity
Boyle, K. Thirty stories
Kroy Wen
Boyle, K. Thirty stories
Let there be honour
Boyle, K. Thirty stories
Loneliest man in the U.S. Army
Boyle, K. Thirty stories
Maiden, maiden
Boyle, K. Thirty stories
Major Alshuster
Boyle, K. Thirty stories
Major engagement in Paris
Boyle, K. Thirty stories
Men
Boyle, K. Thirty stories
Natives don't cry
Boyle, K. Thirty stories
Rest cure
Boyle, K. Thirty stories

Boyle, Kay—*Continued*
Their name is Macaroni
  Boyle, K. Thirty stories
They weren't going to die
  Boyle, K. Thirty stories
This they took with them
  Boyle, K. Thirty stories
Wedding day
  Boyle, K. Thirty stories
White as snow
  Boyle, K. Thirty stories
White horses of Vienna
  Boyle, K. Thirty stories
  First-prize stories, 1919-1957
Winter night
  Boyle, K. Thirty stories
Your body is a jewel box
  Boyle, K. Thirty stories

Boyles, C. S., 1925-
Cowboy Columbus
  Western Writers of America. Hoof
  trails and wagon tracks
Marshal and the mob
  Western Writers of America. Branded
  West

Boylston, Helen (Dore) 1895-
Stuff of dreams
  Mason, P. O. and Mason, J. eds. Fa-
  vorite cat stories of Pamela and James
  Mason

BOYS
Aichinger, I. Private tutor
Aiken, C. P. Silent snow, secret snow
Alford, H. The shorn lamb
Angoff, C. Curly
Atherton, V. The lizard died, too
Aymé, M. Seven-league boots
Babel', I. E. In the basement
Barry, J. Double talk
Beaumont, C. Miss Gentilbelle
Benét, S. V. The die-hard
Blackburn, A. Golden river
Block, A. H. Next time, stay home!
Block, A. R. Gee! Miss Marshall
Block, A. R. Genesis
Brodkey, H. First love and other sor-
  rows
Butler, M. Susie Q
Campbell, W. E. M. Miss Daisy
Carter, R. G. Beneath the saddle
Cather, W. S. The enchanted bluff
Chacel, R. Twlight in extremadura
Champney, L. W. Old stager
Chamson, A. My enemy
Chester, A. As I was going up the stair
Choynowski, P. Boarding house
Chute, B. J. Birthday gift
Chute, B. J. The fiesta
Clayton, J. B. All the petals of all the
  roses in the world
Clayton, J. B. Summer of the insistent
  voices
Clayton, J. B. White circle
Case, V. Touch of tenderness
Coates, R. M. Decline and fall of Perry
  Whitman
Cole, S. New boy
Coombs, C. I. Gadgets aren't everything
Criswell, C. Crying through the lock
Criswell, C. Give your heart to Jesus
Criswell, C. Goddess of Mercy

Criswell, C. You'll be late for your sup-
  per
Curley, D. Saccovanzetti
Daniel, N. Detour to Mashburn's Hill
Eastlake, W. Little Joe
Farque, V. The runaway
Farrell, J. T. Autumn afternoon
Farrell, J. T. Boyhood
Farrell, J. T. Grammar school love
Farrell, J. T. Little Johnny: A fable
Farrell, J. T. Senior prom
Faulkner, W. Ambuscade
Faulkner, W. Race at morning
Faulkner, W. Raid
Faulkner, W. Uncle Willy
Fitzgerald, F. S. K. Freshest boy
Gold, H. Burglars and the boy
Grahame, K. The burglars
Grau, S. A. Joshua
Green, C. Compliments of Caliph Bernie
Green, H. G. Boy with the big tongue
Greene, G. Basement room
Halacy, D. S. Ride the rough string
Hesling, B. The game
Heyert, M. New kid
Jacobson, D. Little pet
Katkov, N. Torn invitation
Kennedy, R. C. Nightcrawlers
Kentfield, C. Chip Canary
Kentfield, C. Johnny's land and Johnny's
  castle
Kentfield, C. River stay 'way from my
  door
Kubly, H. The gray umbrella
Kubly, H. The unmarried bartender
La Farge, O. By the boys themselves
La Farge, O. Touch of greatness
Leflley, R. Cry of the nightingale
Lessing, D. M. Through the tunnel
Livingston, T. M. A show of strength
Lytle, A. N. Mahogany frame
Macauley, R. The invaders
McCourt, E. A. White mustang
Macken, W. The atheist
Macken, W. The lion
Macken, W. The wasteland
Marsh, W. N. Last tag
Maxwell, W. What every boy should
  know
Merritt, M. Death of a kangaroo
Miller, E. M. Green grasshopper
Miller, W. M. The will
Moser, D. The collector
Moser, D. Mr Agruvian and the red-tailed
  hawks
Nicholson, M. The outcast
O'Connor, F. Circle in the fire
O'Connor, F. The river
O'Donovan, J. Little Scotch skirt
O'Donovan, M. The genius
O'Donovan, M. Man of the house
O'Donovan, M. My Œdipus complex
O'Faoláin, S. The confessional
O'Faoláin, S. Judas touch
O'Hara, J. Hotel kid
O'Hara, J. Pardner
Parker, K. A. The fight
Parr, E. Pink
Patten, L. B. Big Black and the bully
Patton, F. G. The homunculus
Pincherle, A. The fall
Robinson, F. M. Dream Street

BOYS—*Continued*

Rutledge, A. H. Blood on the mountain laurels
Ryúnosuke, A. Flatcar
Sampson, C. Love, down in the weeds
Samuel, E. H. The hat-rack
Sandoz, M. Y. Lady of the cornflowers
Saroyan, W. The inventor and the actress
Saroyan, W. Sea and the small boy
Saroyan, W. Sunday zeppelin
Schleyen, M. Back to nature
Schleyen, M. Bad one
Seton, E. T. Boy and the badger
Shaw, I. Peter Two
Skuthorpe, L. Two plates at once
Smith, E. W. Underground episode
Sobel, D. J. Two-timers
Strousse, F. Perfume spray
Summers, H. Black and white and gray
Tarkington, B. Talleyrand Penrod
Thomas, D. The followers
Thomas, D. The peaches
Thomas, D. Prospect of the sea
Thurman, R. Not another word
Vidal, G. The robin
Waldo, E. H. Shadow, shadow on the wall
Wallant, E. L. I held back my hand
Waller, L. Restless ones
Weatherby, K. The pipe
West, A. C. Not Isaac
West, A. C. River's end
West, A. C. Turning page
West, J. The lesson
Wilson, A. Sad fall
Wolfe, T. Paper route
Zawieyski, J. The president calls

    See also Adolescence; Children; Orphans

Boys and girls. Farrell, J. T.

Boys are afraid of girls. De Meyer, J.

Boysi. Allan, G.

BRACELETS

Johns, V. P. Homecoming
Lesiņš, K. Siljonis' jewel
Sansom, W. Mother's bangle

Bracha. Sened, A. and Sened, Y.

Brachvogel, Albert Emil, 1824-1878
Christmas at the Bachs'
Fremantle, A. J. ed. Christmas is here

Brackett, Leigh
Other people
Best science-fiction stories and novels; 9th ser.
So pale, so cold, so fair
Best detective stories of the year (13th annual collection)

Brad Halloran. Kilcrin, I.

Bradbury, Ray, 1920-
All summer in a day
Magazine of fantasy and science fiction. Best from Fantasy and science fiction; 4th ser.
April 2000: the third expedition
Bradbury, R. Martian chronicles
April 2003: the musicians
Bradbury, R. Martian chronicles
April 2005: Usher II
Bradbury, R. Martian chronicles

April 2026: the long years
Bradbury, R. Martian chronicles
August 1999: the earth men
Bradbury, R. Martian chronicles
August 1999: the summer night
Bradbury, R. Martian chronicles
August 2001: the settlers
Bradbury, R. Martian chronicles
August 2002: night meeting
Bradbury, R. Martian chronicles
August 2005: the old ones
Bradbury, R. Martian chronicles
August 2026: there will come soft rains
Bradbury, R. Martian chronicles
The cistern
Bradbury, R. October country
The crowd
Bradbury, R. October country
Day it rained forever
Best American short stories, 1958
December 2001: the green morning
Bradbury, R. Martian chronicles
December 2005: the silent towns
Bradbury, R. Martian chronicles
The dwarf
Bradbury, R. October country
The emissary
Bradbury, R. October country
February 1999: Ylla
Bradbury, R. Martian chronicles
February 2002: the locusts
Bradbury, R. Martian chronicles
February 2003: interim
Bradbury, R. Martian chronicles
Fire balloons
Montgomery, R. B. ed. Best SF
The foghorn
Laughton, C. ed. Tell me a story
Fox and the forest
Laughton, C. ed. Tell me a story
The golden kite, the silver wind
Jennings, F. G. and Calitri, C. J. eds. Stories
Good-by, Grandma
Oberfirst, R. ed. Anthology of best short-short stories, v6
Saturday evening post (Periodical) Saturday evening post stories, 1957
Homecoming
Bradbury, R. October country
Icarus Montgolfier Wright
Magazine of fantasy and science fiction. Best from Fantasy and science fiction; 6th ser.
Illustrated man
Lewis, J. D. ed. Great stories about show business
Jack-in-the-box
Bradbury, R. October country
January 1999: rocket summer
Bradbury, R. Martian chronicles
The jar
Bradbury, R. October country
June 2001:—and the moon be still as bright
Bradbury, R. Martian chronicles
June 2003: way in the middle of the air
Bradbury, R. Martian chronicles
The lake
Bradbury, R. October country
Man upstairs
Bradbury, R. October country

Bradbury, Ray—*Continued*
March 2000: the taxpayer
Bradbury, R. Martian chronicles
Next in line
Bradbury, R. October country
November 2005: the luggage store
Bradbury, R. Martian chronicles
November 2005: the off season
Bradbury, R. Martian chronicles
November 2005: the watchers
Bradbury, R. Martian chronicles
October 2002: the shore
Bradbury, R. Martian chronicles
October 2026: the million-year picnic
Bradbury, R. Martian chronicles
The scythe
Bradbury, R. October country
September 2005: the Martian
Bradbury, R. Martian chronicles
Shopping for death
Best detective stories of the year—1955
Skeleton
Bradbury, R. October country
Small assassin
Bradbury, R. October country
Sneakers
Oberfirst, R. ed. Anthology of best
short-short stories v5
Same as: Summer in the air
Summer in the air
Saturday evening post (Periodical) Sat-
urday evening post stories, 1956
Same as: Sneakers
Sun and shadow
Laughton, C. ed. Tell me a story
There was an old woman
Bradbury, R. October country
Touched with fire
Bradbury, R. October country
2004-05: the naming of names
Bradbury, R. Martian chronicles
Uncle Einar
Bradbury, R. October country
Watchful poker chip of H. Matisse
Bradbury, R. October country
The wind
Bradbury, R. October country
Wonderful death of Dudley Stone
Bradbury, R. October country
Zero hour
Montgomery, R. B. ed. Best SF two
Bradford, Roark, 1896-1948
Child of God
First-prize stories, 1919-1957
How come Christmas?
Posselt, E. ed. A merry, merry Christ-
mas book
Bradshaw, George, 1913-
"The picture wouldn't fit in the stove"
Best American short stories, 1958
Brady, Charles Andrew, 1912-
Jerusalem: the fifteenth Nisan
Hughes, R. ed. All manner of men
Brady, John P. 1918-
December nights in Brooklyn
New voices 2: American writing today
BRAINS, MECHANICAL. See Automata
Brancati, Vitaliano, 1907-
The cavaliere
Slonim, M. L. ed. Modern Italian short
stories

Branch, Claudette Ann (Monelli) 1936-
Apricot and thistle
American vanguard, 1956
Circle of light
New voices 2: American writing today
Branch, Rene, 1930-
Good-bye to spring
American vanguard, 1956
Branch road. Garland, H.
Brand, Christianna, pseud. See Lewis, Mary
Christina
Brand, Max, pseud.
Bulldog
Great dog stories
Brandon, William
Brief enchantment
Saturday evening post (Periodical) Sat-
urday evening post stories, 1956
Brandt, Elsie Cipra
My surprise
Oberfirst, R. ed. Anthology of best
short-short stories v6
BRANDY
Schisgall, O. Intrigue in diamonds
Brave new word. McComas, J. F.
BRAVERY. See Courage
Bravery. Barnsley, A. G.
Bravest of the bulls. Terriss, T.
Brazen locked room. Asimov, I.
BRAZIL
Reid, L. Dehydrated romance
Reid, L. Divorce
Reid, L. Elnea
Reid, L. Granny Bapanira
Reid, L. Irony
Reid, L. A lifetime
Reid, L. Miss Glory
Reid, L. My Lady Happiness
Reid, L. My Lady Happiness, and other
short stories; 12 stories
Reid, L. Nitia
Reid, L. The old man
Reid, L. Sir Pride
Reid, L. Way life is

Rio de Janeiro
Coates, R. M. Friendly game of cards
BREACH OF PROMISE
Harte, B. Colonel Starbottle for the plain-
tiff
Breach of promise. West, J.
Bread alone. O'Hara, J.
The **break.** Jackson, C.
Breakdown. Cook, H. G.
Breakfast at Tiffany's. Capote, T.
Breathe, Coach, breathe! Hall, A.
Breck, Vivian, pseud. See Breckenfeld, Viv-
ian Gurney
Breckenfeld, Vivian Gurney
Touch of Arab
Everygirls horse stories
Brennan, Joseph Payne, 1918-
Calamander chest
Brennan, J. P. Nine horrors and a
dream
Canavan's back yard
Brennan, J. P. Nine horrors and a
dream

BROTHERS AND SISTERS—*Continued*
O'Donovan, J. First love
Porter, K. A. The grave
Schleyen, M. Oh, brother!
Stifter, A. Rock crystal
Stockton, F. R. Asaph
Taylor, P. H. Spinster's tale
Van Doren, M. My son, my son
West, J. Foot-shaped shoes
Williams, T. Portrait of a girl in glass
    See also Brothers; Children; Sisters

BROTHERS-IN-LAW
Anderson, S. Nice girl
Annunzio, G. d' The wake
Bentley, P. E. West Riding love story
Maltz, A. Happiest man on earth
Pincherle, A. Mario
Pincherle, A. The strawberry mark
Walsh, M. Quiet man

Brother's ring. Innerst, I.

Broun, Heywood Campbell, 1888-1939
Jackpot
    Lewis, J. D. ed. Dealer's choice
Last signal
    Collier's (Periodical) Collier's Greatest
    sports stories

Brown, D. MacNab
Car'line
    Oberfirst, R. ed. Anthology of best
    short-short stories v6

Brown, Frederic, 1906-
Answer
    Montgomery, R. B. ed. Best SF three
Expedition
    Magazine of fantasy and science fiction.
    Best from Fantasy and science fiction;
    7th ser.
Keep out
    Conklin, G. ed. Science-fiction adventures in mutation
Placet is a crazy place
    Montgomery, R. B. ed. Best SF two

Brown, Gladys A.
Come back with me
    Oberfirst, R. ed. Anthology of best
    short-short stories v5

Brown, Ivor
Wee bit crude
    Winter's tales, 4

Brown, Jeff
The way I feel
    Teen-age tales, bk 5

Brown, John, 1810-1882
Rab and his friends
    Blaustein, P. M. and Blaustein, A. P.
    eds. Doctors' choice

Brown, Morna Doris MacTaggert, 1907-
Drawn into error
    Crime Writers Association, London.
    Planned departures

Brown, Morris, 1921-
Snow owl
    Best American short stories, 1956

Brown, Thomas Kite, 1916-
Drink of water
    Prize stories, 1958: the O. Henry awards

Brown, Wenzell, 1912-
Anonymous fame
    Mystery Writers of America, inc. A
    choice of murders

Brown, Will C. pseud. See Boyles, C. S.

Brown beauty. Person, W. T.

Brown Jonathan. Ruhen, O.

Bruder, Otto
Little old woman
    Fremantle, A. J. ed. Christmas is here

BRUMMELL, GEORGE BRYAN, 1789-1840
Carroll, S. The shining thing

Brunton, Alexis
This miracle
    Furman, A. L. ed. Everygirls romance
    stories

BRUSH FIRES. See Fires

Brush of the wings. La Farge, O.

The **brute.** Conrad, J.

Brute creation. Jones, G.

Bruyn, Frans de
The drowning
    World prize stories; 2d ser.

Bryning, Frank
Place of the throwing-stick
    Stivens, D. comp. Coast to coast

The **bubble.** Barclay, S. G.

The **bubble.** Hale, N.

BUBBLE GUM. See Chewing-gum

Bubbles. Steele, W. D.

BUCCANEERS. See Pirates

Buchan, John 1st baron Tweedsmuir, 1875-1940
Outgoing of the tide
    Urquhart, F. ed. Scottish short stories

BUCHAREST. See Rumania—Bucharest

Buck, Pearl (Sydenstricker) 1892-
The enemy
    Blaustein, P. M. and Blaustein, A. P.
    eds. Doctors' choice
The frill
    Sterner, L. G. ed. Favorite short stories
Old demon
    Baudin, M. ed. Contemporary short stories v2

Buck in the hills. Clark, W. Van T.

Buck Lamont. Bahr, J.

Buckeridge, Anthony
Call to arms
    Buckeridge, A. comp. In and out of
    school
Jennings runs cross country
    Buckeridge, A. comp. In and out of
    school

Bucket-rider. Kafka, F.

Buckskin empire. Drago, H. S.

Buckskin pensioner. Blackburn, T. W.

Bud Perry's first wife. Caldwell, E.

BUDDHA AND BUDDHISM
Tuong, H. H. Margouillat who chose its
destiny

BUDDHIST PRIESTS
Tuong, H. H. Margouillat who chose its
destiny

Buddies. Verga, G.

Budget of the beasts. Franko, I. I.

BUDGETS, PERSONAL
Knight, R. Third honeymoon
Shaw, I. Main currents of American thought

Budrys, Algis J.
Edge of the sea
  Merril, J. ed. SF: '58
Man who always knew
  Best science-fiction stories and novels: 1956
Nightsound
  Best science-fiction stories and novels; 9th ser.
Nobody bothers Gus
  Merril, J. ed. S-F: ['56]
Silent brother
  Merril, J. ed. SF: '57

Buechler, James
Pepicelli
  Prize stories, 1956: the O. Henry awards

Buechner, Frederick, 1926-
The tiger
  Prize stories, 1955: the O. Henry awards

Buffaloed by a bear. Adams, A.

BUGS. See Insects

Buhet, Gil, 1908-
Siege of Casteilcorbon
  Buckeridge, A. comp. In and out of school

Builder of murderer's bar. Ballard, W. T.

Buist, Ali, 1930-
Days of Jolie
  American vanguard, 1956

BULBS
O'Connor, F. Greenleaf

Bulkhead. Waldo, E. H.

Bull Durham and the vigilantes. Adams, A.

BULL FIGHTERS. See Bullfighters and bullfighting

Bull in a china shop. Gilford, C. B.

Bulldog. Brand, M. pseud.

Bullen, Frank Thomas, 1857-1915
Sea change
  Kemp, P. K. ed. Hundred years of sea stories

Bulletin. Jackson, S.

Bullets lied. MacDonald, J. D.

BULLFIGHTERS AND BULLFIGHT-ING
Blasco Ibanez, V. El Gallardo
Hemingway, E. Capital of the world
Hemingway, E. The undefeated
Smith, E. H. Four o'clock
Terriss, T. Bravest of the bulls

BULLFIGHTING. See Bullfighters and bullfighting

BULLFROGS. See Frogs

BULLS
O'Connor, F. Greenleaf
Scouller, E. Murdoch's bull
  See also Cattle

BULL-TERRIERS
Brand, M. pseud. Bulldog

BUMS. See Tramps

Bunco artists. Charteris, L.

Bunner Sisters. Wharton, E. N. J.

Buntcheh the Silent. Peretz, I. L.

Burdick, Eugene L. 1918- See Lederer, W. J. jt. auth.

BURGLARS. See Thieves

The burglars. Grahame, K.

Burglars and the boy. Gold, H.

BURIAL. See Burials at sea; The dead; Funeral rites and ceremonies

BURIAL, PREMATURE
Poe, E. A. Fall of the House of Usher
Poe, E. A. Premature burial
Rutledge, A. H. Resurrection and the magnolia bloom

The burial. Ervine, St J. G.

BURIAL CUSTOMS. See Funeral rites and ceremonies

BURIALS AT SEA
Maugham, W. S. P. & O.

BURIED ALIVE. See Burial, Premature

BURIED TREASURE. See Treasure-trove

Burk, Carl John
Trumpets in the morning
  Miller, N. ed. New campus writing, no. 2

Burke, Norah, 1907-
My brother, my brother
  World prize stories; 2d ser.

Burkett, Benjamin S.
Onions in the garden
  Oberfirst, R. ed. Anthology of best short-short stories v6

Burla, Yehuda, 1886-
Man and wife
  Tehilla, and other Israeli tales

BURMA
Marshall, E. Heart of Little Shikara

Communism
  See Communism—Burma

Burnet, Dana, 1888-
Giant land
  Tibbets, A. B. ed. Youth, youth, youth

Burnett, Frances (Hodgson) 1849-1924
Behind the white brick
  Lohan, R. ed. Christmas tales for reading aloud

Burnett, Jane
The trophy
  Oberfirst, R. ed. 1955 anthology of best original short-shorts

Burnett, Whit, 1899-
Suffer the little children
  Burnett, W. ed. This is my best humor

Burnett, William Riley, 1899-
Dressing-up
  First-prize stories, 1919-1957

Burnham, Carter, 1901-
Trapping of Tio
  Best detective stories of the year—1955

The burning. Welty, E.

Burning baby. Thomas, D.

Burns, John Horne, 1916-1953
Queen penicillin
  Fenton, C. A. ed. Best short stories of World War II

C

CABALA
Peretz, I. L. The Cabalists

The Cabalists. Peretz, I. L.

CABINET MAKERS
Gilbert, M. F. Scream in a soundproof room

CABINET-WORK
Cave, H. B. Girl shy

Cable, George Washington, 1844-1925
'Sieur George
Thorp, W. ed. Southern reader

CABLE RAILROADS. See Railroads, Cable

Cacciatore, Vera, 1917-
Auction sale
Strachan, W. J. ed. Modern Italian stories

A caddy's diary. Lardner, R. W.

CADET LIFE. See School life

Cadmus Henry, balloon observer. Edmonds, W. D.

Caesar's wife's ear. Bottome, P.

CAFÉS. See Restaurants, lunch rooms, etc.

CAFETERIAS. See Restaurants, lunch rooms, etc.

The cage. Chandler, A. B.

The cake. Maupassant, G. de

CAKES. See Food

Calamander chest. Brennan, J. P.

CALCULATING-MACHINES
Asimov, I. Franchise
Asimov, I. Jokester
Asimov, I. Someday
Balchin, N. God and the machine
Clarke, A. C. The nine billion names of God
Shaara, M. 2066: Election Day

Caldwell, Erskine, 1903-
Advice about women
Caldwell, E. Erskine Caldwell's Gulf Coast stories
Anneve
Caldwell, E. Certain women
Bud Perry's first wife
Caldwell, E. Erskine Caldwell's Gulf Coast stories
Clementine
Caldwell, E. Certain women
Clyde Bickle and Dora
Caldwell, E. Erskine Caldwell's Gulf Coast stories
Daughter
Short, R. W. and Sewall, R. B. eds. Short stories for study
Fifteenth summer
Caldwell, E. Erskine Caldwell's Gulf Coast stories
Gift for Sue
Caldwell, E. Erskine Caldwell's Gulf Coast stories
Girl on the road
Caldwell, E. Erskine Caldwell's Gulf Coast stories
Girl with figurines
Caldwell, E. Erskine Caldwell's Gulf Coast stories

Hat on the bedpost
Caldwell, E. Erskine Caldwell's Gulf Coast stories
Her name was Amelie
Caldwell, E. Erskine Caldwell's Gulf Coast stories
Hilda
Caldwell, E. Certain women
In memory of Judith Courtright
Caldwell, E. Erskine Caldwell's Gulf Coast stories
Kathy
Caldwell, E. Erskine Caldwell's Gulf Coast stories
Last anniversary
Caldwell, E. Erskine Caldwell's Gulf Coast stories
Letters in the mail
Caldwell, E. Erskine Caldwell's Gulf Coast stories
Little candy for Tessie
Caldwell, E. Erskine Caldwell's Gulf Coast stories
Louellen
Caldwell, E. Certain women
Memento
Caldwell, E. Erskine Caldwell's Gulf Coast stories
Miss Paddleford
Caldwell, E. Erskine Caldwell's Gulf Coast stories
Nannette
Caldwell, E. Certain women
The People vs. Abe Lathan: colored
Hall, J. B. and Langland, J. T. eds. Short story
Pride of Miss Stella Sibley
Caldwell, E. Erskine Caldwell's Gulf Coast stories
Selma
Caldwell, E. Certain women
Shooting of Judge Price
Caldwell, E. Erskine Caldwell's Gulf Coast stories
Soquots
Caldwell, E. Erskine Caldwell's Gulf Coast stories
To the chaparral
Caldwell, E. Erskine Caldwell's Gulf Coast stories
Vick Short and the good of the game
Caldwell, E. Erskine Caldwell's Gulf Coast stories
Vicki
Caldwell, E. Certain women

CALENDARS
Asimov, I. Last trump

CALF. See Cattle

The calf. Feierberg, M. Z.

CALIFORNIA
Fuchs, D. Twilight in Southern California

1846-1900
Harte, B. Outcasts of Poker Flat
Harte, B. Tennessee's partner
Hawthorne, H. Gunshot messenger

20th century
Davis, A. L. Mushrooms on the hill
Stegner, W. E. Field guide to the Western birds
Steinbeck, J. The chrysanthemums

CALIFORNIA—*Continued*
Beverly Hills
Fuchs, D. Golden West

Hollywood
Benchley, R. C. Love in Hollywood
Farrell, J. T. $1,000 a week
Fenton, F. The chicken or the egghead
Fitzgerald, F. S. K. Boil some water—
    lots of it
Fitzgerald, F. S. K. No harm trying
Fitzgerald, F. S. K. Teamed with genius
Sullivan, F. Trip to Hollywood

Ranch life
See Ranch life—California

San Francisco
Cather, W. S. Son of the celestial: a
    character
McKimmey, J. Scared cop

Santa Cruz
Connell, E. S. Fisherman from Chihuahua

Calisher, Hortense, 1911-
Christmas carillon
    Prize stories, 1955: the O. Henry
    awards
Night club in the woods
    Prize stories, 1956: the O. Henry
    awards
One of the chosen
    Ribalow, H. U. ed. Treasury of Ameri-
    can Jewish stories
What a thing, to keep a wolf in a cage!
    Prize stories, 1958: the O. Henry
    awards

The **call.** Picard, J.

Call me Joe. Anderson, P.

Call of the wild. London, J.

A **call** on the president. Runyon, D.

Call this land home. Haycox, E.

Call to arms. Buckeridge, A.

Callaghan, Morley Edward, 1903-
Rigmarole
    Nelson, G. E. ed. Cavalcade of the
    North

Called on the carpet. Farrell, J. T.

Callie Daniel. Lochridge, B. H.

CALVES. See Cattle

Calvino, Italo, 1923-
One afternoon, Adam
    Slonim, M. L. ed. Modern Italian short
    stories

Camacho's wedding feast. Gerchunoff, A.

Cameron, Owen, 1905-
Civilized man
    Meredith, S. ed. Bar 6

Camp at Lockjaw. McCord, D. T. W.

Camp in the meadow. Murphy, D.

Campbell, John Wood, 1910-
The idealists
    Healy, R. J. ed. 9 tales of space and
    time

Campbell, William Edward March, 1894-1954
Arrogant shoat
    Campbell, W. E. M. William March
    omnibus

Bill's eyes
    Blaustein, P. M. and Blaustein, A. P.
    eds. Doctors' choice
    Campbell, W. E. M. William March
    omnibus
Cinderella's slipper
    Campbell, W. E. M. William March
    omnibus
Company K
    Campbell, W. E. M. William March
    omnibus
Dirty Emma
    Campbell, W. E. M. William March
    omnibus
Female of the fruit fly
    Campbell, W. E. M. William March
    omnibus
First sunset
    Campbell, W. E. M. William March
    omnibus
The funeral
    Campbell, W. E. M. William March
    omnibus
Happy Jack
    Campbell, W. E. M. William March
    omnibus
I broke my back on a rosebud
    Campbell, W. E. M. William March
    omnibus
Little wife
    Campbell, W. E. M. William March
    omnibus
Memorial to the slain
    Campbell, W. E. M. William March
    omnibus
Miss Daisy
    Campbell, W. E. M. William March
    omnibus
Mist on the meadow
    Campbell, W. E. M. William March
    omnibus
Not worthy of a Wentworth
    Campbell, W. E. M. William March
    omnibus
October Island
    Campbell, W. E. M. William March
    omnibus
    Good housekeeping (Periodical) Editor's
    choice
Personal letter
    Campbell, W. E. M. William March
    omnibus
Send in your answer
    Baudin, M. ed. Contemporary short
    stories v2
She talks good now
    Campbell, W. E. M. William March
    omnibus
Shop in St Louis, Missouri
    Campbell, W. E. M. William March
    omnibus
The slate
    Campbell, W. E. M. William March
    omnibus
This heavy load
    Campbell, W. E. M. William March
    omnibus
Toy bank
    Campbell, W. E. M. William March
    omnibus
Willow fields
    Campbell, W. E. M. William March
    omnibus

Carr, John D.—*Continued*
Death by invisible hands
Queen, E. pseud. ed. Ellery Queen's 13th annual
Incautious burglar
Haycraft, H. and Beecroft, J. eds. Treasury of great mysteries
Same as: Guest in the house
Man who explained miracles
Haycraft, H. and Beecroft, J. eds. Treasury of great mysteries

CARRIAGES AND CARTS
Bates, H. E. Woman who had imagination

Carroll, Lewis, pseud.
Mad tea-party
Sterner, L. G. ed. Favorite short stories

Carroll, Paul Vincent, 1900-
She went by gently
Costain, T. B. and Beecroft, J. eds. More Stories to remember
Garrity, D. A. ed. 44 Irish short stories

Carroll, Sidney
The shining thing
Good housekeeping (Periodical) Editor's choice

Carter, Burnham, 1901-
Thief of diamonds
Best detective stories of the year—1956

Carter, Hodding, 1907-
Rank injustice
Orr, E. and Hammett, E. A. eds. Delta Decameron

Carter, Russell Gordon, 1892-
Beneath the saddle
Humphreville, F. T. ed. In other days

CARTS. See Carriages and carts

CARVING. See Wood carving

Caryatids, an unfinished tale. Blixen, K.

Caryl, Joan, 1920-
For every person in Paris there is a tree
American vanguard, 1956

Cary, Joyce, 1888-1957
Good investment
Davin, D. M. ed. English short stories of today, 2d ser.
Umaru
Davin, D. M. ed. English short stories of today, 2d ser.

Casanova de Seingalt, Giacomo Girolamo, 1725-1798
Rendezvous with M———— M————
Laughton, C. ed. Tell me a story

Case, Victoria, 1897-
Lost wagons
Saturday evening post (Periodical) Saturday evening post stories, 1954
Touch of tenderness
Teen-age tales, bk 5

Case is closed. Rinehart, M. R.

Case of conscience. Bentley, P. E.

Case of conscience. Blish, J.

Case of nerves. Cohen, O. R.

Case of the crimson kiss. Gardner, E. S.

The case of the missing sources. Ashbaugh, D.

Case of the stolen horse. Gerchunoff, A.

Case of the white elephant. Allingham, M.

The case of Valentin Lecormier. Household, G.

The cashier. Voronov, N.

CASHIERS. See Banks and banking

Cask of Amontillado. Poe, E. A.

Casserbanker the Second. Drury, W. P.

Cassill, R. V. 1919-
Biggest band
Fifteen by three
The goldfish
Fifteen by three
The hot girl
New directions 15
Inland years
Prize stories, 1955: the O. Henry awards
Larchmoor is not the world
Fifteen by three
Life of the sleeping beauty
Fifteen by three
The prize
Prize stories, 1956: the O. Henry awards
Romanticizing of Dr Fless
Fifteen by three
When old age shall this generation waste
Prize stories, 1957: the O. Henry awards

The castaway. Maupassant, G. de

CASTAWAYS. See Shipwrecks and castaways

CASTLES
Buhet, G. Siege of Casteilcorbon
Hartley, L. P. Killing bottle

The cat. Colette, S. G.

The cat. Fournier, P.

The cat, a goldfinch, and the stars. Pirandello, L.

Cat and mouse in partnership. Grimm, J. L. K. and Grimm, W. K.

Cat and the cornfield. MacMahon, B.

Cat and the taxidermist. Colette, S. G.

Cat in the jacal. Adams, A.

Cat man. Coombs, C. I.

Cat up in a tree. Sansom, W.

CATACOMBS
Poe, E. A. Cask of Amontillado

CATASTROPHIES. See Accidents

Catch that Martian. Knight, D.

The caterpillar. Hirai, T.

Cates, Robert E. 1930-
Man in black
Oberfirst, R. ed. Anthology of best short-short stories v6

Cathedral of hearts. Gironella, J. M.

Cather, Willa Sibert, 1873-1947
Affair at Grover Station
Cather, W. S. Early stories of Willa Cather
The best years
Cather, W. S. Five stories
Clemency of the court
Cather, W. S. Early stories of Willa Cather

Cather, Willa S.—*Continued*
Conversion of Sum Loo
　Cather, W. S. Early stories of Willa
　Cather
Count of Crow's Nest
　Cather, W. S. Early stories of Willa
　Cather
Dance at Chevalier's
　Cather, W. S. Early stories of Willa
　Cather
The enchanted bluff
　Cather, W. S. Five stories
Eric Hermannson's soul
　Cather, W. S. Early stories of Willa
　Cather
"Fear that walks by noonday"
　Cather, W. S. Early stories of Willa
　Cather
Lou, the prophet
　Cather, W. S. Early stories of Willa
　Cather
Nanette: an aside
　Cather, W. S. Early stories of Willa
　Cather
Neighbour Rosicky
　Cather, W. S. Five stories
　Costain, T. B. and Beecroft, J. eds.
　　More Stories to remember
　Hart, J. D. and Gohdes, C. L. eds.
　　America's literature
　Same as: Neighbor Rosicky
Night at Greenway Court
　Cather, W. S. Early stories of Willa
　Cather
On the divide
　Cather, W. S. Early stories of Willa
　Cather
Paul's case
　Baudin, M. ed. Contemporary short
　　stories v 1
　Cather, W. S. Five stories
　Jennings, F. G. and Calitri, C. J. eds.
　　Stories
Peter
　Cather, W. S. Early stories of Willa
　Cather
The prodigies
　Cather, W. S. Early stories of Willa
　Cather
A resurrection
　Cather, W. S. Early stories of Willa
　Cather
Sentimentality of William Tavener
　Cather, W. S. Early stories of Willa
　Cather
Singer's romance
　Cather, W. S. Early stories of Willa
　Cather
Son of the Celestial: a character
　Cather, W. S. Early stories of Willa
　Cather
Tale of the white pyramid
　Cather, W. S. Early stories of Willa
　Cather
Tom Outland's story
　Cather, W. S. Five stories
Tommy, the unsentimental
　Cather, W. S. Early stories of Willa
　Cather

CATHOLIC BISHOPS. See Bishops,
　Catholic

CATHOLIC CHURCH. See Catholic faith

CATHOLIC CHURCH IN POLAND
　Babel', I. E. Church at Novograd
CATHOLIC FAITH
　Coogan, J. Decline and fall of Augie
　　Sheean
　Daudet, A. Father Gaucher's elixir
　Dostoevskiĭ, F. M. The grand inquisitor
　Elliott, G. P. Brother Quintillian and
　　Dick the chemist
　Farrell, J. T. Hyland family
　James, D. A kind of faith
　Lytle, A. N. Ortiz's Mass
　MacDonagh, D. Duet for organ and
　　strings
　Miller, E. M. Christmas Eve
　O'Faoláin, S. Unholy living and half
　　dying
　O'Hara, J. No mistakes
　Pea, E. Moscardino
　Plunkett, J. The damned
　Plunkett, J. Mercy
　Powers, J. F. Devil was the joker
　Shaw, G. B. Miraculous revenge
CATHOLIC PRIESTS
　Applegate, F. G. Tricks in all trades
　Atherton, G. F. H. Vengence of Padre
　　Arroyo
　Blish, J. Case of conscience
　Blixen, K. Cardinal's third tale
　Carmer, C. L. Vision of the falling priest
　Chesterton, G. K. Blue cross
　Dąbrowska, M. Father Philip
　Daudet, A. Three Low Masses
　Farrell, J. T. Father Timothy Joyce
　Fay, W. Weep not for me
　Guareschi, G. A baptism
　Guareschi, G. The petition
　Kubly, H. Divine ecstasy
　Lavin, M. Wet day
　Lederer, W. J. and Burdick, E. L. Nine
　　friends
　Lofts, N. R. Father Francisco's ointment
　MacMahon, B. Cat and the cornfield
　MacMahon, B. Evening in Ireland
　MacMahon, B. Sound of the bell
　Maupassant, G. de. After
　Maupassant, G. de. The christening
　Maupassant, G. de. In the moonlight
　Maupassant, G. de. Making a convert
　Maupassant, G. de. Moonlight
　Maupassant, G. de. Olive orchard
　Maupassant, G. de. The patron
　Maupassant, G. de. A surprise
　Maupassant, G. de. Shepherd's leap
　Miller, E. M. Scramble
　Moore, G. Julia Cahill's curse
　O'Donovan, M. Peasants
　O'Faoláin, S. Admiring the scenery
　O'Faoláin, S. Broken world
　O'Faoláin, S. Discord
　O'Faoláin, S. Silence of the valley
　O'Faoláin, S. Sinners
　Pevehouse, A. Kachina dolls
　Powers, J. F. Dawn
　Powers, J. F. Death of a favorite
　Powers, J. F. Defection of a favorite
　Powers, J. F. The forks
　Powers, J. F. Losing game
　Powers, J. F. Presence of Grace
　Powers, J. F. Valiant woman
　Powers, J. F. Zeal
　Reid, L. Divorce
　White, W. A. P. Balaam
　Wulzen, A. The priest

Catlin, George
Ba'tiste's story of the medicine bag
Schaefer, J. W. ed. Out West

CATS
Adams, A. Cat in the jacal
Berriault, G. Felis catus
Blackwood, A. Psychical invasion
Boylston, H. D. Stuff of dreams
Bretnor, R. Genius of the species
Carr, A. H. Z. Black kitten
Colette, S. G. The cat
Colette, S. G. Cat and the taxidermist
Colette, S. G. Chance acquaintances
Colette, S. G. Domino
Colette, S. G. Fastagette
Colette, S. G. Little black cat
Colette, S. G. The long-cat
Colette, S. G. Mother cat
Colette, S. G. "Poum"
Colette, S. G. "Prrou"
Colette, S. G. Robin
Colette, S. G. "The she-shah"
Colette, S. G. The Siamese
Colette, S. G. Simpleton
Colette, S. G. The tom-cat
De La Roche, M. Ninth life
Fournier, P. The cat
Freeman, M. E. W. Object of love
Green, C. Serafina caper
Hammett, E. A. Prawns for Penelope
Hardy, J. Anna says cats are like people
Kerr, S. Mister Youth
Macken, W. Lady and the tom
MacMahon, B. Cat and the cornfield
Mankowitz, W. Day Aunt Chaya was buried
Manners, M. Death on little cat's feet
Mason, P. O. and Mason, J. ed. Favorite cat stories of Pamela and James Mason; 10 stories
Maupassant, G. de. Misti
Maupassant, G. de. On cats
Peattie, D. C. and Peattie, L. R. Plutarch's lives
Peretz, I. L. The pious cat
Pincherle, A. The fall
Powers, J. F. Defection of a favorite
Reid, A. The kitten
Roberts, M. C. Tom Ivory, the cat
Sansom, W. Cat up in a tree
Sayers, D. L. Cyprian cat
Seton, E. T. Slum cat
Steele, W. D. Bubbles
Summers, H. Black and white and gray
Van Vechten, C. Feathers
Van Vechten, C. My cat
Warner, S. T. At the Trafalgar Bakery
Weaver, J. Van A. and Wood, P. Far-sighted cat
Williams, T. The malediction
Wright, S. F. Better choice
Zistel, E. Biography

The **cats.** Allen, S.

Cat's-paw. Ellin, S.

CATSKILL MOUNTAINS
Irving, W. Rip Van Winkle

CATTLE
Brophy, J. Prodigal calf
Easton, R. O. Death in October
Feierberg, M. Z. The calf
Foster, B. Trail song
Hankins, J. W. Thaw

Mankowitz, W. Devil and the cow
O'Flaherty, L. Birth
O'Flaherty, L. Cow's death
O'Flaherty, L. Two lovely beasts
Rhodes, E. M. Aforesaid Bates
Rhodes, E. M. Trouble man
Richter, C. The lady
Stuart, J. Chase of the skittish heifer
Stuart, J. Rich men
West, J. Learn to say good-by
West, J. The lesson
See also Bulls

CATTLE DRIVES
Adams, A. Alkaline dust ain't snow
Adams, A. Why the Chisholm Trail forks
Barker, S. O. Trail fever
Boyles, C. S. Cowboy Columbus
Foreman, L. L. Wagon-tongue north
Fox, N. A. Trail medicine
Halacy, D. S. Dry-trail showdown
Loomis, N. M. Maverick factory

CAUCASUS. See Russia—Caucasus

Causey, James, 1924-
Felony
Best science-fiction stories and novels: 1955

A **cavalcade.** Tikhonov, N. S.

The **cavaliere.** Brancati, V.

Cavalleria rusticana. Verga, G.

Cavalry tale. See Hofmannsthal, H. H. Edler von. Tale of the cavalry

Cavanaugh, James Patrick, 1922-
Marking time
New voices 2: American writing today

Cave, Hugh Barnett, 1910-
Extra girl
Ferris, H. J. comp. Girls, girls, girls
Girl shy
Stowe, A. comp. When boy dates girl
Teen-age tales, bk 5

Cave of night. Gunn, J. E.

Cave on Thunder Cloud. Rinehart, M. R.

Caveat emptor. De Camp, L. S. and Pratt, F.

CAVELL, EDITH LOUISA, 1865-1915
Hagedorn, H. Edith Cavell

Caviar. Waldo, E. H.

Caylus, Anne Claude Philippe de Tubieres, comte de, 1692-1765
Fairy gifts
Laughton, C. ed. Tell me a story

Cecchi, Emilio, 1884-
Aquarium
Slonim, M. L. ed. Modern Italian short stories
Visitors
Slonim, M. L. ed. Modern Italian short stories

Cela, Camilo José
Village idiot
Flores, A. ed. Great Spanish stories

Celebrated jumping frog of Calaveras County. Clemens, S. L.

Celebrated sassage factory. Dickens, C.

Celebration. Comito, T.

Celebration for Joe. Gold, H.

Celestial omnibus. Forster, E. M.

Cellini, Benvenuto
Price, J. B. Murder for fine art
CEMETERIES
Angoff, C. Shma Ysroel
Fournier, P. Season of the dead
McConnell, J. Nor dust corrupt
Maupassant, G. de. Graveyard sirens
Maupassant, G. de. Was it a dream?
Porter, K. A. The grave
Singmaster, E. The home-coming
CENSORSHIP OF THE PRESS. See
Liberty of the press
CENSUS
Pohl, F. Census takers
Census takers. Pohl, F.
The centaur. Campion, A.
Century of a lifetime. Johnston, R. T.
CERAMICS. See Potters and pottery
Cerebrative psittacoid. Nearing, H.
CEREMONIES. See Rites and ceremonies
Cernescu, Adrian, 1932-
Daybreak meeting
Short stories v 1
Certain people are gonna wake up and
learn the score is too late. Kober, A.
Chacel, Rosa
Twilight in extremadura
Flores, A. ed. Great Spanish stories
Chaff in the wind. Bates, H. E.
Chaikin, Nancy G.
Bachelor of arts
Best American short stories, 1955
CHAIN GANGS. See Convicts; Prison la-
bor
Chain of command. Rynas, S. A.
CHAINS
Wright, G. Madman's chain
CHAIRS
Hirai, T. Human chair
Châli. Maupassant, G. de
Challenge to the reader. Philips, J. P.
Chamberlain, William
Imitation general
Saturday evening post (Periodical) Sat-
urday evening post stories, 1956
Chambers, Maude L.
Fair exchange
Oberfirst, R. ed. Anthology of best
short-short stories v5
Champion. Lardner, R. W.
The champions. Stuart, J.
Champions of the peaks. Annixter, P. pseud.
Champney, Lizzie W.
Old stager
Humphreville, F. T. ed. In other days
Chamson, André, 1900-
My enemy
Gettman, R. A. and Harkness, B. eds.
Book of stories
Power of words
Lehmann, J. ed. Modern French stories
CHANCE
Butler, E. P. Mascot
Faulkner, W. Chance
Parkinson, E. M. Lucky day

Chance. Faulkner, W.
Chance acquaintances. Colette, S. G.
Chandler, A. Bertram
The cage
Magazine of fantasy and science fiction.
Best from Fantasy and science fiction;
7th ser.
Chandler, David
12 flights up
This week magazine. This week's Sto-
ries of mystery and suspense
Chandler, Raymond, 1888-1959
Big sleep
Haycraft, H. and Beecroft, J. eds.
Treasury of great mysteries
Change in the rules. McKinney, D. L.
Change of heart. Kelso, S. E.
Changing mask. Weigel, H.
CHAPELS. See Churches
CHAPLAINS. See Clergy
CHAPMAN, JOHN, 1774-1847
Malcolmson, A. B. Johnny Appleseed
Chapman, Mildred
Mistaken identity
Oberfirst, R. ed. 1955 anthology of best
original short-shorts
Chariot race. Grazier, J. A.
CHARITIES
Allen, S. The award
Chekhov, A. P. Woman's kingdom
Coppée, F. Baron's two francs
Criswell, C. Goddess of Mercy
Friel, G. Thoughtless
Mansfield, K. Cup of tea
Samuel, E. H. Big givers
Sandoz, M. Y. The visitation
CHARLESTON. See South Carolina—
Charleston
Charlotte. Angoff, C.
Charlotte Russe. Hale, N.
Charm dispelled. Maupassant, G. de
Charmed lives. Gordimer, N.
CHARMS
Cates, R. E. Man in black
Conrad, J. Karain: a memory
Derleth, A. W. Seal of R'lyeh
Jacobs, W. W. Monkey's paw
Charteris, Leslie, 1907-
Arrow of God
Cooke, D. C. ed. My best murder story
Haycraft, H. and Beercroft, J. eds.
Treasury of great mysteries
Bunco artists
Charteris, L. Thanks to The Saint
Careful terrorist
Charteris, L. Thanks to The Saint
Good medicine
Charteris, L. Thanks to The Saint
Happy suicide
Charteris, L. Thanks to The Saint
Mug's game
Lewis, J. D. ed. Dealer's choice
Perfect sucker
Charteris, L. Thanks to The Saint
Unescapable word
Charteris, L. Thanks to The Saint

CHARWOMEN. See Servants—Cleaning women

The **chase.** Apperley, C. J.

Chase of the skittish heifer. Stuart, J.

Chase the crippled dream. Bishop, L.

Chasing mustangs. Adams, A.

Chateaubriand. Epstein, S.

Chatzkel. Angoff, C.

Chaucer, Geoffrey, 1340?-1400
Pardoner's tale
Sterner, L. G. ed. Favorite short stories

CHAUFFEURS. See Servants—Chauffeurs

Chavez, Angelico, 1910-
Ardent commandant
Chavez, A. From an altar screen
Bell that sang again
Chavez, A. From an altar screen
Black ewe
Chavez, A. From an altar screen
Colonel and the santo
Chavez, A. From an altar screen
Fiddler and the angelito
Chavez, A. From an altar screen
Lean years
Chavez, A. From an altar screen
Wake for Don Corsinio
Chavez, A. From an altar screen

Chawdron. Huxley, A. L.

Cheap excursion. Coward, N. P.

CHEATING. See Swindlers and swindling

Checkmate. McLaren, M.

Checkmate. Maupassant, G. de

Cheerful land. Rhodes, E. M.

Cheest. Faulkner, W.

Cheever, John, 1912-
Bus to St James's
Stories
Country husband
Best American short stories, 1955
Cheever, J. Housebreaker of Shady Hill, and other stories
First-prize stories, 1919-1957
Prize stories, 1956: the O. Henry awards
Stories
Day the pig fell into the well
Stories
Enormous radio
Hall, J. B. and Langland, J. T. eds. Short story
Havighurst, W. and others, eds. Selection
Five-forty-eight
Cheever, J. Housebreaker of Shady Hill, and other stories
Prize stories, 1955: the O. Henry awards
Housebreaker of Shady Hill
Cheever, J. Housebreaker of Shady Hill, and other stories
Journal of an old gent
Prize stories, 1957: the O. Henry awards
Just tell me who it was
Cheever, J. Housebreaker of Shady Hill, and other stories
National pastime
Stories
O youth and beauty!
Cheever, J. Housebreaker of Shady Hill, and other stories

Sorrows of gin
Cheever, J. Housebreaker of Shady Hill, and other stories
Trouble of Marcie Flint
Cheever, J. Housebreaker of Shady Hill, and other stories
Worm in the apple
Cheever, J. Housebreaker of Shady Hill, and other stories

CHEFS. See Servants—Cooks

Chekhov, Anton Pavlovich, 1860-1904
The bet
Rosenblum, M. ed. Stories from many lands
Sterner, L. G. ed. Favorite short stories
Betrothed
Chekhov, A. P. Peasants, and other stories
The bishop
Chekhov, A. P. Peasants, and other stories
Gooseberries
Locke, L. G.; Gibson, W. M. and Arms, G. W. eds. Introduction to literature
Short, R. W. and Sewall, R. B. eds. Short stories for study
Gusev
Jarrell, R. ed. Anchor book of stories
In the ravine
Chekhov, A. P. Peasants, and other stories
The lady with the dog
Gettman, R. A. and Harkness, B. eds. Book of stories
The lament
Havighurst, W. and others, eds. Selection
McClennen, J. comp. Masters and masterpieces of the short story
The murder
Chekhov, A. P. Peasants, and other stories
My life: the story of a provincial
Chekhov, A. P. Peasants, and other stories
The New Villa
Chekhov, A. P. Peasants, and other stories
Thurston, J. A. ed. Reading modern short stories
On official business
Hall, J. B. and Langland, J. T. eds. Short story
Peasants
Chekhov, A. P. Peasants, and other stories
Rothschild's fiddle
Jarrell, R. ed. Anchor book of stories
Three years
Chekhov, A. P. Peasants, and other stories
Two tragedies
Blaustein, P. M. and Blaustein, A. P. eds. Doctors' choice
Woman's kingdom
Chekhov, A. P. Peasants, and other stories

Chekov, Anton. See Chekhov, Anton Pavlovich

CHRISTMAS—*Continued*

Miller, E. M. Christmas Eve
Miller, E. M. Christmas present
Milne, A. A. Hint for next Christmas
Moore, C. C. Noel candle
Mottram, R. H. Good old-fashioned Christmas
Munro, H. H. Bertie's Christmas Eve
Munro, H. H. Reginald's Christmas revel
Pagano, J. Signor Santa
Plomer, W. C. F. Friend of her father's
Pohl, F. Happy birthday, dear Jesus
Porter, W. S. Gift of the Magi
Posselt, E. ed. A merry, merry Christmas book; 16 stories
Raymund, B. Last Christmas
Ready, W. B. As it was and as it will be: a Christmas tale
Robb, E. C. White shawl
Rosegger, P. Carpenter's Christmas
Rosten, L. C. Mr Kaplan and the Magi
Runyon, D. Dancing Dan's Christmas
Sansom, W. The ballroom
Schaumann, R. Harvest without seed
Simenon, G. Maigret's Christmas
Soman, F. J. Sweet eighteen
Sørensen, V. The concert
Steffens, L. Miserable merry Christmas
Stifter, A. Rock crystal
Stockton, F. R. Stephen Skarridge's Christmas
Stokl, H. B. On Christmas Eve
Sullivan, F. Crisp new bills for Mr Teagle
Thurman, R. Y. Not another word
Topelius, Z. Christmas with the goblins
West, A. C. No fatted calf
Wiggin, K. D. S. Birds' Christmas carol
Wilson, A. Flat country Christmas
Wodehouse, P. G. Jeeves and the yuletide spirit
Worthington, R. What about Susanna?
Yoder, R. M. Merry Christmas in ten pieces
See also Jesus Christ—Nativity

Christmas at the Bachs'. Brachvogel, A. E.
Christmas bogey. Frank, P.

CHRISTMAS CARDS
Morley, C. D. Worst Christmas story

Christmas carillon. Calishers, H.
Christmas carol. Dickens, C.
Christmas doll. Chute, B. J.
Christmas Eve. Gogol', N. V.
Christmas Eve. Maupassant, G. de
Christmas Eve. Miller, E. M.

CHRISTMAS GIFTS. See Christmas; Gifts
Christmas lovers. Coppée, F.
Christmas memory. Capote, T.
Christmas mystery. Locke, W. J.
Christmas present. Miller, E. M.
Christmas song. Woodson, E. S.
Christmas spectacle. Benchley, R. C.

CHRISTMAS STORIES. See Christmas
Christmas tree. Dickens, C.
Christmas tree and a wedding. Dostoevskiĭ, F. M.

CHRISTMAS TREES
Andersen, H. C. Fir tree
Clingerman, M. The wild wood
Moore, C. C. Legend of the Christmas tree

Christmas trombone. Banks, R. E.
Christmas with the goblins. Topelius, Z.
Christmas wreck. Stockton, F. R.

CHRISTOPHER, SAINT, fl. 3d century
O'Connor, P. The big ferryman

Christopher, John, 1922-
New wine
Montgomery, R. B. ed. Best SF

Chronicle of a demise. Williams, T.
The chrysanthemums. Steinbeck, J.

Church, Francis P.
Is there a Santa Claus?
Lohan, R. ed. Christmas tales for reading aloud

Church, Richard
Elephants in the mirror
Pudney, J. ed. Pick of today's short stories, 9

Church at Novograd. Babel', I. E.
Church cleaning at Lickskillet. Polk, W. T.

CHURCH DECORATION AND ORNAMENT
Babel', I. E. Pan Apolek

CHURCH ENTERTAINMENTS
Benchley, R. C. Christmas spectacle
Carlile, C. The animal fair

CHURCH SCHOOLS
Winters, N. D. Sea shells

CHURCH SOCIABLES. See Church entertainments

CHURCHES
Babel', I. E. In St Valentine's church
Bentley, P. E. Case of conscience
Hall, J. B. In the time of demonstrations
Warner, S. T. The reredos

CHURCHILL, SIR WINSTON LEONARD SPENCER, 1874-
Blassingame, W. Gray Arab of Winston Churchill

CHURCHYARDS. See Cemeteries

Chute, Beatrice Joy, 1913-
Birthday gift
Chute, B. J. Blue cup, and other stories
Blue cup
Chute, B. J. Blue cup, and other stories
Christmas doll
Chute, B. J. Blue cup, and other stories
Escape
Chute, B. J. Blue cup, and other stories
The fiesta
Chute, B. J. Blue cup, and other stories
The jukebox and the Kallikaks
Chute, B. J. Blue cup, and other stories
Costain, T. B. and Beecroft, J. eds. More Stories to remember
The legacy
Chute, B. J. Blue cup, and other stories
Miss Maggie Doons and the wicked city
Chute, B. J. Blue cup, and other stories
The outcasts
Chute, B. J. Blue cup, and other stories
Q for quitclaim
Chute, B. J. Blue cup, and other stories
Rookie cop
Chute, B. J. Blue cup, and other stories
Ski high
Furman, A. L. ed. Teen-age humorous stories

Chute, Beatrice J.—*Continued*
 Three in a stew
  Furman, A. L. ed. Teen-age humorous stories
 Vexation of Barney Hatch
  Chute, B. J. Blue cup, and other stories
CICADA
 Sargent, E. N. Princess in the pecan tree
The **cicatrice.** Gordimer, N.
CIGARETTES. See Smoking
CIGARS. See Smoking
CINCINNATI. See Ohio—Cincinnati
Cinderella's slipper. Campbell, W. E. M.
Cindy Thacker's Christmas dinner. Clayton, J. B.
CINEMA. See Moving pictures
CIPHER AND TELEGRAPH CODES
 King, R. Malice in wonderland
 Poe, E. A. Gold bug
Circe. Welty, E.
Circle in the fire. O'Connor, F.
Circle of light. Branch, C. A. M.
Circuit of the wild swan. Sullivan, A.
CIRCUMCISION
 Babel', I. E. Karl-Yankel
 Yaari, Y. Threefold covenant
CIRCUS
 Aichinger, I. Bound man
 Aymé, M. The dwarf
 Coombs, C. I. Cat man
 Edell, H. Tiger was a lady
 Karlan, A. The wall
 Macken, W. The lion
 Porter, K. A. The circus
  See also Acrobats and acrobatism; Carnival; Menageries
The **circus.** Porter, K. A.
CIRCUS PERFORMERS. See Circus
CIRCUS wrestlers. Colette, S. G.
CIRCUSES. See Circus
The **cistern.** Bradbury, R.
CITIES, IMAGINARY. See Imaginary cities
CITIES AND TOWNS
 Knight, D. Natural state
 Lochridge, B. H. The town
 Winslow, T. S. City folks
  See also Small town life
Citizen in space. Sheckley, R.
CITRON
 Rabinowitz, S. Dead citron
City folks. Winslow, T. S.
CITY LIFE. See Cities and towns
City of Sin. Loomis, N. M.
City of the living. Stegner, W. E.
CIVIL ENGINEERS
 Fuchs, D. Man in the middle of the ocean
CIVIL LIBERTY. See Liberty
CIVIL SERVICE
 Chekhov, A. P. On official business
 Cooper, W. Ball of paper
 Lederer, W. J. and Burdick, E. L. Employment opportunities abroad

Lederer, W. J. and Burdick, E. L. Girl who got recruited
Lederer, W. J. and Burdick, E. L. The sum of tiny things
Maugham, W. S. Door of opportunity
Maugham, W. S. Mackintosh
Rabinowitz, S. The convoy
Waddington, P. Street that got mislaid
CIVIL WAR. See United States—19th century—Civil War
CIVILIZATION
 Oliver, C. Of course
Civilized man. Cameron, O.
Clad, Noel, 1924?-
 Man with a secret
  Saturday evening post (Periodical) Saturday evening post stories, 1956
Clair de lune. See Maupassant, Guy de. Moonlight
CLAIRVOYANCE
 Conrad, J. Secret agent
 Criswell, C. Give your heart to Jesus
 Plomer, W. C. F. Thy neighbour's creed
  See also Fortune telling; Mind reading; Thought transference
Clancy, Dorothy
 The meek Mr Weeks
  Oberfirst, R. ed. Anthology of best short-short stories v5
CLANS AND CLAN SYSTEM
 Brown, I. Wee bit crude
 MacMahon, B. Kings asleep in the ground
CLARE. See Ireland; Provincial and rural—Clare
Clark, Alfred Alexander Gordon, 1900-
 Magnifying glass
  Crime Writers Association, London. Planned departures
 Murderer's luck
  This week magazine. This week's Stories of mystery and suspense
Clark, Walter Van Tilburg, 1909-
 Buck in the hills
  Schaefer, J. ed. Out West
 Hook
  Baudin, M. ed. Contemporary short stories v 1
 Portable phonograph
  Havighurst, W. and others, eds. Selection
 The rapids
  Hall, J. B. and Langland, J. T. eds. Short story
 Wind and the snow of winter
  First-prize stories, 1919-1957
Clarke, Arthur Charles, 1917-
 All the time in the world
  Clarke, A. C. The other side of the sky
 The awakening
  Clarke, A. C. Reach for tomorrow
 Cosmic Casanova
  Clarke, A. C. The other side of the sky
 The curse
  Clarke, A. C. Reach for tomorrow
 Fires within
  Clarke, A. C. Reach for tomorrow
 Forgotten enemy
  Clarke, A. C. Reach for tomorrow

Clarke, Arthur C.—*Continued*
Jupiter five
   Clarke, A. C. Reach for tomorrow
The nine billion names of God
   Clarke, A. C. The other side of the sky
   Montgomery, R. B. ed. Best SF two
No morning after
   Clarke, A. C. The other side of the sky
The other side of the sky
   Clarke, A. C. The other side of the sky
Out of the sun
   Clarke, A. C. The other side of the sky
The parasite
   Clarke, A. C. Reach for tomorrow
The possessed
   Clarke, A. C. Reach for tomorrow
Publicity campaign
   Clarke, A. C. The other side of the sky
Refugee
   Clarke, A. C. The other side of the sky
Rescue party
   Clarke, A. C. Reach for tomorrow
Security check
   Clarke, A. C. The other side of the sky
Songs of the distant earth
   Clarke, A. C. The other side of the sky
The star
   Clarke, A. C. The other side of the sky
Technical error
   Clarke, A. C. Reach for tomorrow
This earth of majesty
   Magazine of fantasy and science fiction. Best from Fantasy and science fiction; 5th ser.
Time's arrow
   Clarke, A. C. Reach for tomorrow
Transience
   Clarke, A. C. The other side of the sky
Trouble with the natives
   Clarke, A. C. Reach for tomorrow
Venture to the moon
   Clarke, A. C. The other side of the sky
   Magazine of fantasy and science fiction. Best from Fantasy and science fiction; 7th ser.
Walk in the dark
   Clarke, A. C. Reach for tomorrow
Wall of darkness
   Clarke, A. C. The other side of the sky
Clarke, Desmond, 1907-
The Islandman
   Garrity, D. A. ed. 44 Irish short stories
CLASS DISTINCTION
Adams, A. Quarternights near the salt licks
Amis, K. My enemy's enemy
Connell, E. S. Beau monde of Mrs Bridge
   See also Social classes; Social status
Classified. Ferber, E.
Claudie. Lochridge, B. H.
Claussen, William Edmunds
Man from Texas
   Western Writers of America. Wild streets
The **Claxtons.** Huxley, A. L.
Clay, George R. 1921-
We're all guests
   Best American short stories, 1956
Clay. Joyce, J.

Clayton, John Bell, 1906-1955
All the petals of all the roses in the world
   Clayton, J. B. Strangers were there
Cindy Thacker's Christmas dinner
   Clayton, J. B. Strangers were there
Empty Sunday, the snow, and the strangers
   Clayton, J. B. Strangers were there
Happy story when seen backwards
   Clayton, J. B. Strangers were there
Incident at Chapman's Switch
   Clayton, J. B. Strangers were there
Last blast of the trumpet
   Clayton, J. B. Strangers were there
Little Bailey girl
   Clayton, J. B. Strangers were there
Little Woodrow
   Clayton, J. B. Strangers were there
Man who looked like a bird
   Clayton, J. B. Strangers were there
Mr Sampsell's thirty-pound diamond
   Clayton, J. B. Strangers were there
Part of the town
   Clayton, J. B. Strangers were there
Short ride up the hollow
   Clayton, J. B. Strangers were there
Silence of the mountains
   Clayton, J. B. Strangers were there
Snowfall on Fourth Street
   Clayton, J. B. Strangers were there
Soft step of the Shawnee
   Clayton, J. B. Strangers were there
Sound that God heard
   Clayton, J. B. Strangers were there
Summer of the insistent voices
   Clayton, J. B. Strangers were there
Sunday ice cream
   Clayton, J. B. Strangers were there
Warm day in November
   Clayton, J. B. Strangers were there
White against winter dawn
   Clayton, J. B. Strangers were there
White circle
   Clayton, J. B. Strangers were there
   First-prize stories, 1919-1957
Clean, well-lighted place. Hemingway, E.
CLEANING
McKinney, D. L. Night man
CLEANING WOMEN. See Servants— Cleaning women
CLEANLINESS. See Baths
Clear case of self-defence. Gollschewsky, E. A.
Clegg, Christine
The picnic
   Miller, N. ed. New campus writing no. 2
Clemency of the court. Cather, W. S.
Clemens, Samuel Langhorne, 1835-1910
Celebrated jumping frog of Calaveras County
   Hart, J. D. and Gohdes, C. L. eds. America's literature
   Same as: Notorious jumping frog of Calaveras County
From "A Connecticut Yankee in King Arthur's Court"
   Gallant, J. ed. Stories of scientific imagination

Clemens, Samuel L.—*Continued*
Man that corrupted Hadleyburg
Hart, J. D. and Gohdes, C. L. eds.
America's literature
Short, R. W. and Sewall, R. B. eds.
Short stories for study
Notorious jumping frog of Calaveras
county
Sterner, L. G. ed. Favorite short stories
Same as: Celebrated jumping frog of
Calaveras County
Professor's yarn
Lewis, J. D. ed. Dealer's choice

Clementine. Caldwell, E.

Clemons, Walter, 1930?-
Dark roots of the rose
Best American short stories, 1957
Summer shower
Prize stories, 1958: the O. Henry
awards

CLERGY
Ali, A. Before death
Allen, S. Sunday morning shift
Anderson, S. Strength of God
Baltenbach, L. J. Parson's dilemma
Barker, S. Fog on Pemble Green
Bentley, P. E. Case of conscience
Caldwell, E. Clementine
Campbell, W. E. M. Mist on the meadow
Chesterton, G. K. Blue cross
Dreiser, T. Doer of the word
Gide, A. P. G. Pastoral symphony
Hammett, E. A. Solomon primitive
Hawthorne, N. Minister's black veil
Jones, G. Price-Parry
Keir, R. H. Sunday punch
Marlett, M. B. G. Purring countess
Newmen, W. C. Protestant Saint Francis
Paulk, G. S. A cup of trust
Rawlings, M. K. Jessamine Springs
Sampson, C. Love, down in the weeds
Sunna. Love is humbug
Thomas, D. The enemies
Thomason, J. W. The preacher calls the
dance
Thomason, J. W. A preacher goes to war
Thomason, J. W. The stars in their
courses
Tolstoi, L. N. Graf. Three hermits
See also Bishops; Cardinals; Catholic priests; Monasticism and religious
orders; Rabbis

CLERGY, ANGLICAN AND EPISCOPAL
Ashton, W. Dearly beloved of Benjamin
Cobb
Bowen, E. Maria
Farrell, M. F. Villainy of Mr Fox
Lochridge, B. H. Hilary Arnold
Patton, F. G. Mimosa blight

CLERGY, CATHOLIC. See Catholic
priests

Clerical error. Clifton, M.

Clerical error. Cozzens, J. G.

CLERKS
Farrell, J. T. Jazz-age clerk
Joyce, J. Counterparts
O'Faoláin, S. Born genius

Clever girl. Joseph Zabara

Clicking of Cuthbert. Wodehouse, P. G.

The **cliff.** Hirai, T.

Clifton, Mark, 1906-
Clerical error
Best science-fiction stories and novels:
1956
Sense from thought divide
Merril, J. ed. S-F: ['56]

Climate of the lost. Bodington, N.

Climbing against death. Major, R. H.

Clingerman, Mildred
Birds can't count
Magazine of fantasy and science fiction.
Best from Fantasy and science fiction; 5th ser.
Merril, J. ed. S-F: ['56]
Last prophet
Magazine of fantasy and science fiction.
Best from Fantasy and science fiction; 5th ser.
Mr Sakrison's halt
Magazine of fantasy and science fiction.
Best from Fantasy and science fiction; 6th ser.
The wild wood
Magazine of fantasy and science fiction.
Best from Fantasy and science fiction; 7th ser.

Clinton, Ed. M.
Small world of M-75
Conklin, G. ed. Science-fiction adventures in mutation

CLIPPER SHIPS. See Sailing vessels

Clive, Mary
Entirely platonic
Winter's tales, 2

The **cloak.** Blixen, K.

Clochette. See Maupassant, G. de. Bellflower

Clock that struck thirteen. Rabinowitz, S.

CLOCKMAKERS. See Clocks and watches

The **clockmender.** O'Brian, P.

CLOCKS AND WATCHES
Gordimer, N. Charmed lives
McNeill, J. Specs and the cuckoo clock
O'Brian, P. The clockmender
Rabinowitz, S. Clock that struck thirteen

A **clod** of earth. Ryūnosuke, A.

Close to the clay. MacMahon, B.

Closed door. Crossen, K. F.

Clothes make the man. Duvernois, H.

Clothes mender. Leskov, N. S.

CLOTHING AND DRESS
Andersen, H. C. Emperor's new clothes
Babcock, H. Temporary gentleman
Bahr, J. Linen suit
Blake, L. J. Those green trousers
Lowry, R. J. C. Glad rags
O'Flaherty, L. New suit
Sansom, W. Outburst
Schleyen, M. Road by example
Smith, E. H. Red dress
Stockton, F. R. Asaph
Weidman, J. The tuxedos
West, J. Battle of the suits
Woolf, V. S. New dress

Cogswell, Theodore R.—*Continued*
Limiting factor
Conklin, G. ed. Science-fiction adventures in mutation
Galaxy science fiction magazine. Third Galaxy reader
Threesie
Davenport, B. ed. Deals with the devil
You know Willie
Merril, J. ed. SF: '58

Cohen, Octavus Roy, 1891-
Always trust a cop
Cooke, D. C. ed. My best murder story
Case of nerves
This week magazine. This week's Stories of mystery and suspense
Last blow
Collier's (Periodical) Collier's Greatest sports stories
Nuts and reasons
Saturday evening post (Periodical) Saturday evening post Carnival of humor
Perfect alibi
Best detective stories of the year—1955

COIN BANKS
Campbell, W. E. M. Toy bank

COLD (DISEASE)
Hale, N. Year I had the colds

Cold equations. Godwin, T.

Cold house. O'Hara, J.

Cold war. Kuttner, H.

Cole, Everett B. 1910-
Exile
Best science-fiction stories and novels: 1955

Cole, Stephen
New boy
Teen-age tales, bk 4

Coleman, Lonnie. See Coleman, William Laurence

Coleman, William Laurence, 1920-
Bird of paradise
Coleman, W. L. Ship's company
King's parade
Coleman, W. L. Ship's company
Legend of good men
Coleman, W. L. Ship's company
Man who smiled awhile
Coleman, W. L. Ship's company
Nick and Letty, their love story
Coleman, W. L. Ship's company
Noblesse oblige
Coleman, W. L. Ship's company
Passion play
Coleman, W. L. Ship's company
Revel below
Coleman, W. L. Ship's company
Take care of our little Nell
Coleman, W. L. Ship's company
The Theban warriors
Coleman, W. L. Ship's company

COLERIDGE, SAMUEL TAYLOR, 1772-1834
Ewen, F. Letter from Coleridge

Colette, pseud. See Colette, Sidonie Gabrielle

Colette, Sidonie Gabrielle, 1873-1954
Ambulance dogs
Colette, S. G. Creatures great and small

Autumn salon
Colette, S. G. Creatures great and small
Bel-Gazou and Buck
Colette, S. G. Creatures great and small
The bitch
Colette, S. G. Creatures great and small
Blue parakeet
Colette, S. G. Creatures great and small
The butterflies
Colette, S. G. Creatures great and small
The cat
Colette, S. G. 7 by Colette
Cat and the taxidermist
Colette, S. G. Creatures great and small
Chance acquaintances
Colette, S. G. 7 by Colette
Chéri
Colette, S. G. 7 by Colette
Circus wrestlers
Colette, S. G. Creatures great and small
Dog show
Colette, S. G. Creatures great and small
Domino
Colette, S. G. Creatures great and small
Fastagette
Colette, S. G. Creatures great and small
Fish man
Colette, S. G. Creatures great and small
French bull-dog
Colette, S. G. Creatures great and small
Gigi
Colette, S. G. 7 by Colette
Gold-fish
Colette, S. G. Creatures great and small
Jealous bitch
Colette, S. G. Creatures great and small
Last of Chéri
Colette, S. G. 7 by Colette
Little black cat
Colette, S. G. Creatures great and small
Live birds and insects
Colette, S. G. Creatures great and small
Lizards, frog, and grasshopper
Colette, S. G. Creatures great and small
The long-cat
Colette, S. G. Creatures great and small
"Look!"
Colette, S. G. Creatures great and small
Monsieur Rouzade's little sow
Colette, S. G. Creatures great and small
Mother cat
Colette, S. G. Creatures great and small
My mother's house
Colette, S. G. 7 by Colette
October
Colette, S. G. Creatures great and small
Old lady and the bear
Colette, S. G. Creatures great and small
Poucette
Colette, S. G. Creatures great and small
"Poum"
Colette, S. G. Creatures great and small
"Prrou"
Colette, S. G. Creatures great and small
Ricotte
Colette, S. G. Creatures great and small
Robin
Colette, S. G. Creatures great and small
Rock pool
Colette, S. G. Creatures great and small
Salivation by suggestion
Colette, S. G. Creatures great and small

COMMENCEMENTS
Chaikin, N. G. Bachelor of arts
Langdon, J. Blue serge suit
O'Connor, F. Late encounter with the enemy
COMMERCIAL TRAVELERS
Caldwell, E. Louellen
     See also Salesmen and salesmanship
Commings, Joseph
Great hunger
     Mystery Writers of America, inc. For tomorrow we die
Through the looking glass
     Mystery Writers of America, inc. Big time mysteries
Commissar in Connecticut. Ware, L.
Common denominator. Bates, H. E.
COMMUNISM
Farrell, J. T. Comrade Stanley
Farrell, J. T. The dialectic
Karp, D. Death warrant
Russell, B. A. W. R. 3d earl. Dean Acheson's nightmare

Asia
Lederer, W. J. and Burdick, E. L. Everyone has ears
Lederer, W. J. and Burdick, E. L. Lucky, Lucky Lou #2

Burma
Lederer, W. J. and Burdick, E. L. Nine friends

Hungary
Dery, T. Behind the brick wall

Mexico
Miller, E. M. Habit of murder

Poland
O'Sullivan-Barra, J. The password

Russia
Abernathy, R. Heirs apparent
Babel', I. E. Evening
Babel', I. E. Italian sunshine
Babel', I. E. Life and adventures of Matthew Pavlichenko
Babel', I. E. Oil
Babel', I. E. Salt

United States
Farrell, J. T. Saturday night in Paris

Vietnam
Lederer, W. J. and Burdick, E. L. Lessons of war
Company K. Campbell, W. E. M.
Company office. Samuel, E. H.
COMPETITIVE EXAMINATIONS. See Examinations
Complication. Maupassant, G. de
Compliments of Caliph Bernie. Green, C.
COMPOSERS. See Musicians—Composers
Compound B. Fink, D. H.
Compounded interest. Reynolds, M.
COMPULSORY LABOR. See Convict labor
COMPUTING MACHINES. See Calculating machines

Comrade Governor. Samuel, E. H.
Comrade Stanley. Farrell, J. T.
CONCENTRATION CAMPS
Boyle, K. Winter night
Farrell, J. T. Saturday night in America
Fournier, P. Season of the dead
     See also World War, 1939-1945—Prisoners and prisons
Concerning a treaty with France. Drury, W. P.
The **concert.** Sørensen, V.
CONCERTS
Davies, R. Benefit concert
Shrubb, P. List of all people
CONDEMNED PRISONERS. See Prisoners, Condemned
The **condor** and the guests. Connell, E. S.
CONDORS
Connell, E. S. The condor and the guests
CONDUCT OF LIFE
Bohnsack, E. J. School teacher
Enright, E. The bookkeepers
Tolstoi, L. N. Graf. Dialogue among clever people
CONDUCTORS (MUSIC) See Musicians—Conductors
CONFEDERATE STATES OF AMERICA
     See also Southern States; United States—19th century—Civil War

Army
Carter, H. Rank injustice
Marquand, J. P. Jack Still
Confessing. Maupassant, G. de
CONFESSION (CATHOLIC)
McKune, J. W. Between the skunk and the locket
Maupassant, G. de. Making a convert
O'Donovan, M. First confession
O'Faoláin, S. The confessional
O'Faoláin, S. Sinners
The **confession.** Maupassant, G. de
Confession. Sitan, J. M.
The **confessional.** O'Faoláin, S.
CONFIRMATION
Maupassant, G. de. Madame Tellier's establishment
Conflict. Gardner, C.
CONFUCIUS, 551-478 B.C.
Cook, B. G. Chinese fishing
Conger eel. O'Flaherty, L.
CONGRESSES AND CONVENTIONS
Wilson, E. Mrs Golightly and the first convention
CONGRESSMEN. See United States. Congress
CONJURING
Ellin, S. Moment of decision
     See also Magic
The **conjuror.** Chopelas, J.
CONJURORS. See Conjuring
Conn, Frederick
Coda
     Miller, N. ed. New campus writing, no. 2

Coppard, Alfred Edgar, 1878-1957
Arabesque: the mouse
McClennen, J. comp. Masters and masterpieces of the short story
Cherry tree
Havighurst, W. and others, eds. Selection
Dusky Ruth
Laughton, C. ed. Tell me a story
Judith
Costain, T. B. and Beecroft, J. eds. Stories to remember
Willie Waugh
Gettman, R. A. and Harkness, B. eds. Book of stories

Coppée, François, 1842-1908
Baron's two francs
Fremantle, A. J. ed. Christmas is here
Christmas lovers
Fremantle, A. J. ed. Christmas is here
The louis-d'or
Lohan, R. ed. Christmas tales for reading aloud

Copper Dahlia. Kersh, G.

COPYREADERS. See Journalists

Cora. Le Vino, E. G.

Coralee's burden-bearer. Polk, W. T.

Corda. Lesins, K.

CORK. See Ireland, Provincial and rural—Cork

Corkery, Daniel, 1878-
The awakening
Garrity, D. A. ed. 44 Irish short stories
O'Donovan, M. ed. Modern Irish short stories
The return
Garrity, D. A. ed. 44 Irish short stories

Corle, Edwin, 1906-
Bank holiday
Schaefer, J. W. ed. Out West

CORMORANTS
O'Flaherty, L. Wounded cormorant

CORN
Giono, J. The corn dies
The **corn** dies. Giono, J.

Cornered. Fox, N. A.

Coroner story. Baillie-Grohman, W. A.

CORONERS
Baillie-Grohman, W. A. Coroner story

Corporal Hardy. Danielson, R. E.

Corporal Nat. Mowery, W. B.

The **corpse** in the Statue of Liberty. Woolrich, C.

CORPSES. See The dead

CORPULENCE
Dicks, J. R. Man on a diet
Mankowitz, W. Too much man
Maupassant, G. de. Toine
Wells, H. G. Truth about Pyecraft

CORRESPONDENCE. See Letters, Stories about

CORSICA
Maupassant, G. de. Corsican bandit

Corsican bandit. Maupassant, G. de

CORTÉS, HERNANDO, 1485-1547
Blassingame, W. Strange fate of El Morzillo

Cory, Edith, 1930-
Hero's children
Stanford short stories, 1955

Cosmic Casanova. Clarke, A. C.

Cosmic expense account. Kornbluth, C. M.

COSSACKS
Babel', I. E. Afonka Bida
Babel', I. E. My first goose

Costigan, Mack, pseud. See Miller, Ed Mack

Costly outing. Maupassant, G. de

COSTUME. See Clothing and dress

COTSWOLD HILLS. See England, Provincial and rural—Cotswold Hills

Cottage for August. Kyd, T. pseud.

Cottage in Galilee. Samuel, E. H.

Cottrell, Dorothy (Wilkinson) 1902-
Mysterious box
Saturday evening post (Periodical) Saturday evening post stories, 1954
Wilderness orphan
Teen-age tales, bk 5

COUGARS. See Pumas

COUNSELING
Fonger, H. Lead me home

COUNSELS. See Law and lawyers

The **Count.** Bahr, J.

Count Lothar's heart. Boyle, K.

Count of Crow's Nest. Cather, W. S.

COUNTERFEITERS
Allingham, M. Money to burn
Chambers, M. L. Fair exchange
Clark, A. A. G. Magnifying glass
Doyle, Sir A. C. Adventure of the engineer's thumb
Lipman, C. and Lipman, M. Dilemma of Grampa Dubois

Counterparts. Joyce, J.

Counterspy. Edwards, K.

Countess Kathleen O'Shea
Davenport, B. ed. Deals with the devil

Counting the waves. Farrell, J. T.

Country doctor. Kafka, F.

Country excursion. Maupassant, G. de

Country husband. Cheever, J.

COUNTRY LIFE

England
Bates, H. E. Death of a huntsman

Israel
Samuel, E. H. Cottage in Galilee

Maine
Medici, R. Quiet

Mexico
Smith, E. H. Manolo

Russia
Tolstoǐ, A. N. Graf. Mishka Nalymov
Tolstoǐ, A. N. Graf. The ravines
Tolstoǐ, A. N. Graf. A week in Turenevo

Vermont
Fisher, D. F. C. Nothing ever happens

Country mice. Faulkner, W.

CREOLES
LaMar, N. Creole love song
CRETE
Drury, W. P. Concerning a treaty with France
CREW. See Rowing
Crewe. De La Mare, W. J.
Crews, Susie (Pepper)
Newspapers in heaven
Orr, E. and Hammett, E. A. eds. Delta Decameron
CRICKET
Beith, J. H. Pip's first cricket match
Hughes, J. G. Master of the golden game
Johnston, R. T. Century of a lifetime
Johnston, R. T. A1 at Lord's
Johnston, R. T. Century of a lifetime; 5 stories
Johnston, R. T. Cricket in the blood
Johnston, R. T. Eternal triangle
Johnston, R. T. Woman with a past
MacDonell, A. G. Match at Fordenden
Cricket in the blood. Johnston, R. T.
CRIME AND CRIMINALS
Andreev, L. N. Seven who were hanged
Aymé, M. Dermuche
Aymé, M. Walker-through-walls
Canning, V. Dr Kang's white egret coat
Chapman, M. Mistaken identity
Doyle, Sir A. C. Final problem
Kersh, G. Murderer's eye
McKimmey, J. Scared cop
Maugham, W. S. Episode
Maupassant, G. de. A madman
Millar, K. Guilt-edged blonde
Ōgai, M. Takasebune
Pincherle, A. The caretaker
Pincherle, A. The terror of Rome
Williams, T. One arm

See also Convicts; Juvenile delinquency; Murder stories; Mystery and detective stories; and names of particular crimes: e.g. Embezzlement; Theft

Identification
Stewart, J. I. M. Was he Morton?
Crime for Llewellyn. Waldo, E. H.
Crime must have a stop. White, W. A. P.
CRIME OF PASSION. See Crime passionnel
CRIME PASSIONNEL
Tolstoĭ, L. N. Graf. Kreutzer sonata
Criminal mind. MacDonald, J. D.
CRIMINALS. See Crime and criminals
Crimson paw. Eberhart, M. G.
The **cripple.** Maupassant, G. de
CRIPPLES
Campbell, W. E. M. I broke my back on a rosebud
Campbell, W. E. M. Miss Daisy
Clayton, J. B. Little Bailey girl
Hodgson, J. Different Christmas
Kapelner, A. Walking, running people
Lee, R. J. Moth and the star
Lowry, R. J. C. Little baseball world
MacMahon, B. Chicken-Licken
Maupassant, G. de. "Bell"
Maupassant, G. de. Bellflower

Maupassant, G. de. The cripple
O'Connor, F. Good country people
Sandoz, M. Y. Crutches of Uncle Celestin
Smith, E. H. The decision
The **crisis.** Gordon, A.
A **crisis.** Maupassant, G. de
Crisp new bills for Mr Teagle. Sullivan, F.
Crispin, Edmund, pseud. See Montgomery, Robert Bruce
Crispin Hough. Rew, K.
Criswell, Charles
Come in come in
Criswell, C. Nobody knows what the stork will bring, and other stories
Crying through the lock
Criswell, C. Nobody knows what the stork will bring, and other stories
Give your heart to Jesus
Criswell, C. Nobody knows what the stork will bring, and other stories
Goddess of Mercy
Criswell, C. Nobody knows what the stork will bring, and other stories
The hobby
Criswell, C. Nobody knows what the stork will bring, and other stories
Jocasta
Criswell, C. Nobody knows what the stork will bring, and other stories
Linden trees
Criswell, C. Nobody knows what the stork will bring, and other stories
Moment of truth
Criswell, C. Nobody knows what the stork will bring, and other stories
Nobody knows what the stork will bring
Criswell, C. Nobody knows what the stork will bring, and other stories
To see once more
Criswell, C. Nobody knows what the stork will bring, and other stories
Wreath for the living
Criswell, C. Nobody knows what the stork will bring, and other stories
You'll be late for supper
Criswell, C. Nobody knows what the stork will bring, and other stories
Critchell, Laurence Sanford, 1918-
Flesh and blood
Fenton, C. A. ed. Best short stories of World War II
CROATAN INDIANS
Rutledge, A. Lost colony
CROCODILES
Kipling, R. Elephant's child
See also Alligators
Croix de cuisine. Polk, W. T.
CRO-MAGNON. See Man, Prehistoric
Cronin, Archibald Joseph, 1896-
Provost's tale
Urquhart, F. ed. Scottish short stories
Crooked man. Beaumont, C.
Crooked nail. O'Rourke, F.
The **crop.** Polk, W. T.
Cross, Eric, 1905-
Jury case
O'Donovan, M. ed. Modern Irish short stories
Saint Bakeoven
Garrity, D. A. ed. 44 Irish short stories

Dark trail. Elston, A. V.

Dark woman of the sonnets. Brodkey, H.

The darkest hour. Picard, J.

Darling, please believe me. Byrd, J. J.

DARWINISM. See Evolution

A dash of spring. Finney, J.

Date for Dorothy's party. Teal, V.

Date with a stranger. Madden, H. T.

DATING. See Courtship

Daudet, Alphonse, 1840-1897
  Father Gaucher's elixir
    Hall, J. B. and Langland, J. T. eds. Short story
  Last class
    Rosenblum, M. ed. Stories from many lands
  Pope's mule
    Costain, T. B. and Beecroft, J. eds. Stories to remember
  Three Low Masses
    Lohan, R. ed. Christmas tales for reading aloud

Daughter. Caldwell, E.

Daughter of the Confederacy. Eisenberg, F.

DAUGHTERS. See Fathers and daughters; Mothers and daughters; Parent and child

Daughter's grave. Rabinowitz, S.

DAUGHTERS-IN-LAW
  Chekhov, A. P. In the ravine
  Ryūnosuke, A. A clod of earth

David and Bathsheba. Bible. Old Testament

David and Goliath. Bible. Old Testament

David's bower. Shenhar, Y.

Davidson, Avram
  The golem
    Magazine of fantasy and science fiction. Best from Fantasy and science fiction; 5th ser.
    Merril, J. ed. S-F: ['56]
  Help! I am Dr Morris Goldpepper
    Galaxy science fiction magazine. Third Galaxy reader
  King's evil
    Magazine of fantasy and science fiction. Best from Fantasy and science fiction; 6th ser.
  Mr Stilwell's stage
    Magazine of fantasy and science fiction. Best from Fantasy and science fiction; 7th ser.
  My boy friend's name is Jello
    Magazine of fantasy and science fiction. Best from Fantasy and science fiction; 4th ser.
  Necessity of his condition
    Queen, E. pseud. ed. Ellery Queen's awards: 12th ser.
  Now let us sleep
    Merril, J. ed. SF: '58

Davies, John
  Ghost wore a monocle
    This week magazine. This week's Stories of mystery and suspense

Davies, Rhys, 1903-
  Benefit concert
    Jones, G. ed. Welsh short stories
  Nature of man
    Jones, G. ed. Welsh short stories

Davis, Alice Lee
  Mushrooms on the hill
    Oberfirst, R. ed. 1955 anthology of best original short-shorts

Davis, Dorothy Salisbury
  Matter of public notice
    Queen, E. pseud. ed. Ellery Queen's awards: 12th ser.

Davis, Eileen
  Natural thing
    Ferris, H. J. comp. Girls, girls, girls

Davis, Harold Lenoir, 1896-
  Old man Isbell's wife
    Schaefer, J. W. ed. Out West

Davis, Mamie
  Flip of a coin
    Oberfirst, R. ed. Anthology of best short-short stories, v6
  Warned by Satan
    Oberfirst, R. ed. Anthology of best short-short stories v5

Davis, Pearl Ann
  Homesteading
    Oberfirst, R. ed. Anthology of best short-short stories v5

Davis, Richard Harding, 1864-1916
  Her first appearance
    Lewis, J. D. ed. Great stories about show business

Davis, Wesley Ford, 1921-
  Lady Luck and the guardian angel
    Stanford short stories, 1955
  The undertow
    Best American short stories, 1956
    Stanford short stories, 1955

Dawkins, Mary Lucile, 1927-
  Pop the blue balloon
    Stanford short stories, 1954

Dawn. Powers, J. F.

Dawn flighting. O'Brian, P.

Dawson, Peter, pseud. See Glidden, Jonathan H.

Day, Clarence, 1874-1935
  Father and the cook
    Costain, T. B. and Beecroft, J. eds. More Stories to remember

Day Lewis, Cecil, 1904-
  Operation glazier
    Buckeridge, A. comp. In and out of school

Day after Thanksgiving. Kane, H. T.

The day all traffic stopped. Wells, R. W.

Day Aunt Chaya was buried. Mankowitz, W.

Day before summer. Ashbaugh, D.

Day before Yom Kippur. Rabinowitz, S.

A day in Toledo. Solomon, B. P.

Day in Venice. Tecchi, B.

Day it rained forever. Bradbury, R.

Day like any other. Gallant, M.

Day of Atonement. Brinig, M.

Day of glory. Brookhouser, F.

Death of a favorite. Powers, J. F.

Death of a huntsman. Bates, H. E.

Death of a kangaroo. Merritt, M.

Death of an actor. Bernstein, D.

Death of Dolgushov. Babel', I. E.

Death of Elder Saul. Gerchunoff, A.

Death of Francisco. Sylvester, W.

Death of Iván Ilých. Tolstoï, L. N. Graf

Death of Lully. Huxley, A. L.

Death of Monseigneur. Saint Simon, L. de R. duc de

Death of Socrates. Plato

Death of the little glassblower. Adams, A.

Death on a foggy morning. Lockridge, F. L. D. and Lockridge, R.

Death on Christmas Eve. Ellin, S.

Death on little cat's feet. Manners, M.

DEATH PENALTY. See Capital punishment

Death the proud brother. Wolfe, T.

Death warrant. Karp, D.

DEATHBED SCENES
Bradbury, R. Good-by, Grandma
Polk, W. T. My mother's Uncle Hal
Turgenev, I. S. District doctor

Debatable point. Gilchrist, D.

DEBATES AND DEBATING
Gilchrist, D. Debatable point

The debtor. Phillips, B. M.

DECADENCE. See Degeneration

De Camp, Lyon Sprague, 1907-
Judgment Day
Best science-fiction stories and novels: 1956
See also Howard, R. E. jt. auth.

De Camp, Lyon Sprague, 1907- and Pratt, Fletcher, 1897-1956
Caveat emptor
Davenport, B. ed. Deals with the devil

De Caylus, Comte. See Caylus, Anne Claude Philippe de Tubieres, comte de

DECEIT. See Truthfulness and falsehood

December morning. Ressler, R. D.

December nights in Brooklyn. Brady, J. P.

December 2001: the green morning. Bradbury, R.

December 2005: the silent towns. Bradbury, R.

December's glad song. Heintz, V.

DECEPTION. See Hoaxes

Deceptions of Marie-Blanche. Gallant, M.

A decidedly innocent man. Manners, M.

The decision. O'Hara, J.

The decision. Smith, E. H.

Decision for a star. Miller, E. M.

Decline and fall of a purist. Smith, E. W.

Decline and fall of Augie Sheean. Coogan, J.

Decline and fall of Perry Whitman. Coates, R. M.

Decline of sport. White, E. B.

DECORATION DAY. See Memorial Day

DECORATIONS OF HONOR
Maupassant, G. de. How he got the Legion of Honor

Decoy. Sweeney, C. L.

Dee, Bert
The revolt of machines
Oberfirst, R. ed. Anthology of best short-short stories, v5

De Eds, Joanne
And the moon rose on Yellowhammer
Stanford short stories, 1958

Deeps of the sea. Steiner, G.

DEER
Rawlings, M. K. Jody finds the fawn
Rutledge, A. H. Demon of the ocean
Rutledge, A. H. Not to the victor

DEER HUNTING
Babcock, H. Shirttail
Clark, W. Van T. Buck in the hills
Faulkner, W. Race at morning
Triem, F. Quest buck

Deer slayer. Annixter, P. pseud.

Defeat. Boyle, K.

Defection of a favorite. Powers, J. F.

DEFECTIVES AND DELINQUENTS
Cather, W. Paul's case

Defence in depth. Samuel, E. H.

DeFord, Miriam Allen, 1888-
Time trammel
Davenport, B. ed. Deals with the devil

DEFORMITIES
Lowry, R. J. C. Artie Bell
Welty, E. Petrified man
See also Monsters

DEGENERATES
Chandler, R. Big sleep
West, A. C. Upper room

DEGENERATION
Faulkner, W. Wash

Dehydrated romance. Reid, L.

De La Mare, Walter John, 1873-1956
Crewe
Ridler, A. B. comp. Best ghost stories
Seaton's aunt
Davin, D. M. ed. English short stories of today, 2d ser.

De La Roche, Mazo, 1885-
Ninth life
Mason, P. O. and Mason, J. eds. Favorite cat stories of Pamela and James Mason

Delayed hearing. Nemerov, H.

Deledda, Grazia, 1871-1936
Golden crucifix
Fremantle, A. J. ed. Christmas is here
Sardinian fox
Slonim, M. L. ed. Modern Italian short stories

De Leeuw, Adèle Louise, 1899-
Easy does it
Everygirls adventure stories
Girl to the rescue
Everygirls adventure stories
If wishes were horses
Everygirls horse stories

DIABETES
Wilson, A. Sad fall

DIALECT STORIES
Macken, W. Currach race

English—Yorkshire

Baring-Gould, S. Tom a' Tuddlams

French Canadian

Thomson, E. W. Old Man Savarin

Irish

Brooks, W. Officer Mulvaney and the hot buttered pig
Dreiser, T. St Columba and the river
MacMahon, B. Cat and the cornfield
MacMahon, B. Close to the clay
MacMahon, B. Evening in Ireland
MacMahon, B. Plain people of England
MacMahon, B. Red petticoat
MacMahon, B. Sound of the bell
MacMahon, B. Sunday afternoon. Sunny

Jewish

Kober, A. Music in the air
Kober, A. Paintner in the Bronx

Middle West

Clemens, S. L. Celebrated jumping frog of Calaveras County
Garland, H. Under the lion's paw

Mountain Whites (Southern States)

Carlile, C. The animal fair

Negro

Albee, G. S. Little Hiram
Alexander, S. White boat
Allan, G. Boysi
Harris, J. C. Mr Rabbit nibbles up the butter
Leonard, N. H. Rich
Paul, L. No more trouble for Jedwick
Stuart, R. M. Duke's Christmas

New England

Benet, S. V. The devil and Daniel Webster
Freeman, M. E. W. Revolt of mother
Stockton, F. R. Christmas wreck

Scotch

Bird, W. R. When a boy's a man
Duke, W. Hallowe'en party
Gaitens, E. Wee nip
Gilpatric, G. The artful Mr Glencannon
Graham, R. B. C. Beattock for Moffat
Mackenzie, O. C. Something different
MacLellan, R. The mennans
Rhodes, E. M. Beyond the desert

Southern

Faulkner, W. Mule in the yard
Faulkner, W. Race at morning
Faulkner, W. Two soldiers
Faulkner, W. Wash
Hammett, E. A. Solomon primitive
Harris, G. W. Rare ripe garden-seed
McMullen, J. A. Old Pro
Polk, W. T. Dark house and a bloody fight
Pridgen, T. Eighteen oak ties
Rawlings, M. K. Cocks must crow
Rawlings, M. K. Gal young un
Rawlings, M. K. Jacob's ladder
Roberts, E. M. On the mountainside
Smith, E. V. Prelude

The **dialectic.** Farrell, J. T.
Dialogue. Allen, S.
Dialogue among clever people. Tolstoi, L. N. Graf

DIAMOND CUTTERS
Eberhart, M. G. Deadly is the diamond
Diamond dilemma. Evans, E.
Diamond guitar. Capote, T.

DIAMONDS
Doyle, Sir A. C. Adventure of the Mazarin stone
Eberhart, M. G. Deadly is the diamond
Gilbert, M. F. One-tenth man
Maupassant, Guy de. The necklace
Runyon, D. Dancing Dan's Christmas
Sandoz, M. Y. At the Spanish custom-house
Schisgall, O. Intrigue in diamonds
Stewart, J. I. M. Very odd case
Diamonds in paradise. Queen, E. pseud.

DIARIES (STORIES IN DIARY FORM)
Cheever, J. Journal of an old gent
Ellis, H. F. Vexations of A. J. Wentworth, B. A.
Farrell, J. T. To whom it may concern
Lardner, R. W. A caddy's diary
Lardner, R. W. I can't breathe
Maupassant, G. de. At the spa
Maupassant, G. de. The horla
Maupassant, G. de. My twenty-five days
Maupassant, G. de. Our friends the English
Pangborn, E. Angel's egg

DIARIES, STORIES ABOUT
Bayley, J. Some demon's mistress
Reid, L. Elnea
Stewart, J. I. M. Dangerfield's diary
Van Doren, M. The diary
The **diary.** Van Doren, M.

DICE. See Gambling

Dick, Philip K. 1928-
Impostor
Montgomery, R. B. ed. Best SF two
Dickens, Charles, 1812-1870
Celebrated sassage factory
Laughton, C. ed. Tell me a story
Child's story
Dickens, C. Christmas stories
Christmas carol
Lohan, R. ed. Christmas tales for reading aloud
Christmas tree
Dickens, C. Christmas stories
Devil and Mr Chips
Davenport, B. ed. Deals with the devil
Doctor Marigold
Dickens, C. Christmas stories
Going into society
Dickens, C. Christmas stories
Haunted house
Dickens, C. Christmas stories
Holly-tree
Dickens, C. Christmas stories
I am born
Costain, T. B. and Beecroft, J. eds. Stories to remember
Lazy tour of two idle apprentices
Dickens, C. Christmas stories

Dickens, Charles—*Continued*
Life of Our Lord
Lohan, R. ed. Christmas tales for reading aloud
Message from the sea
Dickens, C. Christmas stories
Mrs Lirriper's legacy
Dickens, C. Christmas stories
Mrs Lirriper's lodgings
Dickens, C. Christmas stories
Mugby Junction
Dickens, C. Christmas stories
No thoroughfare
Dickens, C. Christmas stories
Nobody's story
Dickens, C. Christmas stories
Perils of certain English prisoners
Dickens, C. Christmas stories
Poor relation's story
Dickens, C. Christmas stories
Sam Weller makes his bow
Costain, T. B. and Beecroft, J. eds. More Stories to remember
Schoolboy's story
Dickens, C. Christmas stories
Seven poor travellers
Dickens, C. Christmas stories
Somebody's luggage
Dickens, C. Christmas stories
Story of the goblins who stole a sexton
Lohan, R. ed. Christmas tales for reading aloud
Tom Tiddler's ground
Dickens, C. Christmas stories
What Christmas is as we grow older
Dickens, C. Christmas stories
Wreck of the Golden Mary
Dickens, C. Christmas stories
Dickinson, William H. 1899-
Roses
Oberfirst, R. ed. Anthology of best short-short stories v5
Dicks, Judson R. 1927-
Man on a diet
Oberfirst, R. ed. Anthology of best short-short stories v6
Dickson, Carter, pseud. See Carr, John Dickson
Dickson, Gordon R. See Anderson, Poul, jt. auth.
Didn't he ramble. Oliver, C.
The **die**-hard. Benét, S. V.
Diego Suarez story. St John, O.
Dieppe. Shapiro, L.
Dieste, Rafael
Stuffed parrot
Flores, A. ed. Great Spanish stories
Different Christmas. Hodgson, J.
Dig that crazy grave! Bloch, R.
Digging the Weans. Nathan, R.
Di Grasso. Babel', I. E.
Dilemma of Grampa Dubois. Lipman, C. and Lipman, M.
Dill pickle. Mansfield, K.
Dine, Deborah R.
The fund
Oberfirst, R. ed. 1955 anthology of best original short-shorts

DINERS. See Restaurants, lunch rooms, etc.
Dinesen, Isak, pseud. See Blixen, Karen
Dingle, Aylward Edward, 1874-1947
Bound for Rio Grande
Kemp, P. K. ed. Hundred years of sea stories
Dingo. Annixter, P. pseud.
DINGOES
Annixter, P. pseud. Dingo
DINING. See Dinners
Dinner for the philosopher. Moretti, U.
DINNERS
Arabian nights. Barmecide feast
Blixen, K. Babette's feast
Bowen, E. Her table spread
Chekhov, A. P. Woman's kingdom
Connell, E. S. The condor and the guests
Hale, N. Charlotte Russe
Kubly, H. Halloween party
Samuel, E. H. Fish suppers
The **diplomat.** Duck, T.
DIPLOMATIC LIFE
Piper, H. B. He walked around the horses
Zamfirescu, A. D. I. Popescu of the boundaries
See also Consuls
DIPLOMATS. See Diplomatic life
DIPLOMAT'S wife. Boyle, K.
The **dipper.** Rinehart, M. R.
DIPTERA
Smilansky, M. Barhash
DIRIGIBLE BALLOONS. See Air-ships
Dirty Emma. Campbell, W. E. M.
DISABLED. See Cripples; Invalids
DISAPPEARANCES
Dickens, C. Celebrated sassage factory
King, R. Malice in wonderland
Maupassant, G. de. At the church door
Stewart, J. I. M. The ribbon
Woollcott, A. Vanishing lady
Yellen, S. The passionate shepherd
See also Invisibility
DISASTERS. See Accidents; Fires; Floods; Shipwrecks and castaways; Storms
Discipline. Wain, J.
Discord. O'Faoláin, S.
Discourager of hesitancy. Stockton, F. R.
DISCOVERIES (IN SCIENCE) See Inventions
DISCRIMINATION IN HOUSING
McGerr, P. Some with a flattering word
DISESASES. See names of diseases: e.g. Cancer (Disease); Cold (Disease)
DISEASES, FEIGNED. See Malingering
DISFIGUREMENTS. See Face—Abnormities and deformities
DISGUISES. See Impersonations
DISHONESTY. See Honesty
The **disinherited.** Hendry, J. F.
DISMAL SWAMP. See Virginia—Dismal Swamp

Disorder and early sorrow. Mann, T.
DISORDERS OF PERSONALITY. See
  Personality, Disorders of
Displaced person. O'Connor, F.
DISPLACED PERSONS. See World War,
  1939-1945—Displaced persons
DISSENTERS
  Sandburg, C. Girl from the queer people
Distaff strategy. Francis, B.
Distler, Alan J.
  Set her down
  Fenner, P. R. ed. Heroes, heroes, heroes
DISTILLING, ILLICIT
  Rawlings, M. K. Gal young un
District doctor. Turgenev, I. S.
The diver. Blixen, K.
DIVERS (PERSONS) See Diving
Divided horsecloth
  Laughton, C. ed. Tell me a story
Divine ecstasy. Kubly, H.
DIVINE HEALING. See Faith cure; Miracles
DIVING
  Harmon, M. Big splash
  Maugham, W. S. Gigolo and gigolette
  Sylvester, W. Death of Francisco
DIVING, SUBMARINE
  Derleth, A. W. Seal of R'lyeh
  Eadie, T. Story of Michels
  Hemingway, E. After the storm
  Whitehill, J. Terry Bindle
  Whitehill, J. Young man with a spear
DIVINING-ROD
  Wells, K. M. We hire a witch
DIVORCE
  Bodington, N. Climate of the lost
  Bourla, Y. At a glance
  Clay, G. R. We're all guests
  Enright, E. The playground
  Gallant, M. About Geneva
  Gellhorn, M. E. Till death us do part
  Gerchunoff, A. Divorce
  Gordimer, N. The cicatrice
  Gordimer, N. My first two women
  Hale, N. Full life
  Hale, N. Sheltered
  Harss, L. An agreement
  O'Donovan, J. Desert islands
  Raphaelson, S. Lost on 44th Street
  Reid, L. Divorce
  Saroyan, W. Reader of "The World Almanac for 1944"
  Wharton, E. N. J. Autres temps
  Wharton, E. N. J. Other two
  Wharton, E. N. J. Souls belated
    See also Marriage problems
Divorce. Gerchunoff, A.
Divorce case. Maupassant, G. de
DIVORCÉES. See Divorce
Dixie. Crabtree, P.
Dixon, Harry Vernor
  Trapped!
  This week magazine. The week's Stories
    of mystery and suspense
Do you like it here? O'Hara, J.
Dobbs Ferry. See New York (State)—Dobbs
  Ferry

DOBERMAN PINSCHERS
  Burt, O. W. Washed out
Dobhal, Purushotam
  Contrary teacher
    World prize stories; 2d ser.
Doc Mellhorn and the pearly gates. Benét,
  S. V.
Doctor and Mrs Parsons. O'Hara, J.
Dr Borosky. Lochridge, B. H.
Doctor Faustus
  Davenport, B. ed. Deals with the devil
Dr Heidegger's experiment. Hawthorne, N.
Dr Kang's white egret coat. Canning, V.
Doctor Marigold. Dickens, C.
Dr Southport Vulpes's nightmare. Russell,
  B. A. W. R. 3d earl
DOCTORS. See Dentists; Physicians
Doctor's son. O'Hara, J.
Document 1. Weiss, P.
DODGE CITY. See Kansas—Dodge City
Dodger fan. Stanton, W.
Dodgson, Charles Lutwidge. See Carroll,
  Lewis, pseud.
Dodie and the boogerman. Williams, V.
The doe and the gantlet. Stadley, P.
Doer of the word. Dreiser, T.
The dog. Annixter, P. pseud.
DOG BREEDS
  Annixter, P. pseud. His man
The dog died first. Fischer, B.
Dog eater. Russell, C. M.
Dog in my life. McMullen, J. A.
DOG RACING
  Dahl, R. Mr Feasey
Dog show. Colette, S. G.
DOG SHOWS
  Prescott, J. B. Ribbon for Ginger
Dog that wouldn't talk. Blochman, L. G.
DOGS
  Adams, S. H. Such as walk in darkness
  Annixter, P. pseud. Champions of the
    peaks
  Annixter, P. pseud. Dingo
  Annixter, P. pseud. The dog
  Annixter, P. pseud. Hunting horn, and
    other dog stories; 13 stories
  Annixter, P. pseud. Stronger force
  Annixter, P. pseud. Tiger hound
  Babcock, H. Miss Priss
  Balchin, N. The master
  Blackwood, A. Psychical invasion
  Blochman, L. G. Dog that wouldn't talk
  Bradbury, R. The emissary
  Brier, H. M. Thoroughbred
  Brown, J. Rab and his friends
  Byrd, J. J. First year
  Clayton, J. B. Warm day in November
  Coburn, W. Orneriest three
  Coleman, W. L. Take care of our little
    Nell
  Colette, S. G. Ambulance dogs
  Colette, S. G. The bitch
  Colette, S. G. French bull-dog
  Colette, S. G. Jealous bitch

DOGS—*Continued*

Colette, S. G. Poucette
Doyle, Sir A. C. Hound of the Basker-
villes
Eberhart, M. G. Crimson paw
Eberhart, M. G. Mr Wickwire's "gun
moll"
Edmonds, W. D. Honor of the county
Fisher, D. F. C. The apprentice
Foster, B. Night of terror
Fournier, P. The dogs
Gardner, I. B. Heart of a hero
Germann, R. F. The talking dog
Goehring, D. Towser the terrific
Great dog stories; 10 stories
Grey, Z. Don
Halacy, D. S. Lucky goes fishing
Hardy, W. G. Czech dog
Harris, A. W. The unique conception
Hawkins, J. and Hawkins, W. Look out
for John Tucker!
Jenkins, W. F. Propagandist
Jenkins, W. F. Skag with the queer head
Jones, G. Brute creation
Kantor, M. That Greek dog
Kelton, E. Yellow Devil
Kjelgaard, J. A. Right as rain
Lampman, B. H. Blinker was a good dog
Lang, D. Tramp, the sheep dog
London, J. Call of the wild
London, J. White Fang
McCormack, N. Lazy-bones
Macken, W. Foreign fish
McMullen, J. A. Bill sells a "bill of goods"
McMullen, J. A. Dog in my life
McMullen, J. A. Old Pro
McMullen, J. A. Old Pro, and four other
stories; 5 stories
McMullen, J. A. Sam dreams a dream
McMullen, J. A. Sampson and the blue
"Delilahs"
Mann, T. Tobias Mindernickel
Maupassant, G. de. Francis
Maupassant, G. de. Semillante
Maupassant, G. de. The watchdog
Moretti, U. I had this dog
Mowat, F. Last husky
Nye, H. L. Jerry
Philips, J. P. Hunting day
Quentin, P. pseud. Puzzle for Poppy
Reynolds, M. And thou beside me
Rhine, R. Margaret and Wilbur keep
Moses
Robertson, F. C. Bonehead
Russell, C. M. Dog eater
Russell, E. F. Into your tent I'll creep
Smith, E. H. The gift
Stafford, J. In the zoo
Taber, G. B. Just a little havoc
Tamási, A. Flashes in the night
Terhune, A. P. The grudge
Waldo, E. H. Tiny and the monster
Waugh, E. On guard
Welch, D. Mr Digby and the talking dog
West, A. C. No fatted calf
Western Writers of America. Hound dogs
and others; 15 stories
Wharton, E. N. J. Kerfol
Williams, B. A. Mine enemy's dog
Williamsom, H. Redeye
Wodehouse, P. G. Episode of the dog
McIntosh

Wodehouse, P. G. Very shy gentleman
Yaari, Y. Shepherd and his dog
See also Bird dogs; Dog breeds;
Dogs, War use of; also names of par-
ticular breeds: e.g. Foxhounds, etc.

DOGS, WAR USE OF
Annixter, P. pseud. Choirboy
Annixter, P. pseud. Krag of the K-9's
Burt, O. W. Washed out
Fournier, P. The dogs

Dollar a kiss. Guldager, C.

DOLLS
Chute, B. J. Christmas doll
Pevehouse, A. Kachina dolls

Dolorosa, here I come. Haycox, E.

Domestic idyll. Peretz, I. L.

Domestic peace. Peretz, I. L.

Domino. Colette, S. G.

The **dominoes.** McIlnay, R. D.

Dominions beyond. Moore, W.

Don. Grey, Z.

Don Jones. Anderson, P. and Dickson, G. R.

Doña Berta. Alas, L.

DONATIONS. See Gifts

The **donkey.** Maupassant, G. de

DONKEYS. See Asses and mules

Donna Santa's sin. Verga, G.

Don't believe a word she says. Gresham,
W. L.

Don't call me by my right name. Purdy, J.

Don't delve too deeply. Pincherle, A.

Don't let no cracked-pot lay his fishbooks
on your chronium. Kober, A.

Don't take no for an answer. Garrett, G.

Don't wait up for me tonight. Woolrich, C.

DOOMSDAY. See Judgement Day

Door of opportunity. Maugham, W. S.

The **doorbell.** Keller, D. H.

DOORS
Kuttner, H. Threshold

The **doorstop.** Bretnor, R.

Doppo, Kunikida, 1871-1908
Meat and potatoes
McKinnon, R. N. ed. The heart is alone

DORDOGNE. See France, Provincial and
rural—Dordogne

Doretta. Baldini, A.

Dorling, Henry Taprell, 1883-
Little drop o' leaf
Kemp, P. K. ed. Hundred years of sea
stories

Dormant. Van Vogt, A. E.

Dorrance, Ward Allison, 1904-
Devil on a hot afternoon
Best American short stories, 1956

Dostoevskiĭ, Fedor Mikhaĭlovich, 1821-1881
Christmas tree and a wedding
Dostoevskiĭ, F. M. Best short stories of
Dostoevsky
Dream of a ridiculous man
Dostoevskiĭ, F. M. Best short stories of
Dostoevsky

Dostoevskiĭ, Fedor M.—*Continued*
A gentle creature
Dostoevskiĭ, F. M. Best short stories of Dostoevsky
The grand inquisitor
Gettman, R. A. and Harkness, B. eds. Book of stories
The honest thief
Dostoevskiĭ, F. M. Best short stories of Dostoevsky
Notes from the underground
Dostoevskiĭ, F. M. Best short stories of Dostoevsky
The peasant Marey
Dostoevskiĭ, F. M. Best short stories of Dostoevsky
Short, R. W. and Sewall, R. B. eds. Short stories for study
White night
Dostoevskiĭ, F. M. Best short stories of Dostoevsky

Dostoevsky, Fyodor. See Dostoevskiĭ, Fedor Mikhaĭlovich

Double pins. Maupassant, G. de

Double skull, slow burn, and a ping. Coogan, J.

Double surprise. Towery, J. G.

Double talk. Barry, J.

Doublecross. Wray, J.

Doubtful happiness. Maupassant, G. de

Douglas, Ronald Macdonald
Woman of the roads
Urquhart, F. ed. Scottish short stories

Douglass, Donald McNutt
The perfectionist
Queen, E. pseud. Ellery Queen's awards: 10th ser.

The dove. Lesiņš, K.

DOVES. See Pigeons

Dow, David
Ol' Nick's wife
Stanford short stories, 1958

Dowdey, Clifford, 1904-
The Duke's brigade
Saturday evening post (Periodical) The Post Reader of Civil War stories
Weep not for them
Saturday evening post (Periodical) The Post Reader of Civil War stories

Downey, Harris
The hobo
Best American short stories, 1956
The hunters
First-prize stories, 1919-1957
The song
Best American short stories, 1957

Downs, Cecil. See Downs, K. jt. auth.

Downs, Kaye, and Downs, Cecil
A drink on the house
Oberfirst, R. ed. Anthology of best short-short stories v5

Doyle, Adrian Conan, 1910-1955
Lover of the Coral Glades
Oberfirst, R. ed. Anthology of best short-short stories v6

Doyle, Sir Arthur Conan, 1859-1930
Adventure of Black Peter
Doyle, Sir A. C. Treasury of Sherlock Holmes

Adventure of Charles Augustus Milverton
Doyle, Sir A. C. Treasury of Sherlock Holmes
Adventure of Shoscombe Old Place
Doyle, Sir A. C. Treasury of Sherlock Holmes
Adventure of the Abbey Grange
Doyle, Sir A. C. Treasury of Sherlock Holmes
Adventure of the Beryl Coronet
Doyle, Sir A. C. Treasury of Sherlock Holmes
Adventure of the Blue Carbuncle
Doyle, Sir A. C. Treasury of Sherlock Holmes
Sandrus, M. Y. ed. Famous mysteries
Adventure of the dancing men
Doyle, Sir A. C. Treasury of Sherlock Holmes
Adventure of the devil's foot
Doyle, Sir A. C. Treasury of Sherlock Holmes
Adventure of the dying detective
Doyle, Sir A. C. Treasury of Sherlock Holmes
Adventure of the empty house
Doyle, Sir A. C. Treasury of Sherlock Holmes
Adventure of the engineer's thumb
Doyle, Sir A. C. Treasury of Sherlock Holmes
Adventure of the Mazarin stone
Doyle, Sir A. C. Treasury of Sherlock Holmes
Adventure of the missing three-quarter
Collier's (Periodical) Collier's Greatest sports stories
Adventure of the priory school
Doyle, Sir A. C. Treasury of Sherlock Holmes
Adventure of the second stain
Doyle, Sir A. C. Treasury of Sherlock Holmes
Adventure of the six Napoleons
Doyle, Sir A. C. Treasury of Sherlock Holmes
Adventure of the speckled band
Aymar, B. ed. Treasury of snake lore
Doyle, Sir A. C. Treasury of Sherlock Holmes
McMaster, J. ed. Stories to remember
Sterner, L. G. ed. Favorite short stories
Archery contest
Langford, W. F. ed. Book of better stories
Boscombe Valley mystery
Sandrus, M. Y. ed. Famous mysteries
Croxley master
Costain, T. B. and Beecroft, J. eds. More Stories to remember
Final problem
Doyle, Sir A. C. Treasury of Sherlock Holmes
Five orange pips
Doyle, Sir A. C. Treasury of Sherlock Holmes
The "Gloria Scott"
Doyle, Sir A. C. Treasury of Sherlock Holmes
Greek interpreter
Doyle, Sir A. C. Treasury of Sherlock Holmes

Doyle, Sir Arthur C.—*Continued*

His law bow
Doyle, Sir A. C. Treasury of Sherlock Holmes

Hound of the Baskervilles
Doyle, Sir A. C. Treasury of Sherlock Holmes

How the brigadier slew the fox
Welcome, J. and Orchard, V. eds. Best hunting stories

Musgrave ritual
Doyle, Sir A. C. Treasury of Sherlock Holmes

Naval treaty
Doyle, Sir A. C. Treasury of Sherlock Holmes

Problem of Thor Bridge
Doyle, Sir A. C. Treasury of Sherlock Holmes

Red-headed League
Doyle, Sir A. C. Treasury of Sherlock Holmes

Reigate puzzle
Doyle, Sir A. C. Treasury of Sherlock Holmes

Silver Blaze
Doyle, Sir A. C. Treasury of Sherlock Holmes
Schwed, P. and Wind, H. W. eds. Great stories from the world of sport

Study in scarlet
Doyle, Sir A. C. Treasury of Sherlock Holmes

Through the veil
Costain, T. B. and Beecroft, J. eds. More Stories to remember

Parodies, travesties, etc.

Harte, B. Stolen cigar case by A. Co-n D-le

Doyle, Maura

Vicarious experience
Hughes, R. ed. All manner of men

DRAFT, MILITARY. See Military service, Compulsory

Drago, Harry Sinclair, 1888-

All the brothers were bad
Drago, H. S. Their guns were fast

Born bad
Drago, H. S. Their guns were fast

Buckskin empire
Western Writers of America. Hoof trails and wagon tracks

Dusty saddles
Drago, H. S. Their guns were fast

Ghost of the Cimarron
Drago, H. S. Their guns were fast

Long winter
Drago, H. S. Their guns were fast

Raw land
Drago, H. S. Their guns were fast

Sagebrush champion
Western Writers of America. Wild horse roundup

The Spanish Kid
Drago, H. S. Their guns were fast

Washout at Ute Crossing
Drago, H. S. Their guns were fast

DRAKES. See Ducks

DRAMATISTS

Simak, C. D. Shadow show

Drawing of the Curranwood badgers. O'Brian, P.

Drawing room B. O'Hara, J.

Drawn into error. Brown, M. D. M.

The **dream.** Angoff, C.

Dream of a ridiculous man. Dostoevskiĭ, F. M.

Dream of love. Farrell, J. T.

Dream of winter. Lehmann, R.

Dream Street. Robinson, F. M.

Dream trespass. Blackwood, A.

Dream woman. Collins, W.

Dreaming is a private thing. Asimov, I.

DREAMS

Asimov, I. Dreaming is a private thing
Benét, S. V. End to dreams
Blackwood, A. Dream trespass
Dostoevskiĭ, F. M. Dream of a ridiculous man
Maugham, W. S. Lord Mountdrago
Maupassant, G. de. Dreams
Peretz, I. L. Journey in time
Plunkett, J. Mercy
Rabinowitz, S. Only son, the mother, and Elijah the Prophet
Reid, L. My Lady Happiness
Russell, B. A. W. R. 3d earl. Dean Acheson's nightmare
Russell, B. A. W. R. 3d earl. Dr Southport Vulpes's nightmare
Russell, B. A. W. R. 3d earl. Eisenhower's nightmare
Russell, B. A. W. R. 3d earl. Existentialist's nightmare
Russell, B. A. W. R. 3d earl. Mathematician's nightmare
Russell, B. A. W. R. 3d earl. Metaphysician's nightmare
Russell, B. A. W. R. 3d earl. Mr Bowdler's nightmare
Russell, B. A. W. R. 3d earl. Psychoanalyst's nightmare
Russell, B. A. W. R. 3d earl. Queen of Sheba's nightmare
Russell, B. A. W. R. 3d earl. Stalin's nightmare
Russell, R. Put them all together, they spell monster
Sandoz, M. Y. Souvenir of Hammam Meskoutine
Schulz, B. My father joins the fire brigade
Shaw, I. Age of reason
Toland, S. Wedding ring

Dreams. Maupassant, G. de

DREDGING

Kentfield, C. Place for lovers in the summertime

Dreiser, Theodore, 1871-1945

Convention
Dreiser, T. Best short stories of Theodore Dreiser

Doer of the word
Dreiser, T. Best short stories of Theodore Dreiser

Free
Dreiser, T. Best short stories of Theodore Dreiser

Khat
Dreiser, T. Best short stories of Theodore Dreiser

Dreiser, Theodore—*Continued*

Lost Phoebe
 Dreiser, T. Best short stories of Theo-
  dore Dreiser
McEwen of the shining slave makers
 Dreiser, T. Best short stories of Theo-
  dore Dreiser
Marriage—for one
 Dreiser, T. Best short stories of Theo-
  dore Dreiser
My brother Paul
 Dreiser, T. Best short stories of Theo-
  dore Dreiser
Nigger Jeff
 Dreiser, T. Best short stories of Theo-
  dore Dreiser
Old neighborhood
 Dreiser, T. Best short stories of Theo-
  dore Dreiser
Phantom gold
 Dreiser, T. Best short stories of Theo-
  dore Dreiser
Prince who was a thief
 Dreiser, T. Best short stories of Theo-
  dore Dreiser
St Columba and the river
 Dreiser, T. Best short stories of Theo-
  dore Dreiser
Second choice
 Hart, J. D. and Gohdes, C. L. eds.
  America's literature
The shadow
 Dreiser, T. Best short stories of Theo-
  dore Dreiser

The **dress**. Thomas, D.

Dresser, Daniel
White army
 Gallant, J. ed. Stories of scientific imag-
  ination

Dresser, Davis, 1904-
Dead man's code
 Mystery Writers of America, inc. Crime
  for two
Human interest stuff
 Mystery Writers of America, inc. Big
  time mysteries

DRESSES. See Clothing and dress

Dressing room secret. Shaw, G. B.

Dressing-up. Burnett, W. R.

DRESSMAKERS
Maupassant, G. de. Bellflower
Pincherle, A. A pair of spectacles

DREYFUS, ALFRED, 1859-1935
Rabinowitz, S. Dreyfus in Kasrilevka

Dreyfus in Kasrilevka. Rabinowitz, S.

Dribbling fool. Olgin, J.

DRILL AND MINOR TACTICS
West, J. Love, death, and the ladies' drill
 team

Drink of water. Brown, T. K.

A **drink** on the house. Downs, K. and
 Downs, C.

DRINKING BOWLS. See Drinking vessels

DRINKING VESSELS
Household, G. Treasure hunt

**DRINKS AND DRINKING (IN RE-
 LIGION, FOLKLORE, ETC.)**
Lesiņš, K. Wine of eternity

Drive from the San Saba to the Concho.
 Adams, A.

DRIVERS, AUTOMOBILE. See Automobile drivers

Driving lesson. Wallace, F. L.

The **drought**. Bilenchi, R.

Drought. Ward, L. L.

DROUGHTS
Rhodes, E. M. Aforesaid Bates

Drowned man. Maupassant, G. de

DROWNING
Bjornson, B. The father
Bradbury, R. The lake
Kentfield, C. River stay 'way from my
 door
Lesiņš, K. The secret
Lowry, R. J. C. Guys from Ray's Place
Macken, W. The sailor
Marsh, W. N. Last tag
O'Connor, F. The river
Pincherle, A. Taboo
Salcher, P. The octopus
Welty, E. Wide net
West, A. C. Song of the barrow

The **drowning**. Bruyn, F. de

Droz, Gustave, 1832-1895
I take supper with my wife
 Lohan, R. ed. Christmas tales for read-
  ing aloud

Drug for the Major. Household, G.

DRUG HABIT. See Narcotic habit

DRUGS
Pohl, F. What to do until the analyst
 comes
Simak, C. D. Retrograde evolution
Wells, H. G. New accelerator

DRUGSTORES
MacDonald, J. D. Homicidal hiccup

DRUMMERS. See Commercial travelers

The **drunkard**. O'Donovan, M.

DRUNKARDS
Adams, A. Trotter's sack of salt
Alexander, D. Man who went to Taltavul's
Allen, S. Southern accent
Caldwell, E. Last anniversary
Cheever, J. O youth and beauty!
Clayton, J. B. Happy story when seen
 backwards
Coates, R. M. In a foreign city
Curley, D. The ship
Farrell, J. T. Short story
Fischer, B. Sam Rall's private ghost
Ivins, D. Favored son
Lofts, N. R. Happy Christmas
MacMahon, B. Chicken-Licken
Mankowitz, W. Bonifas the cobbler
Maupassant, G. de. An enthusiast
Maupassant, G. de. Waiter, a bock!
O'Faoláin, S. An enduring friendship
O'Flaherty, L. The fight
Porter, W. S. Blackjack bargainer
Pritchett, V. S. Pocock passes
Rosmond, B. No sense of humor
Shultz, W. H. Shirts off their backs
Smith, E. W. Gates ajar
Stafford, J. In the zoo
Taylor, P. H. Spinster's tale
West, A. Upper room
 See also Alcoholism

DRUNKENNESS. See Alcoholism; Drunkards

Drury, W. P.
Casserbanker the Second
Kemp, P. K. ed. Hundred years of sea stories
Concerning a treaty with France
Kemp, P. K. ed. Hundred years of sea stories

DRY CLEANING. See Cleaning

DRY-GOODS
Stockton, F. R. Piece of red calico

Dry rock. Shaw, I.

Dry-trail showdown. Halacy, D. S.

DRYADS
Stockton, F. R. Old Pipes and the dryad

DUAL PERSONALITY
Dostoevskiĭ, F. M. Notes from the underground
Stevenson, R. L. Strange case of Dr Jekyll and Mr Hyde

DUBLIN. See Ireland—Dublin

Dublin Fusilier. Plunkett, J.

Dubonnet, Renée, 1922-
Arab officer
American vanguard, 1956

The **duchess** and the jeweller. Woolf, V. S.

The **Duchess** and the Smugs. Frankau, P.

Duchoux. Maupassant, G. de

Duck, Toni
The diplomat
Oberfirst, R. ed. Anthology of best short-short stories v6

Duck and the rabbit. Lowry, R. J. C.

DUCK PIN BOWLING. See Bowling

DUCK SHOOTING
Gordon, A. First hunt
Ilyenkov, V. Foma Zabotkin
Lytle, A. N. The guide
Lytle, A. N. Mahogany frame
Maupassant, G. de. Love
O'Brian, P. Dawn flighting
Stegner, W. E. Blue-winged teal

Duck soup. Macken, W.

DUCKS
Hearn, L. Oshidori
McLaverty, M. Wild duck's nest
West, A. C. Turning page

Ducovny, Amram Martin, 1927-
I am the athlete, the chosen
New voices 2: American writing today

DUDE RANCHES
Jameson, C. G. Smart guy

A **duel.** Maupassant, G. de

The **duel** [another story] Maupassant, G. de

DUELING
Maupassant, G. de. A duel
Maupassant, G. de. The duel [another story]
Verga, G. Cavalleria rusticana

Duels. See Dueling

Duet for organ and strings. MacDonagh, D.

Duke, Madelaine, 1919-
Manuel at full moon
Pudney, J. ed. Pick of today's short stories, 9

Duke, Winifred
Hallowe'en party
Urquhart, F. ed. Scottish short stories

The **Duke's** brigade. Dowdey, C.

Duke's children. O'Donovan, M.

Duke's Christmas. Stuart, R. M.

Dulce domum. Grahame, K.

Dumas, Alexandre, 1802-1870
Man who lived four thousand years
Costain, T. B. and Beecroft, J. eds. Stories to remember

Du Maurier, Daphne, 1907-
The birds
Costain, T. B. and Beecroft, J. eds. Stories to remember
Good housekeeping (Periodical) Editor's choice

Dumb Martian. Harris, J. B.

Dumbest man in the Army. Sneider, V. J.

Dumitriu, Petru, 1924-
Family jewels
Short stories v 1

Duncan, Eva
Silent voice
Oberfirst, R. ed. 1955 anthology of best original short-shorts

Duncan, Lois, 1934-
April
Seventeen (Periodical) Seventeen's stories

Dunsany, Edward John Moreton Drax Plunkett, 18th baron, 1878-1957
Deal with the devil
Davenport, B. ed. Deals with the devil
Kith of the Elf-folk
Garrity, D. A. ed. 44 Irish short stories
Misadventure
Magazine of fantasy and science fiction. Best from Fantasy and science fiction; 4th ser.

Dunsany, Lord. See Dunsany, Edward John Moreton Drax Plunkett, 18th baron

Duranty, Walter, 1884-1957
The parrot
First-prize stories, 1919-1957

Duras, Marguerite, 1914-
The boa
Lehmann, J. ed. Modern French stories

Durland, Frances
Heart turned inward
Furman, A. L. ed. Everygirls romance stories

Dusky Ruth. Coppard, A. E.

Dust and the serpent. Crane, L.

Dust of death. Asimov, I.

Dusty saddles. Drago, H. S.

DUTCH EAST INDIES. See Indonesia, Republic of

DUTCH IN INDONESIA
Conrad, J. Almayer's folly

DUTCH IN THE UNITED STATES
Irving, W. Legend of Sleepy Hollow
Irving, W. Rip Van Winkle

Dutourd, Jean, 1920-
Young patriot
Burnett, W. ed. This is my best humor

DUTY
Blixen, K. Country tale
Gray, C. North of the corduroy
Duty to live. Asch, S.
Duvernois, Henri, 1875-1937
Clothes make the man
Oberfirst, R. ed. Anthology of best short-short stories v5
The **dwarf.** Aymé, M.
The **dwarf.** Bradbury, R.
DWARFS
Aymé, M. Martin the novelist
Bradbury, R. The dwarf
Clayton, J. B. Summer of the insistent voices
Dickens, C. Going into society
Huxley, A. L. Sir Hercules
Karlen, A. The wall
Vidal, G. Erlinda and Mr Coffin
DWELLINGS. See Houses
Dworzan, Helene L. 1925-
Almighty power
New voices 2: American writing today
DYING. See Death

E

Each an explorer. Asimov, I.
Each in his generation. Burt, M. S.
Eadie, Thomas
Story of Michels
Fenner, P. R. ed. Heroes, heroes, heroes
EAGLES
Mannix, J. Our best friend is an eagle
Eagles and the trumpets. Plunkett, J.
EARLY CHRISTIANS. See Christians, Early
Early marriage. Richter, C.
EARP, WYATT BERRY STAPP, 1848-1929
Claussen, W. E. Man from Texas
EARTH
Clarke, A. C. Fires within
McConnell, J. Nor dust corrupt
Porges, A. The ruum
EARTH, DESTRUCTION OF
Clarke, A. C. The curse
Clarke, A. C. No morning after
Leiber, F. The big trek
Richardson, R. S. Xi effect
See also End of the world
EARTHQUAKES
Smith, E. H. Repeat performance
Earth's holocaust. Hawthorne, N.
EAST AFRICA. See Africa
EAST SIDE. See New York (City)—East Side
EASTER
O'Faoláin, S. Unholy living and half dying
Zimmerman, M. Important wish
Eastlake, William
Little Joe
Best American short stories, 1955

Quiet chimneys
Best American short stories, 1956
Unhappy hunting grounds
Best American short stories, 1957
Easton, Robert Olney
Death in October
Schaefer, J. W. ed. Out West
Easy does it. De Leeuw, A. L.
EATING CONTESTS. See Dinners
Eberhart, Mignon (Good) 1899-
Bermuda grapevine
Eberhart, M. G. Deadly is the diamond, and three other novelettes of murder
Crimson paw
Eberhart, M. G. Deadly is the diamond, and three other novelettes of murder
Deadly is the diamond
Eberhart, M. G. Deadly is the diamond, and three other novelettes of murder
Mr Wickwire's "gun moll"
Mystery Writers of America, inc. A choice of murders
Murder in waltz time
Eberhart, M. G. Deadly is the diamond, and three other novelettes of murder
Spider
Cooke, D. C. ed. My best murder story
Wagstaff pearls
This week magazine. This week's Stories of mystery and suspense
ECCENTRICS AND ECCENTRICITIES
Enright, E. One for the collection
Echoes. Blixen, K.
Eckard, Alma Kline
Sharp as the broken cup
Hughes, R. ed. All manner of men
The **eclipse.** Enright, E.
Edell, Harold
Tiger was a lady
Teen-age tales, bk 3
Edelman, Marek, 1922-
Last stand in the Warsaw ghetto
Schwarz, L. W. ed. Feast of Leviathan
Edge of sound. Woodward, G.
Edge of the sea. Budrys, A. J.
EDINBURGH. See Scotland—Edinburgh
Edith Cavell. Hagedorn, H.
EDITORS. See Journalists; Sport writers
Edmonds, Walter Dumaux, 1903-
Cadmus Henry, balloon observer
Fenner, P. R. comp. Brother against brother
Honor of the county
Great dog stories
Edmondson, G. C.
Rescue
Magazine of fantasy and science fiction. Best from Fantasy and science fiction; 7th ser.
Edna's husband. Farrell, J. T.
EDUCATION
Hale, L. P. Agamemnon's career
Lochridge, B. H. Will Davis
MacMahon, B. White blackbird
Spears, R. S. Sheriff's educated son
Stuart, J. Split cherry tree
See also Evening and continuation schools; School life; Teachers

EDUCATION, MILITARY. See Military
education

EDUCATION, RELIGIOUS. See Religious
education

EDUCATIONAL MEASUREMENTS. See
Examinations

Edwards, Kelley
Counterspy
Montgomery, R. B. ed. Best SF three

EELS
O'Flaherty, L. Conger eel

Effigy of war. Boyle, K.

The egg. Anderson, S.

Eggertsson, Jochum M.
Blue Fairy
World prize stories; 2d ser.

EGGS
Anderson, S. The egg
Household, G. Eggs as ain't

Eggs as ain't. Household, G.

EGOISM
Hawthorne, N. Egotism; or, The bosom
serpent
Mansfield, K. Dill pickle
Maugham, W. S. Door of opportunity

Egotism; or, The bosom serpent. Hawthorn,
N.

EGYPT
Shaw, I. Walking wounded

To 640

Cather, W. S. Tale of the white pyramid
Cook, B. G. Egyptian fishing

Egyptian fishing. Cook, B. G.

Ehrenfreund, Norbert, 1922-
Woman and child
American vanguard, 1956

Eidman, Leslie, 1935-
Oranges
American vanguard, 1956

Eight minutes to kill. Symons, J.

Eight years in the making. Mankowitz, W.

Eighteen oak ties. Pridgen, T.

Eighth circle of Gehenna. Peretz, I. L.

Eighty-yard run. Shaw, I.

Eisele, Albert, 1896-
The vigil
Hughes, R. ed. All manner of men

Eisenberg, Frances, 1912-
Daughter of the Confederacy
Burnett, W. ed. This is my best humor

Eisenhower's nightmare. Russell, B. A. W.
R. 3d earl

Elaine. Bates, H. E.

Elam, Richard M.
Expedition Pluto
Elam, R. M. Teen-age super science
stories
First man into space
Elam, R. M. Teen-age super science
stories
Flight of the Centaurus
Elam, R. M. Teen-age super science
stories

Ghost ship of space
Elam, R. M. Teen-age super science
stories
Mercy flight to Luna
Elam, R. M. Teen-age super science
stories
Mystery eyes over earth
Elam, R. M. Teen-age super science
stories
Peril from outer space
Elam, R. M. Teen-age super science
stories
Race around the sun
Elam, R. M. Teen-age super science
stories
Space steward
Elam, R. M. Teen-age super science
stories

ELECTIONS
Asimov, I. Franchise
Cushman, D. Old Copper Collar
Rhodes, E. M. The numismatist
Shaara, M. 2066: Election Day

ELECTRIC APPARATUS AND APPLI-
ANCES
Gold, H. An afternoon with the appliances

ELECTRIC CIRCUITS
Hamilton, D. Archie catches it

ELECTROMAGNETIC SCREENS. See
Shielding (Electricity)

ELECTROMAGNETIC SHIELDS. See
Shielding (Electricity)

ELEPHANTS
Annixter, P. pseud. Secret place
Chesterton, G. K. Elusive companion of
Parson White
Hunter, H. H. Pancho and the elephant
Kipling, R. Elephant's child
Williams, W. S. Elephant's child

Elephant's child. Kipling, R.

Elephant's child. Williams, W. S.

Elephants in the mirror. Church, R.

ELEVATORS
Dunsany, E. J. M. D. P. 18th baron. Misadventure

Eleven o'clock. Pritchett, V. S.

11 o'clock bulletin. Turner, R.

Eleventh juror. Starrett, V.

Elijah the prophet. Fineman, I.

ELIXIR OF LIFE. See Rejuvenation

Elk tooth dress. Johnson, D. M.

Ellin, Stanley, 1917?-
Best of everything
Ellin, S. Mystery stories
The betrayers
Ellin, S. Mystery stories
The Blessington Method
Mystery Writers of America, inc. A
choice of murders
Queen, E. pseud. ed. Ellery Queen's
awards: 11th ser.
Broker's special
Best detective stories of the year—1956
Ellin, S. Mystery stories
Cat's-paw
Ellin, S. Mystery stories
Death on Christmas Eve
Ellin, S. Mystery stories

Everything is wild. Thurber, J.

Everything satisfactory. O'Hara, J.

EVIL. See Good and evil

EVIL EYE
Brennan, J. P. Death in Peru

Evils of Spain. Pritchett, V. S.

EVOLUTION
Blish, J. Battle of the unborn
Clarke, A. C. The possessed
Cogswell, T. R. Limiting factor
Godwin, T. You created us
Grinnell, D. pseud. Lysenko maze
Guin, W. Volpla
Jenkins, W. F. Skag with the queer head
Kuttner, H. Cold war
McDowell, W. Veiled island
Neville, K. Experiment station
Nourse, A. E. Family resemblance
Russell, E. F. This one's on me
St Clair, M. Age of prophecy
Waldo, E. H. Love of heaven
Wallace, F. L. Impossible voyage home
White, J. The conspirators
Wright, S. F. Better choice

Evolution of Saxby. Bates, H. E.

Ewen, Frederic, 1899-
Letter from Coleridge
New voices 2: American writing today

Ewing, Juliana Horatia (Gatty) 1841-1885
Peace egg
Fremantle, A. J. ed. Christmas is here

Ex parte. Lardner, R. W.

Examination for lieutenant. Forester, C. S.

EXAMINATIONS
Folinsbee, J. P. Final question
Forester, C. S. Examination for lieutenant

EXCAVATIONS (ARCHEOLOGY)
Bates, H. E. Roman figures
Cather, W. S. Tom Outland's story
Doyle, Sir A. C. Through the veil

EXCEPTIONAL CHILDREN. See Children, Gifted

EXCHANGE OF IDENTITY. See Dual personality; Impersonations

Exclusive luxury of Enoch Oates. Chesterton, G. K.

EX-CONVICTS
Clayton, J. B. Little Woodrow
Dery, T. Love

The **excursionists.** Cardozo, N.

EXECUTIONS AND EXECUTIONERS
Kafka, F. In the penal colony
MacMahon, B. Foxy-haired lad
O'Donovan, M. Guests of the nation
Woolrich, C. Guillotine
See also Hanging

EXERCISE
Purdy, J. You may safely gaze

Exile. Cole, E. B.

The **exile.** Stewart, J. I. M.

Exile of paradise island. Albee, G. S.

EXILES. See Refugees

Exile's return. MacMahon, B.

EXISTENTIALISM
Russell, B. A. W. R. 3d earl. Existentialist's nightmare

Existentialist's nightmare. Russell, B. A. W. R. 3d earl

Expectation of life. O'Donovan, M.

Expedition Pluto. Elam, R. M.

EXPEDITIONS, ARCTIC. See Arctic regions

Experiment station. Neville, K.

EXPRESS SERVICE
Farrell, J. T. Called on the carpet

Employees
Farrell, J. T. Memento mori

EXPURGATED BOOKS
Russell, B. A. W. R. 3d earl. Mr Bowdler's nightmare

EXTORTION. See Blackmail

EXTRA girl. Cave, H. B.

EXTRA-SENSORY PERCEPTION. See Thought-transference

EYE
Surgery
Kersh, G. Murderer's eye

The **eye** of a soldier. Household, G.

Eye of God in paradise. Lessing, D. M.

EYEGLASSES
Huxley, A. L. The monocle
Kober, A. Certain people are gonna wake up and learn the score is too late
Rendina, L. J. C. My heart saw you

Eyes of the cat. Macken, W.

F

Fable IX. Saroyan, W.

Fable of the wise piker who had the kind of talk that went. Ade, G.

FABLES
Ade, G. Fable of the wise piker who had the kind of talk that went
Aymé, M. Dermuche
Hearn, L. Oshidori
Schwarz, L. W. Leviathan and the fox
Sørensen, V. Two legends
See also Allegories

FABULOUS brew. Hay, J.

Fabulous quest. Rutledge, A. H.

FACE
Abnormities and deformities
Household, G. Letter to a sister

The **face.** Benson, E. F.

Face at the window. Sansom, W.

Face from Atlantis. Gordimer, N.

The **face** is familiar, but—. Shulman, M.

Face like a pound of butter. Angoff, C.

Face next door. Holder, W.

Face of destiny. Moscardelli, N.

Face of the war. Wolfe, T.

Face on the wall. Lucas, E. V.

Face within the face. Schorer, M.

FAMILY LIFE—*Continued*

Connell, E. S. Beau monde of Mrs Bridge
Duncan, L. April
Enright, E. Flight to the islands
Enright, E. Nancy
Epstein, S. Jingle bells
Evans, C. Father in Sion
Ewing, J. H. G. Peace egg
Farrell, J. T. Hyland family
Farrell, J. T. Monday is another day
Farrell, J. T. Only son
Ferber, E. Classified
Ferber, E. Holiday
Fisher, D. F. C. Married children
Fisher, D. F. C. Scylla and Charybdis
Gibbons, S. Saturday afternoon
Green, H. The grey bird
Hall, J. B. Near the margin of the bay
Huxley, A. L. The Claxtons
Knight, R. Third honeymoon
Levinson, N. In the beginning
Lyberaki, M. The other Alexander
Macauley, R. Windfall
Macauley, R. The wishbone
Mann, T. Disorder and early sorrow
Marlett, M. B. G. Second chance
Maupassant, G. de. A family
Maupassant, G. de. My Uncle Jules
Maxwell, W. What every boy should know
Medici, R. Quiet
Neola, pseud. Mad about motors
O'Donovan, J. Lady soloist
O'Donovan, J. One of the family
O'Donovan, M. The paragon
Peretz, I. L. Morning in a basement
Pickens, L. Consolation prize
Porter, K. A. Old mortality
Pritchett, V. S. Lion's den
Pritchett, V. S. The sniff
Rao, R. Akkayya
Reid, L. A lifetime
Saroyan, W. Bill McGee's brother
Sarver, L. J. Percheron
Shaw, I. Sunny banks of the River Lethe
Sherburne, Z. From mother . . . with love
Summers, H. Black and white and gray
Thurman, R. Y. Not another word
Tolstoĭ, A. N. Graf. Mishka Nalymov
Tolstoĭ, A. N. Graf. A week in Turenevo
Upshaw, H. My brother's voice
Verga, G. Consolation
Welty, E. Kin
Welty, E. Why I live at the P. O.
Wilson, A. Et Dona Ferentes
Winslow, T. S. Cycle of Manhattan
Worthington, R. What about Susanna?
    See also Aunts; Brothers; Brothers and sisters; Children; Family chronicles; Fathers; Grandfathers; Grandmothers; Home; Mothers; Sisters; Uncles

Family of five. Fitzsimmons, P. M.

Family resemblance. Nourse, A. E.

FAMILY REUNIONS

Bowles, P. F. Frozen fields
Criswell, C. Jocasta

Family tree. Barrett, B. L.

The **fanatic**. Pincherle, A.

FANATICISM

Allen, S. The Blood of the Lamb

FANCY DRESS PARTIES. See Masquerades

FANTASIES

Abernathy, R. Grandma's lie soap
Abernathy, R. Heirs apparent
Albee, G. S. Exile of paradise island
Albee, G. S. Little Hiram
Aldiss, B. W. Let's be frank
Allen, S. Public hating
Andersen, H. C. Happy family
Andersen, H. C. The nightingale
Anderson, P. The immortal game
Anderson, P. Man who came early
Aymé, M. Martin the novelist
Aymé, M. The walker-through-walls
Banks, R. E. Littlest people
Banks, R. E. The short ones
Beaumont, C. Crooked man
Benét, S. V. By the waters of Babylon
Benét, S. V. Doc Mellhorn and the pearly gates
Benét, S. V. Judgment in the mountains
Benét, S. V. King of the Cats
Bixby, J. One way street
Blixen, K. The diver
Blixen, K. Immortal story
Borgese, E. M. The rehearsal
Bradbury, R. The crowd
Bradbury, R. Icarus Montgolfier Wright
Bradbury, R. Jack-in-the-box
Bradbury, R. The scythe
Bradbury, R. Skeleton
Bradbury, R. Small assassin
Bradbury, R. There was an old woman
Bradbury, R. Uncle Einar
Bradbury, R. The wind
Bradbury, R. Wonderful death of Dudley Stone
Brooks, W. R. Mr Whitcomb's genie
Brown, F. Answer
Budrys, A. J. Nobody bothers Gus
Burnett, F. H. Behind the white brick
Butler, F. To the wilderness I wander
Carroll, L. pseud. Mad tea-party
Causey, J. Felony
Clarke, A. C. Wall of darkness
Clingerman, M. Birds can't count
Clingerman, M. Last prophet
Clingerman, M. Mr Sakrison's halt
Clingerman, M. The wild wood
Coates, R. M. Autumn fable
Collier, J. Devil, George, and Rosie
Collier, J. Thus I refute Beelzy
Cross, E. Saint Bakeoven
Davidson, A. Now let us sleep
Dreiser, T. McEwen of the shining slave makers
Dunsany, E. J. M. D. P. 18th baron. Kith of the Elf-folk
Eustis, H. Mister Death and the red-headed woman
Finney, J. Of missing persons
Fitzgerald, F. S. K. Outside the cabinet-maker's
Forster, E. M. Celestial omnibus
Friborg, A. C. Careless love
Gallico, P. W. Lost hour
Germann, R. F. The talking dog
Gironella, J. M. Cathedral of hearts
Gogol', N. V. The nose
Henderson, Z. Anything box
Henderson, Z. Wilderness
Hilton, J. Lost horizon

FARM LIFE—*Continued*

Italy

Bacchelli, R. Etruscan harvest

Kansas

Trigg, P. E. Second chance

Middle West

Cather, W. S. Neighbour Rosicky
Garland, H. Under the lion's paw
Ward, L. L. Drought

Nebraska

Cather, W. S. On the divide

New England

Freeman, M. E. W. Revolt of mother

Palestine

Sened, A. and Sened, Y. Bracha
Shenhar, Y. Pitfalls of love

Russia

Chekhov, A. P. Gooseberries
Franko, I. I. Les's widow's household

South Carolina

Lowry, R. J. C. Little car in Virginia

South Dakota

Garland, H. Among the corn-rows

Southern States

Davis, W. F. Lady Luck and the guardian angel

Tennessee

Warren, R. P. Blackberry winter

Texas

Porter, K. A. Noon wine

Wales

Goodwin, G. Sitting of eggs
West, A. C. The monocrats
Williams, D. J. Pwll-yr-Onnen

The West

Cather, W. S. Lou, the prophet
Garland, H. Main-travelled roads
Garland, H. Up the Coolly

Wisconsin

Ferber, E. Farmer in the dell
FARM TENANCY. See Tenant farming
Farmer in the dell. Ferber, E.
FARMERS. See Farm life
Farmer's wife. Maupassant, G. de
Farque, Verdie
The runaway
Oberfirst, R. ed. Anthology of best
short-short stories v6
Farrell, James Thomas, 1904–
Accident
Farrell, J. T. Omnibus of short stories
After the sun has risen
Farrell, J. T. Omnibus of short stories
Autumn afternoon
Farrell, J. T. Omnibus of short stories
Baby Mike
Farrell, J. T. Omnibus of short stories
A baptism in Italy
Farrell, J. T. French girls are vicious,
and other stories

Benefits of American life
Hall, J. B. and Langland, J. T. eds.
Short story
Boyhood
Farrell, J. T. Omnibus of short stories
Boys and girls
Farrell, J. T. Dangerous woman, and
other stories
Bride of Christ
Farrell, J. T. Omnibus of short stories
Called on the carpet
Farrell, J. T. Omnibus of short stories
Comrade Stanley
Farrell, J. T. Omnibus of short stories
Counting the waves
Farrell, J. T. Omnibus of short stories
Dangerous woman
Farrell, J. T. Dangerous woman, and
other stories
The dialectic
Farrell, J. T. Omnibus of short stories
Dream of love
Farrell, J. T. French girls are vicious,
and other stories
Edna's husband
Farrell, J. T. Dangerous woman, and
other stories
Episode in a dentist's office
Farrell, J. T. Omnibus of short stories
Fall of Machine Gun McGurk
Farrell, J. T. Omnibus of short stories
Fate of a hero
Farrell, J. T. Omnibus of short stories
Father Timothy Joyce
Farrell, J. T. Omnibus of short stories
French girls are vicious
Farrell, J. T. French girls are vicious,
and other stories
Getting out the vote for the working
class
Farrell, J. T. Omnibus of short stories
Grammar school love
Farrell, J. T. Dangerous woman, and
other stories
High-school star
Farrell, J. T. Omnibus of short stories
Hyland family
Farrell, J. T. Omnibus of short stories
I want to meet a French girl
Farrell, J. T. French girls are vicious,
and other stories
I'm dancing Frances
Farrell, J. T. Dangerous woman, and
other stories
It's cold in the Alps
Farrell, J. T. Dangerous woman, and
other stories
Jazz-age clerk
Farrell, J. T. Omnibus of short stories
Joe
Farrell, J. T. Dangerous woman, and
other stories
Joe Eliot
Farrell, J. T. Omnibus of short stories
Kilroy was here
Farrell, J. T. French girls are vicious,
and other stories
Life adventurous
Farrell, J. T. Omnibus of short stories
Little Johnny: a fable
Farrell, J. T. Dangerous woman, and
other stories

Farrell, James T.—*Continued*

Love story of our time
  Farrell, J. T. Omnibus of short stories
Lunch hour: 1923
  Farrell, J. T. Omnibus of short stories
Memento mori
  Farrell, J. T. Dangerous woman, and
    other stories
Mr Gremmer
  Farrell, J. T. Omnibus of short stories
Monday is another day
  Farrell, J. T. Omnibus of short stories
Norman Allen
  Farrell, J. T. Dangerous woman, and
    other stories
Omar James
  Farrell, J. T. Omnibus of short stories
Olsen
  Farrell, J. T. Omnibus of short stories
$1,000 a week
  Farrell, J. T. Omnibus of short stories
Only son
  Farrell, J. T. Omnibus of short stories
Pat McGee
  Farrell, J. T. Omnibus of short stories
Patsy Gilbride
  Farrell, J. T. Omnibus of short stories
The philosopher
  Farrell, J. T. Omnibus of short stories
Quest
  Farrell, J. T. Omnibus of short stories
Rendezvous
  Farrell, J. T. French girls are vicious,
    and other stories
Ruth and Bertram
  Farrell, J. T. French girls are vicious,
    and other stories
Saturday night
  Farrell, J. T. Omnibus of short stories
Saturday night in America
  Farrell, J. T. Dangerous woman, and
    other stories
Saturday night in Paris
  Farrell, J. T. Dangerous woman, and
    other stories
Scrambled eggs and toast
  Farrell, J. T. Omnibus of short stories
Senior prom
  Farrell, J. T. Dangerous woman, and
    other stories
Short story
  Farrell, J. T. Omnibus of short stories
Sorel
  Farrell, J. T. Omnibus of short stories
Sport of kings
  Farrell, J. T. Omnibus of short stories
Street scene
  Farrell, J. T. Omnibus of short stories
Success story
  Farrell, J. T. Dangerous woman, and
    other stories
Sunday in April
  Farrell, J. T. Omnibus of short stories
Teamster's payday
  Farrell, J. T. Omnibus of short stories
They ain't the men they used to be
  Farrell, J. T. French girls are vicious,
    and other stories
They don't know what time it is
  Farrell, J. T. French girls are vicious,
    and other stories

To whom it may concern
  Farrell, J. T. Omnibus of short stories
Tommy Gallagher's crusade
  Farrell, J. T. Omnibus of short stories
Triumph of Willie Collins
  Farrell, J. T. Omnibus of short stories
Whoopee for the new deal!
  Farrell, J. T. Omnibus of short stories
Yesterday's love
  Farrell, J. T. Omnibus of short stories
Young artist
  Farrell, J. T. Omnibus of short stories
Young convicts
  Farrell, J. T. Omnibus of short stories

Farrell, Kathleen
George finds freedom
  Winter's tales, 3

Farrell, M. F.
Villainy of Mr Fox
  Welcome, J. and Orchard, V. eds. Best
    hunting stories

FASCISM
Mann, T. Mario and the magician

FASHION. See Clothing and dress

FASHION MODELS. See Models, Fashion
  (Persons)

Fashionable tiger. Ferry, J.

Fast, Howard Melvin, 1914-
Spoil the child
  Schaefer, J. W. ed. Out West
Where are your guns?
  Ribalow, H. U. ed. Treasury of Ameri-
    can Jewish stories

Fastagette. Colette, S. G.

FASTENINGS
Hedgecock, L. J. Zipper trouble

FAT. See Corpulence

Fatal gesture. Foote, J. T.

Fate of a hero. Farrell, J. T.

The **father**. Babel', I. E.

The **father**. Bjørnson, B.

The **father**. Maupassant, G. de

Father and I. Lagerkvist, P. F.

Father and the cook. Day, C.

Father Christmas. McLaverty, M.

Father Francisco's ointment. Lofts, N. R.

Father Gaucher's elixir. Daudet, A.

Father image. Block, A. R.

Father in Sion. Evans, C.

Father Judas. Maupassant, G. de

Father Philip. Dąbrowska, M.

Father Timothy Joyce. Farrell, J. T .

Father-to-be. Bellow, S.

FATHERS
Angoff, C. Something about my father
Bates, H. E. Go, lovely rose
Bjørnson, B. The father
Cantwell, J. Act of faith
Clay, G. R. We're all guests
Fowler, M. D. Man of distinction
Gale, Z. Bill's little girl
Hardy, F. Good as ever
McClellan, D. S. Salt
McCord, J. Somewhere out of nowhere
Maupassant, G. de. The father
Maupassant, G. de. Monsieur Parent

FATHERS—*Continued*

Maupassant, G. de. Old Amable
O'Donovan, J. Black magic
O'Donovan, J. My father loved roses
Shaw, I. Sunny banks of the River Lethe
    See also Fathers and daughters; Fathers and sons

FATHERS AND DAUGHTERS

Aymé, M. Roll of daughters
Babel', I. E. The father
Boyle, K. Episode in the life of an ancestor
Byrd, J. J. Out of the darkness
Caldwell, E. Anneve
Caldwell, E. Girl with figurines
Caldwell, E. Hilda
Carr, A. H. Z. Black kitten
Cather, W. S. Count of Crow's Nest
Cheever, J. Sorrows of gin
Chute, B. J. The legacy
Clegg, C. The picnic
Clemons, W. Summer shower
Conrad, J. Almayer's folly
Davis, R. H. Her first appearance
D'Elia, R. The spoiled one
Fitzgerald, F. S. K. Babylon revisited
Forster, E. M. Road from Colonus
Gallant, M. Wing's chips
Hawthorne, N. Rappaccini's daughter
Hecht, B. Actor's blood
Household, G. Constant lover
Hunt, M. F. Pair of lovers
James, D. A kind of faith
Maupassant, G. de. The spasm
Pincherle, A. Rain in May
Prentice, H. Equinox
Rabinowitz, S. Daughter's grave
Rabinowitz, S. Hodel
Rich, C. M. My sister's marriage
Rutledge, A. The standing tomb
Schweitzer, G. Not a child anymore
Sherburne, Z. From mother . . . with love
Williams, T. Yellow bird
    See also Parent and child

FATHERS AND SONS

Aldrich, T. B. White feather
Babel', I. E. A letter
Barker, D. Trip to Paris
Barrett, B. L. Filial regard
Beauchamp, D. D. The best year
Beigel, U. The balancing man
Bellow, S. Seize the day
Bjørnson, B. The father
Block, A. R. Father image
Block, A. R. One moment of truth
Block, A. R. Sunday morning
Block, R. E. Americanisation of Shadrach Cohen
Bowles P. F. Frozen fields
Boyle, K. Rest cure
Branch, R. Good-bye to spring
Burnett, W. Suffer the little children
Chekhov, A. P. My life: the story of a provincial
Clayton, J. B. Happy story when seen backwards
Clayton, J. B. Sound that God heard
Coates, R. M. Storms of childhood
Collier, J. Ah, the university
Collier, J. Thus I refute Beelzy
Cooper, E. Invisible boy
Cooper, W. Moral choice
Cozzens, J. G. Total stranger

Criswell, C. Crying through the lock
Danischewsky, H. Judgment of Mr Moyshe
Deming, R. Custody
Divided horsecloth
Dow, D. Ol' Nick's wife
Faulkner, W. Barn burning
Garrett, G. A hard row to hoe
Garrett, G. The king of the mountain
Garrett, G. The lion hunter
Garrett, G. The rivals
Grau, S. A. Hunter's home
Hemingway, E. My old man
Ivins, D. Favored son
Jones, G. Wat Pantathro
Kafka, F. The judgment
La Farge, O. Brush of the wings
Lagerkvist, P. F. Father and I
Lochridge, B. H. Birdie Keller
Mabry, T. D. Indian feather
MacMahon, B. Sunday afternoon. Sunny
Marquand, J. P. The end game
Matheson, R. The test
Maupassant, G. de. Hautot and his son
Maupassant, G. de. Little one
Meyers, L. My father and the Indians
Miller, E. M. Pay and the uniform
Morton, C. Walnut bed
Oakes, P. Lion in the house
O'Donovan, M. My Œdipus complex
O'Flaherty, L. The blow
O'Hara, J. Bread alone
Picard, J. The fox
Polk, W. T. The patriot
Pritchett, V. S. Fly in the ointment
Purdy, J. Color of darkness
Purdy, J. Cutting edge
Rabinowitz, S. Lottery ticket
Richter, C. Sea of grass
Rutledge, A. H. Fabulous quest
Saroyan, W. Aram Saeetyujkfogl
Saroyan, W. Palo
Saroyan, W. Reader of "The World Almanac for 1944"
Saroyan, W. Return to the pomegranate trees
Saroyan, W. Whole voyald, and other stories
Shenton, E. Son he'd never met
Spears, R. S. Sheriff's educated son
Stafford, J. A reunion
Stegner, W. E. Blue-winged teal
Stegner, W. E. City of the living
Strong, L. A. G. Prongs
Stuart, J. Split cherry tree
Swados, H. Present for the boy
Thurber, J. More alarms at night
Van Druten, J. Gavin
Van Scoyk, B. Home from camp
Welty, E. Ladies in spring
Zawieyski, J. The president calls
    See also Parent and child

FATHERS-IN-LAW

Block, A. R. Whipping boy
Montross, L. S. Good wife for a young doctor

Faulkner, William, 1897-

All the dead pilots
    Hall, J. B. and Langland, J. T. eds. Short story
Ambuscade
    Saturday evening post (Periodical) The Post Reader of Civil War stories

Fear. Maupassant, G. de
Fear. Straw, C. S.
"Fear that walks by noonday." Cather, W. S.
Fearing, Kenneth, 1902-
    Three wives too many
        Best detective stories of the year (12th
        annual collection)
FEAST OF LIGHTS. See Hanukkah
    (Feast of Lights)
FEASTS. See Festivals
Feathers. Van Vechten, C.
February 1999: Ylla. Bradbury, R.
February 2002: the locusts. Bradbury, R.
February 2003: interim. Bradbury, R.
Fecundity. Maupassant, G. de
Fedor Kuzmich of the conservatoire.
    Trifonov, Y.
FEEBLE-MINDED
    Bachrach, S. F. Walk-away kid
    French, J. Love is a flaming angel
    Hall, J. B. In the time of demonstrations
    Lardner, R. W. Haircut
    Maupassant, G. de. Bertha
    Porter, K. A. He
    Rawlings, M. K. The shell
    Sansom, W. Game of billiards
    Todd, R. Big wheel
    Welty, E. Lily Daw and the three ladies
        See also Idiocy
Feet upon the mountains. Spiegler, G. R.
Feierberg, Mordecai Zeeb, 1874-1899
    The calf
        Schwarz, L. W. ed. Feast of Leviathan
Felis catus. Berriault, G.
Felony. Causey, J.
Felsen, Gregor, 1916-
    Why rustlers never win
        Meredith, S. ed. Bar 6
Felsen, Henry Gregor. See Felsen, Gregor
Felts, Josephine Noyes
    Winning of Dark Boy
        Everygirls horse stories
Female of the fruit fly. Campbell, W. E. M.
Feminine men. Maupassant, G. de
FEMINISM
    Pincherle, A. Don't delve too deeply
The fence. Simak, C. D.
FENCES
    Kelton, E. Coward
FENCES (RECEIVERS OF STOLEN
    GOODS) See Receiving stolen goods
FENCING
    Olgin, J. Lucky touch
    Sansom, W. The big stick
Feng, Meng-lung, 1574?-1645
    Canary murders
        Feng, M. Stories from a Ming collection
    Fairy's rescue
        Feng, M. Stories from a Ming collection
    Journey of the corpse
        Feng, M. Stories from a Ming collection
    Lady who was a beggar
        Feng, M. Stories from a Ming collection
    Pearl-sewn shirt
        Feng, M. Stories from a Ming collection

Story of Wu Pao-an
    Feng, M. Stories from a Ming collection
Wine and dumplings
    Feng, M. Stories from a Ming collection
Fenton, Edward, 1917-
    Broken Christmas
        Fremantle, A. J. ed. Christmas is here
Fenton, Frank, 1904-
    The chicken or the egghead
        Healy, R. J. ed. 9 tales of time and
        space
Ferber, Edna, 1887-
    Afternoon of a faun
        Ferber, E. One basket
    Barn cuts off the view
        Ferber, E. One basket
    Blue blood
        Ferber, E. One basket
    Blue glasses
        Ferber, E. One basket
    Classified
        Ferber, E. One basket
    Every other Thursday
        Ferber, E. One basket
    Farmer in the dell
        Ferber, E. One basket
    Gay old dog
        Ferber, E. One basket
    Gigolo
        Ferber, E. One basket
    Glamour
        Ferber, E. One basket
    Grandma isn't playing
        Ferber, E. One basket
    Hey! Taxi!
        Ferber, E. One basket
    Holiday
        Ferber, E. One basket
    Home girl
        Ferber, E. One basket
    Keep it holy
        Ferber, E. One basket
    Light touch
        Ferber, E. One basket
    Long distance
        Ferber, E. One basket
    Maternal feminine
        Ferber, E. One basket
    Molly Brandeis takes hold
        Schwarz, L. W. ed. Feast of Leviathan
    Un morso doo pang
        Ferber, E. One basket
    Mother knows best
        Ferber, E. One basket
    No room at the Inn
        Ferber, E. One basket
    Nobody's in town
        Ferber, E. One basket
    Old Lady Mandle
        Ferber, E. One basket
        Kobler, F. ed. Her children call her
        blessed
    Old Man Minick
        Baudin, M. ed. Contemporary short sto-
        ries v2
        Ferber, E. One basket
    Our very best people
        Ferber, E. One basket
    Sudden sixties
        Ferber, E. One basket
    That's marriage
        Ferber, E. One basket

Fisher, Dorothea F.—*Continued*

Saint of the Old Seminary
  Fisher, D. F. C. Harvest of stories

Scylla and Charybdis
  Fisher, D. F. C. Harvest of stories

Sex education
  Fisher, D. F. C. Harvest of stories

"Through pity and terror. . ."
  Fisher, D. F. C. Harvest of stories

Uncle Giles
  Fisher, D. F. C. Harvest of stories

"Vive Guignol!"
  Fisher, D. F. C. Harvest of stories

Washed window
  Fisher, D. F. C. Harvest of stories

Fisher, Dorothy Canfield. See Fisher, Dorothea Frances (Canfield)

Fisher, Vardis, 1895-
The scarecrow
  Schaefer, J. W. ed. Out West

Fisherman from Chihuahua. Connell, E. S.

FISHERMEN
Boyle, K. Herring piece
Boyle, K. How Bridie's girl was won
Clarke, D. The Islandman
Combs, P. Man on the beach
Corkery, D. The awakening
Maupassant, G. de. At sea
Maupassant, G. de. Drowned man
Maupassant, G. de. Selfishness
Maupassant, G. de. The victim
Moldi. Net fishers
O'Flaherty, L. Conger eel
O'Flaherty, L. The landing
O'Flaherty, L. The oar
Peretz, I. L. Miracles on the sea
Poe, E. A. Descent into the Maelström
Sandoz, M. Y. Friends
Wallenius, K. M. Bare land
  See also Fishing

FISHES
Annixter, P. pseud. Flounder, flounder in the sea
Li Fu-yen. Man who became a fish
O'Faoláin, S. The trout
Picard, J. The fish
  See also Fishing; Muskellunge; Salmon; Sea food; Sharks

FISHING
Block, A. H. Next time, stay home!
Connell, E. S. I'll take you to Tennessee
Cook, B. G. Chinese fishing
Cook, B. G. Egyptian fishing
Cook, B. G. Greek fishing
Cook, B. G. Old English fishing
Cook, B. G. Truth is stranger than fishin'; 5 stories
Cook, B. G. We get set for a long jump
Ferguson, R. His lucky day
Foote, J. T. Fatal gesture
Foote, J. T. A wedding gift
Gordon, C. Old Red
Grau, S. A. Joshua
Graves, J. Green fly
Holappa, P. Pastoral
Jensen, M. A. Juggin' for cats in the Big Muddy
Lesiņš, K. Siljonis' jewel
Lowry, R. J. C. Hero in New York
Maupassant, G. de. The hole

Nagibin, Y. Night guest
O'Brian, P. Happy despatch
O'Brian, P. Last pool
O'Brian, P. The return
O'Flaherty, L. The rockfish
Person, W. T. Measure of an angler
Person, W. T. Won by a tail
Rinehart, M. R. Hijack and the game
Smith, E. W. An angler comes to life
Smith, E. W. Decline and fall of a purist
Smith, E. W. Most-remembered pools
Welty, E. Ladies in spring
Welty, E. Wide net
Wylie, P. Affair of the ardent amazon
Wylie, P. Light tackle
Wylie, P. Man who loved a joke
Wylie, P. Plane down—hurricane area
Wylie, P. Smuggler's cove
Wylie, P. Treasure cruise
Wylie, P. Treasure cruise and other Crunch and Des stories; 6 stories
  See also Fishermen

Implements and appliances
Cook, B. G. Truth is stranger than fishin'; 5 stories

Fishing excursion. Maupassant, G. de

FISHING TACKLE. See Fishing—Implements and appliances

FIST FIGHTING. See Fighting, Hand-to-hand

Fitch, Ahlene
Faithful fool
  Oberfirst, R. ed. Anthology of best short-short stories v5

Fitch, George Helgeson, 1877-1915
The Greek double cross
  Saturday evening post (Periodical) Saturday evening post Carnival of humor

Fitness of Sean O'Fallon. Fox, N. A.

Fitzgerald, Francis Scott Key, 1896-1940
Afternoon of an author
  Fitzgerald, F. S. K. Afternoon of an author
Author's house
  Fitzgerald, F. S. K. Afternoon of an author
Babylon revisted
  Baudin, M. ed. Contemporary short stories v2
  Costain, T. B. and Beecroft, J. eds. More Stories to remember
  Locke, L. G.; Gibson, W. M. and Arms, G. W. eds. Introduction to literature
Basil and Cleopatra
  Fitzgerald, F. S. K. Afternoon of an author
Bernice bobs her hair
  Jennings, F. G. and Calitri, C. J. eds. Stories
Boil some water—lots of it
  Fitzgerald, F. S. K. Afternoon of an author
Crazy Sunday
  Lewis, J. D. ed. Great stories about show business
Design in plaster
  Fitzgerald, F. S. K. Afternoon of an author

Fitzgerald, Francis S. K.—*Continued*
Forging ahead
Fitzgerald, F. S. K. Afternoon of an author
Freshest boy
Havighurst, W. and others, eds. Selection
News of Paris—fifteen years ago
Fitzgerald, F. S. K. Afternoon of an author
Night at the fair
Fitzgerald, F. S. K. Afternoon of an author
No harm trying
Fitzgerald, F. S. K. Afternoon of an author
One interne
Blaustein, P. M. and Blaustein, A. P. eds. Doctors' choice
One trip abroad
Fitzgerald, F. S. K. Afternoon of an author
Outside the cabinet-maker's
Fitzgerald, F. S. K. Afternoon of an author
Teamed with genius
Fitzgerald, F. S. K. Afternoon of an author

Fitzsimmons, Paul M.
Family of five
Teen-age tales, bk 6

Five-forty-eight. Cheever, J.
Five orange pips. Doyle, Sir A. C.
Five per cent of paradise. Mankowitz, W.
The **fix.** Haner, R.
Fixed fight. Rowland, S.
FLAGSTADT, M. JEANNETTE, 1919-
Flower show
Oberfirst, R. ed. 1955 anthology of best original short-shorts
The **flame**-knife. Howard, R. E. and De-Camp, L. S.
Flame-out. Harvey, F. L.
Flanagan, Thomas
Customs of the country
Queen, E. pseud. ed. Ellery Queen's awards: 11th ser.
This will do nicely
Queen, E. pseud. ed. Ellery Queen's awards: 10th ser.
FLASHBACKS. See Retrospective stories
Flashes in the night. Tamási, A.
Flat country Christmas. Wilson, A.
Flatcar. Ryûnosuke, A.
FLATS. See Apartment houses
Flaubert, Gustave, 1821-1880
Simple heart
Thurston, J. A. ed. Reading modern short stories
Flavors of exile. Lessing, D. M.
FLEAS
Mankowitz, W. Battersea miracle
Fleg, Edmond, 1874-
Boy prophet
Schwarz, L. W. ed. Feast of Leviathan
Flesh and blood. Critchell, L. S.
Fleur-de-Blé. Lemonnier, C

FLIES
Langelaan, G. The fly
Flight. Lessing, D. M.
Flight. Steinbeck, J.
Flight into disaster. Gardner, E. S.
Flight of Betsey Lane. Jewett, S. O.
Flight of the Centaurus. Elam, R. M.
Flight pattern. Knapp, S. E.
Flight to France. Jovine, F.
Flight to the islands. Enright, E.
Flint and fire. Fisher, D. F. C.
Flip of a coin. Davis, M.
FLOATS (PARADES)
Ostroff, A. La bataille des fleurs
Floherty, John Joseph, 1882-
Shipwreck and sacrifice
Fenner, P. R. ed. Heroes, heroes, heroes
Yellow terror
Fenner, P. R. ed. Heroes, heroes, heroes
FLOODS
Fitzsimmons, P. M. Family of five
Lowry, R. J. C. Floodwater! Floodwater!
MacLeish, R. Night of disaster
Samuel, E. H. When the cloud burst
Floodwater! Floodwater! Lowry, R. J. C.
FLORENCE. See Italy—Florence
Florentine. Maupassant, G. de
FLORICULTURE. See Gardens and gardening
FLORIDA
Garrett, G. The king of the mountain
Hunt, M. F. Pair of lovers
Rawlings, M. K. Gal young un
Rawlings, M. K. Jacob's ladder

20th century
O'Connor, F. Stroke of good fortune
Rawlings, M. K. Jessamine Springs
Rawlings, M. K. Pelican's shadow

Key West
Vidal, G. Erlinda and Mr Coffin
Vidal, G. Three stratagems

St Petersburg
Lardner, R. W. Golden honeymoon
Flounder, flounder in the sea. Annixter, P. pseud.
FLOWER GARDENING. See Gardens and gardening
Flower show. Flagstadt, M. J.
Flowers, John Owen, 1909-
Bus stop
Oberfirst, R. ed. Anthology of best short-short stories v5
FLOWERS
Bontempelli, M. Honesty
Jenkins, R. Flowers
See also Gardens and gardening; also names of particular flowers, e.g. Roses
FLUTE PLAYERS. See Musicians—Flute players
FLY. See Flies
The **fly.** Langelaan, G.
The **fly.** Mansfield, K.

FOREIGN CORRESPONDENTS. See Journalists

Foreign fish. Macken, W.

FOREIGN LEGION (FRENCH ARMY)
Boyle, K. They weren't going to die

FOREIGN SERVICE. See Civil service

Foreman, Leonard London, 1901-
Wagon-tongue north
Western Writers of America. Hoof trails and wagon tracks

FORENAMES. See Names, Personal

The forest. Picard, J.

Forester, Cecil Scott, 1899-
Examination for lieutenant
Wood, E. R. ed. Contemporary short stories
The hostage
Hudson, D. ed. Modern English short stories, 2d ser.
Some kinds of bad luck
Lewis, J. D. ed. Dealer's choice

FORESTERS
Munro, H. H. The interlopers

FORESTS AND FORESTRY
Blackwood, A. Man whom the trees loved
Blackwood, A. The wendigo

Forests and pastures. Franko, I. I.

The forge. Prévost, J.

FORGERIES, LITERARY. See Literary forgeries and mystifications

FORGERY
Gilbert, M. F. Income tax mystery
See also Counterfeiters

FORGERY OF WORKS OF ART
Bradshaw, G. "The picture wouldn't fit in the stove"

Forgetful man. Balchin, N.

Forging ahead. Fitzgerald, F. S. K.

FORGIVENESS
Blixen, K. Of hidden thoughts and of heaven
Tolstoi, L. N. Graf. Long exile

Forgiveness. Maupassant, G. de

Forgotten enemy. Clarke, A. C.

Forgotten mother. Fisher, D. F. C.

Forgotten poet. Nabokov, V. V.

The forks. Powers, J. F.

FORMOSA
Sneider, V. J. Pail of oysters

Forrestier, Michael
Gifts to my people
Queen, E. pseud. ed. Ellery Queen's awards: 11th ser.

Forster, Edward Morgan, 1879-
Celestial omnibus
Locke, L. G.; Gibson, W. M. and Arms, G. W. eds. Introduction to literature
McClennen, J. comp. Masters and masterpieces of the short story
Thurston, J. A. ed. Reading modern short stories
Road from Colonus
Havighurst, W. ed. Masters of the modern short story
Story of the siren
Jarrell, R. ed. Anchor book of stories

FORTUNE-TELLING
Criswell, C. Give your heart to Jesus
See also Palmistry

Forty years on. Lofts, N. R.

Fossi, Paavo
Moments
World prize stories; 2d ser.

Foster, Bennett
Killer at bay
Western Writers of America. Branded West
Night of terror
Western Writers of America. Hound dogs and others
Thief by choice
Meredith, S. ed. Bar 6
Trail song
Western Writers of America. Hoof trails and wagon tracks

Foster, Michael, 1904-
Spotlight
Saturday evening post (Periodical) Saturday evening post stories, 1956

FOSTER CHILDREN
Maupassant, G. de. In the country
Maupassant, G. de. Mademoiselle Pearl
Maupassant, G. de. The orphan
Ringwood, G. P. Little ghost
Seidenberg, E. S. Amelia
Sneider, V. J. Child of the regiment
Stafford, J. In the zoo
Weed, A. Matter of months
See also Foundlings; Orphans

Foundation of the city. Maeterlinck, M.

FOUNDLINGS
Dickens, C. No thoroughfare

FOUNTAIN OF YOUTH. See Rejuvenation

Four annas. Weston, C. G.

Four freedoms. Newhouse, E.

Four generations and four wills. Peretz, I. L.

Four in one. Knight, D.

Four meetings. James, H.

Four men and a box. Barnard, L. G.

Four-minute mile Rackowe, A.

Four o'clock. Smith, E. H.

Four o'clock bell. Ruskin, S.

Four seasons. Stewart, J. I. M.

Four sides of a triangle. Yellen, S.

Fournier, Pierre, 1916-
The animals
Fournier, P. Beasts and men
Lehmann, J. ed. Modern French stories
The cat
Fournier, P. Beasts and men
The dogs
Fournier, P. Beasts and men
Gaston
Fournier, P. Beasts and men
The horses
Fournier, P. Beasts and men
House of blood
Fournier, P. Beasts and men
Season of the dead
Fournier, P. Beasts and men

Fourth cockatoo. Meller, L.

French, Joan, 1926-
 Love is a flaming angel
 New voices 2: American writing today
FRENCH AND INDIAN WAR. See
 United States—18th century—French
 and Indian War, 1755-1763
French bull-dog. Colette, S. G.
FRENCH CANADIAN DIALECT. See
 Dialect stories—French Canadian
FRENCH CANADIANS
 Murphy, R. There was a bigger one
 Thomson, E. W. Old Man Savarin
French Enoch Arden. Maupassant, G. de
French girls are vicious. Farrell, J. T.
FRENCH IN AFRICA
 Camus, A. Adulterous woman
 Maupassant, G. de. Marroca
FRENCH IN CANADA
 Fontaine, R. L. Crown relents
FRENCH IN GERMANY
 Beauquey, M. In the other's shoes
FRENCH IN HAITI
 Gold, H. Encounter in Haiti
FRENCH IN INDIA
 Maupassant, G. de. Châli
FRENCH IN ITALY
 Maupassant, G. de. Sisters Rondoli
FRENCH IN NORWAY
 Blixen, K. Babette's feast
FRENCH IN THE UNITED STATES
 Cather, W. S. Count of Crow's Nest
 Cather, W. S. Night at Greenway Court
 Catlin, G. Ba'tiste's story of the medicine
 bag
 Cave, H. B. Extra girl
FRENCH LANGUAGE
 Chamson, A. Power of words
 Kroner, J. On Saturday afternoons

 Composition and exercises
 Aymé, M. The proverb

 Study and teaching
 Barrett, B. L. Victim of a lust
FRENCH POLITICS. See Politics—
 France
French scarecrow. Maxwell, W.
FRENCH SOLDIERS. See Soldiers,
 French
Fresh milk. Gerchunoff, A.
Freshest boy. Fitzgerald, F. S. K.
FRIARS. See Monks
Friborg, Albert Compton, 1930-
 Careless love
 Best science-fiction stories and novels:
 1955
 Magazine of fantasy and science fiction.
 Best from Fantasy and science fic-
 tion; 4th ser.
Friday is a lucky day. Muldur, N.
Friel, George
 Thoughtless
 Urquhart, F. ed. Scottish short stories
Friend in need. Maugham, W. S.
Friend of her father's. Plomer, W. C. F.
Friend of the family. Boyle, K.

Friend of the family. O'Donovan, J.
Friend of the family. Samuel, E. H.
Friendly game of cards. Coates, R. M.
FRIENDS. See Friendship
FRIENDS, SOCIETY OF
 Carmer, C. L. Quaker girl and the rock-
 ing ghost
 Russell, B. A. W. R. 3d earl. Stalin's
 nightmare
 West, J. First day finish
 West, J. Music on the Muscatatuck
 West, J. Pacing goose
Friends. Sandoz, M. Y.
Friends of Petro. Kirch, J. A.
Friends of the friends. James, H.
FRIENDSHIP
 Angoff, C. Beryl der Croomer
 Balchin, N. Among friends
 Blakiston, N. Mrs Webster
 Corkery, D. The awakening
 Farrell, J. T. The dialectic
 Feng, M. Journey of the corpse
 Feng, M. Story of Wu Pao-an
 Hale, N. Full life
 Harte, B. Tennessee's partner
 Kober, A. Good-by to palship
 Millholland, R. Roaring Pittsburgh Dan
 O'Faoláin, S. One true friend
 Patton, F. G. The game
 Pincherle, A. Jewellery
 Pohl, F. Pythias
 Porter, W. S. After twenty years
 Sandoz, M. Y. Friends
 Smith, E. W. Jeff Coongate and the
 stolen crony
 Smith, E. W. One-eyed poacher's revenge
 Smith, E. W. Specific gravity of Jeff
 Coongate
 Spark, M. Portobello Road
 Unamuno y Jugo, M. de. Abel Sanchez
 Van Doren, M. The little house
 Ward, L. L. Tomorrow afternoon
 Yates, R. Really good jazz piano
Friendship. Pincherle, A.
FRIGHT. See Fear
Frightened ones. Marlett, M. B. G.
Frightened pilot. Harvey, F. L.
The frill. Buck, P. S.
Frisbie—Santa's helper. Coombs, C. I.
Fritz, Jean
 Bottle night
 Seventeen (Periodical) Seventeen's
 stories
FROGS
 Clemens, S. L. Celebrated jumping frog
 of Calaveras County
 Clemens, S. L. Notorious jumping frog
 of Calaveras County
From "A Connecticut Yankee in King Ar-
 thur's Court." Clemens, S. L.
From mother . . . with love. Sherburne, Z.
From the diary of one not born. Singer,
 I. B.
From the mouse to the hawk. Henderson, D.
Fronds of corn. Bartlett, P.
FRONTIER AND PIONEER LIFE
 Bill, E. E. The rose
 Case, V. Lost wagons

FUTURE TIME. See Time

Fu-yen, Li. See Li Fu-yen

Fyfe, H. B.
In value deceived
Gallant, J. ed. Stories of scientific imagination

G

GI story. Queen, E. pseud.

Gable, Betty Lee, 1927-
November love
American vanguard, 1956

Gable window. Lovecraft, H. P. and Derleth, A. W.

Gaby, Alex
Fifty-two miles to terror
Saturday evening post (Periodical) Saturday evening post stories, 1956

Gadarene swine. Allen, S.

Gadgets aren't everything. Coombs, C. I.

Gaeglers and the wild geese. Macken, W.

Gaitens, Edward
Wee nip
Urquhart, F. ed. Scottish short stories

Gal young un. Rawlings, M. K.

Galdos, Benito Perez. See Perez Galdos, Benito

Gale, Zona, 1874-1938
Bill's little girl
Jennings, F. G. and Calitri, C. J. eds. Stories

GALICIA. See Poland

Gallagher, Frank
Leaping trout
Garrity, D. A. ed. 44 Irish short stories

Gallant, Mavis
About Geneva
Gallant, M. The other Paris
Autumn day
Gallant, M. The other Paris
Day like any other
Gallant, M. The other Paris
Deceptions of Marie-Blanche
Gallant, M. The other Paris
Going ashore
Gallant, M. The other Paris
The legacy
Gallant, M. The other Paris
One morning in June
Gallant, M. The other Paris
The other Paris
Gallant, M. The other Paris
The picnic
Gallant, M. The other Paris
Poor Franzi
Gallant, M. The other Paris
Señor Pinedo
Gallant, M. The other Paris
Wing's chips
Gallant, M. The other Paris

El Gallardo. Blasco Ibañez, V.

GALLERIES, ART. See Art galleries and museums

Gallico, Paul William, 1897-
Lost hour
Saturday evening post (Periodical) Saturday evening post stories, 1955
Never take no for an answer
Good housekeeping (Periodical) Editor's choice
Silent hostages
Saturday evening post (Periodical) Saturday evening post stories, 1956
Thicker than water
Collier's (Periodical) Collier's Greatest sports stories
Verna
Lewis, J. D. ed. Great stories about show business
The world of Babe Ruth
Saturday evening post (Periodical) Saturday evening post stories, 1954

Galouye, Daniel F.
Sanctuary
Magazine of fantasy and science fiction. Best from Fantasy and science fiction; 4th ser.

Galsworthy, John, 1867-1933
Acme
Lewis, J. D. ed. Great stories about show business
Quality
McMaster, J. ed. Stories to remember
Ultima Thule
Costain, T. B. and Beecroft, J. eds. More Stories to remember

Galway Bay. O'Flaherty, L.

Gambler, the nun and the radio. Hemingway, E.

GAMBLERS. See Gambling

Gambler's choice. Francis, W. H.

GAMBLING
Amundson, G. Man of parts
Arthur, R. Satan and Sam Shay
Bohnsack, E. J. The odds
Clemens, S. L. Celebrated jumping frog of Calaveras County
Collier, J. Ah, the university
Collins, W. Terribly strange bed
Coppee, F. The louis-d'or
Dunsany, E. J. M. D. P. 18th baron. Deal with the devil
Farrell, J. T. Sport of kings
Harte, B. Outcasts of Poker Flat
Horn, H. Old man
Lawrence, D. H. Rocking-horse winner
Lowry, R. J. C. Guys from Ray's Place
Maugham, W. S. Facts of life
Perret, J. The fly
Runyon, D. Blood pressure
Smith, L. W. Ace in the hole
Tolstoi, L. N. Graf. Recollections of a billiard-marker
Wilde, P. Pillar of fire
See also Lotteries; Wagers

The game. Beigel, U.

The game. Hesling, B.

The game. Patton, F. G.

GAME AND GAME BIRDS. See Duck shooting

GAME COCKS. See Cock fighting; Roosters

Gate-leg table. St John, M. L.

The **gates**. Strong, L. A. G.

Gates ajar. Smith, E. W.

GAUCHOS
Gerchunoff, A. The herdsman

Gaudeamus igitur. O'Donovan, J.

The **gauger**. Machen, W.

Gault, William Campbell
Million dollar gesture
Best detective stories of the year (13th annual collection)

The **gavel**. Miller, R. M.

Gavin. Van Druten, J.

Gay, Florence, 1910-
Bird of the air
New voices 2: American writing today

Gay old dog. Ferber, E.

Gay young call. Martin, B. F.

Gedali. Babel', I. E.

Gee! Miss Marshall. Block, A. R.

GEESE
O'Flaherty, L. Fairy goose
Rutledge, A. H. Phantom huntsmen
West, J. Pacing goose

GEHENNA. See Hell

Geier, Chester S.
Environment
Conklin, G. ed. Strange adventures in science fiction

GEISHA GIRLS
Mailer, N. K. Paper house

Gellhorn, Martha Ellis, 1908-
For better for worse
Gellhorn, M. E. Two by two
For richer for poorer
Gellhorn, M. E. Two by two
In sickness and in health
Gellhorn, M. E. Two by two
Same as: Smell of lilies
Till death us do part
Gellhorn, M. E. Two by two

GEMS. See Precious stones

GENEALOGY
Garrett, G. The accursed huntsman

GENERALS
Miller, E. M. Decision for a star

General's ring. Lagerlof, S. O. L.

Genesis. Block, A. R.

Genesis. Reichenstein, S.

GENETICS. See Evolution

GENIE. See Jinn

GENIUS
Babel', I. E. Awakening
See also Children, Gifted

The **genius**. O'Donovan, M.

Genius of the species. Bretnor, R.

The **geniuses**. Franklin, M.

Gentle counsels. Balchin, N.

A **gentle** creature. Dostoevskiĭ, F. M.

Gentleman caller. Johns, V. P.

Gentleman from Cracow. Singer, I. B.

Gentleman in blue. Stallings, L.

Genuine blend of bluegrass and bourbon. Adams, A.

George finds freedom. Farrell, K.

GEORGIA
20th century
O'Connor, F. A good man is hard to find

Gerchunoff, Alberto, 1883-1950
The Anthem
Gerchunoff, A. Jewish Gauchos of the Pampas
Camacho's wedding feast
Gerchunoff, A. Jewish Gauchos of the Pampas
Case of the stolen horse
Gerchunoff, A. Jewish Gauchos of the Pampas
Death of Elder Saul
Gerchunoff, A. Jewish Gauchos of the Pampas
Divorce
Gerchunoff, A. Jewish Gauchos of the Pampas
First furrow
Gerchunoff, A. Jewish Gauchos of the Pampas
Fresh milk
Gerchunoff, A. Jewish Gauchos of the Pampas
The herdsman
Gerchunoff, A. Jewish Gauchos of the Pampas
In the beginning
Gerchunoff, A. Jewish Gauchos of the Pampas
Lamentations
Gerchunoff, A. Jewish Gauchos of the Pampas
Miraculous doctor
Gerchunoff, A. Jewish Gauchos of the Pampas
New immigrants
Gerchunoff, A. Jewish Gauchos of the Pampas
Old colonist
Gerchunoff, A. Jewish Gauchos of the Pampas
The owl
Gerchunoff, A. Jewish Gauchos of the Pampas
Plundered orchard
Gerchunoff, A. Jewish Gauchos of the Pampas
The poet
Gerchunoff, A. Jewish Gauchos of the Pampas
Revolution
Gerchunoff, A. Jewish Gauchos of the Pampas
Sad and lonely one
Gerchunoff, A. Jewish Gauchos of the Pampas
The shower
Gerchunoff, A. Jewish Gauchos of the Pampas
The siesta
Gerchunoff, A. Jewish Gauchos of the Pampas
Silver candelabra
Gerchunoff, A. Jewish Gauchos of the Pampas
Same as: Silver candlestick
Silver candlestick
Schwarz, L. W. ed. Feast of Leviathan
Same as: Silver candelabra

Gerchunoff, Alberto—*Continued*
  Social call
    Gerchunoff, A. Jewish Gauchos of the
      Pampas
  Song of songs
    Gerchunoff, A. Jewish Gauchos of the
      Pampas
  Story of Miryam
    Gerchunoff, A. Jewish Gauchos of the
      Pampas
  Threshing wheat
    Gerchunoff, A. Jewish Gauchos of the
      Pampas
  Witches
    Gerchunoff, A. Jewish Gauchos of the
      Pampas

GERMAN SOLDIERS. See Soldiers, German

Germann, Robert F.
  The talking dog
    Good housekeeping (Periodical) Editor's choice

GERMANS IN AFRICA, SOUTH
  Gordimer, N. The white goddess and the
    mealie question

GERMANS IN AUSTRALIA
  Rowlands, L. "And what part of Europe
    do you come from?"

GERMANS IN FRANCE
  Boyle, K. Defeat
  Boyle, K. They weren't going to die
  Boyle, K. Thirty stories
  Fisher, D. F. C. In the eye of the storm
  Fisher, D. F. C. "Through pity and terror. . ."
  Maupassant, G. de. A duel
  Maupassant, G. de. Jolly fellow
  Maupassant, G. de. Mademoiselle Fifi
  Maupassant, G. de. Mother Savage
  O'Neill, A. Survival

GERMANS IN ITALY
  Levi, C. Massacre of Vallucciole
  Marceau, F. Armistice in Venice

GERMANS IN PALESTINE
  Yaari, Y. Threefold covenant

GERMANS IN POLAND
  Edelman, M. Last stand in the Warsaw
    ghetto

GERMANS IN THE UNITED STATES
  Gordimer, N. Face from Atlantis
  Kornbluth, C. M. Cosmic expense account

GERMANY

1918-date

  Lessing, D. M. Eye of God in paradise
  Truax, L. Man alone

Berlin

  Boyle, K. Carnival of fear

Heidelberg

  Stafford, J. My blithe, sad bird

Strasbourg

  Sansom, W. Beauty and beast

Germelshausen. Gerstäcker, F. W. C.

Gerstäcker, Friedrich Wilhelm Christian,
    1816-1872
  Germelshausen
    Costain, T. B. and Beecroft, J. eds.
      Stories to remember

Getting off the altitude. Lessing, D. M.

Getting out the vote for the working class.
    Farrell, J. T.

GETTYSBURG, BATTLE OF, 1863
  Thomason, J. W. The stars in their
    courses

Gettysburg bugle. Queen, E. pseud

GHETTOS. See Jews—Segregation

Ghost at his shoulder. Le May, A.

Ghost horse. Lance, L.

The ghost-maker. Pohl, F.

Ghost of a chance. Waldo, E. H.

Ghost of the Cimarron. Drago, H. S.

Ghost of the graveyard. Rutledge, A. H.

Ghost of the River Octagon. Carmer, C. L.

Ghost ship. Middleton, R. B.

Ghost ship of space. Elam, R. M.

GHOST SHIPS
  Middleton, R. B. Ghost ship

GHOST STORIES. See Ghosts

Ghost town. Elston, A. V.

Ghost wore a monocle. Davies, J.

GHOST WRITING. See Writing, Automatic

GHOSTS
  Aichinger, I. Ghosts on the lake
  Angioletti, G. B. Poor ghost
  Bécquer, G. A. Master Pérez the organist
  Benson, E. F. The face
  Blackwood, A. Empty house
  Blackwood, A. Psychical invasion
  Blackwood, A. Smith: an episode in a
    lodging house
  Blackwood, A. The wendigo
  Blackwood, A. With intent to steal
  Bowen, E. Apple tree
  Brandon, W. Brief enchantment
  Brontë, E. J. Hand at the window
  Carmer, C. L. The bewitched eggshell
  Carmer, C. L. Bond of reunion
  Carmer, C. L. Bride of Apollo
  Carmer, C. L. Ghost of the River Octagon
  Carmer, C. L. Harp notes in the mist
  Carmer, C. L. The haunted farmhouse
  Carmer, C. L. How ocean-born Mary came
    back from the dead
  Carmer, C. L. Lavender evening dress
  Carmer, C. L. The lone grave
  Carmer, C. L. Most-haunted town
  Carmer, C. L. Pair of gloves
  Carmer, C. L. Phantom merry-go-round
  Carmer, C. L. Pirate ghosts of Dismal
    Swamp
  Carmer, C. L. Quaker girl and the rocking
    ghost
  Carmer, C. L. The screaming ghost, and
    other stories; 21 stories
  Carmer, C. L. Screaming ghost of Saratoga
  Carmer, C. L. The singing river
  Carmer, C. L. Tale of the white dove

Gille, Jules
  The Marie-Helene
    World prize stories; 2d ser.
Gillese, John Patrick
  The typewriter
    Hughes, R. ed. All manner of men
Gilmore, Leroy H.
  Last five percent
    Oberfirst, R. ed. 1955 anthology of best
      original short-shorts
Gilpatric, Guy, 1896-1950
  The artful Mr Glencannon
    Saturday evening post (Periodical) Sat-
      urday evening post Carnival of hu-
      mor
Gimmicks three. Asimov, I.
Gimpel the fool. Singer, I. B.
Gioconda smile. Huxley, A. L.
Giono, Jean, 1895-
  Corn dies
    Lehmann, J. ed. Modern French stories
    Short, R. W. and Sewall, R. B. eds.
      Short stories for study
GIPSIES
  Blixen, K. Caryatids, an unfinished tale
  Byrne, D. Tale of my aunt Jenepher's
    wooing
  Lewis, A. The wanderers
  MacMahon, B. Broken lyre
  MacMahon, B. Cat and the cornfield
      See also Tinkers
The **girl.** Smith, G.
Girl at the Granada. Fox, N. A.
The **girl** from Ciociaria. Pincherle, A.
Girl from the queer people. Sandburg, C.
Girl growing up. Schleyen, M.
Girl had guts. Waldo, E. H.
Girl in the Humbert. Sandoz, M.
Girl named Dora. Reynolds, Q. J.
Girl next door. Collins, P. T.
The **girl** of my dreams. Malamud, B.
Girl on the beach. O'Farrell, W.
Girl on the bus. Sansom, W.
Girl on the road. Caldwell, E.
Girl shy. Cave, H. B.
Girl to the rescue. De Leeuw, A. L.
Girl who got recruited. Lederer, W. J. and
    Burdick, E. L.
Girl with figurines. Caldwell, E.
Girl with her heels set on half moons.
    Haupt, Z.
The **girl** with the burgundy lips. Blochman,
    L. G.
Girl with the glow. Frank, H.
GIRLS
  Bendine, L. F. Tender touch
  Bodington, N. Climate of the lost
  Bodington, N. An idyll
  Breckenfeld, V. G. Touch of Arab
  Brodkey, H. Laurie dressing
  Chute, B. J. Christmas doll
  Colette, S. G. Gigi
  Criswell, C. Nobody knows what the
    stork will bring
  Duck, T. The diplomat

Enright, E. Nancy
Enright, E. The operator
Enright, E. When the bough breaks
Fisher, D. F. C. The apprentice
Green, H. The grey bird
Hoyt, M. No sum too small
Lambert, J. Tall as the stars
Lewin, I. Ring for Kathy's birthday
Lofts, N. R. Heaven in your hand
Lowry, R. J. C. Guys from Ray's Place
McCarthy, A. Q. No second coming
Marquand, J. P. Children's page
O'Connor, F. Temple of the Holy Ghost
O'Donovan, J. Big Bertha
O'Donovan, J. Gaudeamus igitur
Sansom, W. Alicia
Stafford, J. Bad characters
Stuady, A. Little Miss Big Shot
Tolstoĭ, L. N. Graf. Little girls wiser
    than their elders
Warner, A. S. On the hoof
West, J. Mr Cornelius, I love you
Wright, J. Colour of death
      See also Adolescence
Girls on the tenth floor. Allen, S.
Gironella, José María
  Cathedral of hearts
    Flores, A. ed. Great Spanish stories
Give your heart to Jesus. Criswell, C.
Glad rags. Lowry, R. J. C.
GLADIATORS
  Rowland, S. Fixed fight
Gladius Dei. Mann, T.
GLADNESS. See Happiness
Gladstone's candlestick. Montgomery, R. B.
Glamor comes hard. Haynes, N.
Glamour. Ferber, E.
Glanville, Brian, 1931-
  The hero
    Pudney, J. ed. Pick of today's short
      stories, 9
Glaspell, Susan, 1882-1948
  Jury of her peers
    Baudin, M. ed. Contemporary short
      stories v3
GLASS
  Williams, T. Portrait of a girl in glass
The **glass** bridge. Arthur, R.
The **glass** jaw. Yellen, S.
Glaze, Andrew
  Slightly different story
    World prize stories; 2d ser.
A **gleam.** Mann, T.
Glen, Emilie, 1919-
  Dark pearl
    New voices 2: American writing today
Glidden, Jonathan H. 1907-1957
  Long gone
    Western Writers of America. Branded
      West
The **"Gloria** Scott." Doyle, Sir A. C.
Glory in the daytime. Parker, D. R.
GLOVES
  Carmer, C. L. Pair of gloves
GLUTTONS (ANIMALS) See Wolver-
    ines

GLUTTONY
Enright, E. Paper palace
Kober, A. Poor Goldie
Pincherle, A. Appetite

GNOMES. See Fairies

Go be insulted when a fella hands you a compliment. Kober, A.

The go-between. Pincherle, A.

Go, lovely rose. Bates, H. E.

GOATHERDS. See Goats

GOATS
Newcomb, E. Grand slam
O'Flaherty, L. Wild goat's kid
Pirandello, L. Black kid
Rabinowitz, S. Enchanted tailor

GOBLINS. See Fairies

GOD
Clarke, A. C. The star
Horowitz, E. God's agents have beards
Miller, E. M. Last barrier
Tolstoĭ, L. N. Graf. What men live by

God and the machine. Balchin, N.

God is good to a Jew. Hecht, B.

Godden, Rumer, 1907-
The oyster
Winter's tales, 2

Goddess in granite. Young, R. F.

Goddess of mercy. Criswell, C.

Godfrey, Leslie
Craving
Pudney, J. ed. Pick of today's short stories, 9

GODS
Little, D. H. Chinese god
Ovid. Atalanta's race

God's agents have beards. Horowitz, E.

God's ravens. Garland, H.

The godson. Tolstoĭ, L. N. Graf

Godwin, Tom, 1915-
Cold equations
Best science-fiction stories and novels: 1955
Montgomery, R. B. ed. Best SF three
Last victory
Best science-fiction stories and novels; 9th ser.
You created us
Best science-fiction stories and novels: 1956

Goehring, Damaris
That last buckskin
Western Writers of America. Wild horse roundup
Towser the terrific
Western Writers of America. Hound dogs and others

GOETHE, JOHANN WOLFGANG VON, 1749-1832
Sandoz, M. Y. An apparition

Gogol, Nicolai. See Gogol', Nikolaĭ Vasil'evich

Gogol', Nikolaĭ Vasil'evich, 1809-1852
Christmas Eve
Fremantle, A. J. ed. Christmas is here
The nose
Jarrell, R. ed. Anchor book of stories

Going ashore. Gallant, M.

Going downhill together. Lofts, N. R.

Going into exile. O'Flaherty, L.

Going into society. Dickens, C.

Going to Naples. Welty, E.

Gold, Herbert, 1924-
An afternoon with the appliances
New directions 15
Aristotle and the hired thugs
Fifteen by three
Burglars and the boy
Fifteen by three
Celebration for Joe
Fifteen by three
Prize stories, 1956: the O. Henry awards
Encounter in Haiti
Prize stories 1957: the O. Henry awards
Heart of the artichoke
Fifteen by three
Susanna at the beach
Fifteen by three

Gold, Horace Leonard
Man of parts
Healy, R. J. ed. 9 tales of time and space

GOLD
Henderson, D. From the mouse to the hawk

Gold bug. Poe, E. A.

Gold-fish. Colette, S. G.

Gold from Argentina. Fisher, D. F. C.

GOLD MINES AND MINING
Ballard, W. T. Builder of murderer's bar
London, J. All Gold Canyon
Turner, W. O. Proud diggers
See also Mines and mining

Goldben, Jack, 1929-
Kelly
American vanguard, 1956

Goldberg, Leah
Growing up
Schwarz, L. W. ed. Feast of Leviathan

Golden crucifix. Deledda, G.

Golden Eagle Ordinary. Polk, W. T.

GOLDEN honeymoon. Lardner, R. W.

The golden kite, the silver wind. Bradbury, R.

Golden river. Blackburn, A.

Golden wedding. Suckow, R.

Golden West. Fuchs, D.

GOLDFINCHES. See Finches

The goldfish. Cassill, R. V.

Goldie Tabak. Angoff, C.

Goldstein, Clifford H. 1920-
Invisible barriers
Oberfirst, R. ed. Anthology of best short-short stories v6

The golem. Davidson, A.

Golem of Prague. Bin Gorion, M. J.

GOLF
Lardner, R. W. A caddy's diary
Lardner, R. W. Mr Frisbie
Marshall, R. Haunted major
Ormond, S. K. All's fair
Rinehart, M. R. Tish plays the game
Temple, W. H. The eternal duffer
Wodehouse, P. G. Clicking of Cuthbert
Wodehouse, P. G. Heart of a goof

Gollschewsky, E. A.
  Clear case of self-defence
    Stivens, D. comp. Coast to coast
Gombrowicz, Witold
  Premeditated crime
    Ordon, E. ed. 10 contemporary Polish
    stories
Gomez. Smith, E. H.
Gone to freedom. Hopkins, J. G. E.
The Gonzaga manuscripts. Bellow, S.
GOOD AND EVIL
  Blixen, K. Tales of two old gentlemen
  Hawthorne, N. Great Stone Face
  Hawthorne, N. Young Goodman Brown
  Pritchett, V. S. The saint
  Tolstoï, L. N. Graf. The Devil's per-
    sistent, but God is resistant
Good as ever. Hardy, F.
Good business with sentiment. Mankowitz,
  W.
Good-by, Grandma. Bradbury, R.
Good-by to palship. Kober, A.
Good-bye to spring. Branch, R.
Good corn. Bates, H. E.
Good country people. O'Connor, F.
"Good fellow's" wife. Garland, H.
Good for two drinks. Adams, A.
Good investment. Cary, J.
A good man is hard to find. O'Connor, F.
Good medicine. Charteris, L.
Good memory. Lofts, N. R.
Good morning, Miss Dove. Patton, F. G.
Good old-fashioned Christmas. Mottram,
  R. H.
Good reasons. Maupassant, G. de
Good-tempered fellow. Verdad
Good time Bessie. Bromfield, L.
Good wife for a young doctor. Montross,
  L. S.
Good woman. Purdy, J.
Goodman, Paul, 1916-
  Memorial synagogue
    Ribalow, H. U. ed. Treasury of Ameri-
    can Jewish stories
Goodwin, Geraint, 1903-1941
  Sitting of eggs
    Jones, G. ed. Welsh short stories
Gooseberries. Chekhov, A. P.
Gorbatov, Boris Leont'evich
  Man is born
    Loaf sugar, and other Soviet stories
Gordimer, Nadine
  A bit of young life
    Gordimer, N. Six feet of the country
  Charmed lives
    Gordimer, N. Six feet of the country
  The cicatrice
    Gordimer, N. Six feet of the country
  Clowns in clover
    Gordimer, N. Six feet of the country
  Enemies
    Gordimer, N. Six feet of the country
  Face from Atlantis
    Gordimer, N. Six feet of the country

Happy event
  Gordimer, N. Six feet of the country
Horn of plenty
  Gordimer, N. Six feet of the country
My first two women
  Gordimer, N. Six feet of the country
  Jennings, F. G. and Calitri, C. J. eds.
  Stories
Out of season
  Gordimer, N. Six feet of the country
Six feet of the country
  Gordimer, N. Six feet of the country
The smell of death and flowers
  Gordimer, N. Six feet of the country
A wand'ring minstrel, I
  Gordimer, N. Six feet of the country
Which new era would that be?
  Gordimer, N. Six feet of the country
The white goddess and the mealie ques-
  tion
  Gordimer, N. Six feet of the country
Gordon, Arthur, 1912-
  The crisis
    Oberfirst, R. ed. Anthology of best
    short-short stories v6
  First hunt
    Teen-age tales, bk 4
  The spell
    This week magazine. This week's Sto-
    ries of mystery and suspense
  Terror beneath the sea
    Saturday evening post (Periodical) Sat-
    urday evening post stories, 1955
  The warning
    This week magazine. This week's Sto-
    ries of mystery and suspense
Gordon, Caroline, 1895-
  Brilliant leaves
    Thorp, W. ed. Southern reader
  Old Red
    McClennen, J. comp. Masters and mas-
    terpieces of the short story
Gospel according to Matthew. Bible. New
  Testament. Matthew
Gospel according to St Luke. Bible. New
  Testament. Luke
Goss, John Mayo, 1892-
  Bird song
    First-prize stories, 1919-1957
GOSSIP
  Hawthorne, N. Mr Higginbotham's ca-
    tastrophe
  O'Hara, J. Other women's households
  Pincherle, A. Mario
  Plumtree, C. Innuendo
  Verga, G. Donna Santa's sin
  Welty, E. Petrified man
  West, J. Love, death, and the ladies' drill
    team
Gould, John
  Pioneers in Maine
    Lohan, R. ed. Christmas tales for read-
    ing aloud
GOURMETS
  Beaumont, C. Infernal bouillabaisse
GOVERNESSES
  Nabokov, V. V. Mademoiselle O
  Osterman, M. Fraulein
  Seymour, M. Theresa
GOVERNMENT EMPLOYEES. See Civil
  service

Greville Fane. James, H.

Grey, Zane, 1872-1939
Don
Great dog stories

The **grey** bird. Green, H.

Grey shroud. Horner, A.

Grey's ghost. Stewart, J. I. M.

Griffin, John Howard, 1920-
Whole world in his hands
New voices 2: American writing today

Griffith, Wyn, 1890-
Ifan Owen and the grey rider
Jones, G. ed. Welsh short stories

Grimm, Jacob Ludwig Karl, 1785-1863, **and Grimm, Wilhelm Karl,** 1786-1859
Cat and mouse in partnership
Jarrell, R. ed. Anchor book of stories

Grinnell, David, pseud.
Lysenko maze
Conklin, G. ed. Science-fiction adventures in mutation

GROCERY TRADE
Gold, H. Heart of the artichoke

Groch, Judith
Junior year is dull
Seventeen (Periodical) Seventeen's stories

Groninger, William
Acorn for Jamie
Stowe, A. comp. When boy dates girl

Groszmann, Lore, 1928-
Boy-friend-in-law
American vanguard, 1956

GROTTOES. See Caves

Growing old. Maupassant, G. de

Growing pains on Broadway. Tekeyan, C.

Growing stone. Camus, A.

Growing up. Goldberg, L.

The **growth.** Hale, N.

Gruber, Frank, 1904-
Ask me another
Cooke, D. C. ed. My best murder story

The **grudge.** Terhune, A. P.

Guardians of Mobali. Ruhen, O.

Guareschi, Giovanni, 1908-
A baptism
Burnett, W. ed. This is my best humor
The petition
Slonim, M. L. ed. Modern Italian short stories

GUERRILLAS
O'Faoláin, S. The patriot

Guest, Anna, 1913?-
Beauty is truth
Seventeen (Periodical) Stories from Seventeen
Momentito
New voices 2: American writing today

The **guest.** Camus, A.

The **guest.** Kubly, H.

Guest in the house. See Carr, J. D. Incautious burglar

GUESTS
Hale, N. Sheltered
Kubly, H. The guest

Lardner, R. W. Liberty Hall
Nash, O. Stranger in the house
O'Connor, F. Temple of the Holy Ghost
Somerville, E. A. O. and Martin, V. F.
Lisheen races, second-hand
Wodehouse, P. G. Uncle Fred Flits

Guests of the nation. O'Donovan, M.

The **guide.** Lytle, A. N.

Guide to the Muniment Room. Macauley, R.

GUIDES (HUNTING)
La Farge, O. Old Century's river
Smith, E. W. Men, women and wilderness

GUIGNOL. See Puppets and puppet-plays

Guillemot Rock. Maupassant, G. de

Guillotine. Woolrich, C.

Guilloux, Louis, 1899-
Man's name
Lehmann, J. ed. Modern French stories

GUILT
Pincherle, A. The fall
See also Sin

Guilt-edged blonde. Millar, K.

Guilty as charged. Porges, A.

Guin, Wyman
Volpla
Galaxy science fiction magazine. Third Galaxy reader

GUINEA-PIGS
Breuer, M. J. Hungry guinea pig

The **guitar.** Kahana, B.

GUITAR PLAYERS. See Musicians—Guitar players

Guldager, Carl
Dollar a kiss
Teen-age tales, bk 3

Gulick, Bill. See Gulick, Grover C.

Gulick, Grover C. 1916-
"Conquest"
Gulick, G. C. White men, red men, and mountain men
Fire-water fiasco
Gulick, G. C. White men, red men, and mountain men
Hexed rifle
Gulick, G. C. White men, red men, and mountain men
Kid that rode with death
Western Writers of America. Wild horse roundup
Marriage of Moon Wind
Western Writers of America. Branded West
Squaw fever
Gulick, G. C. White men, red men, and mountain men
Trouble with traders
Gulick, G. C. White men, red men, and mountain men

GULLS
Annixter, P. pseud. Seekonk, the tale of a sea gull
O'Flaherty, L. His first flight

The **gun.** London, D. H.

Gun at his back. Hawkins, J. and Hawkins, W.

Gun dog. Annixter, P. pseud.

Gunn, James E.
Cave of night
Merril, J. ed. S-F: ['56]
Wherever you may be
Galaxy science fiction magazine. Five
Galaxy short novels
Gunn, Neil Miller, 1891-
Tax-gatherer
Urquhart, F. ed. Scottish short stories
GUNNING. See Shooting
Gunshot messenger. Hawthorne, H.
GUNSMITHING
White, S. E. Long rifle
Gunther, Max
The prisoner
Saturday evening post (Periodical) Sat-
urday evening post stories, 1957
Gusev. Chekhov, A. P.
Gustafson, Grace
The web
Oberfirst, R. ed. Anthology of best
short-short stories v5
Guthrie, Alfred Bertram, 1901-
The way West
Western Writers of America. Hoof
trails and wagon tracks
Guy de Maupassant. Babel', I. E.
Guys from Ray's Place. Lowry, R. J. C.
Gyarfas, Miklos
Louis Kossuth at Kisgomboc
Juhasz, W. and Rothberg, A. A. eds.
Flashes in the night
GYMNASTICS
Olgin, J. Full twists
See also Acrobats and acrobatism
GYPSIES. See Gipsies

H

Haber, Richard Mayer, 1920?-
Journey to Milan
New voices 2: American writing today
Habit of loving. Lessing, D. M.
Habit of murder. Miller, E. M.
Hacking around. Lineaweaver, M.
Hadas, Auraham
Mating season
World prize stories; 2d ser.
Hadley, James D.
The blue crane
Orr, E. and Hammett, E. A. eds. Delta
Decameron
Hadow, Lyndall
Freedom for Laura
Stivens, D. comp. Coast to coast
Hagedorn, Hermann, 1882-
Edith Cavell
Fenner, P. R. ed. Heroes, heroes,
heroes
HAIL
Ward, L. L. Drought
HAIR
Branch, C. A. M. Apricot and thistle
Fitzgerald, F. S. K. Bernice bobs her
hair

Maupassant, G. de. One phase of love
Porter, W. S. Gift of the Magi
Schwartz, A. Anna's haircut
Haircut. Lardner, R. W.
HAIRDRESSING
Maupassant, G. de. The mask
See also Barbers; Beauty, Personal
Hairless Mexican. Maugham, W. S.
Hairy hand. Sandoz, M. Y.
Hai's well. Barash, A.
HAITI
Capote, T. House of flowers
Gold, H. Encounter in Haiti
Halacy, Dan S. 1920-
Dry-trail showdown
Western Writers of America. Hoof
trails and wagon tracks
Lucky goes fishing
Western Writers of America. Hound
dogs and others
Ride the rough string
Western Writers of America. Wild
horse roundup
Halcyon sea. Detzortzis, D.
Hale, Lucretia Peabody, 1820-1900
Agamemnon's career
Nash, O. comp. I couldn't help laugh-
ing
Hale, Nancy, 1908-
The bubble
Hale, N. Empress's ring
But one buttonhole needful
Hale, N. Empress's ring
Charlotte Russe
Hale, N. Empress's ring
Copley-Plaza
Hale, N. Empress's ring
Empress's ring
Hale, N. Empress's ring
First day of school
Hale, N. Empress's ring
The fox
Hale, N. Empress's ring
Full life
Hale, N. Empress's ring
The growth
Hale, N. Empress's ring
How would you like to be born
Hale, N. Empress's ring
Inside
Hale, N. Empress's ring
Miss August
Hale, N. Empress's ring
Mocha cakes
Hale, N. Empress's ring
New order
Hale, N. Empress's ring
Object of virtue
Hale, N. Empress's ring
On the beach
Hale, N. Empress's ring
People in places
Hale, N. Empress's ring
The place and the time
Hale, N. Empress's ring
Readville stars
Hale, N. Empress's ring
Secret garden
Hale, N. Empress's ring

Hale, Nancy—*Continued*
    Sheltered
        Hale, N. Empress's ring
    Slow boat to China
        Prize stories, 1958: the O'Henry awards
    Snows of childhood
        Hale, N. Empress's ring
    Some day I'll find you
        Hale, N. Empress's ring
    A summer's long dream
        Best American short stories, 1957
    Year I had the colds
        Hale, N. Empress's ring
Half-crown. Plunkett, J.
Half-holiday. Huxley, A. L.
The half-mile. Beachcroft, T. O.
HALF-SISTERS
    Tomlinson, N. Pretty surprise
Haliburton, Thomas Chandler, 1796-1865
    Beating the smuggling game
        Nelson, G. E. ed. Cavalcade of the North
Hall, Andrew
    Breathe, Coach, breathe
        Furman, A. L. ed. Teen-age humorous
        stories
    Saved by the belle
        Furman, A. L. ed. Teen-age humorous
        stories
Hall, Holworthy, pseud. See Porter, Harold
    Everett
Hall, James B.
    Action time in twilight
        Fifteen by three
    In the time of demonstrations
        Fifteen by three
    The lion and the chalice
        Fifteen by three
    Near the margin of the bay
        Fifteen by three
    Spot in history
        Fifteen by three
Hall, Meta
    Height of love
        Furman, A. L. ed. Everygirls romance
        stories
Hall, Nellie M.
    Right bait
        Oberfirst, R. ed. 1955 anthology of best
        original short-shorts
Halliday, Brett, pseud. See Dresser, Davis
Hallmarked. Macken, W.
HALLOWEEN
    Duke, W. Hallowe'en party
    Kubly, H. Halloween party
Hallowe'en party. Duke, W.
Halloween party. Kubly, H.
HALLUCINATIONS AND ILLUSIONS
    Aymé, M. Wine of Paris
    Bradbury, R. The cistern
    Chester, A. As I was going up the stair
    Dreiser, T. Lost Phoebe
    Fischer, B. Sam Rall's private ghost
    Gresham, W. L. Don't believe a word she
        says
    Lovecraft, H. P. and Derleth, A. W.
        Shadow out of space
    Merrit, M. Death of a kangaroo
    Sandoz, M. Y. Lady of the cornflowers
    Sansom, W. Murder
        See also Ghosts

HALOS
    Aymé, M. State of grace
    Aymé, M. Grace
Halper, Albert, 1904-
    My mother's love story
        Ribalow, H. U. ed. Treasury of Amer-
        ican Jewish stories
    Warm matzos
        Schwarz, L. W. ed. Feast of Leviathan
Halsey, Dabney
    The miniature
        Oberfirst, R. ed. Anthology of best
        short-short stories v6
Hamamah. Shami, Y.
Hamblett, Charles
    Love is a fading memory
        Pudney, J. ed. Pick of today's short
        stories, 9
Hameiri, Avigdor, 1890-
    Three halutzot
        Kobler, J. ed. Her children call her
        blessed
Hamilcar, Jack, 1910-
    Uncle Hannibal
        Oberfirst, R. ed. 1955 anthology of best
        original short-shorts
Hamilton, Dale
    Archie catches it
        Furman, A. L. ed. Teen-age humorous
        stories
Hamilton, Margaret
    Jenny Stairy's hat
        Urquhart, F. ed. Scottish short stories
Hammett, Evelyn Allen
    Mattie dear
        Orr, E. and Hammet, E. A. eds. Delta
        Decameron
    Prawns for Penelope
        Orr, E. and Hammet, E. A. eds. Delta
        Decameron
    Solomon primitive
        Orr, E. and Hammet, E. A. eds. Delta
        Decameron
HAND
    Le Fanu, J. S. Narrative of the ghost of a
        hand
Hand at the window. Brontë, E. J.
HAND-TO-HAND FIGHTING. See Fight-
    ing, Hand-to-hand
Handful of earth. Mankowitz, W.
Hands off. Sheckley, R.
Handsome is as handsome does. Pritchett,
    V. S.
HANDWRITING. See Writing
Haner, R.
    The fix
        Oberfirst, R. ed. Anthology of best
        short-short stories v6
HANGING
    Adams, A. Marshal of Cow Springs
    Aichinger, I. Speech under the gallows
    Bradford, R. Child of God
    Harte, B. Tennessee's partner
    Masefield, J. Anty Bligh
    Stuart, J. Sunday afternoon hanging

Hankins, Jack W.
Black Satin
Everygirls horse stories
Thaw
Furman, A. L. ed. Everygirls romance
stories
Hanley, Gerald, 1916-
Private means
Winter's tales, 1
Hannukah money. Rabinowitz, S.
Hans Brueckner on the edge of the sea.
O'Brian, P.
Hansen, Dorothy E. S.
Junior's at an age
Furman, A. L. ed. Everygirls romance
stories
HANUKKAH (FEAST OF LIGHTS)
Rabinowitz, S. Hannukah money
Happiest man on earth. Maltz, A.
Happily ever after. Huxley, A. L.
HAPPINESS
Lesinš, K. One-day land
Maupassant, G. de. Happiness
Reid, L. My Lady Happiness
Tolstoĭ, L. N. Graf. Ilyas
White, R. State of well-being
Happiness. Maupassant, G. de
Happy as a sandboy. Samuel, E. H.
Happy birthday. Epstein, S.
Happy birthday, dear Jesus. Pohl, F.
Happy Christmas. Lofts, N. R.
Happy despatch. O'Brian, P.
Happy ending. Loomis, A. F.
Happy event. Gordimer, N.
Happy family. Andersen, H. C.
Happy holiday abroad. Sansom, W.
Happy Indian laughter. La Farge, O.
Happy Jack. Campbell, W. E. M.
Happy Prince. Wilde, O.
Happy story when seen backwards. Clayton,
J. B.
Happy suicide. Charteris, L.
Happy was the soldier! Rosten, L. C.
Hard case. Arthur, R.
A hard row to hoe. Garrett, G.
Hard way. Leonard, E.
Hardest thing in the world. Kobler, F.
Hardesty, Rollen, 1906-
Anatomy lesson
Oberfirst, R. ed. Anthology of best
short-short stories v6
Hardy, Frank
Good as ever
Stivens, D. comp. Coast to coast
Hardy, Joanne, 1936-
Anna says cats are like people
Stanford short stories, 1957
Hardy, Thomas, 1840-1928
Thieves who couldn't help sneezing
Lohan, R. ed. Christmas tales for read-
ing aloud
Three strangers
Costain, T. B. and Beecroft, J. eds.
More Stories to remember
Short, R. B. and Sewall, R. W. eds.
Short stories for study

Hardy, William George, 1896-
Czech dog
Nelson, G. E. ed. Cavalcade of the
North
Hare, Cyril, pseud. See Clark, Alfred Alex-
ander Gordon
HARLEM. See New York (City)—Harlem
Harmon, Margaretta
Big splash
Furman, A. L. ed. Everygirls sports
stories
HARMONICA, MOUTH. See Mouth organ
HARMONICA PLAYERS. See Musicians
—Harmonica players
Harmony. Fain, W.
Harmony. Lardner, R. W.
Harp notes in the mist. Carmer, C. L.
Harper, James
Perils for trial
Kemp, P. K. ed. Hundred years of sea
stories
HARPISTS. See Musicians—Harpists
Harrington, John
Only the trade winds know
Teen-age tales, bk 5
Harris, Anthony W.
The unique conception
Miller, N. ed. New campus writing,
no. 2
Harris, George Washington, 1814-1869
Rare ripe garden-seed
Thorp, W. ed. Southern reader
Harris, Joel Chandler, 1848-1908
Mr Rabbit nibbles up the butter
Thorp, W. ed. Southern reader
Harris, John Beynon, 1903-
Dumb Martian
Montgomery, R. B. ed. Best SF
Una
Montgomery, R. B. ed. Best SF two
Harris, Mark, 1922-
Bang the drum slowly
Schwed, P. and Wind, H. W. eds. Great
stories from the world of sport
Harris, Raymond
Hippo and the tortoise
Buckeridge, A. comp. In and out of
school
Harriss, Robert Preston, 1903-
The house
Welcome, J. and Orchard, V. eds. Best
hunting stories
Harrod, Margaret E. 1910-
Bent twig
Oberfirst, R. ed. Anthology of best
short-short stories v6
HARRODSBURY. See Kentucky—Har-
rodsbury
Harss, Luis, 1936-
An agreement
Stanford short stories, 1957
Arrest
Stanford short stories, 1956
Harte, Bret, 1836-1902
Colonel Starbottle for the plaintiff
Hart, J. D. and Gohdes, C. L. eds.
America's literature

Harte, Bret—*Continued*
How Santa Claus came to Simpson's Bar
  Lohan, R. ed. Christmas tales for read-
  ing aloud
Luck of Roaring Camp
  Hart, J. D. and Gohdes, C. L. eds.
  America's literature
Muck-a-Muck
  Hart, J. D. and Gohdes, C. L. eds.
  America's literature
Outcasts of Poker Flat
  Lewis, J. D. ed. Dealer's choice
Stolen cigar case by A. Co-n-D-le
  McMaster, J. ed. Stories to remember
Tennessee's partner
  Schaefer, J. W. ed. Out West

About
Hawthorne, H. Gunshot messenger

Harte, Francis Bret. See Harte, Bret

Hartley, Frank P.
The poacher
  Oberfirst, R. ed. Anthology of best
  short-short stories v5

Hartley, Leslie Poles, 1895-
Killing bottle
  Davin, D. M. ed. English short stories
  of today, 2d ser.
Per far l'amore
  Winter's tales, 1

Harvest without seed. Schaumann, R.

HARVESTING
Giono, J. The corn dies
Smilansky, M. Barhash
  See also Threshing

Harvey, Frank L.
Flame-out
  Harvey, F. L. Jet
Frightened pilot
  Harvey, F. L. Jet
Saturday evening post (Periodical)
  Saturday evening post stories, 1954
Murder in the sky
  Harvey, F. L. Jet
Runaway bomber
  Harvey, F. L. Jet
Scramble nighthawk!
  Harvey, F. L. Jet
Stand by to bail out!
  Harvey, F. L. Jet
Test jump
  Teen-age tales, bk 6
Volunteer assignment
  Harvey, F. L. Jet

Harvey, William Fryer, 1885-1937
The tool
  Ridler, A. B. comp. Best ghost stories

Harvey Riddle. Lochridge, B. H.

Hasas, Haïm, 1897-
It's she
  Schwarz, L. W. ed. Feast of Leviathan
The wanderer
  Tehilla, and other Israeli tales

The hat. Brodahl, G.

Hat on the bedpost. Caldwell, E.

Hat-rack. Samuel, E. H.

HATE
Allen, S. Public hating
Chamson, A. My enemy
Enright, E. The bookkeepers

Faulkner, W. The rosary
Knight, D. The country of the kind
Pincherle, A. The perfect game

HATS
Adams, A. Blue bird swooping down like
  a pigeon hawk
Chesterton, G. K. Unpresentable appear-
  ance of Colonel Crane
Peretz, I. L. Shtraimel
Perkins, F. B. Devil-puzzlers
Rabinowitz, S. On account of a hat

Hattie. Lochridge, B. H.

Haunted corpse. Pohl, F.

The haunted farmhouse. Carmer, C. L.

Haunted hour. Purdy, K. W.

Haunted house. Dickens, C.

HAUNTED HOUSES. See Ghosts

Haunted island. Blackwood, A.

Haunted major. Marshall, R.

Haupt, Zygmunt, 1907-
Girl with her heels set on half moons
  New Directions in prose and poetry, 16

Hautot and his son. Maupassant, G. de

Hautot, father and son. See Maupassant, G.
  de. Hautot and his son

HAVANA. See Cuba—Havana

Haven't we been nice to you? Sommers,
  M. O.

HAWAIIAN ISLANDS
Stevenson, R. L. Bottle imp
Stevenson, R. L. Isle of Voices

The hawk. O'Flaherty, L.

HAWKERS. See Peddlers and peddling

Hawkins, Sir Anthony Hope, 1863-1933
Love's conundrum
  Costain, T. B. and Beecroft, J. eds.
  Stories to remember

Hawkins, Desmond, 1908-
Man and a fox
  Wood, E. R. ed. Contemporary short
  stories

Hawkins, John, 1910- **and Hawkins, Ward,**
  1912
Cop without a badge
  Saturday evening post (Periodical)
  Saturday evening post stories, 1954
  Tibbets, A. B. ed. Youth, youth, youth
Gun at his back
  Best detective stories of the year—1956
Look out for John Tucker!
  Teen-age tales, bk 6
Matter of life and death
  Cooke, D. C. ed. My best murder story
Young and scared
  Saturday evening post (Periodical)
  Saturday evening post stories, 1957

Hawkins, Ward, 1912- See Hawkins, J.
  jt. auth.

HAWKS
Clark, W. Van T. Hook
Moser, D. The collector
Moser, D. Mr Agruvian and the red-tailed
  hawks
O'Flaherty, L. The hawk

Hawks over Shem. Howard, R. E. and
  DeCamp, L. S.

Hawthorne, Hildegarde, 1871?-1952
  Gunshot messenger
    Humphreville, F. T. ed. In other days
  Jack Jouett's ride
    Fenner, P. R. ed. Heroes, heroes, heroes
Hawthorne, Nathaniel, 1804-1864
  Dr Heidegger's experiment
    Hart, J. D. and Gohdes, C. L. eds.
    America's literature
  Earth's holocaust
    Hart, J. D. and Gohdes, C. L. eds.
    America's literature
  Egotism; or, The bosom serpent
    Aymar, B. ed. Treasury of snake lore
  Ethan Brand
    Hart, J. D. and Gohdes, C. L. eds.
    America's literature
  Great carbuncle
    Havighurst, W. and others, eds. Selection
  Great Stone Face
    Costain, T. B. and Beecroft, J. eds.
    Stories to remember
  Minister's black veil
    Hart, J. D. and Gohdes, C. L. eds.
    America's literature
    Jennings, F. G. and Calitri, C. J. eds.
    Stories
  Mr Higginbotham's catastrophe
    Short, R. W. and Sewall, R. B. eds.
    Short stories for study
  Rappaccini's daughter
    Hart, J. D. and Gohdes, C. L. eds.
    America's literature
    Sterner, L. G. ed. Favorite short stories
  Young Goodman Brown
    Gettman, R. A. and Harkness, B. eds.
    Book of stories
    Hart, J. D. and Gohdes, C. L. eds.
    America's literature
    Locke, L. G.; Gibson, W. M. and Arms,
    G. W. eds. Introduction to literature
Hay, Ian, pseud. See Beith, John Hay
Hay, Jacob
  Fabulous brew
    Saturday evening post (Periodical)
    Saturday evening post stories, 1957
Haycox, Ernest, 1899-1950
  At Wolf Creek tavern
    Haycox, E. Last rodeo
  Born to conquer
    Haycox, E. Last rodeo
  Call this land home
    Western Writers of America. Hoof
    trails and wagon tracks
  Dolorosa, here I come
    Haycox, E. Last rodeo
  Farewell to the years
    Haycox, E. Last rodeo
  Fourth son
    Haycox, E. Last rodeo
  High wind
    Western Writers of America. Wild
    streets
  Last rodeo
    Haycox, E. Last rodeo
  Old Glory
    Haycox, E. Last rodeo
  One more river
    Haycox, E. Last rodeo
  One star by night
    Haycox, E. Last rodeo

Question of blood
  Schaefer, J. W. ed. Out West
Things remembered
  Haycox, E. Last rodeo
Haynes, Dorothy K. 1918-
  The head
    Urquhart, F. ed. Scottish short stories
Haynes, Nelma
  Glamor comes hard
    Teen-age tales, bk 5
Hazard, N. Rowland
  Right line
    Oberfirst, R. ed. Anthology of best
    short-short stories v6
Hazaz, Hayim. See Hasas, Haïm
Hazzaz, Hayyim. See Hasas, Haïm
He. Lessing, D. M.
He? Maupassant, G. de
He. Porter K. A.
He don't plant cotton. Powers, J. F.
He found his fortune in the Delta. Orr, E.
He had collided with lead in Texas. Adams,
  A.
He loved me truly. Bailey, B. and Walworth, D.
He should never have become a painter.
  Moretti, U.
He walked around the horses. Piper, H. B.
He walked through the fields. Shamir, M.
HEAD (ANATOMY, HUMAN)
  Sandoz, M. Y. Slow-motion crime
The head. Haynes, D. K.
HEAD-HUNTERS
  Ruhen, O. Head-hunters of Ianagl
  Russell, J. Price of the head
Head-hunters of Ianagl. Ruhen, O.
Head of a sad angel. Chester, A.
Headlines. Oberfirst, R.
Health card. Yerby, F. G.
HEALTH RESORTS, WATERING-
    PLACES, ETC.
  Maupassant, G. de. At the spa
Healy, Raymond J.
  Great Devon mystery
    Healy, R. J. ed. 9 tales of time and
    space
Hearn, Lafcadio, 1850-1904
  Mujina
    Laughton, C. ed. Tell me a story
  Oshidori
    Laughton, C. ed. Tell me a story
HEART
                Diseases
  Cather, W. S. Neighbour Rosicky
  Horgan, P. Heart attack
  Patton, F. G. The homunculus
Heart attack. Horgan, P.
The heart is a lofty citadel. Rubin, L.
Heart of a goof. Wodehouse, P. G.
Heart of a hero. Gardner, I. B.
Heart of darkness. Conrad, J.
Heart of furious fancies. McClintic, W.
Heart of Little Shikara. Marshall, E.
Heart of the artichoke. Gold, H.

Heart turned inward. Durland, F.

Heart's desire. Tomlinson, H. M.

Heath, W. L.
  Most valuable player
  Teen-age tales, bk 5

The heathen. Annixter, P. pseud.

HEAVEN
  Aymé, M. Legend of Poldevia
  Benét, S. V. Doc Mellhorn and the pearly gates
  Blixen, K. Of hidden thoughts and of heaven
  Bradford, R. Child of God
  Linklater, E. Kind Kitty
  Peretz, I. L. Two deathbeds
  Temple, W. H. The eternal duffer
  See also Future life

Heaven in your hand. Lofts, N. R.

Heaven-sent. Miller, E. M.

HEBREW LANGUAGE

  Study and teaching
  Berg, L. Snowball man and Holy Writ

HEBREWS. See Jews

Hecht, Ben, 1893-
  Actor's blood
  Lewis, J. D. ed. Great stories about show business
  God is good to a Jew
  Ribalow, H. U. ed. Treasury of American Jewish stories
  Miracle of the fifteen murderers
  Blaustein, P. M. and Blaustein, A. P. eds. Doctors' choice

Hedge between. Armstrong, C.

Hedgecock, L. J. 1896-
  Zipper trouble
  Oberfirst, R. ed. 1955 anthology of best original short-shorts

Hee-haw! Warner, S. T.

Heggen, Thomas, 1919-1949
  The birthmark
  Fenton, C. A. ed. Best short stories of World War II

Heidelberg. See Germany—Heidelberg

Height of love. Hall, M.

Heine, Heinrich, 1797-1856
  On a seder night
  Schwarz, L. W. ed. Feast of Leviathan

Heinlein, Robert Anson, 1907-
  Black pits of Luna
  Gallant, J. ed. Stories of scientific imagination
  Blowups happen
  Montgomery, R. B. ed. Best SF two

Heintz, Velma
  December's glad song
  Oberfirst, R. ed. 1955 anthology of best original short-shorts

HEIRLOOMS
  Doyle, Sir A. C. Musgrave ritual
  Wells, M. The coverlid

HEIRS. See Inheritance and succession

Heirs apparent. Abernathy, R.

HELL
  Asimov, I. Brazen locked room
  Asimov, I. Gimmicks three

Benét, S. V. Doc Mellhorn and the pearly gates

Collier, J. Devil, George, and Rosie

McCormack, F. Hell-bent

Peretz, I. L. Eighth circle of Gehenna

Peretz, I. L. Two deathbeds

Hell-bent. McCormack, F.

Hell of mirrors. Hirai, T.

Hell-ship voyage. Lubback, A. B.

Hellinger, Mark, 1903-1947
  Encouragement
  Lewis, J. D. ed. Great stories about show business

Hellman, Sam
  Toll bridge
  Saturday evening post (Periodical) Saturday evening post Carnival of humor

Hello again, darling. Allen, S.

Help! I am Dr Morris Goldpepper. Davidson, A.

Help her to believe. Olsen, T.

Hemingway, Ernest, 1898-
  After the storm
  Kemp, P. K. ed. Hundred years of sea stories
  Capital of the world
  McClennen, J. comp. Masters and masterpieces of the short story
  Thurston, J. A. ed. Reading modern short stories
  Clean, well-lighted place
  Hart, J. D. and Gohdes, C. L. eds. America's literature
  Fifty grand
  Schwed, P. and Wind, H. W. eds. Great stories from the world of sport
  Gambler, the nun and the radio
  Lewis, J. D. ed. Dealer's choice
  In another country
  Hall, J. B. and Langland, J. T. eds. Short story
  Hart, J. D. and Gohdes, C. L. eds. America's literature
  Short, R. W. and Sewall, R. B. eds. Short stories for study
  My old man
  Havighurst, W. and others, eds. Selection
  Now I lay me
  Gettman, R. A. and Harkness, B. eds. Book of stories
  Old man at the bridge
  Costain, T. B. and Beecroft, J. eds. More Stories to remember
  Short happy life of Francis Macomber
  Locke, L. G.; Gibson, W. M. and Arms, G. W. eds. Introduction to literature
  Ten Indians
  Thurston, J. A. ed. Reading modern short stories
  The undefeated
  Baudin, M. ed. Contemporary short stories v2
  Havighurst, W. ed. Masters of the modern short story
  Jennings, F. G. and Calitri, C. J. eds. Stories

Henderson, Dion, 1921-
  From the mouse to the hawk
  Queen, E. pseud. ed. Ellery Queen's awards: 11th ser.

Henderson, Zenna, 1917-
Anything box
Merril, J. ed. SF: '57
Food to all flesh
Montgomery, R. B. ed. Best SF three
Pottage
Magazine of fantasy and science fiction.
Best from Fantasy and science fiction;
5th ser.
Merril, J. ed. S-F: ['56]
Wilderness
Merril, J. ed. SF: '58
Hendry, J. F. 1913-
The disinherited
Urquhart, F. ed. Scottish short stories
Henry, O. pseud. See Porter, William Sydney
Henson, Iris
Orchids and fishing togs
Oberfirst, R. ed. 1955 anthology of best
original short-shorts
Her first ball. Mansfield, K.
Her name was Amelie. Caldwell, E.
Her shadow love. Heuman, W.
Her table spread. Bowen, E.
Herbert, Frank, 1920-
Nightmare blues
Best science-fiction stories and novels:
1955
Herbert, Frederick Hugh, 1897-
Husband trouble
Saturday evening post (Periodical) Saturday evening post stories, 1954
Herbie solves a mystery. Wouk, H.
The herdsman. Gerchunoff, A.
Here is the news. Stewart, J. I. M.
HEREDITY
Adams, A. Strong on the breed
Byrne, D. Tale of my aunt Jenepher's
wooing
Grinnell, D. pseud. Lysenko maze
O'Hara, J. The decision
Hergesheimer, Joseph, 1880-1954
The crystal chandelier
Saturday evening post (Periodical). The
Post Reader of Civil War stories
Rebel Trace
Saturday evening post (Periodical). The
Post Reader of Civil War stories
Heriot, C. D.
Poltergeist
Winter's tales, 3
Heritage portrait. Stewart, J. I. M.
Hermann, Georg, pseud. See Borchardt,
Georg Hermann
Herman's day. Swados, H.
The hermit. Maupassant, G. de
HERMITS
Dickens, C. Tom Tiddler's ground
Maupassant, G. de. The hermit
Tolstoï, L. N. Graf. Three hermits
The hero. Glanville, B.
Hero by mistake. Brenner, A.
Hero in New York. Lowry, R. J. C.

HEROES
Crane, S. Mystery of heroism
Jackson, C. R. The break
See also Courage
HEROINES. See Heroes
HEROISM. See Heroes
Hero's children. Cory, E.
Herring piece. Boyle, K.
Hershfeld, Carl, 1921-
The key
American vanguard, 1956
Hershman, Morris
Proposal perilous
Mystery Writers of America, inc. For
love or money
Hesling, Bernard
The game
Stivens, D. comp. Coast to coast
Heuman, William
Brooklyns lose
Schwed, P. and Wind, R. W. eds. Great
stories from the world of sport
Her shadow love
Saturday evening post (Periodical) Saturday evening post stories, 1955
Rookie of the year
Teen-age tales, bk 6
Hewitt, Joan
Stardust
Hughes, R. ed. All manner of men
Hexed rifle. Gulick, G. C.
Hey sailor, what ship? Olsen, T.
Hey! Taxi! Ferber, E.
Heyday of the blood. Fisher, D. F. C.
Heyert, Murray
New kid
Jennings, F. G. and Calitri, C. J. eds.
Stories
Heyliger, William, 1884-
Shouting violet
Tibbets, A. B. ed. Youth, youth, youth
Hibben, Frank Cummings, 1910-
Massacre in Peralta Canyon
Humphreville, F. T. ed. In other days
HIDING-PLACES (SECRET CHAMBERS, ETC.)
Derleth, A. W. House in the valley
Higgins, Frank Victor
Resting sands
Oberfirst, R. ed. Anthology of best
short-short stories v6
HIGH SCHOOL LIFE. See School life
High-school star. Farrell, J. T.
HIGH SCHOOLS. See School life
High tide. Marquand, J. P.
High wind. Haycox, E.
Higher standards. Wilson, A.
A highly remockable chimpaneze with a
head chuck-fulla grain matter. Kober,
A.
HIGHWAYMEN. See Brigands and robbers
HIGHWAYS. See Roads
Hijack and the game. Rinehart, M. R.
Hilaire and the Maréchal Pétard. Boyle, K.
Hilary Arnold. Lochridge, B. H.

Hilborn, Norman C.
A bargain's a bargain
Oberfirst, R. ed. Anthology of best short-short stories v5

Hilda. Caldwell, E.

Hill, Arnold, 1918-
Miss Gillespie and the Micks
Garrity, D. A. ed. 44 Irish short stories

Hill, Pati. See Hill, Patricia

Hill, Patricia, 1921-
Ben
Best American short stories, 1958

Hilsher, John M.
New perspective
Oberfirst, R. ed. Anthology of best short-short stories v5

Hilton, James, 1900-1954
Lost horizon
Costain, T. B. and Beecroft, J. eds. More Stories to remember

HINDUS IN AUSTRALIA
Abdullah, M. K. Grandfather tiger

HINDUS IN FRANCE
Godden, R. The oyster

Hippo and the tortoise. Harris, R.

Hippolyte's claim. Maupassant, G. de

Hirai, Tarō, 1894-
The caterpillar
Hirai, T. Japanese tales of mystery and imagination
The cliff
Hirai, T. Japanese tales of mystery and imagination
Hell of mirrors
Hirai, T. Japanese tales of mystery and imagination
Human chair
Hirai, T. Japanese tales of mystery and imagination
Psychological test
Hirai, T. Japanese tales of mystery and imagination
Red chamber
Hirai, T. Japanese tales of mystery and imagination
The traveler with the pasted rag picture
Hirai, T. Japanese tales of mystery and imagination
The twins
Hirai, T. Japanese tales of mystery and imagination
Two crippled men
Hirai, T. Japanese tales of mystery and imagination

HIRED GIRLS. See Servants—Hired girls

HIRED MEN. See Servants—Hired men

HIROSHIMA. See Japan—Hiroshima

His Excellency. Montanelli, I.

His first flight. O'Flaherty, L.

His first point. Prishvin, M. M.

His gin. Tekeyan, C.

His last adventure. Wenter, J.

His last bow. Doyle, Sir A. C.

His lucky day. Ferguson, R.

His man. Annixter, P. pseud.

"His wife's deceased sister." Stockton, F. R.

Hisao, Juran
Mother and son
World prize stories; 2d ser.

HISTORIANS
Bahr, J. Eminent historian

HISTORIC HOUSES, ETC.
James, H. The birthplace

HISTORICAL RESEARCH
Asimov, I. Dead past

Hit and run. Olgin, J.

Hit and run. Schweitzer, G.

HIT-AND-RUN DRIVERS
Hawkins, J. and Hawkins, W. Cop without a badge

HITCHHIKERS
Lowry, R. J. C. Little car in Virginia
Samuel, E. H. Tremp

Hłasko, Marek, 1931-
Most sacred words of our life
Ordon, E. ed. 10 contemporary Polish stories

HOAXES
O'Rourke, F. Stretch in time
Pincherle, A. The film test
See also Humor—Practical jokes

The **hobby.** Criswell, C.

The **hobo.** Downey, H.

Hobo God. James, M.

HOBOES. See Tramps

Hobson's choice. Bester, A.

HOCKEY
Raddall, T. H. Man from Cap D'Amour

Hodel. Rabinowitz, S.

Hodgson, John
Different Christmas
Winter's tales, 3

Hodgson, William Hope, 1878-1918
Island of the Ud
Stead, C. ed. Great stories of the South Sea Islands

Hoffman, Ida Belle
Mirror showed darkness
Oberfirst, R. ed. 1955 anthology of best original short-shorts
Time for smiles
Oberfirst, R. ed. Anthology of best short-short stories v6

Hofmannsthal, Hugo Hofmann, Edler von, 1874-1929
Tale of the cavalry
Jarrell, R. ed. Anchor book of stories
Same as: Cavalry tale
Tale of the 672nd night
Thurston, J. A. ed. Reading modern short stories

Hogan, David, pseud. See Gallagher, Frank

HOGS. See Pigs

Holappa, Pentti
Pastoral
World prize stories; 2d ser.

Holder, William
Face next door
Best detective stories of the year—1956

HOLDUPS. See Robbery

The **hole.** Maupassant, G. de

Holiday. Ferber, E.

HOLIDAYS. See names of particular holidays; also Vacations

Holland, Marion
Crazy over horses
Everygirls horse stories

Holly-tree. Dickens, C.

HOLLYHOCKS
Chavez, A. Lean years

Hollywood. See California—Hollywood

Holman, Jessie
Hunting is for men
Bronfeld, S. ed. Treasury of new short fiction

Holman, Marguerite
Power of suggestion
Oberfirst, R. ed. Anthology of best short-short stories v6

Holmes, Llewellyn Perry, 1895-
Blaze Face
Western Writers of America. Wild horse roundup

Holmes, Marjorie Rose
Reflection of Luanne
Ferris, H. J. comp. Girls, girls, girls

Holmes, Oliver Wendell, 1809-1894
Elsie Venner arouses Master Bernard's suspicions
Aymar, B. ed. Treasury of snake lore

HOLY LAND. See Palestine

Holy morning. Roberts, E. M.

Holy night. Lagerlöf, S. O. L.

Holy Six. Thomas, D.

Home. Faulkner, W.

Home again for Mr Muff. Orr, E.

HOME COMING
Boorstein, R. S. Another man like Johnny
Carlen, E. A. The sky had fallen
Garland, H. Return of a private
Garland, H. Up the Coolly
Markewich, R. Return to the Bronx
Moore, G. Home sickness
Patton, F. G. Loving hands at home
Van Doren, M. Home with Hazel
West, A. C. No fatted calf

The **home**-coming. Singmaster, E.

Home-coming. West, J.

Home for Consuela. Orr, E.

Home for Passover. Rabinowitz, S.

Home from camp. Van Scoyk, B.

Home from the sea. Polk, W. T.

Home girl. Ferber, E.

Home of the human race. Saroyan, W.

Home sickness. Moore, G.

Home there's no returning. Kuttner, H. and Moore, C. L.

Home town. O'Rourke, F.

Home with Hazel. Van Doren, M.

HOMECOMING. See Home coming

Homecoming. Bradbury, R.

Homecoming. Johns, V. P.

HOMES. See Houses

HOMES (INSTITUTIONS) See Almshouses and workhouses; Old age homes

Homesteader's wife. Fox, N. A.

HOMESTEADING
Davis, P. A. Homesteading
Fox, N. A. Homesteader's wife
See also Frontier and pioneer life

Homicidal hiccup. MacDonald, J. D.

Homicide expert. Treat, L.

HOMOSEXUALITY
Beaumont, C. Crooked man
Boyle, K. Count Lothar's heart
Coleman, W. L. The Theban warriors
James, H. The pupil
Mason, M. Saul
Maupassant, G. de. Paul's mistress
O'Donovan, J. Bait
Vidal, G. Pages from an abandoned journal
Vidal, G. Three stratagems
Williams, T. One arm

The **homunculus.** Patton, F. G.

HONDURAS
Carr, A. F. Black beach

The **honest** thief. Dostoevskiĭ, F. M.

HONESTY
Adams, A. Trust and betrayal
Lipman, C. and Lipman, M. Dilemma of Grampa Dubois

Honesty. Bontempelli, M.

Honey, don't you mix, honey, you butt out. Kober, A.

HONEYMOONS
Garrett, G. The sleeping beauty
See also Marriage; Marriage problems

HONG KONG. See China—Hong Kong

Honk-honk breed. White, S. E.

Honor of the County. Edmonds, W. D.

Honorable opponent. Simak, C. D.

The **hoofer.** Miller, W. M.

HOOK. Clark, W. Van T.

HOPI INDIANS
Applegate, F. G. Indian divorce

Hopkins, J. G. E.
Gone to freedom
Hughes, R. ed. All manner of men

Hopkinson, Henry Thomas, 1905-
Mountain madness
Schwed, P. and Wind, H. W. eds. Great stories from the world of sport

Hopkinson, Tom. See Hopkinson, Henry Thomas

Horace Chooney, M. D. West, J.

Horgan, Paul, 1903-
Heart attack
Saturday evening post (Periodical) Saturday evening post stories, 1955
Water in the wilderness
Humphreville, F. T. ed. In other days

The **horla.** Maupassant, G. de

Horn, Holloway, 1886-
Old man
Costain, T. B. and Beecroft, J. eds. More Stories to remember

Horn of plenty. Gordimer, N.

Horner, Antony, 1924-
Grey shroud
Pudney, J. ed. Pick of today's short stories, 9

Horns of plenty. Annixter, P. pseud.

Horowitz, Emmanuel, 1910-
God's agents have beards
  Ribalow, H. U. ed. Treasury of American Jewish stories

The horrible. Maupassant, G. de

HORROR STORIES
Armstrong, C. Laugh it off
Blackwood, A. The wendigo
Bradbury, R. Homecoming
Bradbury, R. Man upstairs
Brennan, J. P. Calamander chest
Brennan, J. P. Canavan's back yard
Brennan, J. P. Death in Peru
Brennan, J. P. On the elevator
Brennan, J. P. Slime
Derleth, A. W. House in the valley
Derleth, A. W. Mask of Cthulhu; 6 stories
Derleth, A. W. Return of Hastur
Derleth, A. W. Sandwin compact
Derleth, A. W. Seal of R'lyeh
Derleth, A. W. Something in wood
Derleth, A. W. Whippoorwills in the hills
Doyle, Sir A. C. Adventure of the speckled band
Faulkner, W. Rose for Emily
Jacobs, W. W. Monkey's paw
Lovecraft, H. P. and Derleth, A. W. Wentworth's day
Maupassant, G. de. Father Judas
Maupassant, G. de. The horla
Mergendahl, C. Secret recipe
Poe, E. A. Descent into the Maelström
Poe, E. A. Fall of the House of Usher
Poe, E. A. Tell-tale heart
Pohl, F. Let the ants try
Williams, T. Desire and the black masseur

Horse for the colonel. Evarts, H. G.

Horse herd lost to Cheyennes. Adams, A.

HORSE RACING
Bagnold, E. Grand National
Byram, G. Wonder horse
Doyle, Sir A. C. Silver Blaze
Dunsany, E. J. M. D. P. 18th baron. Deal with the devil
Fain, W. Harmony
Faulkner, W. Cheest
Faulkner, W. Damon and Pythias unlimited
Grazier, J. A. Chariot race
Hemingway, E. My old man
Horn, H. Old man
Lawrence, D. H. Rocking-horse winner
Macken, W. The fair lady
O'Flaherty, L. Black mare
Runyon, D. Pick the winner
Samuel, E. H. Moshe Bey
Shaw, I. Tip on a dead jockey
Somerville, E. A. O. and Martin, V. F. Lisheen races, second-hand
Tolstoï, L. N. Graf. Vronsky's steeplechase
Van Loan, C. E. Last chance
West, J. First day finish
  See also Jockeys

Horse show. Ingram, B.

HORSE SHOWS
Ingram, B. Horse show

Horse that crossed the world. Blassingame, W.

Horse that saved a million lives. Blassingame, W.

HORSE THIEVES
Adams, A. El Lobo's sweetheart
Lamson, D. A. Oh, once in my saddle
Tolstoï, A. N. Graf. Arkhip

HORSE-TRADING
Faulkner, W. Spotted horses

HORSE TRAINING. See Horses

Horseback. Kubly, H.

HORSEBACK RIDING. See Horsemanship

HORSEMANSHIP
Barrett, B. L. Family tree
Bates, H. E. Death of a huntsman
Lambert, J. Tall as the stars
McNeile, H. C. Man in ratcatcher
Welcome, J. Red coats galloping

HORSES
Adams, A. Black-waxy near Waxahachie
Adams, A. Chasing mustangs
Adams, A. Horse herd lost to Cheyennes
Adams, A. Scared horses on the Navidad
Allen, M. P. The Mudhen, V. S.
Annixter, P. pseud. Champions of the peaks
Aramilev, I. Berendey
Babel', I. E. Afonka Bida
Babel', I. E. Argamak
Babel', I. E. Chesniki
Babel', I. E. Remount officer
Babel', I. E. Story of a horse
Bailey, J. Run for the strip
Barker, S. O. Macho
Beauchamp, D. D. The best year
Blassingame, W. Copenhagen and the Iron Duke
Blassingame, W. Gray Arab of Winston Churchill
Blassingame, W. His kingdom for a horse; 12 stories
Blassingame, W. Horse that crossed the world
Blassingame, W. Horse that saved a million lives
Blassingame, W. Horses of Joan of Arc
Blassingame, W. How Rienzi's name was changed to Winchester
Blassingame, W. Justin Morgan
Blassingame, W. Stonewall Jackson and Old Sorrel
Blassingame, W. Strange fate of El Morzillo
Blassingame, W. Trojan horse
Blassingame, W. Truxton against Greyhound
Blassingame, W. Warrior and the First World War
Boyle, K. Episode in the life of an ancestor
Breckenfeld, V. G. Touch of Arab
Brooks, W. R. Mr Pope rides again
Byram, G. Wonder horse
Champney, L. W. Old stager
Cluff, G. B. Pearly gates are open
Coburn, W. Orneriest three
"Dalesman." Irish dream
De Leeuw, A. L. If wishes were horses
Doyle, Sir A. C. Adventure of Shoscombe Old Place

HORSES—*Continued*
Doyle, Sir A. C. Silver Blaze
Drago, H. S. Sagebrush champion
Evarts, H. G. Horse for the colonel
Everygirls horse stories; 12 stories
Faulkner, W. Spotted horses
Felts, J. N. Winning of Dark Boy
Fisher, V. The scarecrow
Folinsbee, J. P. Storm
Folinsbee, P. Big Tex
Fournier, P. The horses
Fox, N. A. Wild leather
Goehring, D. That last buckskin
Gulick, G. C. Kid that rode with death
Halacy, D. S. Ride the rough string
Hankins, J. W. Black Satin
Holland, M. Crazy over horses
Holmes, L. P. Blaze Face
Hoyt, M. No sum too small
Ingram, B. Horse show
Jones, G. Wat Pantathro
Kasson, H. Nonie
Kjelgaard, J. A. Rebel horse
Lambert, J. Tall as the stars
Lance, L. Ghost horse
Lesinš, K. Bek
McCourt, E. A. White mustang
Maupassant, G. de. Coco
Meyers, B. Devil Dust
Montgomery, R. G. King of the mesa
O'Flaherty, L. Black mare
Oliver, C. Star above it
Osgood, L. Birthday gift
Patten, L. B. Big Black and the bully
Payne, S. Black outlaw
Person, W. T. Brown beauty
Rhodes, E. M. Loved I not honor more
Sarver, L. J. Percheron
Shami, Y. Hamamah
Sheehy, E. Black mare
Somerville, E. A. O. and Martin, V. F.
    Lisheen races, second-hand
Somerville, E. A. O. and Martin, V. F.
    A misdeal
Steele, W. D. Blue Murder
Stegner, W. E. The colt
Steinbeck, J. The gift
Steinbeck, J. The promise
Tolstoĭ, L. N. Graf. Kholstomer
Trollope, A. Nappie's grey horse
Warner, A. S. On the hoof
Western Writers of America. Wild horse
    roundup; 14 stories
Wyckoff, J. To be a cowboy
The **horses**. Fournier, P.

Horse's ha. Thomas, D.

Horses of Joan of Arc. Blassingame, W.

Horseshoes. Lardner, R. W.

HOSPITALITY
Lesinš, K. Fiery descent of old Koris
    See also Guests; Visiting
HOSPITALS AND SANATORIUMS
Daneshvar, S. Narges
Detzortzis, D. Halcyon sea
Hale, N. Miss August
Hale, N. New order
King, M. P. Pair of shoes
O'Brian, P. Voluntary patient
O'Kelly, S. Nan Hogan's house
Pincherle, A. Sick boy's winter
Rothberg, A. A. Roman portrait

Rutledge, A. H. Vanishing of Pegram
Samuelson, R. Day of rest
Sandoz, M. Y. Leaning rock
Williams, W. C. Jean Beicke
The **hostage**. Forester, C. S.
HOSTAGES
Forester, C. S. The hostage
The **hot** girl. Cassill, R. V.
Hot pig. Millholland, R.
HOT RODDERS. See Automobile drivers
Hot weather jokes. Pincherle, A.
Hotel kid. O'Hara, J.
HOTELS, TAVERNS, ETC.
Babel', I. E. Lyubka the Cossack
Balchin, N. Mine host
Bradbury, R. Day it rained forever
Brennan, J. P. On the elevator
Byrd, J. J. Darling, please believe me
Caldwell, E. Hilda
Comisso, G. Mario's riches
Cullingford, G. Kill and cure
Devaulx, N. Madame Parpillon's inn
Dickens, C. Holly-tree
Dickens, C. Sam Weller makes his bow
Eberhart, M. G. Bermuda grapevine
Farrell, J. T. I'm dancing Frances
Frankau, P. The Duchess and the Smugs
Hale, N. Copley-Plaza
Irving, W. Stout gentleman
Kubly, H. The guest
Kubly, H. The unmarried bartender
Lawrence, D. H. Samson and Delilah
O'Faoláin, S. Silence of the valley
Pritchett, V. S. The aristocrat
Pritchett, V. S. Many are disappointed
Pritchett, V. S. Things as they are
Sansom, W. Eventide
Stegner, W. E. The volunteer
Warner, S. T. Under new management
Wright, R. Big black, good man
Hound music. Niehuis, C. C.
Hound of the Baskervilles. Doyle, Sir A. C.
HOUNDS
Adams, A. Rich in hounds
Niehuis, C. C. Hound music
Street, H. Proud possessor
Hour after Westerly. Coates, R. M.
The **house**. Harriss, R. P.
House below the street. Patton, F. G.
House called Magnolia. Curley, D.
HOUSE DECORATION. See Interior
    decoration
HOUSE FLIES. See Flies
House in Bel Air. Allen, S.
House in the valley. Derleth, A. W.
House of blood. Fournier, P.
House of flowers. Capote, T.
House of many rooms. White, R.
House of pain. Shaw, I.
HOUSE PARTIES
Durland, F. Heart turned inward
Ellin, S. House party
Fuchs, D. Golden West
Fuchs, D. Twilight in southern California
Gordimer, N. A wand'ring minstrel, I.
Lewis, D. B. W. Ring out, wild bells
Stafford, J. Maggie Meriwether's rich ex-
    perience

Howard, Robert E.—_Continued_
Shadows in Zamboula
Howard, R. E. Conan the barbarian
A witch shall be born
Howard, R. E. Conan the barbarian
Howard, Robert Ervin, 1906-1936, and De Camp, Lyon Sprague, 1907-
Blood-stained god
Howard, R. E. and De Camp, L. S. Tales of Conan
The flame-knife
Howard, R. E. and De Camp, L. S. Tales of Conan
Hawks over Shem
Howard, R. E. and De Camp, L. S. Tales of Conan
Road of the eagles
Howard, R. E. and De Camp, L. S. Tales of Conan
Howland, Rosemary
Magic night
Teen-age tales, bk 5
Run sheep, run
Ferris, H. J. comp. Girls, girls, girls
Something like love
Furman, A. L. ed. Everygirls romance stories
Hoys, Dudley
King Dron
Skelton, P. ed. Animals all
Hoyt, Murray
No sum too small
Everygirls horse stories
Hubbard, Lafayette Ronald, 1911-
Tough old man
Norton, A. M. ed. Space police
Hubbard, P. M.
Botany Bay
Magazine of fantasy and science fiction. Best from Fantasy and science fiction; 5th ser.
Hubert and Minnie. Huxley, A. L.
HUCKSTERS. See Peddlers and peddling
Hudson, Flexmore
"I don't blame you, Ernie!"
Stivens, D. comp. Coast to coast
HUDSON RIVER
Irving, W. Legend of Sleepy Hollow
HUDSON'S BAY COMPANY
Parker, Sir G. bart. Prairie vagabond
Hughes, John Gledwyn
Master of the golden game
World prize stories; 2d ser.
Hughes, Langston, 1902-
One Friday morning
Ferris, H. J. comp. Girls, girls, girls
Hughes, Richard Arthur Warren, 1900-
The stranger
Jones, G. ed. Welsh short stories
Hughes, Vadonna Jean
Swede
Furman, A. L. ed. Everygirls sports stories
Hugo Kertchak, builder. See Schaefer, J. W. Man from far away
Hull, Edna Mayne
The patient
Conklin, G. ed. Science-fiction adventures in mutation

Human chair. Hirai, T.
Human interest stuff. Dresser, D.
Humble drama. Maupassant, G. de
Humiliation. Maupassant, G. de
Humming bird. Johnson, O. M.
HUMOR
Adams, A. Bogged to the saddle skirts in the story
Adams, A. Uncle Dave Hapfinger in heaven
Alarcón, P. A. de. Three-cornered hat
Ashbaugh, D. The case of the missing sources
Asimov, I. Jokester
Atkinson, H. Jumping jeweller of Lavender Bay
Aymé, M. Roll of daughters
Aymé, M. Walker-through-walls
Babcock, H. Cousin Quesenberry Butts and the boiled owl
Babel', I. E. Awakening
Benchley, R. C. Ladies wild
Borchardt, H. The peepshow
Bradbury, R. There was an old woman
Bradbury, R. Watchful poker chip of H. Matisse
Brooks, W. Officer Mulvaney and the hot buttered pig
Brooks, W. R. Mr Pope rides again
Butler, E. P. Mascot
Chesterton, G. K. Elusive companion of Parson White
Chesterton, G. K. Exclusive luxury of Enoch Oates
Chesterton, G. K. Improbable success of Mr Owen Hood
Chesterton, G. K. Tales of the long bow; 8 stories
Chesterton, G. K. Ultimate ultimatum of the League of the Long Bow
Chesterton, G. K. Unobtrusive traffic of Captain Pierce
Chesterton, G. K. Unprecedented architecture of Commander Blair
Chesterton, G. K. Unpresentable appearance of Colonel Crane
Chesterton, G. K. Unthinkable theory of Professor Green
Clemens, S. L. Celebrated jumping frog of Calaveras County
Clemens, S. L. From "Connecticut Yankee in King Arthur's Court"
Cobb, I. S. "Speaking of operations—"
Cohen, O. R. Nuts and reasons
Connell, R. E. The last of the flatfeet
Coombs, C. I. Gadgets aren't everything
Duvernois, H. Clothes make the man
Felsen, G. Why rustlers never win
Fitch, G. H. The Greek double cross
Foote, J. T. A wedding gift
Gilpatric, G. The artful Mr Glencannon
Grahame, K. The burglars
Graves, L. The pig-bristle slugger
Gulick, G. C. Marriage of Moon Wind
Hale, L. P. Agamemnon's career
Harris, J. B. Una
Hedgecock, L. J. Zipper trouble
Hellman, S. Toll bridge
Household, G. The brides of Solomon
Household, G. Eggs as ain't
Huxley, A. L. Cynthia
Johnson, N. The laughing death

HUMOR—*Continued*

Johnston, R. T. A1 at Lord's
Johnston, R. T. Century of a lifetime
Johnston, R. T. Century of a lifetime; 5 stories
Johnston, R. T. Cricket in the blood
Johnston, R. T. Eternal triangle
Johnston, R. T. Woman with a past
Kipling, R. Unsavoury interlude
Knight, D. Catch that Martian
Kober, A. And I am the attorney for the plaintiff
Kober, A. Certain people are gonna wake up and learn the score is too late
Kober, A. Don't let no cracked-pot lay his fishhooks on your chronium
Kober, A. Even the averitch incompoop's got a little egg nest put away
Kober, A. Go be insulted when a fella hands you a compliment
Kober, A. A highly remockable chimpaneze with a head chuck-fulla grain matter
Kober, A. Honey, don't you mix, honey, you butt out
Kober, A. I wouldn't be your partner if you came beggin' me on your two bent knees
Kober, A. I'da never found out about it, essept came the accident
Kober, A. I'm not gonna cowtail to that bubble-headed bastid, if it's the last thing I do!
Kober, A. It'll be too late then. You just wait and see!
Kober, A. The lady and the fox
Kober, A. One for the book
Kober, A. Oooh, what you said; 19 stories
Kober, A. Paintner in the Bronx
Kober, A. Poor Goldie
Kober, A. A red-faced chief who's just come offa the Indian reservoir
Kober, A. Some people are just plumb crazy
Kober, A. What's a girl supposed to do— sit aroun' and twill her thumbs?
Kober, A. The whole audience woulda bust right out laughin'
Kober, A. Y'say ya not saddisfied
Lardner, R. Horseshoes
Lardner, R. W. Some like them cold
Leacock, S. My financial career
Lesinš, K. Tailor and the wolves
McCord, D. T. W. Camp at Lockjaw
MacMahon, B. Red petticoat
Mankowitz, W. Day Aunt Chaya was buried
Mankowitz, W. Devil and the cow
Mankowitz, W. Five per cent of paradise
Marquis, D. O'Meara at Troy
Miller, E. M. Nine rosaries to St Stanislaus Kostka
Miller, W. M. Canticle for Leibowitz
Munro, H. H. The bag
Munro, H. H. The interlopers
Munro, H. H. Schartz-Metterklume method
Munro, H. H. Story teller
Nash, O. Stranger in the house
Nearing, H. Cerebrative psittacoid
Nourse, A. E. Family resemblance
Oliver, C. Transformer

O'Malley, F. W. Shipping the claret to port
Pagano, J. Signor Santa
Peretz, I. L. The pious cat
Porter, W. S. After twenty years
Porter, W. S. Furnished room
Raine, N. R. Tugboat Annie quotes the law
Rhine, R. Margaret and Wilbur keep Moses
Rhodes, E. M. Sticky Pierce, diplomat
Rinehart, M. R. Baby blimp
Rinehart, M. R. Best of Tish; 12 stories
Rinehart, M. R. Cave on Thunder Cloud
Rinehart, M. R. The dipper
Rinehart, M. R. Hijack and the game
Rinehart, M. R. Mind over motor
Rinehart, M. R. Salvage
Rinehart, M. R. Simple lifers
Rinehart, M. R. Strange journey
Rinehart, M. R. Tish does her bit
Rinehart, M. R. Tish goes to jail
Rinehart, M. R. Tish marches on
Rinehart, M. R. Tish plays the game
Rosenberg, E. C. Mrs Rivkin grapples with the drama
Rosten, L. C. Mr Kaplan and the Magi
Runyon, D. A call on the president
Russell, B. A. W. R. 3d earl. Mr Bowdler's nightmare
Rynas, S. A. Chain of command
Saroyan, W. Fable IX
Seton, E. T. Slum cat
Somerville, E. A. O. and Martin, V. F. Lisheen races, second-hand
Stephens, J. A rhinoceros, some ladies, and a horse
Stockton, F. R. Piece of red calico
Stockton, F. R. Remarkable wreck of the "Thomas Hyke"
Stockton, F. R. Transferred ghost
Suhl, Y. With the aid of the One Above
Sullivan, F. Crisp new bills for Mr Teagle
Sullivan, F. Jukes family
Sullivan, F. The ugly mollusk
Tarkington, B. Miss Rennsdale accepts
Tarkington, B. Talleyrand Penrod
Temple, W. H. The eternal duffer
Thurber, J. More alarms at night
Thurber, J. Secret life of Walter Mitty
Thurber, J. You could look it up
Upson, W. H. I'm a natural-born salesman
Waldo, E. H. Never underestimate
Welch, D. Mr Digby and the talking dog
Willans, G. Skool
Winslow, H. My own true love story
Wodehouse, P. G. Artistic career of Corky
Wodehouse, P. G. The aunt and the sluggard
Wodehouse, P. G. Bertie changes his mind
Wodehouse, P. G. Clustering round young Bingo
Wodehouse, P. G. Episode of the dog McIntosh
Wodehouse, P. G. Jeeves and the impending doom
Wodehouse, P. G. Jeeves and the kid Clementina
Wodehouse, P. G. Jeeves and the old school chum

HUMOR—*Continued*

Wodehouse, P. G. Jeeves and the song of songs

Wodehouse, P. G. Jeeves and the unbidden guest

Wodehouse, P. G. Jeeves and the yuletide spirit

Wodehouse, P. G. Jeeves takes charge

Wodehouse, P. G. Love that purifies

Wodehouse, P. G. Ordeal of young Tuppy

Wodehouse, P. G. Rummy affair of old Biffy

Wodehouse, P. G. Selected stories; 15 stories

Wodehouse, P. G. Uncle Fred Flits

Practical jokes

Allen, S. Girls on the tenth floor

Caldwell, E. Letters in the mail

Maupassant, G. de. Practical joke

Maupassant, G. de. Question of Latin

Munro, H. H. Bertie's Christmas Eve

Munro, H. H. Open window

Munro, H. H. Reginald's Christmas revel

O'Hara, J. Pardner

Sansom, W. Man of parts

Sansom, W. The smile

Smith, E. W. Jeff Coongate and the stolen crony

Smith, E. W. Short, happy death of Jeff Coongate

Wylie, P. Man who loved a joke

HUMOROUS STORIES. See Humor

Humphreville, Frances T. 1909-

Moll Cramer, Witch of Woodbury
Humphreville, F. T. ed. In other days

HUNCHBACKS

Marotta, G. In a lane of Naples

Van Druten, J. Gavin

West, J. Breach of promise

Hundredth centennial. Hyman, M.

HUNGARIANS IN THE UNITED STATES

Seid, R. Red necktie

HUNGARY

Household, G. Roll out the barrel

20th century

Dery, T. Love

Gyarfas, M. Louis Kossuth at Kisgomboc

Szabó, P. Mother's tears in the Bukk Mountains

Communism

See Communism—Hungary

HUNGER

Maupassant, G. de. A vagabond

The **hunger.** Beaumont, C.

Hunger. Yezierska, A.

Hunger artist. Kafka, F.

Hungry guinea pig. Breuer, M. J.

Hunt, Mary Fassett

Pair of lovers
Stanford short stories, 1955

The **hunt.** Brennan, J. P.

The **hunted.** Baudin, M.

Hunter, Evan, 1926-

Chinese puzzle
Best detective stories of the year—1955

First offense
Best detective stories of the year—1956

Last spin
Best detective stories of the year (12th annual collection)

Ticket to death
Best detective stories of the year—1955

Hunter, Herbert H. 1910-

Pancho and the elephant
Oberfirst, R. ed. 1955 anthology of best original short-shorts

The **hunter.** Wormser, R.

HUNTERS. See Hunting

The **hunters.** Downey, H.

Hunter's home. Grau, S. A.

HUNTING

Babcock, H. Great day in the morning!

Babcock, H. Miss Priss

Babcock, H. Son of a bishop

Brown, M. Snow owl

Connell, R. E. Most dangerous game

"Dalesman." Irish dream

Emshwiller, C. Hunting machine

Farrell, M. F. Villainy of Mr Fox

Faulkner, W. The bear

Faulkner, W. Old people

Hawkins, D. Man and a fox

Hemingway, E. Short happy life of Francis Macomber

Holman, J. Hunting is for men

Kantor, M. Voice of Bugle Ann

Kjelgaard, J. A. Pat'tidge dog

McMullen, J. A. Old Pro

McNeile, H. C. Man in ratcatcher

Marshall, E. Heart of Little Shikara

Maupassant, G. de. Cock crowed

Maupassant, G. de. Deaf-mute

Maupassant, G. de. Guillemot Rock

Maupassant, G. de. Love

Maupassant, G. de. White wolf

Murphy, R. There was a bigger one

Oakes, P. Lion in the house

O'Brian, P. Drawing of the Curranwood badgers

Sassoon, S. L. The mister

Smith, E. W. Courtship of Jeff Coongate

Smith, E. W. One-eyed poacher's revenge

Tolstoĭ, L. N. Graf. Desire stronger than necessity

Tolstoĭ, L. N. Graf. Full day's hunting

Trollope, A. Nappie's grey horse

Wormser, R. The hunter

See also Bird hunters; Deer hunting; Duck shooting; Fox hunting; Shooting; Trappers

Accidents

Berriault, G. Stone boy

Hunting day. Philips, J. P.

HUNTING DOGS. See Dogs; Foxhounds; Hounds

Hunting horn. Annixter, P. pseud.

HUNTING GUIDES. See Guides (Hunting)

Hunting is for men. Holman, J.

Hunting machine. Emshwiller, C.

Hunting problem. Sheckley, R.

HURDLE-RACING

Olgin, J. Last hurdle

The **hurkle** is a happy beast. Waldo, E. H.

I

Iatridis, Julia
Michali's night
World prize stories; 2d ser.

Ibañez, Vicente Blasco. See Blasco Ibañez, Vicente

Ibn-Sahav, Ari, 1899-
Moroccans at the Wailing Wall
Frank, M. Z. ed. Sound the great trumpet

Ibn-Zahav, Ari. See Ibn-Sahav, Ari

Icarus Montgolfier Wright. Bradbury, R.

ICE HOCKEY. See Hockey

ICE SKATING. See Skating

Ice storm. Barry, J.

ICELAND

10th century
Anderson, P. Man who came early

ICONS
Mankowitz, W. The portrait

I'd have gambled my life on her. Adams, A.

I'da never found out about it, essept came the accident. Kober, A.

Ida Sims. Lochridge, B. H.

Idea in the back of my brother's head. Saroyan, W.

Ideal man. O'Hara, J.

IDEALISM
Hawthorne, N. Great Stone Face

The **idealist.** Donovan, M.

The **idealist.** Household, G.

The **idealist.** Campbell, J. W.

Ideas die hard. Asimov, I.

Idenborough. Warner, S. T.

IDIOCY
Cela, C. J. Village idiot
Faulkner, W. Kingdom of God
See also Feeble-minded; Insanity

IDIOTS. See Idiocy

IDOLS AND IMAGES
Ruhen, O. Road to Heaven

An **idyl.** Maupassant, G. de

An **idyll.** Bodington, N.

Ieli. Verga, G.

If Lizzie tells. Van Doren, M.

If not higher. Peretz, I. L.

If only. Van Doren, M.

If people would only think. Allen, S.

If wishes were horses. De Leeuw, A. L.

Ifan Owen and the grey rider. Griffith, W.

IGUANA. See Lizards

IKONS. See Icons

I'll fight you. Brooks, J.

I'll take you to Tennessee. Connell, E. S.

ILLEGITIMACY
Alas, L. Doña Berta
Babel', I. E. Sin of Jesus
Bentley, P. E. Isabella, Isabella
Carroll, P. V. She went by gently
Doyle, Sir A. C. Adventure of the priory school
Faulkner, W. Wash
Lowry, R. J. C. Marie

Lyberaki, M. The other Alexander
MacMahon, B. Exile's return
MacMahon, B. "So early in the morning, O!"
MacMahon, B. Sunday afternoon. Sunny
Maupassant, G. de. Simon's papa
O'Donovan, J. Two brass candlesticks
O'Donovan, M. Legal aid
Thomas, D. Just like little dogs

Illep and the whale. Wallenius, K. M.

ILLICIT AFFAIRS. See Marriage problems

ILLINOIS
Maxwell, W. Trojan women

Chicago
Farrell, J. T. Kilroy was here
Farrell, J. T. Ruth and Bertram
Ferber, E. Blue blood

ILLITERACY
Maugham, W. S. The verger

ILLNESS
Chekhov, A. P. Gusev
Cullum, W. Punch bowl
Gallant, M. Day like any other
Graham, R. B. C. Beattock for Moffat
Hale, N. The growth
Heriot, C. D. Poltergeist
Kentfield, C. Mortality
Riahovsky, V. The mother
Ward, L. L. Winter wheat
West, A. C. Narcissus unto echo
West, J. The linden trees
See also Invalids

ILLUSIONS. See Hallucinations and illusions

Illustrated man. Bradbury, R.

ILLUSTRATORS
James, H. Real thing

Ilyas. Tolstoĭ, L. N. Graf

Ilyenkov, Vasily
Foma Zabotkin
Loaf sugar, and other Soviet stories

I'm a natural-born salesman. Upson, W. H.

I'm coming in. Bell, J. N.

I'm dancing Frances. Farrell, J. T.

I'm lucky—I'm an orphan. Rabinowitz, S.

I'm murdering Mr Massington. Brennan, J. P.

I'm not gonna cowtail to that bubble-headed bastid, if it's the last thing I do! Kober, A.

I'm scared. Finney, J.

IMAGES AND IDOLS. See Idols and images

IMAGINARY ANIMALS. See Animals, Mythical

IMAGINARY CITIES
Gerstäcker, F. W. C. Germelshausen

IMAGINARY KINGDOMS
Anderson, P. The barbarian
Howard, R. E. Black colossus
Howard, R. E. Conan the barbarian; 5 stories
Howard, R. E. Devil in iron
Howard, R. E. Shadows in the moonlight

IRELAND, PROVINCIAL AND RURAL
—*Continued*

Macken, W. The gauger
Macken, W. Green hills
Macken, W. Green hills, and other stories; 21 stories
Macken, W. Hallmarked
Macken, W. Hurling match
Macken, W. The king
Macken, W. The lady and the tom
Macken, W. The proud man
Macken, W. The river
Macken, W. The sailor
Macken, W. Tuesday's children
Macken, W. The wasteland
Macken, W. Young Turk
O'Donovan, M. Domestic relations; 15 stories
O'Donovan, M. Peasants
O'Donovan, M. That Ryan woman
O'Faoláin, S. Lord and master
O'Faoláin, S. Silence of the valley
O'Flaherty, L. Child of God
O'Flaherty, L. Post office
O'Kelly, S. Nan Hogan's house
Phelan, J. Bell Wethers
Plunkett, J. Eagles and the trumpets
Plunkett, J. Wearin' of the green
Sassoon, S. L. The mister

Clare

Collier, J. Lady on the grey

Cork

O'Faoláin, S. Up the bare stairs

County Kerry

Walsh, M. Quiet man

Irish, William, pseud. See Woolrich, Cornell

IRISH DIALECT. See Dialect stories—Irish

Irish dream. "Dalesman."

Irish eyes. Bahr, J.

IRISH IN ENGLAND
MacMahon, B. Plain people of England

IRISH IN GREECE
Marquis, D. O'Meara at Troy

IRISH IN SPAIN
Saroyan, W. Mr Feeney's cheval

IRISH IN THE UNITED STATES
Coogan, J. Decline and fall of Augie Sheean
Dreiser, T. St Columba and the river
Farrell, J. T. Monday is another day
Farrell, J. T. Only son
Farrell, J. T. Saturday night
Farrell, J. T. Tommy Gallagher's crusade
Fox, N. A. Fitness of Sean O'Fallon
Moore, G. Home sickness
O'Faoláin, S. Born genius
Pickens, L. Consolation prize
Swados, H. Fawn, with a bit of green
Shepley, J. The machine
West, A. C. Upper room

IRISH SOLDIERS. See Soldiers, Irish

IRON AND STEEL INDUSTRY
Millholland, R. Hot pig

Iron lady. Richter, C.

The **iron** of war. Lederer, W. J. and Burdick, E. L.

IRONY
Porter, W. S. Gift of the Magi
See also Satire

Irony. Reid, L.

Irrepressible sergeant. Bahr, J.

IRRIGATION
Matscher, A. College water wagon

Irving, Washington, 1783-1859
Legend of Sleepy Hollow
Costain, T. B. and Beecroft, J. eds. Stories to remember
Short, R. W. and Sewall, R. B. eds. Short stories for study
Legend of the Arabian astrologer
Hart, J. D. and Gohdes, C. L. eds. America's literature
Legend of the Moor's legacy
Sandrus, M. Y. ed. Famous mysteries
Sterner, L. G. ed. Favorite short stories
Rip Van Winkle
Hart, J. D. and Gohdes, C. L. eds. America's literature
Swayze, B. ed. Short story magic
Stout gentleman
Hart, J. D. and Gohdes, C. L. eds. America's literature

Irwin, Inez (Haynes) 1873-
Spring flight
First-prize stories, 1919-1957

Is he dead? Elliott, G.

Is there a Santa Claus? Church, F. P.

Isabella, Isabella. Bentley, P. E.

Ishikawa, Tatsuzo
A witch
World prize stories; 2d ser.

Island festival. Comisso, G.

Island of the Ud. Hodgson, W. H.

The **Islandman.** Clarke, D.

ISLANDS
Albee, G. S. Exile of paradise island
Bates, H. E. Summer in Salandar
Blackwood, A. Haunted island
Campbell, W. E. M. October Island
Lawrence, D. H. Man who loved islands

Isle of Voices. Stevenson, R. L.

ISRAEL BEN ELIEZER, BA'AL SHEM-TOB, called **BESHT,** 1700-1760
Koteliansky, S. S. Salvation of a soul

ISRAEL
Samuel, E. H. Big givers
Samuel, E. H. Friend of the family
Samuel, E. H. 1959
Samuel, E. H. One of us
Samuel, E. H. Tremp
See also Palestine

Country life
See Country life—Israel

Farm life
See Farm life—Israel

Israel Zvi. Shenhar, Y.

ISTANBUL. See Turkey—Istanbul

It may never happen. Pritchett, V. S.

It opens the sky. Waldo, E. H.

It takes a tough hombre. Loomis, N. M.

ITALIAN SOLDIERS. See Soldiers, Italian

Italian sunshine. Babel', I. E.

ITALIANS
Welty, E. Going to Naples

ITALIANS IN FRANCE
Boyle, K. Effigy of war
Boyle, K. Their name is Macaroni

ITALIANS IN THE UNITED STATES
Malamud, B. The prison
Pagano, J. Signor Santa
Weidman, J. The tuxedos

ITALY

20th century
Huxley, A. L. Little Mexican
Mann, T. Mario and the magician
Pincherle, A. Bitter honeymoon
Rudd, H. Devil's Plain

Army
Hofmannsthal, H. H. Edler von. Tale of the cavalry

Assisi
Gallico, P. W. Never take no for an answer

Farm life
See Farm life—Italy

Florence
Huxley, A. L. Little Mexican
Huxley, A. L. Young Archimedes
James, H. Madonna of the future

Naples
Marotta, G. In a lane of Naples
Welty, E. Going to Naples

Padua
Hawthorne, N. Rappaccini's daughter
Huxley, A. L. Little Mexican

Pisa
Garrett, G. The strong man

Rome (City)
Blixen, K. Cardinal's third tale
Calisher, H. What a thing, to keep a wolf in a cage!
Malamud, B. Behold the key
Moretti, U. This is where we are
Price, J. B. Murder for fine art
Sansom, W. Roman holiday
Sansom, W. A woman seldom found
Wharton, E. N. J. Roman fever

Venice
Farrell, J. T. A baptism in Italy
Hartley, L. P. Per far l' amore
Marceau, F. Armistice in Venice
Roth, C. Tree of liberty
Sansom, W. Venice
Tecchi, B. Day in Venice

ITALY, PROVINCIAL AND RURAL
Bilenchi, R. The drought
Comisso, G. Mario's riches
Deledda, G. Sardinian fox
Farrell, J. T. A baptism in Italy
Seidenberg, E. S. Amelia
Silone, I. Along dusty roads and behind hedges
Silone, I. Return to Fontamara
Tombari, F. Miracle at Frusaglia

ITINERANT CLERGY
Griffith, W. Ifan Owen and the grey rider
See also Clergy

ITINERANT PREACHERS. See Itinerant clergy

It'll be too late then. You just wait and see! Kober, A.

It's a good life. Robinson, C.

It's all a question of degree. Bernari, C.

It's all very crazy. Mayer, A. I.

It's cold in the Alps. Farrell, J. T.

It's dark in here. Lowry, R. J. C.

It's nothing to boast about. Simonne

It's she. Hasas, H.

Ivanov, Vsevolod Viacheslavovich, 1895?-
The kid
Hall, J. B. and Langland, J. T. eds. Short story

Ivins, Ann, 1929-
Summer sun
American vanguard, 1956

Ivins, David, 1928-
Favored son
American vanguard, 1956

J

Jack-in-the box. Bradbury, R.

Jack Jouett's ride. Hawthorne, H.

Jack Still. Marquand, J. P.

JACKASSES. See Asses and mules

Jackpot. Broun, H. C.

JACKSON, ANDREW, PRESIDENT U.S.
1767-1845
Blassingame, W. Truxton against Greyhound

Jackson, Charles Reginald, 1903-
The break
Baudin, M. ed. Contemporary short stories v3

Jackson, Dorothy V. S.
Gift of love
Everygirls adventure stories
Night filled with music
Seventeen (Periodical) Stories from Seventeen

Jackson, Joseph H. 1912-
Pastorale
American vanguard, 1956
Winter Sunday
New voices 2: American writing today

Jackson, Shirley, 1920-
Bulletin
Magazine of fantasy and science fiction. Best from Fantasy and science fiction; 4th ser.
The lottery
McClennan, J. comp. Masters and masterpieces of the short story
Lovely night
Ferris, H. J. comp. Girls, girls, girls

Jackson, Shirley—*Continued*
One ordinary day, with peanuts
Best American short stories, 1956
Magazine of fantasy and science fiction.
Best from Fantasy and science fiction; 5th ser.
Merril, J. ed. S-F: ɪ'56ɪ
The tooth
Baudin, M. ed. Contemporary short stories v3
Jackson, Stonewall. See Jackson, Thomas Jonathan
JACKSON, THOMAS JONATHAN, 1824-1863
Blassingame, W. Stonewall Jackson and Old Sorrel
Jacob and the Indians. Benét, S. V.
Jacobs, William Wymark, 1863-1943
Monkey's paw
McMaster, J. ed. Stories to remember
Swayze, B. ed. Short story magic
Jacob's ladder. Rawlings, M. K.
Jacobson, Dan, 1929-
Little pet
Stanford short stories, 1958
Two women
Stanford short stories, 1958
Jacobus de Voragine
Saint Theodora
Hall, J. B. and Langland, J. T. eds. Short story
Jagger from Jaggertown. Adams, A.
JAILS. See Prisoners and prisons
Jake Hoover's pig. Linderman, F. B.
Jake was a tomboy. O'Neill, J.
JAM SESSIONS. See Jazz music
James, Arthur
Something to talk with
Western Writers of America. Hound dogs and others
James, Denise
In memory of John
Stanford short stories, 1957
A kind of faith
Stanford short stories, 1956
James, Henry, 1843-1916
Beast in the jungle
Hamalian, L. and Volpe, E. L. eds. Ten modern short novels
James, H. Selected short stories
The birthplace
James, H. Selected short stories
"Europe"
Gettman, R. A. and Harkness, B. eds. Book of stories
Four meetings
James, H. Selected short stories
Friends of the friends
Ridler, A. B. comp. Best ghost stories
Greville Fane
Hall, J. B. and Langland, J. T. eds. Short story
International episode
James, H. Selected short stories
Jolly corner
James, H. Selected short stories
Lesson of the Master
Hart, J. D. nd Gohdes, C. L. eds. America's literature

Madonna of the future
Havighurst, W. ed. Masters of the modern short story
Maud-Evelyn
Thurston, J. A. ed. Reading modern short stories
Middle years
James, H. Selected short stories
The pupil
James, H. Selected short stories
Short, R. W. and Sewall, R. B. eds. Short stories for study
Real thing
James, H. Selected short stories
Locke, L. G.; Gibson, W. M. and Arms, G. W. eds. Introduction to literature
James, Montagu Rhodes, 1862-1936
Lost hearts
Ridler, A. B. comp. Best ghost stories
Jameson, Colin G.
Smart guy
Oberfirst, R. ed. Anthology of best short-short stories v5
Jameson, Malcolm, 1891-1945
Hobo God
Greenberg, M. ed. All about the future
Jameson, Storm, 1897-
The mask
Winter's tales, 1
Janey Mary. Plunkett, J.
JANITORS
Malamud, B. The bill
West, J. Battle of the suits
January 1999: rocket summer. Bradbury, R.
Janvier, Ivan
Thing
Best science-fiction stories and novels: 1956
Janvier, Paul, pseud. See Budrys, Algis J.
JAPAN
Doppo, K. Meat and potatoes
Ishikawa, T. A witch
Kan, K. Laughing at the dead
Mailer, N. K. Paper house
Naoya, S. The patron Saint
Ōgai, M. Takasebune
Riichi, Y. Spring came on a horse-drawn cart
Ryunosuke, A. A clod of earth
Ryunosuke, A. Flatcar

19th-20th century
Buck, P. S. The enemy

Hiroshima
Plomer, W. C. F. Thy neighbour's creed

Karuizawa
Macauley, R. The mind is its own place
JAPANESE IN MANCHURIA
Katai, T. A soldier
JAPANESE SOLDIERS. See Soldiers, Japanese
Japanese tea-set. Samuel, E. H.
The **jar.** Bradbury, R.
Jarnés, Benjamín, 1888-
Saint Alexis
Flores, A. ed. Great Spanish stories
Jazz-age clerk. Farrell, J. T.

JAZZ MUSIC
  Baldwin, J. Sonny's blues
  Beaumont, C. Black country
  Bloch, R. Dig that crazy grave!
  Johns, V. P. Mr Hyde-de-Ho
  Oliver, C. Didn't he ramble

Je ne comprends pas. Lowry, R. J. C.

Jealous bitch. Colette, S. G.

JEALOUSY
  Colette, S. G. The cat
  Faulkner, W. Jealousy
  Fitzgerald, F. S. K. Design in plaster
  Maupassant, G. de. Am I insane?
  Maupassant, G. de. The confession
  Maupassant, G. de. Mad?
  Maupassant, G. de. One evening
  Unamuno y Jugo, M. de. Abel Sanchez
  Van Doren, M. Wild justice

Jealousy. Faulkner, W.

Jean Beicke. Williams, W. C.

JEANNE D'ARC, SAINT. See Joan of
  Arc, Saint

Jearey, Bertram Frederick
  Single-handed fight with a lion
    Skelton, P. ed. Animals all

Jeeves and the impending doom. Wodehouse, P. G.

Jeeves and the kid Clementina. Wodehouse,
  P. G.

Jeeves and the old school chum. Wodehouse,
  P. G.

Jeeves and the song of songs. Wodehouse,
  P. G.

Jeeves and the unbidden guest. Wodehouse,
  P. G.

Jeeves and the yuletide spirit. Wodehouse,
  P. G.

Jeeves takes charge. Wodehouse, P. G.

Jeff Coongate and the stolen crony. Smith,
  E. W.

Jeff Peters as a personal magnet. Porter,
  W. S.

Jenkins, Robin
  Flowers
    Urquhart, F. ed. Scottish short stories

Jenkins, William Fitzgerad, 1896-
  Plague
    Conklin, G. ed. Strange adventures in
      science fiction
  Propagandist
    Gallant, J. ed. Stories of scientific im-
      agination
  Skag with the queer head
    Conklin, G. ed. Science-fiction adven-
      tures in mutation
  Symbiosis
    Gallant, J. ed. Stories of scientific im-
      agination
  The Wabbler
    Montgomery, R. B. ed. Best SF three

Jennings runs cross country. Buckeridge, A.

Jenny Stairy's hat. Hamilton, M.

Jensen, Marion A.
  Juggin' for cats in the Big Muddy
    Oberfirst, R. ed. Anthology of best
      short-short stories v5

Jericho, Jericho, Jericho. Lytle, A. N.

Jerry. Nye, H. L.

JERUSALEM. See Palestine—Jerusalem

Jerusalem: the fifteenth Nisan. Brady, C. A.

Jessamine Springs. Rawlings, M. K.

JESTERS. See Fools and jesters

JESUITS
  Franko, I. I. The plague

JESUS CHRIST
  Aymé, M. Dermuche
  Babel', I. E. Sin of Jesus
  Bible. New Testament. Matthew
  Bradford, R. How come Christmas?
  Deledda, G. Golden crucifix
  Dickens, C. Life of Our Lord
  Household, G. The eye of a soldier
  Saneatsu, M. John, on hearing Judas'
    explanation
  Saneatsu, M. Judas' explanation

        Nativity
  Bible. New Testament. Luke
  Lagerlöf, S. O. L. Holy night
  Sharp, W. St Bride of the Isles
  Supervielle, J. Ox and the ass at the
    manger

JET PROPULSION. See Rocket ships

JEWELERS
  Woolf, V. S. The duchess and the jeweller

Jewellery. Pincherle, A.

JEWELRY
  Doyle, Sir A. C. Adventure of the Beryl
    Coronet
  Dumitriu, P. Family jewels
  Maupassant, G. de. False gems
  Maupassant, G. de. The jewels
  Pincherle, A. Jewellery
  Rohmer, S. pseud. Mystery of the van-
    ishing treasure
      See also Bracelets; Diamonds; Neck-
        laces; Rings

JEWELS. See Jewelry; Precious stones

The jewels. Maupassant, G. de.

Jewett, Sarah Orne, 1849-1909
  Flight of Betsey Lane
    Laughton, C. ed. Tell me a story

JEWISH DIALECT. See Dialect stories—
  Jewish

JEWISH QUESTION. See Jews

JEWISH RITES AND CEREMONIES.
  See Jews—Rites and ceremonies

JEWS
  Babel, I. E. Awakening
  Babel, I. E. In the basement
  Blackwood, A. Strange adventures of a
    private secretary in New York
  Farrell, J. T. Tommy Gallagher's crusade
  Frank, W. D. Under the dome: Aleph
  Hasas, H. The wanderer
  Hecht, B. God is good to a Jew
  Household, G. Children's crusade
  Levin, M. Maurie finds his medium
  Malamud, B. Angel Levine
  Peretz, I. L. Four generations and four
    wills
  Peretz, I. L. The orphan
  Peretz, I. L. Pious cat
  Peretz, I. L. Supreme sacrifice

JEWS—*Continued*

Peretz, I. L. A teacher's tales
Rabinowitz, S. Day before Yom Kippur
Rosenberg, E. C. Mrs Rivkin grapples
    with the drama
Samuel, E. H. Moshe Bey
Schiller, M. B. Now is the time
Schulberg, B. W. Passport to nowhere
Shaw, I. Act of faith
Suhl, Y. With the aid of the One Above
Zangwill, I. Sabbath breaker

Antiquities

Samuel, E. H. For the tourists

Colonization

Gerchunoff, A. In the beginning

Persecutions

Asch, S. Duty to live
Babel', I. E. First love
Babel', I. E. Story of my dovecot
Picard, J. The darkest hour

Religion

Abramowitz, S. J. A nap, prayers, and
    strawberries
Angoff, C. The Ostrovskys
Fineman, I. Elijah the prophet
Klein, A. The minyan

Rites and ceremonies

Gerchunoff, A. Lamentations
Perl, P. Man in Israel
Picard, J. The Parnes is taught a lesson
Picard, J. The sin
Scheiner, F. Old man had four wives
Weidman, J. The Kinnehórrah
    See also Passover

Segregation

Chute, B. J. The outcasts
Edelman, M. Last stand in the Warsaw
    ghetto

JEWS IN AUSTRALIA
Stedman, S. Stroke of a master

JEWS IN CHINA
Blixen, K. Immortal story

JEWS IN EGYPT
Samuel, E. H. Boy babies

JEWS IN ENGLAND
Danischewsky, M. Judgment of Mr
    Moyshe
Mankowitz, W. Mendelman fire
Maugham, W. S. Alien corn
Pritchett, V. S. The scapegoat
Zangwill, I. Prodigal son

JEWS IN GERMANY
Barash, A. In Marburg
Heine, H. On a seder night
Picard, J. The brother
Picard, J. The call
Picard, J. The darkest hour
Picard, J. The fish   n
Picard, J. The forest
Picard, J. The fox
Picard, J. Lottery ticket
Picard, J. The marked one
Picard, J. The marked one, and twelve
    other stories; 13 stories
Picard, J The Parnes is taught a lesson
Picard, J. Raphael and Recha

Picard, J. The sin
Picard, J. Two mothers
Picard, J. The wooer
Sulkin, S. The plan

JEWS IN HUNGARY
Rabinowitz, S. The fiddle

JEWS IN IRELAND
Murdoch, I. Something special

JEWS IN ITALY
Malamud, B. Lady of the lake
Malamud, B. The last Mohican
Miller, A. Monte Saint Angelo
Roth, C. Tree of liberty

JEWS IN MOROCCO
Ibn-Sahav, A. Moroccans at the Wailing
    Wall

JEWS IN NETHERLANDS
Peretz, I. L. Miracles on the sea

JEWS IN NEW YORK (CITY) See Jews
    in the United States—New York
    (City)

JEWS IN PALESTINE
Auerbach, E. On the threshold
Auerbach, E. Wild growth
Barash, A. Hai's well
Pitman, S. C. Baby is born in Israel
Reichenstein, S. Genesis
Deubeni, A. Watchman and the wall
Shenhar, Y. Street symphony
Smilansky, M. Story of a love
Tabib, M. 1917

JEWS IN POLAND
Asch, S. Yechiel's Sabbath mother
Babel', I. E. Berestechko
Babel', I. E. Crossing into Poland
Babel', I. E. Gedali
Babel', I. E. The Rabbi
Edelman, M. Last stand in the Warsaw
    ghetto
Kuncewiczowa, M. S. A turban
Singer, I. B. Old man

JEWS IN RUSSIA
Babel', I. E. First love
Babel', I. E. Karl-Yankel
Babel', I. E. Rabbi's son
Babel', I. E. Story of my dovecot
Franko, I. I. To the light!
Gerchunoff, A. In the beginning
Mankowitz, W. Bonifas the cobbler
Mankowitz, W. Day Aunt Chaya was
    buried
Mankowitz, W. Finest pipe-maker in
    Russia
Mankowitz, W. Law-breaker
Rabinowitz, S. The convoy
Rabinowitz, S. Town of the little people
Roth, J. Menuchim says mamma

**JEWS IN THE ARGENTINE REPUB-
LIC**
Gerchunoff, A. The Anthem
Gerchunoff, A. Camacho's wedding feast
Gerchunoff, A. Case of the stolen horse
Gerchunoff, A. Death of Elder Saul
Gerchunoff, A. Divorce
Gerchunoff, A. Fresh milk
Gerchunoff, A. The herdsman
Gerchunoff, A. Jewish Gauchos of the
    Pampas; 26 stories
Gerchunoff, A. Lamentations
Gerchunoff, A. Miraculous doctor

K

KABBALA. See Cabala

Kachina dolls. Pevehouse, A.

Kafka, Franz, 1883-1924
Bucket-rider
Jarrell, R. ed. Anchor book of stories
Country doctor
Jarrell, R. ed. Anchor book of stories
Locke, L. G.; Gibson, W. M. and Arms,
G. W. eds. Introduction to literature
Great Wall of China
Short, R. W. and Sewall, R. B. eds.
Short stories for study
Hunger artist
Thurston, J. A. ed. Reading modern
short stories
In the penal colony
Hall, J. B. and Langland, J. T. eds.
Short story
The judgment
Gettman, R. A. and Harkness, B. eds.
Book of stories
Married couple
Thurston, J. A. ed. Reading modern
short stories

Kahana, Batya, 1901-
The guitar
Schwarz, L. W. ed. Feast of Leviathan

Kalinovsky, G.
Quiet post
Loaf sugar, and other Soviet stories

Kan, Kikuchi, 1888-1948
Laughing at the dead
McKinnon, R. N. ed. The heart is
alone

Kane, Harnett, Thomas, 1910-
Day after Thanksgiving
Fenner, P. R. comp. Brother against
brother

KANGAROOS
Cottrell, D. W. Wilderness orphan

Kanin, Garson
Damnedest thing
Merril, J. ed. SF: '57

KANSAS
Boyle, K. Episode in the life of an ancestor
Connell, E. S. Color of the world
Connell, E. S. The condor and the guests

19th century
Bailey, J. Run for the strip

Abilene
Haycox, E. High wind

Dodge City
Claussen, W. E. Man from Texas

Farm life
See Farm life—Kansas

Frontier and pioneer life
See Frontier and pioneer life—
Kansas

Kantor, MacKinlay, 1904-
Grave grass quivers
Costain, T. B. and Beecroft, J. eds.
More Stories to remember

Last bullet
Oberfirst, R. ed. Anthology of best
short-short stories v6
Night of panic
This week magazine. This week's Stories of mystery and suspense
No enemy
Saturday evening post (Periodical) The
Post Reader of Civil War stories
Silent grow the guns
Fenner, P. R. comp. Brother against
brother
That Greek dog
Great dog stories
Unseen witness
Saturday evening post (Periodical) Saturday evening post stories, 1954
Voice of Bugle Ann
Costain, T. B. and Beecroft, J. eds.
Stories to remember

Kapelner, Alan
Walking, running people
New voices 2: American writing today

Kaplan, Ralph, 1904-
Night my brother came home
Ribalow, H. U. ed. Treasury of American Jewish stories

Karain: a memory. Conrad, J.

Karbovskaya, Varvara
Bondage
Loaf sugar, and other Soviet stories

Karchmer, Sylvan, 1914-
Bond
Ribalow, H. U. ed. Treasury of American Jewish stories

KARELIANS
Wallenius, K. M. Merciless and merciful
sea

Karl-Yankel. Babel', I. E.

Karlen, Arno
The wall
Miller, N. ed. New campus writing,
no. 2

Karner, Erwin F.
One big error
Oberfirst, R. ed. Anthology of best
short-short stories v6

Karp, David, 1922-
Death warrant
Saturday evening post (Periodical) Saturday evening post stories, 1954

Karp, Deborah B. 1924-
Carmi
Ribalow, H. U. ed. Treasury of American Jewish stories

Karroo of the jungle. Pringle, M. T.

KARUIZAWA. See Japan—Karuizawa

Kasson, Helen
Nonie
Mystery Writers of America, inc. A
choice of murders

Kastle, Herbert D.
The enemies
Meredith, S. ed. Bar 6

Katai, Tayama, 1872-1930
A soldier
McKinnon, R. N. ed. The heart is alone

Kathy. Caldwell, E.

Katov, Norman, 1918-
Torn invitation
Tibbets, A. B. ed. Youth, youth, youth
Katz, Shlomo
Second Lieutenant, U.S.A. Res.
Ribalow, H. U. ed. Treasury of American Jewish stories
Kavanagh, Patrick, 1905-
Football
Garrity, D. A. ed. 44 Irish short stories
Kavinoky, Bernice, 1914-
Retaliation
New voices 2: American writing today
Kay, Teresa
Captain Luba and the white dress
Hughes, R. ed. All manner of men
Kaylin, Walter
Blaze of glory
Teen-age tales, bk 5
Lady on the island
Saturday evening post (Periodical) Saturday evening post stories, 1954
Kazuo, Hirotsu, 1891-
One night
McKinnon, R. N. ed. The heart is alone
Keele, Francis
Telegraph mystery
Teen-age tales, bk 4
Keep it holy. Ferber, E.
Keep out. Brown, F.
Keep your pity. Boyle, K.
The **keeper.** Maupassant, G. de
Keepers of the river dam. Annixter, P. pseud.
Keir, Richard H.
Sunday punch
Teen-age tales, bk 5
Keller, David Henry, 1880-
The doorbell
Conklin, G. ed. Strange adventures in science fiction
Kelly, Eleanor (Mercein) 1880-
Basquerie
Costain, T. B. and Beecroft, J. eds. Stories to remember
Kelly. Goldben, J.
Kelso, S. E. 1904-
Change of heart
Oberfirst, R. ed. Anthology of best short-short stories v6
Kelton, Elmer
Coward
Western Writers of America. Wild streets
Yellow Devil
Western Writers of America. Hound dogs and others
Kemp, Peter Kemp
"So we'll drink. . ."
Kemp, P. K. ed. Hundrded years of sea stories
Kennedy, Maurice
Vladivostok
Winter's tales, 2
Kennedy, Raymond C.
Nightcrawlers
Hughes, R. ed. All manner of men
Kennel and the stud. Surtees, R. S.

Kentfield, Calvin, 1924-
The angel and the sailor
Kentfield, C. The angel and the sailor
Bell of charity
Kentfield, C. The angel and the sailor
Chip Canary
Kentfield, C. The angel and the sailor
Dancer's cricket
Kentfield, C. The angel and the sailor
Innocence descending
Kentfield, C. The angel and the sailor
Johnny's land and Johnny's castle
Kentfield, C. The angel and the sailor
Mortality
Kentfield, C. The angel and the sailor
Place for lovers in the summertime
Kentfield, C. The angel and the sailor
River stay 'way from my door
Kentfield, C. The angel and the sailor
Round giant
Kentfield, C. The angel and the sailor
KENTUCKY
Cobb, I. S. Snake Doctor
Gordon, C. Old Red
Roberts, E. M. On the mountainside
Warren, R. P. Blackberry winter

Harrodsbury
Carmer, C. L. The lone grave
KENYA COLONY AND PROTECTORATE
Cope, J. No tea for the Memsahib
KERCHIEFS. See Scarves
Kerfol. Wharton, E. N. J.
Kerouac, Jack. See Kerouac, John
Kerouac, John, 1922-
Billowy trip in the world
New Directions in prose and poetry, 16
The Mexican girl
Best American short stories, 1956
Kerr, Sophie, 1880-
Mister Youth
Mason, P. O. and Mason, J. eds. Favorite cat stories of Pamela and James Mason
KERRY, COUNTY. See Ireland—County Kerry
Kersh, Gerald, 1909-
Ali the Terrible Turk
Schwed, P. and Wind, H. W. eds. Great stories from the world of sport
Copper Dahlia
Montgomery, R. B. ed. Best SF two
Murderer's eye
Saturday evening post (Periodical) Saturday evening post stories, 1957
Woman who wouldn't stay dead
Saturday evening post (Periodical) Saturday evening post stories, 1955
Kessary, Ouri
Twilight over Jerusalem
World prize stories; 2d ser.
Key, Alexander, 1904-
Caroliny Trail
Humphreville, F. T. ed. In other days
The **key.** Hershfeld, C.
KEYS. See Locks and keys
Khan, Ismith Mohamed, 1925-
In the subway
New voices 2: American writing today

Khat. Dreiser, T.
Kholstomer. Tolstoi, L. N. Graf
The **kid.** Ivanov, V. V.
Kid in command. Marmur, J.
Kid learns. Faulkner, W.
Kid stuff. Asimov, I.
Kid stuff. Pages, W.
Kid stuff. Queen, E. pseud.
Kid that rode with death. Gulick, G. C.
KIDNAPPING
  Block, L. What son tells everything?
  Bodington, N. An idyll
  Doyle, Sir A. C. Adventure of the priory
    school
  Doyle, Sir A. C. Greek interpreter
Kilcrin, Isabel
  Brad Halloran
    Seventeen (Periodical) Stories from
    Seventeen
Kill and cure. Cullingford, G.
Killer at bay. Foster, B.
Killer in the club car. Savage, D.
Killers die young. Turner, R.
Killing bottle. Hartley, L. P.
Kilroy was here. Farrell, J. T.
Kin. Welty, E.
Kind Kitty. Linklater, E.
A **kind** of faith. James, D.
Kindergarten. Simak, C. D.
Kindly. Sansom W.
Kindly stranger. Household, G.
KINDNESS
  Altice, C. W. Captain's queen
  Gilmore, L. H. Last five percent
KINDNESS TO ANIMALS. See Animals
  —Treatment
King, Mary Paula, 1909-
  Pair of shoes
    Good housekeeping (Periodical) Editor's
    choice
King, Rufus, 1893-
  Agree—or die
    King, R. Malice in wonderland
  Body in the pool
    King, R. Malice in wonderland
  Body in the rockpit
    Best detective stories of the year—1956
    King, R. Malice in wonderland
  Let her kill herself
    King, R. Malice in wonderland
  Malice in wonderland
    King, R. Malice in wonderland
    Queen, E. pseud. ed. Ellery Queen's
    awards: 12th ser.
  Miami papers please copy
    King, R. Malice in wonderland
    Queen, E. pseud. ed. Ellery Queen's
    awards: 11th ser.
  Pills of Lethe
    King, R. Malice in wonderland
  To remember you by
    King, R. Malice in wonderland
The **King.** Babel', I. E.
The **King.** Macken, W.
King Dron. Hoys, D.

King of Kanga. Phillpotts, E.
King of the bees. MacMahon, B.
King of the Cats. Benét, S. V.
King of the desert. O'Hara, J.
King of the mesa. Montgomery, R. G.
The **king** of the mountain. Garrett, G.
King waits. Ashton, W.
Kingdom of God. Faulkner, W.
KINGDOMS, IMAGINARY. See Imagi-
  ginary kingdoms
KINGS AND RULERS
  Blixen, K. Converse at night in Copen-
    hagen
  Lewis, S. Let's play king
  Saint Simon, L. de R. duc de. Death of
    Monseigneur
Kings asleep in the ground. MacMahon, B.
King's evil. Davidson, A.
King's parade. Coleman, W. L.
King's son. Maupassant, G. de
The **kinnehórrah.** Weidman, J.
KINSHIP
  Caldwell, E. Soquots
Kintner, Jean Rodney, 1915-
  Spring fever
    American vanguard, 1956
KIOWA INDIANS
  Garland, H. Lone Wolf's old guard
Kipling, Rudyard, 1865-1936
  Elephant's child
    Laughton, C. ed. Tell me a story
  House surgeon
    Ridler, A. B. comp. Best ghost stories
  Lost legion
    Swayze, B. ed. Short story magic
  Maltese cat
    Schwed, P. and Wind, H. W. eds. Great
    stories from the world of sport
  Mowgli's brothers
    Costain, T. B. and Beecroft, J. eds.
    Stories to remember
  "Rikki-tikki-tavi"
    Aymar, B. ed. Treasury of snake lore
  Strange ride of Morrowbie
    Costain, T. B. and Beecroft, J. eds.
    More Stories to remember
  Unsavoury interlude
    Nash, O. comp. I couldn't help laughing
Kirch, James A.
  Friends of Petro
    Mystery Writers of America, inc. For
    tomorrow we die
  The stranger on horseback
    Mystery Writers of America, inc. A
    choice of murders
KIRGHIZ
  Ivanov, V. V. The kid
Kirkbride, Celia, 1924-
  Lucky break
    Oberfirst, R. ed. Anthology of best
    short-short stories v6
The **kiss.** Babel', I. E.
The **kiss.** Maupassant, G. de
The **kiss** at Croton Falls. Shaw, I.
Kitchen kill. Craig, J.

Kitchen knife. Warner, S. T.

The kite. Maugham, W. S.

KITES
Maugham, W. S. The kite

Kith of the Elf-folk. Dunsany, E. J. M. D. P. 18th baron

The **kitten**. Reid, A.

KITTENS. See Cats

Kjelgaard, James Arthur, 1910-1959
Pat'tidge dog
Western Writers of America. Hound dogs and others
Rebel horse
Western Writers of America. Wild horse roundup
Right as rain
Western Writers of America. Hound dogs and others
Tiger's heart
Teen-age tales, bk 5

Kjelgaard, Jim. See Kjelgaard, James Arthur

Klaxon
The search
Buckeridge, A. comp. In and out of school

Klein, Alexander, 1918-
The minyan
Ribalow, H. U. ed. Treasury of American Jewish stories

Klein, Jenny Machlowitz
Yisgadal
Ribalow, H. U. ed. Treasury of American Jewish stories

KLEPTOMANIA
Slesar, H. Trouble with Ruth

Klimek, Lester D.
Mood music rumble
Oberfirst, R. ed. Anthology of best short-short stories v6

Klimo, Jake
Ship's bell
Teen-age tales. bk 4

Kline, Alexander S.
The three rings
Orr, E. and Hammett, E. A. eds. Delta Decameron

KLONDIKE
London, J. Call of the wild

Knapp, Sally Elizabeth, 1918-
Fair play
Furman, A. L. ed. Everygirls sports stories
Flight pattern
Everygirls adventure stories

Kneale, Nigel
Putting away of Uncle Quaggin
Hudson, D. ed. Modern English short stories; 2d ser.

The **knife**. Lynch, J. A.

Knight, Damon
Catch that Martian
Conklin, G. ed. Strange adventures in science fiction
The country of the kind
Merril, J. ed. S-F: ['56]

Four in one
Montgomery, R. B. ed. Best SF three
Man in the jar
Galaxy science fiction magazine. Third Galaxy reader
Natural state
Greenberg, M. ed. All about the future
Strange station
Merril, J. ed. SF: '57
World without children
Galaxy science fiction magazine. Five Galaxy short novels
You're another
Magazine of fantasy and science fiction. Best from Fantasy and science fiction; 5th ser.

Knight, Ralph
Third honeymoon
Saturday evening post (Periodical) Saturday evening post stories, 1957

KNIGHTS AND KNIGHTHOOD
Tieck, J. L. Fair Eckbert

The **knot-hole**. Fisher, D. F. C.

Kober, Arthur, 1900-
And I am the attorney for the plaintiff
Kobler, A. Oooh, what you said!
Certain people are gonna wake up and learn the score is too late
Kober, A. Oooh, what you said!
Don't let no cracked-pot lay his fishhooks on your chronium
Kober, A. Oooh, what you said!
Even the averitch incomepoop's got a little egg nest put away
Kober, A. Oooh, what you said!
Go be insulted when a fella hands you a compliment
Kober, A. Oooh, what you said!
Good-by to palship
Lewis, J. D. ed. Great stories about show business
A highly remockable chimpaneze with a head chuck-fulla grain matter
Kober, A. Oooh, what you said!
Honey, don't you mix, honey, you butt out
Kober, A. Oooh, what you said!
I wouldn't be your partner if you came beggin' me on your two bent knees
Kober, A. Oooh, what you said!
I'da never found out about it, essept came the accident
Kober, A. Oooh, what you said!
I'm not gonna cowtail to that bubble-headed bastid, if it's the last thing I do!
Kober, A. Oooh, what you said!
It'll be too late then. You just wait and see!
Kober, A. Oooh, what you said!
The lady and the fox
Kober, A. Oooh, what you said!
Music in the air
Schwarz, L. W. ed. Feast of Leviathan
Nobody can beat Freidkin's meats
Ribalow, H. U. ed. Treasury of American Jewish stories
One for the book
Kober, A. Oooh, what you said!

L

LABOR AND LABORING CLASSES
Bentley, P. E. "You see. . ."
Chekhov, A. P. My life: the story of a provincial
Dickens, C. Nobody's story
Franko, I. I. Borislav is laughing
Petrescu, C. They pay with their lives
Saroyan, W. Winter vineyard workers

LABOR DEMONSTRATIONS
Schiller, M. B. Now is the time

LABOR UNIONS. See Trade unions

LABORERS. See Labor and laboring classes

LADDERS
Sansom, W. Vertical ladder

Ladies in spring. Welty, E.

Ladies in the library. Vidal, G.

LADIES' MAIDS. See Servants—Maids

Ladies wild. Benchley, R. C.

The **lady.** Richter, C.

The **lady** and the fox. Kober, A.

The **lady** and the lash. Evarts, H. G.

The **lady** and the tom. Macken, W.

The **lady**-killer. O'Donovan, J.

Lady luck and the guardian angel. Davis, W. F.

Lady of my own. Seide, M.

Lady of the cornflowers. Sandoz, M. Y.

Lady of the lake. Malamud, B.

Lady on the grey. Collier, J.

Lady on the island. Kaylin, W.

The **lady**, or the tiger? Stockton, F. R.

Lady soloist. O'Donovan, J.

Lady who was a beggar. Feng, M.

Lady with the dog. Chekhov, A. P.

La Farge, Oliver, 1901-
All the young men
    Schaefer, J. W. ed. Out West
Bright faces
    La Farge, O. Pause in the desert
Brush of the wings
    La Farge, O. Pause in the desert
By the boys themselves
    La Farge, O. Pause in the desert
The bystander
    La Farge, O. Pause in the desert
Happy Indian laughter
    La Farge, O. Pause in the desert
John the revelator
    La Farge, O. Pause in the desert
Mr Skidmore's gift
    La Farge, O. Pause in the desert
Old Century's river
    La Farge, O. Pause in the desert
Old men's plans
    Meredith, S. ed. Bar 6
Pause in the desert
    La Farge, O. Pause in the desert
Prelude to reunion
    La Farge, O. Pause in the desert
Resting place
    Best American short stories, 1955
    La Farge, O. Pause in the desert

Runaway honeymoon
    Saturday evening post (Periodical) Saturday evening post stories, 1954
    Same as: To walk in the city streets
La spécialité de M Duclos
    La Farge, O. Pause in the desert
Spud and Cochise
    La Farge, O. Pause in the desert
Thick on the bay
    La Farge, O. Pause in the desert
To walk in the city streets
    La Farge, O. Pause in the desert
    Same as: Runaway honeymoon
Touch of greatness
    La Farge, O. Pause in the desert
Young warrior
    Meredith, S. ed. Bar 5

Laforet, Carmen
The return
    Flores, A. ed. Great Spanish stories

Lagerkvist, Pär Fabian, 1891-
Father and I
    Gettman, R. A. and Harkness, B. eds. Book of stories

Lagerlöf, Selma Ottiliana Lovisa, 1858-1940
General's ring
    Costain, T. B. and Beecroft, J. eds. Stories to remember
Holy night
    Lohan, R. ed. Christmas tales for reading aloud
Legend of the Christmas rose
    Lohan, R. ed. Christmas tales for reading aloud
Silver mine
    Sterner, L. G. ed. Favorite short stories

The **lake.** Bradbury, R.

LAKE MICHIGAN
Macauley, R. The invaders

LAKES
Aichinger, I. Ghosts on the lake

LaMar, Nathaniel
Creole love song
    Best American short stories, 1956

LAMAS
Hilton, J. Lost horizon

Lamb, Charles, 1775-1834
Roast pig
    Langford, W. F. ed. Book of better stories

Lambert, Janet
Tall as the stars
    Everygirls horse stories

Lamble, William B. 1908-
I couldn't understand
    American vanguard, 1956

LAMBS. See Sheep

The **lament.** Chekhov, A. P.

Lamentations. Gerchunoff, A.

Lamp of Alhazred. Lovecraft, H. P. and Derleth, A. W.

Lamp of God. Queen, E. pseud.

Lampman, Ben Hur, 1886-
Blinker was a good dog
    Oberfirst, R. ed. Anthology of best short-short stories v5

LAMPS
Lovecraft, H. P. and Derleth, A. W. Lamp of Alhazred

Lamptey, Jonas
Suspicion
World prize stories; 2d ser.

Lamson, David Albert
Oh, once in my saddle
Schaefer, J. W. ed. Out West

Lance, Long
Ghost horse
Skelton, P. ed. Animals all

Lance. Nabokov, V. V.

Land beyond the river. Stuart, J.

LAND SPECULATION
Garland, H. Under the lion's paw

LAND TENURE
Tolstoi, L. N. Graf. How much land does a man need?

LAND TITLES. See Land tenure

The **landing.** O'Flaherty, L.

Landing party. Marmur, J.

The **landlord.** Pritchett, V. S.

LANDLORD AND TENANT
Malamud, B. The mourners
Pritchett, V. S. The landlord
Stockton, F. R. Stephen Skarridge's Christmas

LANDSLIDES
Bennett, S. Jungle for sale

Lang, Don
Tramp, the sheep dog
Teen-age tales, bk 4

Langdon, John, 1913-
Blue serge suit
Best American short stories, 1957
Prize stories 1957: the O. Henry awards

Langelaan, George
The fly
Merril, J. ed. SF: '58

LANGUAGE AND LANGUAGES
Adams, A. Genuine blend of bluegrass and bourbon
Finney, J. Cousin Len's wonderful adjective cellar

Lanier, Sidney, 1842-1881
Soldier-poet in a Northern prison
Thorp, W. ed. Southern reader

Lapidus. Angoff, C.

LAPLAND
Wallenius, K. M. Bare land
Wallenius, K. M. Illep and the whale
Wallenius, K. M. Merciless and merciful sea
Wallenius, K. M. One-eyed wolf of Kaamas Fell
See also Arctic regions

Larchmoor is not the world. Cassill, R. V.

Lardner, Ring Wilmer, 1885-1933
Alibi Ike
Lardner, R. W. Best short stories of Ring Lardner
Schwed, P. and Wind, H. W. eds. Great stories from the world of sport
Anniversary
Lardner, R. W. Best short stories of Ring Lardner

A caddy's diary
Lardner, R. W. Best short stories of Ring Lardner
Champion
Lardner, R. W. Best short stories of Ring Lardner
Day with Conrad Green
Lardner, R. W. Best short stories of Ring Lardner
Ex parte
Lardner, R. W. Best short stories of Ring Lardner
Thurston, J. A. ed. Reading modern short stories
Golden honeymoon
Lardner, R. W. Best short stories of Ring Lardner
Haircut
Havighurst, W. and others, eds. Selection
Jennings, F. G. and Calitri, C. J. eds. Stories
Lardner, R. W. Best short stories of Ring Lardner
Harmony
Lardner, R. W. Best short stories of Ring Lardner
Horseshoes
Lardner, R. W. Best short stories of Ring Lardner
Nash, O. comp. I couldn't help laughing
Schwed, P. and Wind, R. W. eds. Great stories from the world of sport
Hurry Kane
Lardner, R. W. Best short stories of Ring Lardner
I can't breathe
Lardner, R. W. Best short stories of Ring Lardner
Liberty Hall
Lardner, R. W. Best short stories of Ring Lardner
Lewis, J. D. ed. Great stories about show business
Love nest
Lardner, R. W. Best short stories of Ring Lardner
Maysville minstrell
Lardner, R. W. Best short stories of Ring Lardner
Mr and Mrs Fix-it
Lardner, R. W. Best short stories of Ring Lardner
Mr Frisbie
Lardner, R. W. Best short stories of Ring Lardner
My roomy
Lardner, R. W. Best short stories of Ring Lardner
Old folks' Christmas
Fremantle, A. J. ed. Christmas is here
Lardner, R. W. Best short stories of Ring Lardner
Reunion
Lardner, R. W. Best short stories of Ring Lardner
Some like them cold
Lardner, R. W. Best short stories of Ring Lardner
Saturday evening post (Periodical) Saturday evening post Carnival of humor
Thurston, J. A. ed. Reading modern short stories

Lardner, Ring W.—_Continued_
  There are smiles
    Lardner, R. W. Best short stories of
    Ring Lardner
  Travelogue
    Lardner, R. W. Best short stories of
    Ring Lardner
  Who dealt?
    Baudin, M. ed. Contemporary short sto-
    ries v 1
    Lardner, R. W. Best short stories of
    Ring Lardner
  Zone of quiet
    Blaustein, P. M. and Blaustein, A. P.
    eds. Doctors' choice
    Lardner, R. W. Best short stories of
    Ring Lardner
Last anniversary. Caldwell, E.
Last asset. Wharton, E. N. J.
Last barrier. Miller, E. M.
Last blast of the trumpet. Clayton, J. B.
Last blow. Cohen, O. R.
Last bullet. Kantor, M.
Last chance. Van Loan, C. E.
Last Christmas. Raymund, B.
Last class. Daudet, A.
Last dark step. Manners, M.
Last day. Verga, G.
Last day in Paris. Raphaelson, S.
Last day of summer. Tubb, E. C.
Last dream of the old oak tree. Andersen,
  H. C.
Last five percent. Gilmore, L. H.
Last hurdle. Olgin, J.
Last husky. Mowat, F.
LAST JUDGEMENT. See Judgement day
The last laugh. Peyton, A. H.
Last leaf. Porter, K. A.
Last man alive. Rice, C.
The last Mohican. Malamud, B.
Last night the rain. Beaumont, C.
The last notch. MacDonald, D. B.
Last of Chéri. Colette, S. G.
The last of the flatfeet. Connell, R. E.
Last of the Ledyards. Rutledge, A. H.
Last pool. O'Brian, P.
Last present. Stanton, W.
Last prophet. Clingerman, M.
Last ride. Sansom, W.
The last rodeo. Haycox, E.
Last signal. Broun, H. C.
Last spin. Hunter, E.
Last stand in the Warsaw ghetto. Edel-
  man, M.
Last swimming event. Lavrenev, B. A.
Last tag. Marsh, W. N.
Last thunder song. Neihardt, J. G.
Last trump. Asimov, I.
Last victory. Godwin, T.
Last will and testament. Russell, R.
Last word. Oliver, C. and Beaumont, C.
Last word. Sansom, W.

Late encounter with the enemy. O'Connor,
  F.
The late Mr. Adams. Allen, S.
Latham, Philip, pseud. See Richardson,
  Robert Shirley
LATIN LANGUAGE
  Maupassant, G. de. Question of Latin
LATVIA
Folklore
    See Legends and folk tales—Latvia
Laugh it off. Armstrong, C.
Laughing at the dead. Kan, K.
The laughing death. Johnson, N.
LAUGHTER
  Ruhen, O. Sword of laughter
The launch. Aub, M.
Laura. Brodkey, H.
Laurie dressing. Brodkey, H.
Lavender evening dress. Carmer, C. L.
Lavin, Mary, 1912-
  Story of the widow's son
    Garrity, D. A. ed. 44 Irish short stories
  Wet day
    O'Donovan, M. ed. Modern Irish short
    stories
  The will
    O'Donovan, M. ed. Modern Irish short
    stories
Lavrenev, Boris Andreevich, 1894-
  Last swimming event
    Loaf sugar, and other Soviet stories
The law. Coates, R. M.
LAW AND LAWYERS
  Angoff, C. Natalie and John
  Caldwell, E. Shooting of Judge Price
  Campbell, W. E. M. Cinderella's slipper
  Chute, B. J. Q for quitclaim
  Coates, R. M. The law
  Flanagan, T. This will do nicely
  Gombrowicz, W. Premeditated crime
  Harte, B. Colonel Starbottle for the plain-
    tiff
  Hawkins, J. and Hawkins, W. Cop with-
    out a badge
  Johnson, W. R. The night the stair
    creaked
  Kober, A. And I am the attorney for the
    plaintiff
  La Farge, O. Brush of the wings
  La Farge, O. La spécialité de M Duclos
  McLaren, M. Checkmate
  Macrae, S. Serpent versus Donovan
  Masur, H. Q. $2,000,000 defense
  Maupassant, G. de. A madman
  Melville, H. Bartleby the scrivener
  O'Donovan, M. Legal aid
  O'Faoláin, S. Old master
  Phillips, B. M. The debtor
  Polk, W. T. Coralee's burden-bearer
  Polk, W. T. Telegram from Wanda
  Slesar, H. Day of the execution
  Soldati, M. Nora
  Train, A. C. The bloodhound
  Van Doren, M. Madam X and Madam Y
  Yellen, S. Stoneville Pike
Law and the gun. Fowler, K.
Law belongs to every man. Schleyen, M.
Law-breaker. Mankowitz, W.

LAW CLERKS. See Law and lawyers

LAWN TENNIS. See Tennis

Lawrence, David Herbert, 1885-1930
Man who loved islands
Thurston, J. A. ed. Reading modern short stories
Odor of chrysanthemums
Havighurst, W. ed. Masters of the modern short story
Odour of chrysanthemums
Gettman, R. A. and Harkness, B. eds. Book of stories
Rex
Great dog stories
Rocking-horse winner
Havighurst, W. and others, eds. Selection
Jennings, F. G. and Calitri, C. J. eds. Stories
McClennen, J. comp. Masters and masterpieces of the short story
Samson and Delilah
Jarrell, R. ed. Anchor book of stories
Two blue birds
Locke, L. G.; Gibson, W. M. and Arms, G. W. eds. Introduction to literature
Wintry peacock
Hall, J. B. and Langland, J. T. eds. Short story

Lawrence, Hilda
Roof in Manhattan
Mystery Writers of America, inc. For love or money

LAWYERS. See Law and lawyers

LAY PREACHERS. See Clergy

Layover in El Paso. Lowry, R. J. C.

Lazy-bones. McCormack, N.

Lazy tour of two idle apprentices. Dickens, C.

Leach, Fairall Howard
Surprise visit
Oberfirst, R. ed. Anthology of best short-short stories v6

Leacock, Stephen, 1869-1944
Errors of Santa Claus
Posselt, E. ed. A merry, merry Christmas book
My financial career
Nash, O. comp. I couldn't help laughing
Speculations of Jefferson Thorpe
Nelson, G. E. ed. Cavalcade of the North

Lead me home. Fonger, H.

Leader of the community. Angoff, C.

Leader of the people. Steinbeck, J.

Lean years. Chavez, A.

Leaning rock. Sandoz, M. Y.

Leaping trout. Gallagher, F.

Learn to say good-by. West, J.

Leather jacket. Pavese, C.

Leather pushers. Witwer, H. C.

LEAVE-TAKINGS
Boyle, K. Canals of Mars
O'Flaherty, L. Going into exile
O'Flaherty, L. The parting

The **leavetaking.** Lesiņš, K.

LEBANON
Samuel, E. H. Bribery and corruption

Lecture in Dodge City. Adams, A.

LECTURERS. See Lectures and lecturing

LECTURES AND LECTURING
Adams, A. Lecture in Dodge City

Lederer, William Julius, 1912- **and Burdick, Eugene L.** 1918-
Ambassador and the working press
Lederer, W. J. and Burdick, E. L. The ugly American
Bent backs of Chang 'Dong
Lederer, W. J. and Burdick, E. L. The ugly American
Captain Boning, USN
Lederer, W. J. and Burdick, E. L. The ugly American
Employment opportunities abroad
Lederer, W. J. and Burdick, E. L. The ugly American
Everyone has ears
Lederer, W. J. and Burdick, E. L. The ugly American
Everybody loves Joe Bing
Lederer, W. J. and Burdick, E. L. The ugly American
Girl who got recruited
Lederer, W. J. and Burdick, E. L. The ugly American
How to buy an American junior grade
Lederer, W. J. and Burdick, E. L. The ugly American
The iron of war
Lederer, W. J. and Burdick, E. L. The ugly American
Lessons of war
Lederer, W. J. and Burdick, E. L. The ugly American
Lucky, Lucky Lou #1
Lederer, W. J. and Burdick, E. L. The ugly American
Lucky, Lucky Lou #2
Lederer, W. J. and Burdick, E. L. The ugly American
Nine friends
Lederer, W. J. and Burdick, E. L. The ugly American
Ragtime Kid
Lederer, W. J. and Burdick, E. L. The ugly American
Senator Sir
Lederer, W. J. and Burdick, E. L. The ugly American
Six-foot swami from Savannah
Lederer, W. J. and Burdick, E. L. The ugly American
The sum of tiny things
Lederer, W. J. and Burdick, E. L. The ugly American
The ugly American
Lederer, W. J. and Burdick, E. L. The ugly American
The ugly American and the ugly Sarkhanese
Lederer, W. J. and Burdick, E. L. The ugly American
What would you do if you were president?
Lederer, W. J. and Burdick, E. L. The ugly American

Lee, C. Y. See Li, Chin-yang

Lee, Raymond J. 1910-
Moth and the star
New voices 2: American writing today
Le Fanu, Joseph Sheridan, 1814-1873
Narrative of the ghost of a hand
Ridler, A. B. comp. Best ghost stories
Sir Dominick's bargain
Davenport, B. ed. Deals with the devil
Lefley, Robert, 1927-
The accident
New voices 2: American writing today
Cry of the nightingale
American vanguard, 1956
Left-handed Texan. Miller, E. M.

LEG, ARTIFICIAL. See Artificial limbs

LEGACIES. See Inheritance and succession; Wills

The **legacy.** Chute, B. J.

The **legacy.** Gallant, M.

The **legacy.** Maupassant, G. de

Legal aid. O'Donovan, M.

LEGAL TENDER. See Money

LEGATIONS. See Diplomatic life

Legend in the dust. Evarts, H. G.

Legend of good men. Coleman, W. L.

Legend of Mont-Saint-Michel. Maupassant, G. de

Legend of Poldevia. Aymé, M.

Legend of Sleepy Hollow. Irving, W.

Legend of the Arabian astrologer. Irving, W.

Legend of the Christmas rose. Lagerlöf, S. O. L.

Legend of the Christmas tree. Moore, C. C.

Legend of the Moor's legacy. Irving, W.

Legend of three and four. Bialik, H. N.

Legend of two swimmers. Macauley, R.

LEGENDS, JEWISH. See Legends and folk tales—Hebrew

LEGENDS AND FOLK TALES
Andersen, H. C. Fir tree
Andersen, H. C. Little match girl
Andersen, H. C. What the old man does is always right
Hawthorne, N. Great carbuncle
Lagerlöf, S. O. L. Holy night
Moore, C. C. Legend of the Christmas tree
Moore, C. C. Noel candle
O'Faoláin, S. End of the record
Red King and the witch
Sharp, W. St Bride of the Isles
See also Fables; Fantasies

Arabia
Arabian nights. Barber's tale of his fifth brother
Arabian nights. Barmecide feast
Arabian nights. Sinbad the Sailor's third voyage
Saroyan, W. Shepherd's daughter

China
Feng, M. Fairy's rescue

Denmark
See Legends and folk tales—Scandinavia

France
Maupassant, G. de. Legend of Mont-Saint-Michel

Hebrew
Bialik, H. N. Legend of three and four
Bin Gorion, M. J. Akiba story
Bin Gorion, M. J. Golem of Prague
Bin Gorion, M. J. Tales of demons and dervishes
Joseph Zabara. Clever girl
Koteliansky, S. S. Little man in the jar
Peretz, I. L. Seven good years
Singer, I. B. Gentleman from Cracow
Singer, I. B. Wife killer

Iceland
See Legends and folk tales—Scandinavia

Ireland
Countess Kathleen O'Shea
MacManus, S. Tinker of Tamlacht

Latvia
Lesinš, K. Wine of eternity

Norway
See Legends and folk tales—Scandinavia

North Carolina
Rutledge, A. H. Was he Marshal Ney?

Russia
Tolstoǐ, L. N. Graf. The Devil's persistent, but God is resistant
Tolstoǐ, L. N. Graf. How much land does a man need?
Tolstoǐ, L. N. Graf. Skazka
Tolstoǐ, L. N. Graf. Story of Yemilyan and the empty drum
Tolstoǐ, L. N. Graf. Three hermits

Scandinavia
Andersen, H. C. Emperor's new clothes
Andersen, H. C. Last dream of the old oak tree
Lagerlöf, S. O. L. Legend of the Christmas rose

South Carolina
Rutledge, A. The standing tomb

Spain
Irving, W. Legend of the Arabian astrologer

Sweden
See Legends and folk tales—Scandinavia

United States
Randolph, V. Three wishes

LEGION OF HONOR. See Decorations of honor

LEGITIMACY. See Illegitimacy

Lehmann, Rosamond, 1903-
Dream of winter
Hudson, D. ed. Modern English short stories; 2d ser.
A hut, a sea-grape tree
Winter's tales, 2

Leiber, Fritz, 1910-
The big trek
Magazine of fantasy and science fiction.
.Best from Fantasy and science fic-
tion; 7th ser.
Time in the round
Galaxy science fiction magazine. Third
Galaxy reader
Leigh, James, 1930-
The adventurers: a reminiscence
Miller, N. ed. New campus writing,
no. 2
The visitors
Miller, N. ed. New campus writing,
no. 2
Leila. Samuel, E. H.
Leiningen versus the ants. Stephenson, C.
Leinster, Murray, pseud. See Jenkins, Wil-
liam Fitzgerald
Leipzig. Stiles, B.
Le May, Alan, 1899-
Ghost at his shoulder
Lewis, I. D. ed. Dealer's choice
LEMMINGS
Clarke, A. C. The possessed
The lemon. O'Brian, P.
The lemon. Thomas, D.
Lemonnier, Camille, 1844-1913
Fleur-de-Blé
Fremantle, A. J. ed. Christmas is here
LENINGRAD. See Russia—Leningrad
Leonard, Elmore, 1925-
Hard way
Western Writers of America. Branded
West
Rancher's lady
Western Writers of America. Wild
streets
Leonard, Nancy H.
Rich
Stanford short stories, 1954
LEOPARDS
Dessauer, P. Great leopard hunt
LEPERS. See Leprosy
LEPRECHAUNS. See Fairies
LEPROSY
Rinehart, M. R. The secret
Lernet-Holenia, Alexander Maria, 1897-
Three wise men of Totenleben
Fremantle, A. J. ed. Christmas is here
Leroi, F. Jean
Regeneration of Thomas Larkin
Oberfirst, R. ed. Anthology of best
short-short stories v6
LESBIANISM
Coleman, W. L. Bird of paradise
Hadow, L. Freedom for Laura
O'Donovan, J. Johnnie
Lesinš, Knuts
Bek
Lesinš, K. Wine of eternity
Corda
Lesinš, K. Wine of eternity
Delicate mission
Lesinš, K. Wine of eternity
The dove
Lesinš, K. Wine of eternity

Fiery descent of old Koris
Lesinš, K. Wine of eternity
In the blizzard
Lesinš, K. Wine of eternity
The leavetaking
Lesinš, K. Wine of eternity
Lover's letter
Lesinš, K. Wine of eternity
One-day land
Lesinš, K. Wine of eternity
The secret
Lesinš, K. Wine of eternity
Siljonis' jewel
Lesinš, K. Wine of eternity
String of beads
Lesinš, K. Wine of eternity
Tailor and the wolves
Lesinš, K. Wine of eternity
Toys
Lesinš, K. Wine of eternity
Wine of eternity
Lesinš, K. Wine of eternity
Leskov, Nikolaĭ Semenovich, 1831-1895
Clothes mender
Fremantle, A. J. ed. Christmas is here
Les's widow's household. Franko, I. I.
Lessing, Bruno, pseud. See Block, Rudolph
Edgar
Lessing, Doris May, 1919-
Black Madonna
Winter's tales, 3
Day Stalin died
Lessing, D. M. Habit of loving
Eye of God in paradise
Lessing, D. M. Habit of loving
Flavors of exile
Lessing, D. M. Habit of loving
Flight
Lessing, D. M. Habit of loving
Getting off the altitude
Lessing, D. M. Habit of loving
Habit of loving
Lessing, D. M. Habit of loving
He
Lessing, D. M. Habit of loving
Lucy Grange
Lessing, D. M. Habit of loving
Mild attack of locusts
Lessing, D. M. Habit of loving
Plants and girls
Lessing, D. M. Habit of loving
Pleasure
Lessing, D. M. Habit of loving
Road to the big city
Lessing, D. M. Habit of loving
Through the tunnel
Lessing, D. M. Habit of loving
Wine
Lessing, D. M. Habit of loving
The witness
Lessing, D. M. Habit of loving
The woman
Lessing, D. M. Habit of loving
Words he said
Lessing, D. M. Habit of loving
The lesson. West, J.
Lesson of the Master. James, H.
Lessons of war. Lederer, W. J. and Bur-
dick, E. L.
Let her kill herself. King, R.

Lewis, Sinclair, 1885-1951
  Let's play king
    Lewis, J. D. ed. Great stories about
    show business
  Young Man Axelbrod
    Baudin, M. ed. Contemporary short
    stories v2

Lewisohn, Ludwig, 1882-1955
  Writ of divorcement
    Ribalow, H. U. ed. Treasury of Ameri-
    can Jewish stories

Leyson, Burr Watkins, 1898-
  What it takes
    Fenner, P. R. ed. Heroes, heroes,
    heroes

Li, Chin-yang, 1917-
  Mr Weng's last forbidden dollar
    Oberfirst, R. ed. Anthology of best
    short-short stories v5

Li Fu-yen, fl. 9th century
  Man who became a fish
    Rosenblum, M. ed. Stories from many
    lands

Liang, Cecelia, 1934-
  Firecrackers
    Miller, N. ed. New campus writing,
    no. 2

The liar. Faulkner, W.

The liberation. Stafford, J.

Liberman, M. M. 1922-
  Big Buick to the pyramids
    Prize stories 1957: the O. Henry awards

LIBERTY
  Benét, S. V. Freedom's a hard-bought
    thing
  Campbell, W. E. M. This heavy load
  Sheckley, R. Citizen in space

LIBERTY, STATUE OF. See Statue of
  Liberty, New York

Liberty Hall. Lardner, R. W.

LIBERTY OF THE PRESS
  Clayton, J. B. Incident at Chapman's
    Switch

LIBRARIANS
  Brown, G. A. Come back with me
  Derleth, A. W. Sandwin compact
  Frank, H. Girl with the glow
  Lesiñs, K. Delicate mission
  Plunkett, J. Eagles and the trumpets

LIBRARIES
  Cheever, J. Trouble of Marcie Flint
  Enright, E. Quarter-deck shell

LIES. See Truthfulness and falsehood

LIEUTENANTS. See United States. Army
  —Officers; United States. Navy—
  Officers

LIFE
  Saroyan, W. Home of the human race

LIFE (PHILOSOPHY OF LIFE)
  Hale, N. The growth
  Nabokov, V. V. Lance

LIFE, CHRISTIAN. See Christian life

LIFE, FUTURE. See Future life

Life. O'Flaherty, L.

Life adventurous. Farrell, J. T.

Life and adventures of Matthew Pavlichenko. Babel', I. E.

LIFE GUARDS. See Lifesaving

Life in art. Mankowitz, W.

Life is like that. McMillan, G.

Life of Our Lord. Dickens, C.

Life of the sleeping beauty. Cassill, R. V.

LIFE ON OTHER PLANETS
  Asimov, I. Living space
  Blish, J. Case of conscience
  Brown, F. Placet is a crazy place
  Chandler, A. B. The cage
  Clarke, A. C. Walk in the dark
  Cogswell, T. R. Limiting factor
  Davidson, A. Help! I am Dr Morris
    Goldpepper
  Elam, R. M. Flight of the Centaurus
  Geier, C. S. Environment
  Knight, D. Four in one
  Knight, D. Man in the jar
  Kuttner, H. Gift of gab
  McDowell, W. Veiled island
  Oliver, C. Between the thunder and the
    sun
  Oliver, C. Night
  Oliver, C. Rite of passage
  Oliver, C. Scientific method
  Russell, E. F. Present from Joe
  Shaara, M. Grenville's planet
  Sheckley, R. Mountain without a name
  Sheckley, R. Skulking permit
  Sheckley, R. Ticket to Tranai

LIFE-SAVING. See Lifesaving

Life you save may be your own. O'Connor,
  F.

LIFESAVING
  Macauley, R. Legend of two swimmers

A lifetime. Reid, L.

LIGHT
  Richardson, R. S. Xi effect

LIGHT HOUSES. See Lighthouses

Light tackle. Wylie, P.

Light touch. Ferber, E.

LIGHTHOUSES
  Bradbury, R. The foghorn

Like a motherless child. Berriault, G.

Like Count Palmieri. White, W. A. P.

Lila. Lochridge, B. H.

Lilith, stay away from the door. Stolper,
  B. J. R.

Lily Daw and the three ladies. Welty, E.

LIMA. See Peru—Lima

LIMBS, ARTIFICIAL. See Artificial limbs

LIME-KILNS
  Hawthorne, N. Ethan Brand

Limiting factor. Cogswell, T. R.

Limp-paged album. Sandoz, M. Y.

Linaria. Bontempelli, M.

LINCOLN, ABRAHAM, PRESIDENT
  U.S. 1809-1865
  Bailey, B. and Walworth, D. He loved me
    truly
  Sandburg, C. Lincoln speaks at Gettys-
    burg
  Singmaster, E. The battleground

LINCOLN, SARAH (BUSH) JOHN-
  STON, d. 1869
  Bailey, B. and Walworth, D. He loved
    me truly

Little willow. Towers, F.
Little women's Christmas. Alcott, L. M.
Little Woodrow. Clayton, J. B.
Littlest people. Banks, R. E.
Litwak, Leo
　Making of a clerk
　　Prize stories, 1958: the O. Henry awards
Live birds and insects. Colette, S. G.
Lively friend. Maupassant, G. de
Living space. Asimov, I.
Livingston, Thomas M.
　A show of strength
　　Miller, N. ed. New campus writing, no. 2
Livvie. Welty, E.
Livvie is back. Welty, E.
The lizard died, too. Atherton, V.
LIZARDS
　Williams, T. Night of the Iguana
Lizards, frog, and grasshopper. Colette, S. G.
Llewellyn, Richard
　Now hear the cattle
　　Schwed, P. and Wind, H. W. eds. Great stories from the world of sport
Loaf of bread. Roussakis, I.
Loaf sugar. Paustovsky, K.
The loan. Malamud, B.
LOANS
　Thurman, R. Y. Credit line
　Malamud, B. The loan
LOANS, PERSONAL. See Money-lenders
El Lobo's sweetheart. Adams, A.
Local boy makes good, Moore, J. C.
Lochridge, Betsy (Hopkins)
　Birdie Keller
　　Lochridge, B. H. Blue river
　Callie Daniel
　　Lochridge, B. H. Blue river
　Claudie
　　Lochridge, B. H. Blue river
　Death
　　Lochridge, B. H. Blue river
　Dr Borosky
　　Lochridge, B. H. Blue river
　Foots
　　Lochridge, B. H. Blue river
　Harvey Riddle
　　Lochridge, B. H. Blue river
　Hattie
　　Lochridge, B. H. Blue river
　Hilary Arnold
　　Lochridge, B. H. Blue river
　Ida Sims
　　Lochridge, B. H. Blue river
　Lila
　　Lochridge, B. H. Blue river
　Mary Kiser
　　Lochridge, B. H. Blue river
　Samuel Green
　　Lochridge, B. H. Blue river
　Sarah Brooke
　　Lochridge, B. H. Blue river
　The town
　　Lochridge, B. H. Blue river
　Will Davis
　　Lochridge, B. H. Blue river

The lock. Maupassant, G. de
Locke, William John, 1863-1930
　Christmas mystery
　　Lohan, R. ed. Christmas tales for reading aloud
LOCKOUTS. See Strikes and lockouts
Lockridge, Frances Louise (Davis) and Lockridge, Richard, 1898-
　Death on a foggy morning
　　This week magazine. This week's Stories of mystery and suspense
Lockridge, Richard, 1898- See Lockridge, F. L. D. jt. auth.
LOCKS AND KEYS
　Malamud, B. Behold the key
LOCUSTS
　Gerchunoff, A. Plundered orchard
　Lessing, D. M. Mild attack of locusts
LODGING HOUSES. See Boarding houses
Lofts, Norah (Robinson) 1904-
　All that is necessary
　　Lofts, N. R. Heaven in your hand
　Black Christ of Adlerwald
　　Lofts, N. R. Heaven in your hand
　But I've had everything
　　Lofts, N. R. Heaven in your hand
　Day's journey
　　Lofts, N. R. Heaven in your hand
　Father Francisco's ointment
　　Lofts, N. R. Heaven in your hand
　Forty years on
　　Lofts, N. R. Heaven in your hand
　Gift for a queen
　　Lofts, N. R. Heaven in your hand
　Going downhill together
　　Lofts, N. R. Heaven in your hand
　Good memory
　　Lofts, N. R. Heaven in your hand
　The happy Christmas
　　Lofts, N. R. Heaven in your hand
　Heaven in your hand
　　Lofts, N. R. Heaven in your hand
　Portrait of a mother
　　Lofts, N. R. Heaven in your hand
　Rapunzel, Rapunzel, bind up your hair!
　　Lofts, N. R. Heaven in your hand
　The spellbinders
　　Lofts, N. R. Heaven in your hand
　Vergine con bambino
　　Lofts, N. R. Heaven in your hand
　White man
　　Lofts, N. R. Heaven in your hand
The log. Maupassant, G. de
LOG CABINS
　Smith, E. W. Escape to reality
　Smith, E. W. Woodsmoke from old cabins
Logan, Ben T.
　Not like in the movies
　　Furman, A. L. ed. Everygirls sports stories
　Time is out of the whiskey glass
　　Oberfirst, R. ed. Anthology of best short-short stories v6
LOGGERS. See Lumber industry
LOGGING. See Lumber industry
Lombard books. Stewart, J. I. M.
London, Dale H. 1907-
　The gun
　　Oberfirst, R. ed. Anthology of best short-short stories v6

Luck of Roaring Camp. Harte, B.
Luckiest man in the world. Sheckley, R.
Lucky break. Kirkbride, C.
Lucky burglar. Maupassant, G. de
Lucky day. Parkinson, E. M.
Lucky goes fishing. Halacy, D. S.
Lucky, Lucky Lou #1. Lederer, W. J. and Burdick, E. L.
Lucky, Lucky Lou #2. Lederer, W. J. and Burdick, E. L.
Lucky touch. Olgin, J.
Lucy Grange. Lessing, D. M.
Lula Borrow. Marby, T. D.
Lull, Roderick, 1907?-
  Footnote to American history
    Meredith, S. ed. Bar 6
LUMBER INDUSTRY
  Pridgen, T. Eighteen oak ties
LUMBERING. See Lumber industry
LUNACY. See Insanity
LUNATIC ASYLUMS. See Insane hospitals
Lunch hour: 1923. Farrell, J. T.
LUNCHEONS. See Dinners
LUNCHROOMS. See Restaurants, lunchrooms, etc.
La **Lupa.** Verga, G.
Lyberaki, Margarita
  The other Alexander
    New directions 15
LYING. See Truthfulness and falsehood
Lying in the sun. O'Brian, P.
Lynch, John A. 1922-
  The knife
    Hughes, R. ed. All manner of men
Lynch mob at Cimarron Crossing. Thompson, T.
LYNCHING
  Dreiser, T. Nigger Jeff
    See also Hanging; Murder stories
Lynds, Dennis, 1924-
  Just once more
    New voices 2: American writing today
LYNX
  Barker, E. My dogs has what it takes
Lyon, Dana. See Lyon, Mabel Dana
Lyon, Mabel Dana, 1897-
  Impossible murder
    Mystery Writers of America, inc. For tomorrow we die
Lyons, Augusta Wallace
  First flower
    Best American short stories, 1956
Lysenko maze. Grinnell, D. pseud.
Lytle, Andrew Nelson, 1902-
  Alchemy
    Lytle, A. N. A novel, a novella and four stories
  The guide
    Hall, J. B. and Langland, J. T. eds. Short story
  Jericho, Jericho, Jericho
    Lytle, A. N. A novel, a novella and four stories

Mahogany frame
    Lytle, A. N. A novel, a novella and four stories
  Mr MacGregor
    Lytle, A. N. A novel, a novella and four stories
  Ortiz's Mass
    Lytle, A. N. A novel, a novella and four stories
Lyubka the Cossack. Babel', I. E.

M

M. Belhomme's beast. Maupassant, G. de
M-yes! Beliavsky, P. and Raspevin, A.
MS. found in a Chinese fortune cookie. Kornbluth, C. M.
MA CHOU
  Feng, M. Wine and dumplings
Ma Ku's dying. Thompson, K. M.
Mabry, Thomas Dabney
  Indian feather
    First-prize stories, 1919-1957
Mac loved Mr. Kelly. Tekeyan, C.
Macauley, Robie, 1919-
  Academic style
    Macauley, R. End of pity, and other stories
  Chevigny man
    Macauley, R. End of pity, and other stories
    Prize stories, 1956: the O. Henry awards
  End of pity
    Macauley, R. End of pity, and other stories
  Guide to the Muniment Room
    Macauley, R. End of pity, and other stories
  The invaders
    Macauley, R. End of pity, and other stories
  Legend of two swimmers
    Best American short stories, 1958
    Macauley, R. End of pity, and other stories
  The mind is its own place
    Macauley, R. End of pity, and other stories
  Nest of gentlefolk
    Macauley, R. End of pity, and other stories
  Thin voice
    Macauley, R. End of pity, and other stories
  Windfall
    Macauley, R. End of pity, and other stories
  The wishbone
    Macauley, R. End of pity, and other stories
MACAWS. See Parrots
Macbeth murder mystery. Thurber, J.
McCafferty, Verna
  Old lady's whim
    Oberfirst, R. ed. Anthology of best short-short stories v6

MacLean, Katherine
Pictures don't lie
Montgomery, R. B. ed. Best SF
MacLeish, Roderick, 1926-
Night of disaster
Saturday evening post (Periodical) Saturday evening post stories, 1956
MacLellan, Robert
The mennans
Urquhart, F. ed. Scottish short stories
Macleod, Fiona, pseud. See Sharp, William
McLeod's ordeal. Blake, A.
MacMahon, Bryan, 1909-
Broken lyre
MacMahon, B. Red petticoat, and other stories
Candle is lighting
MacMahon, B. Red petticoat, and other stories
The cat and the cornfield
Garrity, D. A. ed. 44 Irish short stories
MacMahon, B. Red petticoat, and other stories
Chicken-Licken
MacMahon, B. Red petticoat, and other stories
Close to the clay
MacMahon, B. Red petticoat, and other stories
Evening in Ireland
MacMahon, B. Red petticoat, and other stories
Exile's return
MacMahon, B. Red petticoat, and other stories
O'Donovan, M. ed. Modern Irish short stories
Foxy-haired lad
MacMahon, B. Red petticoat, and other stories
King of the bees
MacMahon, B. Red petticoat, and other stories
Kings asleep in the ground
MacMahon, B. Red petticoat, and other stories
Nunnery garden
MacMahon, B. Red petticoat, and other stories
O, lonely moon!
MacMahon, B. Red petticoat, and other stories
Plain people of England
Garrity, D. A. ed. 44 Irish short stories
Red petticoat
MacMahon, B. Red petticoat, and other stories
"So early in the morning, O!"
MacMahon, B. Red petticoat, and other stories
Sound of the bell
MacMahon, B. Red petticoat, and other stories
Sunday afternoon. Sunny
MacMahon, B. Red petticoat, and other stories
Wedding eve
MacMahon, B. Red petticoat, and other stories

White blackbird
MacMahon, B. Red petticoat, and other stories
Winter's tales, 1
Windows of wonder
MacMahon, B. Red petticoat, and other stories
The world is lovely and the world is wide
MacMahon, B. Red petticoat, and other stories
MacManus, Seumas, 1869-
Tinker of Tamlacht
Davenport, B. ed. Deals with the devil
McMillan, Gene
Life is like that
Teen-age tales, bk 4
McMullen, James Abney, 1909-
Bill sells a "bill of goods"
McMullen, J. A. Old Pro, and four other stories
Dog in my life
McMullen, J. A. Old Pro, and four other stories
Old Pro
McMullen, J. A. Old Pro, and four other stories
Sam dreams a dream
McMullen, J. A. Old Pro, and four other stories
Sampson and the blue "Delilahs"
McMullen, J. A. Old Pro, and four other stories
McNeil, Steve
Old enough to drive
Saturday evening post (Periodical) Saturday evening post stories, 1955
Teen-age tales, bk 4
McNeile, Herman Cyril, 1888-1937
Man in ratcatcher
Welcome, J. and Orchard, V. eds. Best hunting stories
McNeill, Janet
Specs and the cuckoo clock
Buckeridge, A. comp. In and out of school
Mac's masterpiece. O'Donovan, M.
Mad? Maupassant, G. de
Mad about motors. Neola, pseud.
Mad tea-party. Carroll, L. pseud.
Mad tea-party. Queen, E. pseud.
Mad woman. See Maupassant, G. de. Madwoman
Madam who saved the state. Polk, W. T.
Madam X and Madam Y. Van Doren, M.
Madame Baptiste. Maupassant, G. de
Madame Hermet. Maupassant, G. de
Madame Parisse. Maupassant, G. de
Madame Parpillon's inn. Devaulx, N.
Madame Tellier's establishment. Maupassant, G. de
Madden, Harry T.
Date with a stranger
Saturday evening post (Periodical) Saturday evening post stories, 1954

Maddux, Rachel, 1913-
Final clearance
Magazine of fantasy and science fiction.
Best from Fantasy and science fiction;
6th ser.

Mademoiselle Fifi. Maupassant, G. de

Mademoiselle O. Nabokov, V. V.

Mademoiselle Pearl. Maupassant, G. de

A **madman.** Maupassant, G. de

Madman's chain. Wright, G.

Madmen's Congress. Papini, G.

MADNESS. See Insanity

Madness of Doctor Montarco. Unamuno y
Jugo, M. de

Madonna of the future. James, H.

MADRID. See Spain—Madrid

The **madwoman.** Maupassant, G. de

Maeterlinck, Maurice, 1862-1949
Foundation of the city
Skelton, P. ed. Animals all

Maggie Meriwether's rich experience. Stafford, J.

MAGIC
Gordon, A. The spell
Hirai, T. The traveler with the pasted
rag picture
Lovecraft, H. P. and Derleth, A. W. The
survivor
MacMahon, B. Close to the clay
Mann, T. Mario and the magician
O'Donovan, J. Black magic
Peretz, I. L. The magician
Stewart, J. I. M. Enigma Jones
See also Conjuring

Magic. Porter, K. A.

Magic barrel. Malamud, B.

Magic night. Howland, R.

The **magician.** Peretz, I. L.

MAGICIANS. See Conjuring; Magic

MAGISTRATES. See Law and lawyers

Magnetism. Maupassant, G. de

Magnifying glass. Clark, A. A. G.

Maguire, R. A.
Reprieve
Pudney, J. ed. Pick of today's short
stories, 9

Mahogany frame. Lytle, A. N.

MAHOMMEDANS. See Mohammedans

Maiden in a tower. Stegner, W. E.

Maiden, maiden. Boyle, K.

MAIDS. See Servants—Maids

Maigret's Christmas. Simenon, G.

MAIL CARRIERS. See Postal service

The **mail** carrier's rock garden. Cooper, G.

Mail for Juniper Hill. Brennan, J. P.

MAILBOXES
Beigel, U. Letterboxes ought to be yellow

Mailer, Norman Kingsley, 1923-
Paper house
Fenton, C. A. ed. Best short stories of
World War II
Prologue: the man who studied Yoga
New short novels, 2

Main currents of American thought. Shaw,
I.

Main road. Pritchett, V. S.

MAINE
Smith, E. W. An angler comes to life
Smith, E. W. Axe on Slumber Lake
Smith, E. W. Escape to reality
Smith, E. W. Gates ajar
Smith, E. W. Men, women and wilderness
Smith, E. W. Most-remembered pools
Smith, E. W. Rum over the dam
Smith, E. W. Specific gravity of Jeff
Coongate
Smith, E. W. Woodsmoke from old cabins

20th century
Rawlings, C. A. Young man on his own

Country life
See Country life—Maine

Mainly about shoes. Wodehouse, P. G.

Majesty of the law. O'Donovan, M.

Major, Ralph H.
Climbing against death
Teen-age tales, bk 5

Major Alshuster. Boyle, K.

Major engagement in Paris. Boyle, K.

Maker of coffins. Bates, H. E.

Making a convert. Maupassant, G. de

Making of a clerk. Litwak, L.

Malamud, Bernard, 1914-
Angel Levine
Malamud, B. Magic barrel
Behold the key
Malamud, B. Magic barrel
The bill
Malamud, B. Magic barrel
The first seven years
Malamud, B. Magic barrel
The girl of my dreams
Malamud, B. Magic barrel
Lady of the lake
Malamud, B. Magic barrel
The last Mohican
Malamud, B. Magic barrel
The loan
Malamud, B. Magic barrel
Magic barrel
Best American short stories, 1955
Malamud, B. Magic barrel
The mourners
Malamud, B. Magic barrel
The prison
Malamud, B. Magic barrel
A summer's reading
Malamud, B. Magic barrel
Take pity
Malamud, B. Magic barrel

MALAY ARCHIPELAGO. See Malaya

MALAYA
Conrad, J. Karain: a memory
Maugham, W. S. The book-bag
Maugham, W. S. Door of opportunity

Malcolmson, Anne (Burnett) 1910-
Johnny Appleseed
Humphreville, F. T. ed. In other days

The **malediction.** Williams, T.

MALEDICTIONS. See Curses

Malice in wonderland. King, R.

MALICIOUS MISCHIEF
Armstrong, C. And already lost
Schleyen, M. Law belongs to every man
MALINGERING
Angoff, C. S. A.
Doyle, Sir A. C. Adventure of the dying detective
MALLARDS. See Ducks
Malleson, Lucy Beatrice, 1899-
Blood will tell
Mystery Writers of America, inc. A choice of murders
Sequel to murder
Mystery Writers of America, inc. For tomorrow we die
Malory, Sir Thomas, 15th century
Sword in the stone
Laughton, C. ed. Tell me a story
Malpass, E. L. 1910-
Return of the moon man
Wood, E. R. ed. Contemporary short stories
When grandfather flew to the moon
Merril, J. ed. SF: '57
Maltese cat. Kipling, R.
Maltz, Albert, 1908-
Happiest man on earth
First-prize stories, 1919-1957
MAN, ISLE OF
Kneale, N. Putting away of Uncle Quaggin
MAN, MECHANICAL. See Automata
MAN, PREHISTORIC
Commings, J. Great hunger
Ruhen, O. The husbandmen
MAN, PRIMITIVE
Ruhen, O. Beautiful pattern
Ruhen, O. Sword of laughter
Ruhen, O. Vision at the spring
Ruhen, O. Woman of Labu
Man about the house. Urquhart, F.
Man alone. Truax, L.
Man among men. Block, A. R.
Man and a fox. Hawkins, D.
The **man** and the snake. Bierce, A.
Man and wife. Burla, Y.
Man and wife. Purdy, J.
Man from Cap D'Amour. Raddall, T. H.
Man from far away. Schaefer, J. W.
Man from Texas. Claussen, W. E.
Man in black. Cates, R. E.
Man in Israel. Perl, P.
Man in pince-nez. Tolstoï, A. N. Graf
Man in ratcatcher. McNeile, H. C.
Man in the black cloak. Plimmer, D.
Man in the jar. Knight, D.
Man in the middle of the ocean. Fuchs, D.
Man is born. Gerbatov, B. L.
Man Jones. Patton, F. G.
Man of distinction. Fowler, M. D.
Man of parts. Amundson, G.
Man of parts. Gold, H. L.
Man of parts. Sansom, W.
Man of the house. O'Donovan, M.

Man of the world. O'Donovan, M.
Man on a diet. Dicks, J. R.
Man on the beach. Combs, P.
Man that corrupted Hadleyburg. Clemens, S. L.
Man upstairs. Bradbury, R.
Man who always knew. Budrys, A. J.
Man who became a fish. Li Fu-yen
Man who came early. Anderson, P.
Man who explained miracles. Carr, J. D.
Man who followed Grandma. Lowry, R. J. C.
The **man** who had no thumbs. Loomis, N. M.
Man who invented sin. O'Faoláin, S.
The **man** who liked lions. Daley, J. B.
Man.who lived four thousand years. Dumas, A.
Man who looked like a bird. Clayton, J. B.
Man who loved a joke. Wylie, P.
Man who loved islands. Lawrence, D. H.
Man who made people mad. Van Doren, M.
Man who quit. Byrd, J. J.
Man who shot snapping turtles. Wilson, E.
Man who smiled awhile. Coleman, W. L.
Man who vanished. Coates, R. M.
The **man** who wasn't scared. Winterton, P.
Man who went to Taltavul's. Alexander, D.
Man whom the trees loved. Blackwood, A.
Man with a secret. Clad, N.
The **man** with the moon in him. Sansom, W.
MANATEES
Annixter, P. pseud. Monarch of the lagoons
MANHATTAN. See New York (City)— Manhattan
MANHUNTS
Connell, R. E. Most dangerous game
Gallagher, F. Leaping trout
See also Escaped convicts
MANIACS. See Insanity
MANIKINS (FASHION MODELS) See Models, Fashion (Persons)
Mankowitz, Wolf, 1924-
Battersea miracle
Pudney, J. ed. Pick of today's short stories, 9
Blottik monopoly
Mankowitz, W. Mendelman fire, and other stories
Bonifas the cobbler
Mankowitz, W. Mendelman fire, and other stories
Day Aunt Chaya was buried
Mankowitz, W. Mendelman fire, and other stories
Devil and the cow
Mankowitz, W. Mendelman fire, and other stories
Eight years in the making
Mankowitz, W. Mendelman fire, and other stories

Mankowitz, Wolf—*Continued*

Finest pipe-maker in Russia
  Mankowitz, W. Mendelman fire, and other stories

Five per cent of paradise
  Mankowitz, W. Mendelman fire, and other stories

Fool is essential
  Mankowitz, W. Mendelman fire, and other stories

Good business with sentiment
  Mankowitz, W. Mendelman fire, and other stories

Handful of earth
  Mankowitz, W. Mendelman fire, and other stories

Law breaker
  Mankowitz, W. Mendelman fire, and other stories

Life in art
  Mankowitz, W. Mendelman fire, and other stories

Mendelman fire
  Mankowitz, W. Mendelman fire, and other stories

Nature's way
  Mankowitz, W. Mendelman fire, and other stories

The portrait
  Mankowitz, W. Mendelman fire, and other stories

Thirty-five minutes from nowhere
  Mankowitz, W. Mendelman fire, and other stories

Too much man
  Mankowitz, W. Mendelman fire, and other stories

La vie en rose
  Mankowitz, W. Mendelman fire, and other stories

Manley-Tucker, Audrie

Wanted—a miracle
  Wood, E. R. ed. Contemporary short stories

Mann, Thomas, 1875-1955

Disorder and early sorrow
  Thurston, J. A. ed. Reading modern short stories

Gladius Dei
  Locke, L. G.; Gibson, W. M. and Arms, G. W. eds. Introduction to literature

A gleam
  Hall, J. B. and Langland, J. T. eds. Short story

Mario and the magician
  Hamalian, L. and Volpe, E. L. eds. Ten modern short novels
  Jennings, F. G. and Calitri, C. J. eds. Stories
  Short, R. W. and Sewall, R. B. eds. Short stories for study

Snow world
  Schwed, P. and Wind, R. W. eds. Great stories from the world of sport

Tobias Mindernickel
  Gettman, R. A. and Harkness, B. eds. Book of stories

Manners, Margaret

Death on little cat's feet
  Mystery Writers of America, inc. Big time mysteries

A decidedly innocent man
  Mystery Writers of America, inc. A choice of murders

Last dark step
  Best detective stories of the year (13th annual collection)

Sybilla
  Mystery Writers of America, inc. For love or money

MANNERS AND CUSTOMS

Connell, E. S. Beau monde of Mrs Bridge
Hale, N. Charlotte Russe
O'Hara, J. Are we leaving tomorrow?

Manning, Olivia

The incurable
  Winter's tales, 2

Mannix, Jule

Our best friend is an eagle
  Teen-age tales, bk 3

Manolo. Smith, E. H.

Man's courage. Blassingame, W.

Man's dignity. Bahr, J.

Man's name. Guilloux, L.

Mansfield, Katherine, 1888-1923

Bliss
  Thurston, J. A. ed. Reading modern short stories

Cup of tea
  Sterner, L. G. ed. Favorite short stories

Dill pickle
  Short, R. W. and Sewall, R. B. eds. Short stories for study

The fly
  Langford, W. F. ed. Book of better stories

Garden party
  Havighurst, W. and others, eds. Selection
  McClennen, J. comp. Masters and masterpieces of the short story
  Thurston, J. A. ed. Reading modern short stories

Her first ball
  McClennen, J. comp. Masters and masterpieces of the short story

Marriage à la mode
  McClennen, J. comp. Masters and masterpieces of the short story

Mary
  Rosenblum, M. ed. Stories from many lands

Miss Brill
  McClennen, J. comp. Masters and masterpieces of the short story

Revelations
  Gettman, R. A. and Harkness, B. eds. Book of stories

The stranger
  Havighurst, W. ed. Masters of the modern short story
  McClennen, J. comp. Masters and masterpieces of the short story

Young girl
  McClennen, J. comp. Masters and masterpieces of the short story

MANSLAUGHTER. See Assassination; Crime and criminals; Murder stories; Mystery and detective stories

Manuel at full moon. Duke, M.

MS found in a Chinese fortune cookie. Kornbluth, C. M.

MANUSCRIPTS
Bellow, S. Gonzaga manuscripts

Many are disappointed. Pritchett, V. S.

Manzini, Gianna, 1902-
Indiscreet madrigal
Slonim, M. L. ed. Modern Italian short stories

MAORIS
Joseph, G. Return of a warrior

Map of love.. Thomas, D.

The **mapmakers.** Pohl, F.

MARATHON DANCES. See Dance marathons

MARBLE WORKERS. See Stone-cutters

Marby, Thomas Dabney
Lula Borrow
Best American short stories, 1957

Marceau, Félicien
Armistice in Venice
Lehmann, J. ed. Modern French stories

March, William, pseud. See Campbell, William Edward March

March-Phillipps, Gus, 1908-
The shires
Welcome, J. and Orchard, V. eds. Best hunting stories

March 2000: the taxpayer. Bradbury, R.

Marchi, Emilio de, 1851-1901
Missing letters
Strachan, W. J. ed. Modern Italian stories

MARDI GRAS
Ostroff, A. La bataille des fleurs

Maré, Antonio
A tragedy
Lohan, R. ed. Christmas tales for reading aloud

Margaret and Wilbur keep Moses. Rhine, R.

Margouillat who chose its destiny. Tuong, H. H.

Maria. Bowen, E.

Marie. Lowry, R. J. C.

The **Marie**-Helene. Gille, J.

MARIHUANA
Kerouac, J. Billowy trip in the world
See also Narcotics

Mario. Pincherle, A.

Mario and fortune. Comisso, G.

Mario and the magician. Mann, T.

MARIONETTES. See Puppets and puppet plays

Mario's riches. Comisso, G.

Mark Twain, pseud. See Clemens, Samuel Langhorne

Mark X. Verga, G.

The **marked** one. Picard, J.

Markewich, Robert, 1919-
Return to the Bronx
Ribalow, H. U. ed. Treasury of American Jewish stories

Markfield, Wallace, 1926-
Ph.D.
Ribalow, H. U. ed. Treasury of American Jewish stories

Markheim. Stevenson, R. L.

Marking time. Cavanaugh, J. P.

Marks, Winston
John's other practice
Best science-fiction stories and novels: 1955

Marlett, Melba Balmat (Grimes) 1909-
Frightened ones
Marlett, M. B. G. Frightened ones
In name only
Marlett, M. B. G. Frightened ones
Matter of record
Marlett, M. B. G. Frightened ones
Purring countess
Marlett, M. B. G. Frightened ones
Second chance
Marlett, M. B. G. Frightened ones

Marlowe, Stephen
The shill
Mystery Writers of America, inc. A choice of murders

Marmur, Jacland, 1901-
Kid in command
Saturday evening post (Periodical) Saturday evening post stories, 1955
Landing party
Saturday evening post (Periodical) Saturday evening post stories, 1956
The young and the brave
Saturday evening post (Periodical) Saturday evening post stories, 1954

Marotta, Giuseppe, 1902-
In a lane of Naples
Slonim, M. ed. Modern Italian short stories

Marquand, John Phillips, 1893-1960
Children's page
Baudin, M. ed. Contemporary short stories v3
The end game
Good housekeeping (Periodical) Editor's choice
Engines of hygeia
New short novels, 2
High tide
Saturday evening post (Periodical) The Post Reader of Civil War stories
Jack Still
Costain, T. B. and Beecroft, J. eds. More Stories to remember
Saturday evening post (Periodical) The Post Reader of Civil War stories
Simon pure
Collier's (Periodical) Collier's Greatest sports stories

Marquis, Don, 1878-1937
O'Meara at Troy
Saturday evening post (Periodical) Saturday evening post Carnival of humor

Marquis de Fumerol. Maupassant, G. de

Marred holiday. Peretz, I. L.

MARRIAGE
Benchley, R. C. Love in Hollywood
Connell, E. S. Arcturus
Curley, D. To ask the hard question is easy

MARRIAGE PROBLEMS—*Continued*

O'Donovan, J. Friend of the family
O'Donovan, M. The paragon
O'Faoláin, S. Lovers of the lake
O'Hara, J. Over the river and through the wood
Parker, D. R. Banquet of crow
Parker, D. R. Big blonde
Philipson, M. H. Third partner
Pincherle, A. The baby
Pincherle, A. Hot weather jokes
Porter, K. A. That tree
Pratolini, V. Mistress of twenty
Quinn, K. Molly on the shore
Reid, L. Elnea
Reid, L. Way life is
Ruhen, O. Beautiful pattern
Ruhen, O. Wisdom of Ragos
Sansom, W. Beauty and beast
Schlunke, E. O. Carnival
Singer, I. B. Gimpel the fool
Singer, I. B. The unseen
Tolstoi, L. N. Graf. Kreutzer sonata
Tuohy, F. Admiral and the nuns
Verdad. Good-tempered fellow
Verga, G. Cavalleria rusticana
Verga, G. Donna Santa's sin
Verga, G. Ieli
Verga, G. La Lupa
Verga, G. Stinkpot
Waldo, E. H. Hurricane trio
Warner, S. T. Idenborough
Wharton, E. N. J. Souls belated
Wilson, A. After the show
Yellen, S. Four sides of a triangle
Yellen, S. Stoneville Pike
Yellen, S. Your children will burn

See also Bigamy; Divorce; Husband and wife

MARRIAGES, INTERNATIONAL. See International marriages

MARRIAGES, INTER-RACIAL. See Inter-racial marriages

Married children. Fisher, D. F. C.

Married couple. Kafka, F.

Marroca. Maupassant, G. de

MARS (PLANET)

Bradbury, R. April 2000: the third expedition
Bradbury, R. April 2003: the musicians
Bradbury, R. April 2005: Usher II
Bradbury, R. April 2026: the long years
Bradbury, R. August 1999: the earth man
Bradbury, R. August 1999: the summer night
Bradbury, R. August 2001 the settlers
Bradbury, R. August 2002: night meeting
Bradbury, R. August 2005: the old ones
Bradbury, R. August 2026: there will come soft rains
Bradbury, R. December 2001: the green morning
Bradbury, R. December 2005: the silent towns
Bradbury, R. February 1999: Ylla
Bradbury, R. February 2002: the locusts
Bradbury, R. February 2003: interim
Bradbury, R. Fire balloons
Bradbury, R. January 1999: rocket summer
Bradbury, R. June 2001: —and the moon be still as bright

Bradbury, R. June 2003: way in the midde of the air
Bradbury, R. March 2000: the taxpayer
Bradbury, R. Martian chronicles; 26 stories
Bradbury, R. November 2005: the luggage store
Bradbury, R. November 2005: the off season
Bradbury, R. November 2005: the watchers
Bradbury, R. October 2002: the shore
Bradbury, R. October 2026: the million-year picnic
Bradbury, R. September 2005: the Martian
Bradbury, R. 2004-05: the naming of names
Edmondson, G. C. Rescue
Jameson, M. Hobo God
Oliver, C. Artifact
White, W. A. P. Balaam
White, W. A. P. Star bride
Williams, J. Asa rule

See also Martians

MARSEILLES. See France—Marseilles

Marsh, Ngaio, 1899-
I can find my way out
Haycraft, H. and Beecroft, J. eds. Treasury of great mysteries

Marsh, Willard N. 1922-
Bus fare to tomorrow
Saturday evening post (Periodical) Saturday evening post stories, 1954
The ethicators
Merril, J. ed. S-F: ['56]
Last tag
Prize stories 1957: the O. Henry awards

Marshal and the mob. Boyles, C. S.

Marshal of Cow Springs. Adams, A.

Marshall, Bruce, 1899-
Brigadier smells a rat
This week magazine. This week's Stories of mystery and suspense

Marshall, Edison, 1894-
Heart of Litte Shikara
Fenner, P. R. ed. Heroes, heroes, heroes
First-prize stories, 1919-1957

Marshall, Robert
Haunted major
Schwed, P. and Wind, H. W. eds. Great stories from the world of sport

MARSHALS. See Sheriffs

MARSHES. See Swamps

Marsten, Richard, pseud. See Hunter, Evan

MARTIANS

Bradbury, R. April 2026: the long years
Bradbury, R. August 1999: the earth men
Bradbury, R. August 1999: The summer night
Bradbury, R. September 2005: the Martian
Brown, F. Keep out
Harris, J. B. Dumb Martian
Jameson, M. Hobo God
Moore, W. Dominions beyond
Moore, W. Second trip to Mars
Simak, C. D. Mirage

See also Mars (Planet)

Martin, Betty Fible, 1907-
Gay young call
New voices 2: American writing today
Martin, Kenneth, 1939-
Spring is here
Pudney, J. ed. Pick of today's short
stories
Martin, Violet Florence. See Somerville,
E. A. O. jt. auth.
Martin the novelist. Aymé, M.
Martyr, Weston, 1885-
Bowman's glory
Schwed, P. and Wind, H. W. eds. Great
stories from the world of sport
MARTYRS
Huxley, A. L. Death of Lully
The martyrs. Allen, S.
Martyr's crown. O'Nolan, B.
Mary. Mansfield, K.
Mary Kiser. Lochridge, B. H.
Mary Smith. Tarkington, B.
MARYLAND

Annapolis
Carmer, C. L. Most-haunted town
Mascot. Butler, E. P.
Masefield, John, 1878-
Anty Bligh
Costain, T. B. and Beecroft, J. eds. More
Stories to remember
Devil and the old man
Davenport, B. ed. Deals with the devil
A memory
Kemp, P. K. ed. Hundred years of sea
stories
The mask. Jameson, S.
The mask. Maupassant, G. de
Mask factory. Papini, G.
MASKS (FOR THE FACE)
Papini, G. Mask factory
MASKS (SCULPTURE)
Walpole, Sir H. Silver mask
Mason, Michael
Saul
Miller, N. ed. New campus writing, no. 2
MASONS (SECRET ORDER) See Free-
masons
MASONS (TRADE) See Bricklayers;
Stone-masons
Masque of the Red Death. Poe, E. A.
MASQUERADES
Cheever, J. Just tell me who it was
Poe, E. A. Masque of the Red Death
MASS
Daudet, A. Three Low Masses
MASSACHUSETTS

Boston
Angoff, C. Curly

Boston—20th century
Hale, N. Copley-Plaza

Cape Cod
Kyd, T. pseud. Cottage for August
Nathan, R. Portrait of Jennie
Massacre in Peralta Canyon. Hibben, F. C.
Massacre of Vallucciole. Levi, C.

MASSACRES
Levi, C. Massacre of Vallucciole
MASSAGE
Kubly, H. Mrs Gordon and the blind
masseur
Masselink, Ben
Prove you love me
Teen-age tales, bk 6
The master. Balchin, N.
Master and servant. Ward, L. L.
Master of the golden game. Hughes, J. G.
Master Pérez the organist. Bécquer, G. A.
Masterson, Whit, pseud. See Wade, Bob,
and Miller, Bill
Masur, Harold Q. 1912-
$2,000,000 defense
Queen, E. pseud. ed. Ellery Queen's
13th annual
MATADORS. See Bullfighters and bull-
fighting
Match at Fordenden. MacDonell, A. G.
MATCHMAKERS. See Marriage brokers
Maternal feminine. Ferber, E.
Mate's choice. Johnsen, J. W.
MATHEMATICIANS
Porges, A. Devil and Simon Flagg
Russell, B. A. W. R. 3d earl. Mathemati-
cian's nightmare
Mathematician's nightmare. Russell,
B. A. W. R. 3d earl
Matheson, Richard, 1926-
Pattern for survival
Magazine of fantasy and science fiction.
Best from Fantasy and science fiction;
5th ser.
The test
Magazine of fantasy and science fiction.
Best from Fantasy and science fiction;
4th ser.
Matinee. Berriault, G.
The matinee. Moore, N.
Mating season. Hadas, A.
MATRIMONIAL AGENCIES. See Mar-
riage brokers
Matscher, Alvina
College water wagon
Oberfirst, R. ed. Anthology of best
short-short stories v6
Matter of facts. Payne, L. V.
Matter of goblins. Stewart, J. I. M.
Matter of life and death. Hawkins, J. and
Hawkins, W.
Matter of months. Weed, A.
Matter of price. Bowen, R. O.
Matter of public notice. Davis, D. S.
Matter of record. Marlett, M. B. G.
A matter of scholarship. White, W. A. P.
Matthews, Marjorie
The innkeeper's daughters
Oberfirst, R. ed. Anthology of best
short-short stories v5
Matthiessen, Peter, 1927?-
Travelin man
Prize stories, 1958: the O. Henry awards
Mattie dear. Hammett, E. A.

Maupassant, Guy de—*Continued*

Bellflower
  Maupassant, G. de. Complete short
    stories
  Same as: Clochette
Benoist
  Maupassant, G. de. Complete short
    stories
Bertha
  Maupassant, G. de. Complete short
    stories
Beside a dead man
  Maupassant, G. de. Complete short
    stories
Blind man
  Maupassant, G. de. Complete short
    stories
Boitelle
  Maupassant, G. de. Complete short
    stories
Bric-a-brac
  Maupassant, G. de. Complete short
    stories
The cake
  Maupassant, G. de. Complete short
    stories
Caresses
  Maupassant, G. de. Complete short
    stories
The castaway
  Maupassant, G. de. Complete short
    stories
Châli
  Maupassant, G. de. Complete short
    stories
Charm dispelled
  Maupassant, G. de. Complete short
    stories
Checkmate
  Maupassant, G. de. Complete short
    stories
Christening
  Maupassant, G. de. Complete short
    stories
The christening ₁another story₁
  Maupassant, G. de. Complete short
    stories
Christmas Eve
  Maupassant, G. de. Complete short
    stories
Cock crowed
  Maupassant, G. de. Complete short
    stories
Coco
  Maupassant, G. de. Complete short
    stories
Coconut-drink vendor
  Maupassant, G. de. Complete short
    stories
Colonel's ideas
  Maupassant, G. de. Complete short
    stories
Complication
  Maupassant, G. de. Complete short
    stories
Confessing
  Maupassant, G. de. Complete short
    stories
The confession
  Maupassant, G. de. Complete short
    stories

The conservatory
  Maupassant, G. de. Complete short
    stories
Consideration
  Maupassant, G. de. Complete short
    stories
Corsican bandit
  Maupassant, G. de. Complete short
    stories
Costly outing
  Maupassant, G. de. Complete short
    stories
Country excursion
  Maupassant, G. de. Complete short
    stories
The cripple
  Maupassant, G. de. Complete short
    stories
A crisis
  Maupassant, G. de. Complete short
    stories
Cry of alarm
  Maupassant, G. de. Complete short
    stories
The dancers
  Maupassant, G. de. Complete short
    stories
Dead woman's secret
  Maupassant, G. de. Complete short
    stories
Deaf-mute
  Maupassant, G. de. Complete short
    stories
Denis
  Maupassant, G. de. Complete short
    stories
The devil
  Maupassant, G. de. Complete short
    stories
Divorce case
  Maupassant, G. de. Complete short
    stories
The donkey
  Maupassant, G. de. Complete short
    stories
Double pins
  Maupassant, G. de. Complete short
    stories
Doubtful happiness
  Maupassant, G. de. Complete short
    stories
Dreams
  Maupassant, G. de. Complete short
    stories
Drowned man
  Maupassant, G. de. Complete short
    stories
Duchoux
  Maupassant, G. de. Complete short
    stories
A duel
  Maupassant, G. de. Complete short
    stories
The duel ₁another story₁
  Maupassant, G. de. Complete short
    stories
The Englishman
  Maupassant, G. de. Complete short
    stories
An enthusiast
  Maupassant, G. de. Complete short
    stories

Maupassant, Guy de—*Continued*

Epiphany
Maupassant, G. de. Complete short
stories

Fair exchange
Maupassant, G. de. Complete short
stories

False gems
Maupassant, G. de. Complete short
stories
Thurston, J. A. ed. Reading modern
short stories
Same as: The jewels

A family
Maupassant, G. de. Complete short
stories

Family affair
Maupassant, G. de. Complete short
stories

Farmer's wife
Maupassant, G. de. Complete short
stories

The father
Maupassant, G. de. Complete short
stories

Father Judas
Maupassant, G. de. Complete short
stories

Fear
Maupassant, G. de. Complete short
stories

Fecundity
Maupassant, G. de. Complete short
stories

Feminine men
Maupassant, G. de. Complete short
stories

First snowfall
Maupassant, G. de. Complete short
stories

Fishing excursion
Maupassant, G. de. Complete short
stories

Florentine
Maupassant, G. de. Complete short
stories

For sale
Maupassant, G. de. Complete short
stories

Forbidden fruit
Maupassant, G. de. Complete short
stories

Forgiveness
Maupassant, G. de. Complete short
stories

Francis
Maupassant, G. de. Complete short
stories

French Enoch Arden
Maupassant, G. de. Complete short
stories

Funeral pile
Maupassant, G. de. Complete short
stories

Good reasons
Maupassant, G. de. Complete short
stories

Graveyard sirens
Maupassant, G. de. Complete short
stories

Growing old
Maupassant, G. de. Complete short
stories

Guillemot Rock
Maupassant, G. de. Complete short
stories

Happiness
Maupassant, G. de. Complete short
stories

Hautot and his son
Maupassant, G. de. Complete short
stories
Same as: Hautot, father and son

He?
Maupassant, G. de. Complete short
stories

The hermit
Maupassant, G. de. Complete short
stories

Hippolyte's claim
Maupassant, G. de. Complete short
stories

The hole
Maupassant, G. de. Complete short
stories

The horla
Maupassant, G. de. Complete short
stories

The horrible
Maupassant, G. de. Complete short
stories

How he got the Legion of Honor
Maupassant, G. de. Complete short
stories

Humble drama
Maupassant, G. de. Complete short
stories

Humiliation
Maupassant, G. de. Complete short
stories
Same as: Rose

An idyl
Maupassant, G. de. Complete short
stories

Impolite sex
Maupassant, G. de. Complete short
stories

In a railway carriage
Maupassant, G. de. Complete short
stories

In port
Maupassant, G. de. Complete short
stories

In the country
Maupassant, G. de. Complete short
stories

In the courtroom
Maupassant, G. de. Complete short
stories

In the moonlight
Maupassant, G. de. Complete short
stories

In the spring
Maupassant, G. de. Complete short
stories

In the wood
Maupassant, G. de. Complete short
stories

The inn
Maupassant, G. de. Complete short
stories

Maupassant, Guy de—*Continued*

Monsieur Parent
  Maupassant, G. de. Complete short stories
Moonlight
  Laughton, C. ed. Tell me a story
  Maupassant, G. de. Complete short stories
  Same as: Clair de lune; In the moonlight
Mother and son!!!
  Maupassant, G. de. Complete short stories
Mother of monsters
  Maupassant, G. de. Complete short stories
Mother Savage
  Maupassant, G. de. Complete short stories
  Same as: Mère Sauvage
Mother Superior's twenty-five francs
  Maupassant, G. de. Complete short stories
Mouche
  Maupassant, G. de. Complete short stories
My landlady
  Maupassant, G. de. Complete short stories
My twenty-five days
  Maupassant, G. de. Complete short stories
My Uncle Jules
  Maupassant, G. de. Complete short stories
My Uncle Sosthenes
  Maupassant, G. de. Complete short stories
My wife
  Maupassant, G. de. Complete short stories
The necklace
  Costain, T. B. and Beecroft, J. eds. Stories to remember
  Jennings, F. G. and Calitri, C. J. eds. Stories
  Maupassant, G. de. Complete short stories
  Rosenblum, M. ed. Stories from many lands
  Sterner, L. G. ed. Favorite short stories
New Year's gift
  Maupassant, G. de. Complete short stories
Night: A nightmare
  Maupassant, G. de. Complete short stories
Noncommissioned officer
  Maupassant, G. de. Complete short stories
A Norman
  Maupassant, G. de. Complete short stories
Normandy joke
  Maupassant, G. de. Complete short stories
Odd feast
  Maupassant, G. de. Complete short stories
Of Doctor Heraclius Gloss
  Maupassant, G. de. Complete short stories

Old Amable
  Maupassant, G. de. Complete short stories
Old man
  Maupassant, G. de. Complete short stories
Old Milon
  Maupassant, G. de. Complete short stories
Old Mongilet
  Maupassant, G. de. Complete short stories
Old objects
  Maupassant, G. de. Complete short stories
Olive orchard
  Maupassant, G. de. Complete short stories
  Same as: Olive grove
On a spring evening
  Maupassant, G. de. Complete short stories
On cats
  Maupassant, G. de. Complete short stories
On the river
  Maupassant, G. de. Complete short stories
One evening
  Maupassant, G. de. Complete short stories
One phase of love
  Maupassant, G. de. Complete short stories
The orderly
  Maupassant, G. de. Complete short stories
The Orient
  Maupassant, G. de. Complete short stories
The orphan
  Maupassant, G. de. Complete short stories
Our friends the English
  Maupassant, G. de. Complete short stories
Our letters
  Maupassant, G. de. Complete short stories
A parricide
  Maupassant, G. de. Complete short stories
A passion
  Maupassant, G. de. Complete short stories
The patron
  Maupassant, G. de. Complete short stories
Paul's mistress
  Maupassant, G. de. Complete short stories
Peculiar case
  Maupassant, G. de. Complete short stories
The peddler
  Maupassant, G. de. Complete short stories
A philosopher
  Maupassant, G. de. Complete short stories
Piece of string
  Maupassant, G. de. Complete short stories

Maupassant, Guy de—*Continued*

Poor Andrew
  Maupassant, G. de. Complete short
    stories
Poor girl
  Maupassant, G. de. Complete short
    stories
A portrait
  Maupassant, G. de. Complete short
    stories
Practical joke
  Maupassant, G. de. Complete short
    stories
The prisoners
  Maupassant, G. de. Complete short
    stories
Putter-to-sleep
  Maupassant, G. de. Complete short
    stories
Queen Hortense
  Maupassant, G. de. Complete short
    stories
Queer night in Paris
  Maupassant, G. de. Complete short
    stories
Question of Latin
  Maupassant, G. de. Complete short
    stories
The rabbit
  Maupassant, G. de. Complete short
    stories
Regret
  Maupassant, G. de. Complete short
    stories
The relic
  Maupassant, G. de. Complete short
    stories
The rendezvous
  Maupassant, G. de. Complete short
    stories
Revenge
  Maupassant, G. de. Complete short
    stories
The revenge [another story]
  Maupassant, G. de. Complete short
    stories
Roger's method
  Maupassant, G. de. Complete short
    stories
Room no. 11
  Maupassant, G. de. Complete short
    stories
Rosalie Prudent
  Maupassant, G. de. Complete short
    stories
Rose
  Laughton, C. ed. Tell me a story
  Same as: Humiliation
Rust
  Maupassant, G. de. Complete short
    stories
A sale
  Maupassant, G. de. Complete short
    stories
Saved
  Maupassant, G. de. Complete short
    stories
The secret
  Maupassant, G. de. Complete short
    stories

Selfishness
  Maupassant, G. de. Complete short
    stories
  Same as: At sea
Semillante
  Maupassant, G. de. Complete short
    stories
Sentiment
  Maupassant, G. de. Complete short
    stories
Shepherd's leap
  Maupassant, G. de. Complete short
    stories
The signal
  Maupassant, G. de. Complete short
    stories
Simon's papa
  Maupassant, G. de. Complete short
    stories
Sisters Rondoli
  Maupassant, G. de. Complete short
    stories
Solitude
  Maupassant, G. de. Complete short
    stories
The spasm
  Maupassant, G. de. Complete short
    stories
The specter
  Maupassant, G. de. Complete short
    stories
Story of a farm girl
  Maupassant, G. de. Complete short
    stories
Strange fancy
  Maupassant, G. de. Complete short
    stories
The substitute
  Maupassant, G. de. Complete short
    stories
Suicides
  Maupassant, G. de. Complete short
    stories
A surprise
  Maupassant, G. de. Complete short
    stories
That pig of a Morin
  Maupassant, G. de. Complete short
    stories
Tobacco shop
  Maupassant, G. de. Complete short
    stories
Toine
  Maupassant, G. de. Complete short
    stories
The tomb
  Maupassant, G. de. Complete short
    stories
Traveler's notes
  Maupassant, G. de. Complete short
    stories
Traveler's story
  Maupassant, G. de. Complete short
    stories
Traveler's tale
  Maupassant, G. de. Complete short
    stories
Traveling
  Maupassant, G. de. Complete short
    stories
True story
  Maupassant, G. de. Complete short
    stories

Maupassant, Guy de—*Continued*

Two little soldiers
  Maupassant, G. de. Complete short stories
The umbrella
  Maupassant, G. de. Complete short stories
The unknown
  Maupassant, G. de. Complete short stories
Useless beauty
  Maupassant, G. de. Complete short stories
  Same as: Vain beauty
A vagabond
  Maupassant, G. de. Complete short stories
The victim
  Maupassant, G. de. Complete short stories
Waiter, a bock!
  Maupassant, G. de. Complete short stories
Walter Schnaffs' adventure
  Maupassant, G. de. Complete short stories
Was it a dream?
  Costain, T. B. and Beecroft, J. eds. More Stories to remember
  Maupassant, G. de. Complete short stories
The watchdog
  Maupassant, G. de. Complete short stories
Way to wealth
  Maupassant, G. de. Complete short stories
Wedding night
  Maupassant, G. de. Complete short stories
White wolf
  Maupassant, G. de. Complete short stories
Who knows?
  Maupassant, G. de. Complete short stories
  Ridler, A. B. comp. Best ghost stories
Wife's confession
  Maupassant, G. de. Complete short stories
The will
  Maupassant, G. de. Complete short stories
Woman's wiles
  Maupassant, G. de. Complete short stories
Wooden shoes
  Maupassant, G. de. Complete short stories
Words of love
  Maupassant, G. de. Complete short stories
The wreck
  Maupassant, G. de. Complete short stories
Yvette
  Maupassant, G. de. Complete short stories

About

Babel', I. E. Guy de Maupassant
Maurie finds his medium. Levin, M.
Maverick factory. Loomis, N. M.

Maxwell, William, 1908-
French scarecrow
  Stories
Trojan women
  Stories
What every boy should know
  Stories
Maybe next week. Baker, L. N.
Mayer, Albert I. 1906-
It's all very crazy
  Furman, A. L. ed. Everygirls sports stories
Mayor calls his family. Wellman, M. W.
MAYORS
Gerchunoff, A. Revolution
Guareschi, G. A baptism
Guareschi, G. The petition
Maysville minstrell. Lardner, R. W.
Mead, Harold
Soldier's farewell
  Saturday evening post (Periodical) Saturday evening post stories, 1957
Measure of an angler. Person, W. T.
Measures of security. Sansom, W.
Meat and potatoes. Doppo, K.
MEAT INDUSTRY AND TRADE. See Slaughtering and slaughter-houses
MEDALS, MILITARY AND NAVAL
Chavez, A. Colonel and the santo
MEDICAL RESEARCH
Wright, R. What you don't know won't hurt you
MEDICAL STUDENTS
Doyle, Sir A. C. Croxley master
Maguire, R. A. Reprieve
Medici, Ruth, 1905-
Quiet
  Oberfirst, R. ed. Anthology of best short-short stories v6
MEDICINE MAN
Porter, W. S. Jeff Peters as a personal magnet
MEDICINES, PATENT, PROPRIETARY, ETC.
Garland, H. Uncle Ethan Ripley
Mankowitz, W. Nature's way
O'Donovan, M. Man of the house
Porter, W. S. Jeff Peters as a personal magnet
MEDIUMS. See Spiritualism
Medusa. Waldo, E. H.
The **meek** Mr Weeks. Clancy, D.
A **meeting.** Maupassant, G. de
Meller, Leslie
Fourth cockatoo
  World prize stories; 2d ser.
Melton, James, 1931-
Religion comes to Pocatello
  Standard short stories, 1957
Melville, Herman, 1819-1891
Bartleby the scrivener
  Short, R. W. and Sewall, R. B. eds. Short stories for study
Billy Budd, foretopman
  Book of stories
Moby Dick's last fight
  Kemp, P. K. ed. Hundred years of sea stories

Memento. Caldwell, E.

Memento homo. Miller, W. M.

Memento mori. Farrell, J. T.

MEMORIAL DAY
Fisher, D. F. C. Memorial Day
Mitchell, M. E. For the honor of the company

Memorial synagogue. Goodman, P.

Memorial to the slain. Campbell, W. E. M.

MEMORY
Shaw, I. Sunny banks of the River Lethe

A memory. Maupassant, G. de

A memory. Welty, E.

Men. Boyle, K.

Men, women and wilderness. Smith, E. W.

MENAGERIES
Fournier, P. The animals

Mendelman fire. Mankowitz, W.

The mennans. MacLellan, R.

MENNONITES
Lincoln, V. E. Morning wishes

MENSERVANTS. See Servants—Menservants

MENTAL ILLNESS
Beaumont, C. Miss Gentilbelle
Beaumont, C. Nursery rhyme
Evans, C. Father in Sion
Fisher, D. F. C. Murder on Jefferson Street
Mosenson, Y. Ashes
O'Brian, P. Voluntary patient
Plunkett, J. Dublin Fusilier
Sansom, W. The man with the moon in him
Wilson, A. Ten minutes to twelve
See also Insanity; Neurasthenia; Neuroses; Personality, Disorders of

MENTAL INSTITUTIONS. See Insane hospitals

MENTAL TESTS
Hirai, T. Psychological test

Menuchim says mamma. Roth, J.

MERCHANDISING
Ferber, E. Molly Brandeis takes hold

MERCHANT MARINE
Harper, J. Perils for trial

MERCHANTS
Blixen, K. Immortal story
Murdoch, I. Something special
Polk, W. T. Supply man
See also Business

Merciless and merciful sea. Wallenius, K. M.

Mercy. Plunkett, J.

Mercy flight to Luna. Elam, R. M.

Mère Sauvage. See Maupassant, G. de. Mother Savage

Mergendahl, Charles
Secret recipe
Best detective stories of the year (13th annual collction)

The merger. Beigel, U.

Merliss, R. R.
The stutterer
Merril, J. ed. S-F: ['56]

Merril, Judith, 1923-
Dead center
Best American short stories, 1955

Merritt, Miriam, 1925-
Death of a kangaroo
Stanford short stories, 1954
No game for children
Stanford short stories, 1955
Till Gabriel blows his horn
Stanford short stories, 1954

Merry Christmas in ten pieces. Yoder, R. M.

The merry dance. Kubly, H.

MESMERISM. See Hypnotism

The message. Asimov, I.

Message delayed. Elston, A. V.

Message for General Washington. Allen, M. P.

Message for Harold. Ullman, V.

Message from the sea. Dickens, C.

The messenger. Peretz, I. L.

MESSENGERS
Saroyan, W. Proud poet

MESSIAH
Bar-Joseph, J. Fettered Messiah

METAMORPHOSIS
Bradbury, R. September 2005: the Martian
Langelaan, G. The fly
Norton, A. M. Mousetrap

Metaphysician's nightmare. Russell, B. A. W. R. 3d earl

METHODISM
Newmen, W. C. Protestant Saint Francis

Mewhu's jet. Waldo, E. H.

The Mexican girl. Kerouac, J.

Mexican interlude. Bahr, J.

MEXICANS IN CALIFORNIA
Connell, E. S. Fisherman from Chihuahua
Steinbeck, J. Flight

MEXICANS IN FRANCE
Boyle, K. This they took with them

MEXICANS IN ITALY
Maugham, W. S. Hairless Mexican

MEXICANS IN THE UNITED STATES
Adams, A. There's my horse's track
Bowman, J. K. El patrón
Cather, W. S. Dance at Chevalier's
Connell, E. S. Fisherman from Chihuahua
Hemingway, E. Gambler, the nun and the radio
Kerouac, J. The Mexican girl
Orr, E. Home for Consuela
West, J. Foot-shaped shoes

MEXICO
Bartlett, P. Fronds of corn
Bradbury, R. Next in line
Brenner, A. Hero by mistake
Cardozo, N. The excursionists
Graves, J. Green fly
Guest, A. Momentito
La Farge, O. Old Century's river

20th Century
Greene, G. Across the bridge
Smith, E. H. Conversation among friends
Smith, E. H. The decision
Smith, E. H. Four o'clock
Smith, E. H. The gift

MEXICO—*Continued*
Smith, E. H. Gomez
Smith, E. H. Justice and Juan Morales
Smith, E. H. Little brown ones
Smith, E. H. Manolo
Smith, E. H. Red dress
Smith, E. H. Repeat performance
Smith, E. H. Sadness of Cruz
Smith, E. H. Similar sauce
Smith, E. H. Small side of Doroteo Arango
Smith, E. H. El Tigre!
Smith, E. H. El Tigre! 16 stories
Smith, E. H. Vaya con Dios
Smith, E. H. Wake for El Gusano
Street, J. H. Grains of paradise

Country life
See Country life—Mexico

Communism
See Communism—Mexico

Mexico City
Liberman, M. M. Big Buick to the pyramids

Social life and customs
Smith, E. H. Conversation among friends
Smith, E. H. Similar sauce

MEXICO CITY. See Mexico—Mexico City
Meyer, John de. See De Meyer, John
Meyers, Barlow, 1902-
Devil Dust
Western Writers of America. Wild horse roundup
Meyers, Lewis
My father and the Indians
Oberfirst, R. ed. Anthology of best short-short stories v5
Miami papers please copy. King, R.
MICE
Field, E. Mouse that didn't believe in Santa Claus
Kubly, H. Mice
Rynas, S. A. Chain of command
Michael and Mary. O'Kelly, S.
Michali's night. Iatridis, J.
Michener, James Albert, 1907-
Airstrip at Konora
Fenton, C. A. ed. Best short stories of World War II
Boar's tooth
Stead, C. ed. Great stories of the South Sea Islands
MICHIGAN
Macauley, R. The wishbone
MICHIGAN, LAKE. See Lake Michigan
Microcosmic god. Waldo, E. H.
Micrometer fever. Millholland, R.
Midas plague. Pohl, F.
MIDDLE AGE
Camus, A. Adulterous woman
Colette, S. G. Chéri
Ferber, E. Sudden sixties
Gordimer, N. Out of season
Lessing, D. M. Habit of loving
Lessing, D. M. The witness
Pincherle, A. Silly old fool
Sansom, W. Dangerous age

Sansom, W. Episode at Gastein
Saroyan, W. Paris and Philadelphia
Spencer, J. L. That old jive
MIDDLE CLASSES
O'Hara, J. Walter T. Carriman
MIDDLE WEST
Connell, E. S. Walls of Ávila

Farm life
See Farm life—Middle West

MIDDLE WESTERN DIALECT. See Dialect stories—Middle Western
Middle years. James, H.
Middleton, Elizabeth H. 1902-
Portrait of my son as a young man
Best American short stories, 1955
Middleton, Richard Barham, 1882-1911
Ghost ship
Kemp, P. K. ed. Hundred years of sea stories
Midnight kill. Fay, W.
Midsummer night madness. O'Faoláin, S.
MIDWIVES
Carroll, P. V. She went by gently
Hill, A. Miss Gillespie and the Micks
Mighty moustache. Thomas, A. W.
MIGRANT LABOR
Saroyan, W. Winter vineyard workers
MIGRATION OF BIRDS. See Birds—Migration
Mild attack of locusts. Lessing, D. M.
Mile-long spaceship. Wilhelm, K.
MILITARY AERONAUTICS. See Aeronautics, Military
MILITARY EDUCATION
Trease, G. Military glory
Military glory. Trease, G.
MILITARY LIFE. See Soldiers; Women in military life; also subdivision Army under various countries, e.g. Great Britain. Army
MILITARY MEDALS. See Medals, Military and naval
MILITARY SCHOOLS. See Military education
MILITARY SERVICE, COMPULSORY
Rinehart, M. R. Tish does her bit
MILITARY TRAINING CAMPS
Litwak, L. Making of a clerk
Yates, R. Jody rolled the bones
MILITARY UNIFORMS. See Uniforms, Military
Milking time. O'Flaherty, L.
MILKMEN
Pritchett, V. S. Eleven o'clock
Millar, Kenneth, 1912-
Guilt-edged blonde
Mystery Writers of America, inc. A choice of murders
Millar, Margaret, 1915-
The couple next door
Mystery Writers of America, inc. A choice of murders
Miller, Arthur, 1915-
Monte Saint Angelo
Ribalow, H. U. ed. Treasury of American Jewish stories

Miller, Bill, 1920-   See Wade, B. jt. auth.

Miller, Cloud, pseud. See Cloud-Miller, Elizabeth

Miller, Ed Mack, 1921-
Christmas Eve
   Miller, E. M. Tales of a flier's faith
Christmas present
   Miller, E. M. Tales of a flier's faith
Decision for a star
   Miller, E. M. Tales of a flier's faith
First Communion Day
   Miller, E. M. Tales of a flier's faith
Green grasshopper
   Miller, E. M. Tales of a flier's faith
Habit of murder
   Miller, E. M. Tales of a flier's faith
Heaven-sent
   Miller, E. M. Tales of a flier's faith
Last barrier
   Miller, E. M. Tales of a flier's faith
Left-handed Texan
   Miller, E. M. Tales of a flier's faith
Mister Wister wins a war
   Miller, E. M. Tales of a flier's faith
Night solo
   Miller, E. M. Tales of a flier's faith
Nine rosaries to St Stanislaus Kostka
   Miller, E. M. Tales of a flier's faith
Officers' club girl
   Miller, E. M. Tales of a flier's faith
Pay and the uniform
   Miller, E. M. Tales of a flier's faith
Purple Spad
   Miller, E. M. Tales of a flier's faith
Race with death
   Hughes, R. ed. All manner of men
   Miller, E. M. Tales of a flier's faith
Red diamond for Miss Detwiler
   Miller, E. M. Tales of a flier's faith
Scramble
   Miller, E. M. Tales of a flier's faith
Tempest of the heart
   Miller, E. M. Tales of a flier's faith
This cockpit my grave
   Miller, E. M. Tales of a flier's faith

Miller, Lion
Available data on the Worp Reaction
   Montgomery, R. B. ed. Best SF three

Miller, Mildred, 1929-
In screaming birth
   New voices 2: American writing today

Miller, Nolan
New life
   Prize stories 1957: the O. Henry awards

Miller, R. DeWitt
Swenson, Dispatcher
   Best science-fiction stories and novels: 1956

Miller, Ruth M.
The gavel
   Teen-age tales, bk 4

Miller, Wade, pseud. See Wade, Bob, and Miller, Bill

Miller, Walter M. 1923-
Blood bank
   Greenberg, M. ed. All about the future
Canticle for Leibowitz
   Best science-fiction stories and novels: 1956
   Magazine of fantasy and science fiction. Best from Fantasy and science fiction; 5th ser.

The hoofer
   Merril, J. ed. S-F: ['56]
Memento homo
   Best science-fiction stories and novels: 1955
The will
   Best science-fiction stories and novels: 1955

MILLERS
Alarcón, P. A. de. Three-cornered hat

Millholland, Ray, 1892?-1956
Big gun
   Millholland, R. Blue Chip Haggerty
Hot pig
   Millholland, R. Blue Chip Haggerty
Micrometer fever
   Millholland, R. Blue Chip Haggerty
Production soldier
   Millholland, R. Blue Chip Haggerty
Roaring Pittsburgh Dan
   Millholland, R. Blue Chip Haggerty
Rough turn
   Millholland, R. Blue Chip Haggerty
Six-o'clock whistle
   Millholland, R. Blue Chip Haggerty
Straw battle helmet
   Millholland, R. Blue Chip Haggerty
Supercharged harmony
   Millholland, R. Blue Chip Haggerty
Temperamental jailbird
   Millholland, R. Blue Chip Haggerty
Tolerance
   Millholland, R. Blue Chip Haggerty
Transformer on the line
   Millholland, R. Blue Chip Haggerty

MILLINERS
Ferber, E. Maternal feminine

Million dollar gesture. Gault, W. C.

MILLIONAIRES
Bernari, C. It's all a question of degree
Park, E. J. How I spent my million

Milne, Alan Alexander, 1882-1956
Hint for next Christmas
   Posselt, E. ed. A merry, merry Christmas book

Mimosa blight. Patton, F. G.

Mind alone. Macgregor, J. M.

The mind is its own place. Macauley, R.

Mind over motor. Rinehart, M. R.

MIND READING
Waldo, E. H. Twink

MINE ACCIDENTS
Lawrence, D. H. Odour of chrysanthemums

Mine enemy's dog. Williams, B. A.

Mine host. Balchin, N.

Miner, Leslie
Psychic
   Oberfirst, R. ed. Anthology of best short-short stories v6

MINERS. See Mines and Mining

MINES AND MINING
Bogza, G. End of Jacob Onisia
Hilborn, N. C. A bargain's a bargain
Lawrence, D. H. Odour of chrysanthemums

MINES AND MINING—*Continued*
  Rhodes, E. M. Long shift
  Savage, L. Crow-bait caravan
     See also Coal mines and mining;
    Silver mines and mining
The **miniature**. Halsey, D.
MINING TOWNS
  Coates, R. M. Storms of childhood
MINISTERS. See Clergy
Minister's black veil. Hawthorne, N.
MINISTERS OF THE GOSPEL. See
  Clergy
MINK FARMING
  Reynolds, Q. J. Girl named Dora
Minor operation. O'Brian, P.
Minority report. Waldo, E. H.
MINUET in G. Angoff, C.
The **minyan**. Agnon, S. J.
The **minyan**. Klein, A.
A **miracle**. Maupassant, G. de
Miracle at Frusaglia. Tombari, F.
Miracle of Hashono Rabo. Rabinowitz, S.
Miracle of the fifteen murderers. Hecht, B.
Miracle play. Elliott, G. P.
MIRACLE PLAYS. See Mysteries and
  miracle plays
MIRACLES
  Campbell, W. E. M. Mist on the meadow
  Maupassant, G. de. A miracle
  Shaw, G. B. Miraculous revenge
Miracles do happen. Queen, E. pseud.
Miracles on the sea. Peretz, I. L.
Miraculous doctor. Gerchunoff, A.
Miraculous revenge. Shaw, G. B.
Mirage. Simak, C. D.
The **mirror**. O'Flaherty, L.
The **mirror**. Singer, I. B.
Mirror days. Beigel, U.
Mirror showed darkness. Hoffman, I. B.
MIRRORS
  Bradbury, R. The dwarf
  Hirai, T. Hell of mirrors
  Singer, I. B. The mirror
Mirrors of Chartres Street. Faulkner, W.
Misadventure. Dunsany, E. J. M. D. P.
  18th baron
A **misdeal**. Somerville, E. A. O. and Martin,
  V. F.
Miserable merry Christmas. Steffens, L.
Mishka Nalymov. Tolstoï, A. N. Graf
Miss August. Hale, N.
Miss Baker. Pritchett, V. S.
Miss Brill. Mansfield, K.
Miss Cudahy of Stowes Landing. Elliott,
  G. P.
Miss Daisy. Campbell, W. E. M.
Miss Gentilbelle. Beaumont, C.
Miss Gillispie and the Micks. Hill, A.
Miss Glory. Reid, L.
Miss Harriet. Maupassant, G. de
Miss Hew. Van Doren, M.

Miss McGillicuddy. Perra, A.
Miss Maggie Doons and the wicked city.
  Chute, B. J.
Miss Morissa. Sandoz, M.
Miss Murphy. Armstrong, C.
Miss Paddleford. Caldwell, E.
Miss Precilla June Jones. Adams, A.
Miss Priss. Babcock, H.
Miss Rennsdale accepts. Tarkington, B.
Miss Sallie of Shot-a-Buck Crossing. Adams,
  A.
Missing letters. Marchi, E. de
Mission: romance! Curtis, M.
MISSIONARIES
  Allen, S. The martyrs
  Bradbury, R. Fire balloons
  Campbell, W. E. M. October Island
  Camus, A. The renegade
  Lofts, N. R. White man
  Marsh, W. N. The ethicators
  Maugham, W. S. Rain
  Maugham, W. S. Vessel of wrath
  Roberts, M. Remarkable conversion of
    the Rev. Thomas Ruddle
  Ruhen, O. Road to Heaven
  Ruhen, O. Woman Molak
  White, R. House of many rooms
MISSIONS
          California
  Gulick, G. C. "Conquest"

          India
  White, R. First voice
MISSISSIPPI
  Faulkner, W. By the people
  Faulkner, W. Raid
  Welty, E. Shower of gold

          Natchez Trace
  Welty, E. A still moment
MISSOURI
  Kantor, M. Voice of Bugle Ann
Mist on the meadow. Campbell, W. E. M.
A **mistake**. Maupassant, G. de
Mistaken identity. Chapman, M.
The **mister**. Sassoon, S. L.
Mr Agruvian and the red-tailed hawks.
  Moser, D.
Mr and Mrs Fix-it. Lardner, R. W.
Mr Bisbee's princess. Street, J. L.
Mr Bowdler's nightmare. Russell,
  B. A. W. R. 3d earl
Mr Cornelius, I love you. West, J.
Mr Costello, hero. Waldo, E. H.
Mister Death and the redheaded woman.
  Eustis, Helen
Mr Digby and the talking dog. Welch, D.
Mr Digby's swindle sheet. Welch D.
Mr Feasey. Dahl, R.
Mr Feeney's cheval. Saroyan, W.
Mr Feldman. Yaffe, J.
Mr Frisbie. Lardner, R. W.
Mr Gremmer. Farrell, J. T.
Mr Harrington's washing. Maugham, W. S.

Mr Higginbotham's catastrophe. Hawthorne, N.

Mr Hyde-de-Ho. Johns, V. P.

Mr Isaacs. Epstein, S.

Mr Kaplan and the Magi. Rosten, L. C.

Mr K*A*P*L*A*N the magnificent. Rosten, L. C.

Mr Kensington's finest hour. McGiffin, L.

Mr Know-All. Maugham, W. S.

Mr Loveday's little outing. Waugh, E.

Mr MacGregor. Lytle, A. N.

Mr Minnenick. Barker, A. L.

Mr Payson's satirical Christmas. Ade, G.

Mr Pope rides again. Brooks, W. R.

Mr. Pruitt. Robin, R.

Mr Rabbit nibbles up the butter. Harris, J. C.

Mr Sakrison's halt. Clingerman, M.

Mr Sampsell's thirty-pound diamond. Clayton, J. B.

Mr Skidmore's gift. La Farge, O.

Mr Stilwell's stage. Davidson, A.

Mr Weng's last forbidden dollar. Li, C.

Mr Whitcomb's genie. Brooks, W. R.

Mr Wickwire's "gun moll." Eberhart, M. G.

Mister Wister wins a war. Miller, E. M.

Mister Youth. Kerr, S.

Misti. Maupassant, G. de

Mistress and the master speak. Panzini, A.

Mrs Baxter's butterfly. Selb, K.

Mrs Brownlow's Christmas party. Allen, W. B.

Mrs Confederington. Walker, M.

Mrs Dixon's devil. Christie, K.

Mrs Golightly and the first convention. Wilson, E.

Mrs Gordon and the blind masseur. Kubly, H.

Mrs Lirriper's legacy. Dickens, C.

Mrs Lirriper's lodgings. Dickens, C.

Mistress of twenty. Pratolini, V.

Mrs Ripley's trip. Garland, H.

Mrs Rivkin grapples with the drama. Rosenberg, E. C.

Mrs Sludge. Balchin, N.

Mrs Webster. Blakiston, N.

Mrs Whitman. O'Hara, J.

Mitchell, E. Lane, 1909-
  Death learns the alphabet
    Oberfirst, R. ed. Anthology of best short-short stories v6

Mitchell, James Leslie, 1901-
  Smeddum
    Urquhart, F. ed. Scottish short stories

Mitchell, Mary E.
  For the honor of the company
    Fenner, P. R. comp. Brother against brother

Mitchell, William Ormand, 1914-
  Princess and the wild ones
    Nelson, G. E. ed. Cavalcade of the North

Mitchison, Naomi Margaret (Haldane) 1897-
  In the family
    Urquhart, F. ed. Scottish short stories

MIXED MARRIAGE. See Marriage, Mixed

MOBILE. See Alabama—Mobile

The moccasins. O'Hara, J.

Mocha cakes. Hale, N.

Model of a judge. Samachson, J.

MODEL RAILROADS. See Railroads—Models

MODELS. See Artists' models

MODELS, CLOTHING. See Models, Fashion (Persons)

MODELS, FASHION (PERSONS)
  Block, A. R. Love is a four letter word

Modern children. Rabinowitz, S.

MODERN GREECE. See Greece, Modern

Modern man in search of a soul. Lovell, V. R.

Mohammed Fripouli. Maupassant, G. de

MOHAMMEDANS
  Ali, A. Before death
  Household, H. The case of Valentin Lecormier
  Inber, V. Nor-Babi's crime
  Samuel, E. H. Before the flood
  Samuel, E. H. Japanese tea-set
  Samuel, E. H. Leila

Moldi
  Net fishers
    World prize stories; 2d ser.

MOLES (ANIMALS)
  Grahame, K. Dulce domum

Moll Cramer, Witch of Woodbury. Huntphreville, F. T.

Molloy, Ruth Branning, 1910-
  Twenty below, at the end of a lane
    Best American short stories, 1956

Molly Brandeis takes hold. Ferber, E.

Molly Morgan. Steinbeck, J.

Molly on the shore. Quinn, K.

Mom makes a wish. Yaffe, J.

Mom sheds a tear. Yaffe, J.

Moment before the rain. Enright, E.

Moment of decision. Ellin, S.

Moment of green laurel. Vidal, G.

Moment of truth. Criswell, C.

Moment of truth. Household, G.

Momentito. Guest, A.

Moments. Fossi, P.

Mona Lisa. O'Donovan, J.

MONACO
Monte Carlo
  Maugham, W. S. Facts of life

Monarch of the lagoons. Annixter, P. pseud

MONASTERIES
  Babel', I. E. End of Saint Hypatius

MONASTICISM AND RELIGIOUS ORDERS
  Daudet, A. Father Gaucher's elixir
  Miller, W. M. Canticle for Leibowitz
  O'Brian, P. Virtuous Peleg

Monday is another day. Farrell, J. T.

Monelli, Claudette. See Branch, Claudette Ann (Monelli)

MONEY
Fitzgerald, F. S. K. Forging ahead
Li, C. Mr Weng's last forbidden dollar
Macauley, R. Windfall
Marshall, B. Brigadier smells a rat
Rabinowitz, S. Hannukah money
Rhodes, E. M. Enchanted valley
Talbot, L. Maundesly J. Chandler

MONEY-LENDERS
Walsh, T. I killed John Harrington

Money to burn. Allingham, M.

MONGOLS
Moore, D. T. Terrible game

MONGOOSES
Kipling, R. "Rikki-tikki-tavi"

Monkey bridge. Dan, T. A. H.

MONKEYS
Keele, F. Telegraph mystery
Warner, S. T. At a monkey's breast
Whitehill, J. Able Baker

Monkey's paw. Jacobs, W. W.

MONKS
Daudet, A. Father Gaucher's elixir
Kantor, M. Unseen witness
Santucci, L. Visions of Fra Gelsomino
    See also Monasticism and religious orders

The **monocle.** Huxley, A. L.

The **monocrats.** West, A. C.

MONOLOGS
Criswell, C. Jocasta
Kober, A. Go be insulted when a fella hands you a compliment
Kober, A. Honey, don't you mix, honey, you butt out
Kober, A. I'da never found out about it, essept came the accident
Kober, A. What's a girl supposed to do—sit aroun' and twill her thumbs?
Lardner, R. W. Haircut
Lardner, R. W. Who dealt?
MacMahon, B. "So early in the morning, O!"

Monsieur Jocasta. Maupassant, G. de

Monsieur Parent. Maupassant, G. de

Monsieur Rouzade's little sow. Colette, S. G.

MONSTERS
Blackwood, A. The wendigo
Bradbury, R. The foghorn
Breuer, M. J. Hungry guinea pig
Clarke, A. C. Time's arrow
Maupassant, G. de. Mother of monsters

MONSTROSITIES. See Monsters

Montague, Margaret Prescott, 1878-
England to America
    First-prize stories, 1919-1957

MONTANA
Cushman, D. Old Copper Collar
McCarthy, M. T. Yellowstone Park

Montanelli, Indro, 1909-
His Excellency
    Slonim, M. L. ed. Modern Italian short stories

MONTE CARLO. See Monaco—Monte Carlo

Monte Saint Angele. Miller, A.

Montgomery, Robert Bruce, 1921-
Gladstone's candlestick
    Oberfirst, R. ed. Anthology of best short-short stories v6

Montgomery, Rutherford George, 1896-
King of the mesa
    Western Writers of America. Wild horse roundup
Voice of Jerome Kildee
    Western Writers of America. Branded West

MONTREAL. See Canada—Montreal

Montross, Lois (Seyster) 1897-
Good wife for a young doctor
    Teen-age tales, bk 3

MONUMENTS. See War memorials

Mood music rumble. Klimek, L. D.

MOON
Clarke, A. C. Venture to the moon
Heinlein, R. A. Black pits of Luna
Thomas, T. L. Far look

Moon of Montezuma. Woolrich, C.

Moon story. Aichinger, I.

Moonlight. Maupassant, G. de.

MOONSHINING. See Distilling, Illicit

Moore, Catherine Lucile, 1911-
No woman born
    Montgomery, R. B. ed. Best SF
    See also Kuttner, H. jt. auth.

Moore, Clement Clarke, 1779-1863
Legend of the Christmas tree
    Lohan, R. ed. Christmas tales for reading aloud
Noel candle
    Lohan, R. ed. Christmas tales for reading aloud

Moore, Dan Tyler
Terrible game
    Saturday evening post (Periodical) Saturday evening post stories, 1956

Moore, David E. 1923-
Fourth wall
    New voices 2: American writing today

Moore, George, 1852-1933
Home sickness
    O'Donovan, M. ed. Modern Irish short stories
Julia Cahill's curse
    Garrity, D. A. ed. 44 Irish short stories

Moore, John Cecil, 1907-
Local boy makes good
    Hudson, D. ed. Modern English short stories; 2d ser.

Moore, Nancy, 1908-
The matinee
    Oberfirst, R. ed. Anthology of best short-short stories v6

Moore, Ward, 1903-
Adjustment
    Magazine of fantasy and science fiction. Best from Fantasy and science fiction; 7th ser.
Dominions beyond
    Best science-fiction stories and novels: 1955
No man pursueth
    Magazine of fantasy and science fiction. Best from Fantasy and science fiction; 6th ser.

Muldur, Nil, 1934-
Friday is a lucky day
    Miller, N. ed. New campus writing, no. 2

Mule in the yard. Faulkner, W.

MULES. See Asses and mules

Mulkerns, Val
World outside
    Garrity, D. A. ed. 44 Irish short stories

MUMMIES
About, E. F. V. Strange will
Bradbury, R. Next in line

MUNITIONS INDUSTRY
Millholland, R. Big gun
Millholland, R. Production soldier
Millholland, R. Six-o'clock whistle
Millholland, R. Transformer on the line

Munro, Hector Hugh, 1870-1916
The bag
    Welcome, J. and Orchard, V. eds. Best hunting stories
Bertie's Christmas Eve
    Fremantle, A. J. ed. Christmas is here
The interlopers
    Swayze, B. ed. Short story magic
Open window
    Ridler, A. B. comp. Best ghost stories
    Sandrus, M. Y. ed. Famous mysteries
Reginald's Christmas revel
    Fremantle, A. J. ed. Christmas is here
Schartz-Metterklume method
    Nash, O. comp. I couldn't help laughing
Story teller
    Laughton, C. ed. Tell me a story

The **murder.** Chekhov, A. P.

Murder. Sansom, W.

Murder at the Vicarage. Christie, A. M.

Murder case. Sørensen, V.

Murder for fine art. Price, J. B.

Murder in the Alps. Quentin, P. pseud.

Murder in the Calais coach. Christie, A. M.

Murder in the cowshed. Vickers, R.

Murder in the sky. Harvey, F. L.

Murder in waltz time. Eberhart, M. G.

Murder me twice. Treat, L.

Murder, obliquely. Woolrich, C.

Murder of Roger Ackroyd. Christie, A. M.

Murder on Jefferson Street, Fisher, D. F. C.

Murder on the 7.16. Stewart, J. I. M.

Murder stops the music. McCloy, H.

MURDER STORIES
Adams, A. Trust and betrayal
Allen, S. Point of view
Anderson, E. Question of habit
Annixter, P. pseud. The dog
Aymé, M. Across Paris
Babel', I. E. Dante Street
Balchin, N. Cards for the colonel
Balzac, Honoré, de. La Grande Bretêche
Beaumont, C. Open house
Beauquey, M. In the other's shoes
Bentley, P. E. No road
Bloch, R. Dig that crazy grave!
Bradbury, R. April 2005: Usher II
Brown, M. D. M. Drawn into error
Brown, W. Anonymous fame
Burkett, B. S. Onions in the garden

Campbell, W. E. M. Dirty Emma
Camus, A. The stranger
Cather, W. S. Affair at Grover Station
Chekhov, A. P. The murder
Clarke, A. A. G. Magnifying glass
Clayton, J. B. Incident at Chapman's Switch
Clayton, J. B. Little Woodrow
Clayton, J. B. Warm day in November
Clemons, W. Dark roots of the rose
Cluff, G. B. Pearly gates are open
Coates, R. M. Accident at the Inn
Coppard, A. E. Judith
Crane, L. Dust and the serpent
Cullingford, G. Kill and cure
Curley, D. The ship
De Meyer, J. Safety for the witness
Deming, R. Custody
Dorrance, W. A. Devil on a hot afternoon
Douglass, D. M. The perfectionist
Downs, K. and Downs, C. A drink on the house
Eberhart, M. G. Bermuda grapevine
Eberhart, M. G. Crimson paw
Eberhart, M. G. Murder in waltz time
Ellin, S. Best of everything
Ellin, S. Broker's special
Ellin, S. Fool's mate
Ellin, S. Orderly world of Mr Appleby
Elston, A. V. Message delayed
Faulkner, W. Jealousy
Faulkner, W. The liar
Faulkner, W. Wash
Faulkner, W. Yo Ho and two bottles of rum
Feng, M. Canary murders
Fischer, B. Sam Rall's private ghost
Flanagan, T. This will do nicely
Forrestier, M. Gifts to my people
Foster, B. Killer at bay
Franklin, M. The geniuses
Glaspell, S. Jury of her peers
Gollschewsky, E. A. Clear case of self-defence
Gombrowicz, W. Premeditated crime
Hardesty, R. Anatomy lesson
Hartley, L. L. Killing bottle
Hawthorne, N. Mr Higginbotham's catastrophe
Hecht, B. Actor's blood
Henderson, D. From the mouse to the hawk
Hirai, T. The cliff
Hirai, T. Psychological test
Hirai, T. Red chamber
Hirai, T. Two crippled men
Huxley, A. L. Gioconda smile
Kantor, M. Grave grass quivers
Keller, D. H. The doorbell
King, R. Agree—or die
King, R. Body in the pool
King, R. Body in the rockpit
King, R. Let her kill herself
King, R. Malice in wonderland
King, R. Pills of Lethe
King, R. To remember you by
La Farge, O. The bystander
Lesinš, K. String of beads
Macrae, S. Serpent versus Donovan
Manners, M. A decidedly innocent man
Marceau, F. Armistice in Venice
Marlett, M. B. G. Purring countess
Marlowe, S. The shill

MUSICIANS—Singers—*Continued*
Boyle, K. Friend of the family
Cather, W. S. Count of Crow's Nest
Cather, W. S. Nanette: an aside
Cather, W. S. Singer's romance
Farrell, J. T. Young artist
Gerchunoff, A. Story of Miryam
Lowry, R. J. C. Passing star
Maugham, W. S. Voice of the turtle
O'Faoláin, S. Born genius
Swados, H. Day the singer fell
Trifonov, Y. Fedor Juzmich of the conservatoire
Van Doren, M. The ballad singer

Trombone players
Banks, R. E. Christmas trombone

Trumpeters
Conn, F. Coda
Cundiff, L. Trumpet man

Violinists
Borgese, E. M. The rehearsal
Burnett, W. Suffer the little children
Chavez, A. Fiddler and the angelito
Chekhov, A. P. Rothschild's fiddle
Kubly, H. The wasp
Lovecraft, H. P. Music of Erich Zann
MacDonagh, D. Duet for organ and strings
Tolstoĭ, L. N. Graf. Albert

MUSKELLUNGE
Young, S. White musky

MUSTACHE
Maupassant, G. de. Good reasons

MUSTANGS. See Horses

MUTATION (BIOLOGY) See Evolution

MUTINY
Doyle, Sir A. C. The "Gloria Scott"
Jackson, D. V. S. Gift of love
Melville, H. Billy Budd, foretopman

Mutiny of Sister Gervaise. Bonn, J. L.

My adventure in Norfolk. Alan, A. J.

My apples. Granat, R.

My blithe, sad bird. Stafford, J.

'My books are my children.' Johnson, P. H.

My boy friend's name is Jello. Davidson, A.

My brother, my brother. Burke, N.

My brother Paul. Dreiser, T.

My brother's voice. Upshaw, H.

My cat. Van Vechten, C.

My dogs had what it takes. Barker, E.

My enemy. Chamson, A.

My enemy's enemy. Amis, K.

My eyes no longer hear. Christensen, B.

My father and the Indians. Meyers, L.

My father joins the fire brigade. Shulz, B.

My father loved roses. O'Donovan, J.

My financial career. Leacock, S.

My first goose. Babel', I. E.

My first two women. Gordimer, N.

My heart saw you. Rendina, L. J. C.

My Lady Happiness. Reid, L.

My landlady. Maupassant, G. de

My life: The story of a provincial. Chekhov, A. P.

My little darling. Allen, S.

My mother's hands. Fontaine, R. L.

My mother's house. Colette, S. G.

My mother's love story. Halper, A.

My mother's Uncle Hal. Polk, W. T.

My name is Cricket. Todd, S. M.

My name is Legion. Vrettos, T.

My Œdipus complex. O'Donovan, M.

My old man. Hemingway, E.

My own true love story. Winslow, H.

"My queer dean." Queen, E. pseud.

My roomy. Lardner, R. W.

My sister was ugly. Moretti, U.

My sister's marriage. Rich, C. M.

My son, my son. Van Doren, M.

My surprise. Brandt, E. C.

My twenty-five days. Maupassant, G. de

My Uncle Jules. Maupassant, G. de

My Uncle Sosthenes. Maupassant, G .de

My wife. Maupassant, G. de

Myers, Ward, L.
Only a miracle
Fenner, P. R. ed. Heroes, heroes, heroes

MYOPIA
Babel', I. E. Line and color

Myself and a rabbit. MacGrian, M.

MYSTERIES AND MIRACLE PLAYS
Ewing, J. H. G. Peace egg

Mysteries of life in an orderly manner. West, J.

Mysterious box. Cottrell, D. W.

MYSTERY AND DETECTIVE STORIES
Alexander, D. Coffee and—
Allingham, M. One morning they'll hang him
Armstrong, C. What would you have done
Arthur, R. Sixty grand missing
Ashbaugh, D. The case of the missing sources
Asimov, I. Dust of death
Asimov, I. Singing bell
Bachrach, S. F. Walk-away kid
Barker, S. Fog on Pemble Green
Barry, J. Inside stuff
Best detective stories of the year (12th annual collection) 12 stories
Best detective stories of the year (13th annual collection) 12 stories
Best detective stories of the year—1955; 12 stories
Blochman, L. G. Swami of Northbank
Bradbury, R. Shopping for death
Burnham, C. Trapping of Tio
Child, C. B. Army of little ears
Christie, A. M. Murder in the Calais coach
Cohen, O. R. Perfect alibi
Commings, J. Great hunger
Cooke, D. C. ed. My best murder story; 14 stories
Coxe, G. H. No loose ends
Cunningham, J. M. **Within the law**
Deming, R. The choice
Douglass, D. M. The perfectionist
Dresser, D. Dead man's code

NAMES, PERSONAL
Chesterton, G. K. Tremendous adventures of Major Brown
Leskov, N. S. Clothes mender
Purdy, J. Don't call me by my right name

Nan Hogan's house. O'Kelly, S.

Nance, Berta Hart
She made the moon shine
Oberfirst, R. ed. 1955 anthology of best original short-shorts

Nancy. Enright, E.

Nanette. Caldwell, E.

Nanette: an aside. Cather, W. S.

Nanni Volpe. Verga, G.

Nanou the shepherdess. Jouhandeau, M.

Naoya, Shiga, 1883-
The patron Saint
McKinnon, R. N. ed. The heart is alone

A nap, prayers, and strawberries. Abramowitz, S. J.

NAPLES. See Italy—Naples

NAPOLÉON I, EMPEROR OF THE FRENCH

Invasion of Russia, 1812
Conrad, J. Warrior's soul

NAPOLEONIC WARS. See France—1800-1815; Napoléon I, Emperor of the French—Invasion of Russia, 1812

Nappie's grey horse. Trollope, A.

Narcissus unto echo. West, A. C.

NARCOTIC HABIT
Faulkner, W. Uncle Willy
Haner, R. The fix

NARCOTICS
Clayton, J. B. Snowfall on Fourth Street
Forrestier, M. Gifts to my people
Goehring, D. Towser the terrific
Green, C. Compliments of Caliph Bernie
Pevehouse, A. Kachina dolls
Wylie, P. Smuggler's cove
See also Narcotic habit; Opium habit; Opium trade

Narges. Daneshvar, S.

Narrative of the ghost of a hand. Le Fanu, J. S.

Nash, Hazel I.
Brooding spirit
Bronfeld, S. ed. Treasury of new short fiction

Nash, Ogden, 1902-
Stranger in the house
Nash, O. comp. I couldn't help laughing

Nasty Kupperman and the Ku Klux Klan. Berg, L.

Natalie and John. Angoff, C.

NATCHEZ TRACE. See Mississippi—Natchez Trace

Nathan, Robert, 1894-
Digging the Weans
Merril, J. ed. SF: '57
Parable of peace and war
Schwarz, L. W. ed. Feast of Leviathan
Portrait of Jennie
Costain, T. B. and Beecroft, J. eds. Stories to remember

National pastime. Cheever, J.

NATIONAL SOCIALISM
Taper, B. Inge
See also Fascism

NATIONALISM
Boyle, K. Effigy of war

Natives don't cry. Boyle, K.

Natural state. Knight, D.

Natural thing. Davis, E.

Nature of man. Davies, R.

Nature's way. Mankowitz, W.

NAVAHO INDIANS
Eastlake, W. Quiet chimneys
La Farge, O. All the young men

NAVAL AERONAUTICS. See Aeronautics, Military

NAVAL AIRPLANES. See Airplanes, Military

NAVAL LIFE. See Seamen; also subdivision Navy under various countries: e.g. Great Britain. Navy; United States. Navy

Naval treaty. Doyle, Sir A. C.

NAVY. See Seamen; also subdivision Navy under various countries: e.g. Great Britain. Navy; United States. Navy; etc.

NAVY OFFICERS. See Great Britain. Navy—Officers; United States. Navy—Officers; etc.

NAZIS. See National socialism

Near miss. Kuttner, H.

Near the margin of the bay. Hall, J. B.

Nearing, Homer, 1915-
Cerebrative psittacoid
Montgomery, B. ed. Best SF

NEARSIGHTEDNESS. See Myopia

Nebel, Frederick
Try it my way
Queen, E. pseud. ed. Ellery Queen's awards: 11th ser.

NEBRASKA
Cather, W. S. The best years
Cather, W. S. The enchanted bluff
Cather, W. S. A resurrection
Stone, N. B. Vengeance trail

Farm life
See Farm life—Nebraska

Necessity of his condition. Davidson, A.

The necklace. Maupassant, G. de

The necklace. Pritchett, V. S.

NECKLACES
Christie, A. M. Murder at the Vicarage
Maupassant, G. de. The necklace
Pritchett, V. S. The necklace
Thompson, L. and Boswell, C. Mystery of the nine clean seals

The need. Coates, M.

Neglect a fire and it spreads. Tolstoǐ, L. N. Graf

Negresses. See Negroes

NEGRO DIALECT. See Dialect stories—Negro

NEGRO LAWYERS. See Law and lawyers

NEGRO SOLDIERS. See Negroes as soldiers

NEGRO TEACHERS. See Teachers

NEGROES

Adams, A. Miss Precilla June Jones
Albee, G. S. Little Hiram
Allen, S. Point of view
Balchin, N. Tinfield mascot
Baldwin, J. Sonny's blues
Benét, S. V. Freedom's a hard-bought thing
Berg, L. Snowball man and Holy Writ
Blassingame, W. Man's courage
Block, A. R. Something borrowed—something blue
Boyle, K. Ben
Boyle, K. Black boy
Bradbury, J. June 2003: way in the middle of the air
Caldwell, E. The people vs. Abe Lathan: colored
Campbell, W. E. M. The funeral
Chute, B. J. Birthday gift
Clayton, J. B. Incident at Chapman's Switch
Conn, F. Coda
Cottrell, D. W. Mysterious box
Crabtree, P. Dixie
Crews, S. P. Newspapers in heaven
Curley, D. A spring
Downey, H. The song
Dreiser, T. Nigger Jeff
Ellison, R. Flying home
Farrell, J. T. Kilroy was here
Farrell, J. T. Norman Allen
Faulkner, W. Bear hunt
Faulkner, W. Sunset
Faulkner, W. That evening sun
French, J. Love is a flaming angel
Gold, H. An afternoon with the appliances
Griffin, J. H. Whole world in his hands
Hammett, E. A. Mattie dear
Hopkins, J. G. E. Gone to freedom
Hughes, L. One Friday morning
Joyce, B. Cocktail hour
Lee, R. J. Moth and the star
Leonard, N. H. Rich
Le Vino, E. G. Cora
Lochridge, B. H. Callie Daniel
Lochridge, B. H. Will Davis
McKinney, D. L. Night man
McLaughlin, R. Short wait between trains
McMullen, J. A. Sampson and the blue "Delilahs"
Malamud, B. Angel Levine
Marby, T. D. Lula Borrow
Matthiessen, P. Travelin man
Maupassant, G. de. Boitelle
Maupassant, G. de. King's son
O'Connor, F. Circle in the fire
Patton, F. G. Piece of luck
Paul, L. No more trouble for Jedwick
Polk, W. T. Coralee's burden-bearer
Polk, W. T. Night the races were supposed to riot
Polk, W. T. Supply man
Porter, K. A. The circus
Porter, K. A. The witness
Purdy, J. Eventide
Rutledge, A. H. Fabulous quest
Rutledge, A. H. Ghost of the graveyard

Rutledge, A. H. Phantom huntsmen
Sommers, M. O. Haven't we been nice to you?
Stuart, R. M. Duke's Christmas
Sunwall, B. Things changed
Swados, H. Day the singer fell
Taylor, P. H. What you hear from 'em?
Truax, L. Man alone
Warren, R. P. Blackberry winter
Welty, E. Livvie
Welty, E. Livvie is back
Welty, E. Worn path
Williams, T. Desire and the black masseur
Wilner, H. Passion for Silver's arm
Wolfe, T. Face of the war
Wright, R. Big, black, good man
Wright, R. What you don't know won't hurt you
Yerby, F. G. Health card

NEGROES AS SERVANTS

Alexander, S. White boat
Allan, G. Boysi
Boyle, K. White as snow
Campbell, W. E. M. She talks good now
Faulkner, W. That evening sun
Gordimer, N. Happy event
Lochridge, B. H. Claudie
Lochridge, B. H. Death
Lochridge, B. H. Foots
Lochridge, B. H. Hattie
Lochridge, B. H. Lila
Porter, K. A. Last leaf
Porter, K. A. Old order
Smith, J. R. To sleep and to wake
Steele, W. D. Can't cross Jordan by myself
Wellman, M. W. Mayor calls his family
See also Servants

NEGROES AS SOLDIERS

McLaughlin, R. Short wait between trains.
Yerby, F. G. Health card
See also Soldiers

NEGROES IN BRAZIL

Camus, A. Growing stone

Neighbor Rosicky. See Cather, W. S. Neighbour Rosicky

NEIGHBORS

Aichinger, I. Window entertainment
Coppard, A. E. Willie Waugh
Faulkner, W. The rosary
Fisher, D. F. C. Murder on Jefferson Street
Powers, J. F. Blue Island
Saroyan, W. The inventor and the actress
Tolstoi, L. N. Graf. Neglect a fire and it spreads

Neighbour Rosicky. Cather, W. S.

Neihardt, John Gneisenau, 1881-
Last thunder song
Schaefer, J. W. ed. Out West

Ne'ilah. Peretz, I. L.

Nellthu. White, W. A. P.

NELSON, HORATIO NELSON, VISCOUNT, 1758-1805
Melville, H. Billy Budd, foretopman

Nemerov, Howard, 1920-
Delayed hearing
Best American short stories, 1958

Nemerov, Howard—*Continued*
Tradition
Prize stories, 1956: the O. Henry awards
Yore
Best American short stories, 1955
Neola, pseud.
Mad about motors
Seventeen (Periodical) Stories from
Seventeen
NEPHEWS
Aymé, M. Legend of Poldevia
Bentley, P. E. Isabella, Isabella
Henderson, D. From the mouse to the
hawk
Lofts, N. R. Forty years on
Verga, G. Nanni Volpe
See also Uncles
NEPHITES
Carmer, C. L. The wandering Nephite
NERO, EMPEROR OF ROME, 37-68
Russell, R. Last will and testament
**NERVOUS BREAKDOWN. See Neuras-
thenia**
Nest of gentlefolk. Macauley, R.
The nester and the unclothed lady. Spears,
R. S.
Net fishers. Moldi
Net nemesis. Coombs, C. I.
Nets are for fish. Worthington, J.
NEURASTHENIA
Brenner, A. E. Turbulence at the lake
Cheever, J. Five-forty-eight
Ferber, E. Long distance
Hoffman, I. B. Time for smiles
Lamble, W. B. I couldn't understand
White, E. B. Second tree from the corner
NEUROSES
Cather, W. S. Paul's case
Elliott, W. Y. Watch in the night
Hale, N. The fox
Seymour, M. Theresa
NEUROTICS. See Neuroses
NEUTRALITY
Stockton, F. R. The skipper and el
Capitan
NEVADA
Clark, W. Van T. Wind and the snow
of winter
Ranch life
See Ranch life—Nevada
Never take no for an answer. Gallico, P. W.
Never underestimate. Waldo, E. H.
Neville, Kris
Experiment station
Conklin, G. ed. Science-fiction adven-
tures in mutation
Overture
Healy, R. J. ed. 9 tales of space and
time
New accelerator. Wells, H. G.
New boy. Cole, S.
New boy in town. Schleyen, M.
New dress. Woolf, V. S.
NEW ENGLAND
Fisher, D. F. C. The bedquilt
Wharton, E. N. J. Angel at the grave

18th century
Humphreville, F. T. Moll Cramer, Witch
of Woodbury
20th century
Coates, R. M. The reward
Farm life
See Farm life—New England
**NEW ENGLAND DIALECT. See Dialect
stories—New England**
New-fangled machinery. Ward, L. L.
NEW GUINEA
Ruhen, O. Beautiful pattern
Ruhen, O. Brown Jonathan
Ruhen, O. Dark of the moon
Ruhen, O. Guardians of Mobali
Ruhen, O. Head-hunters of Ianagl
Ruhen, O. The husbandmen
Ruhen, O. Land of Dahori; 14 stories
Ruhen, O. Road to Heaven
Ruhen, O. Sergeant Pangae, detective
Ruhen, O. Sword of laughter
Ruhen, O. Village of phantom ships
Ruhen, O. Vision at the spring
Ruhen, O. Wisdom of Ragos
Ruhen, O. Woman Molak
Ruhen, O. Woman of Labu
NEW HAMPSHIRE
Benét, S. V. Devil and Daniel Webster
New immigrants. Gerchunoff, A.
NEW JERSEY
Atlantic City
Boyle, K. Ben
Boyle, K. Black boy
Ferber, E. Holiday
New kid. Heyert, M.
New life. Miller, N.
NEW MEXICO
Cather, W. S. Tom Outland's story
Chavez, A. Black ewe
Chavez, A. Fiddler and the angelito
Chavez, A. From an altar screen; 7
stories
Chavez, A. Lean years
Chavez, A. Wake for Don Corsinio
Foster, B. Night of terror
Granat, R. My apples
La Farge, O. Pause in the desert
Rhodes, E. M. Aforesaid Bates
18th century
Chavez, A. Bell that sang again
19th century
Rhodes, E. M. Cheerful land
Rhodes, E. M. No mean city
Richter, C. The lady
20th century
Chavez, A. Colonel and the santo
Rhodes, E. M. Barred door
Santa Fé
Chavez, A. Ardent commandant
Savage, L. Traitor town
New order. Hale, N.
**NEW ORLEANS. See Louisiana—New
Orleans**
New Orleans. Faulkner, W.

New perspective. Hilsher, J. M.

NEW PLANETS. See Planets

New suit. O'Flaherty, L.

New Villa. Chekhov, A. P.

New wine. Christopher, J.

NEW WORLDS. See Future, Stories of the; Interplanetary voyages

NEW YEAR
Andersen, H. C. Little match girl
Leskov, N. S. Clothes mender
Ritchie, L. A. da C. Pleasure of their company
Wilson, A. Ten minutes to twelve

NEW YEAR'S EVE. See New Year

New Year's gift. Maupassant, G. de

NEW YORK (CITY)
Knight, D. Natural state
Schleyen, M. Wonderful town

19th century
Wharton, E. N. J. Bunner Sisters
Winslow, T. S. Cycle of Manhattan

20th century
Chute, B. J. Miss Maggie Doons and the wicked city
Ferber, E. Keep it holy
Ferber, E. Nobody's in town
Gellhorn, M. E. In sickness and in health
Lowry, R. J. C. Mystery bus ride
Lowry, R. J. C. New York call girl
Nathan, R. Portrait of Jennie
Runyon, D. Blood pressure
Weidman, J. The tuxedos
Wolfe, T. Alone

East Side
Lowry, R. J. C. Long for this word

Greenwich Village
Allen, S. Girls on the tenth floor
Garrett, G. The seacoast of Bohemia
Malamud, B. The prison
Porter, W. S. Last leaf
Rainer, D. Room at the Inn

Harlem
Baldwin, J. Sonny's blues
Winslow, T. S. City folks

Manhattan
Allen, S. The purpose and the name
Beigel, U. Victoria at night
Capote, T. Breakfast at Tiffany's
Chute, B. J. Rookie cop
Coates, R. M. The oracle
Farrell, J. T. They don't know what time it is
Melville, H. Bartleby the scrivener
Tekeyan, C. N.Y. is all ours!
Turner, R. 11 o'clock bulletin
West, A. C. Upper room
Wharton, E. N. J. After Holbein
Wolfe, T. Death the proud brother

Queens
Mailer, N. K. Prologue: the man who studied Yoga

NEW YORK (STATE)

18th century
Irving, W. Rip Van Winkle

Dobbs Ferry
Carmer, C. L. Wraith on Cedar Street

Saratoga Springs
Carmer, C. L. Screaming ghost of Saratoga

New York call girl. Lowry, R. J. C.

New York girls. Dever, J.

Newcomb, Ellsworth
Grand slam
Furman, A. L. ed. Everygirls romance stories

Newhouse, Edward, 1911-
The ambassador
Prize stories, 1958: The O. Henry awards
Four freedoms
Fenton, C. A. ed. Best short stories of World War II
Poker game
Lewis, J. D. ed. Dealer's choice

NEWLYWEDS. See Marriage; Marriage problems

Newmen, Wiley Clifford
Protestant Saint Francis
Orr, E. and Hammett, E. A. eds. Delta Decameron

News from Chelsea. Sansom, W.

News of Paris—fifteen years ago. Fitzgerald, F. S. K.

NEWS PHOTOGRAPHY. See Photography, Journalistic

NEWSBOYS
Saroyan, W. Home of the human race
Saroyan, W. Love of London
Wolfe, T. Paper route

NEWSPAPER PUBLISHERS. See Journalists

NEWSPAPER WORK. See Journalists

Newspapers in heaven. Crews, S. P.

Next in line. Bradbury, R.

Next stop. Housley, A.

Next time, stay home! Block, A. H.

Next to godliness. Pittinger, V.

Next to last bullet. Derby, M. pseud.

Next-to-last dance of the season. O'Hara, J.

NEY, MICHEL, DUC D'ELCHINGEN, PRINCE DE LA MOSKOWA, 1769-1815
Rutledge, A. H. Was he Marshal Ney?

NICE. See France—Nice

Nice girl. Anderson, S.

Nicholas, St. See Santa Claus

Nicholson, Margaret
The outcast
Oberfirst, R. ed. 1955 anthology of best original short-shorts

Nick and Letty, their love story. Coleman, W. L.

Nickleman, Henry, pseud. See Cather, Willa

Nicolas. O'Brian, P.

Niehuis, Charles C.
Hound music
Western Writers of America. Hound dogs and others

Nielsen, Helen
  You can't trust a man
    Best detective stories of the year—1955
Nigger Jeff. Dreiser, T.
Night. Oliver, C.
Night: A nightmare. Maupassant, G. de
Night at Galon-Uchaf. Jones, G.
Night at Greenway Court. Cather, W. S.
Night at the fair. Fitzgerald, F. S. K.
Night club in the woods. Calisher, H.
NIGHT COURTS. See Trials
Night filled with music. Jackson, D. V. S.
Night flight. Johnson, J. W.
Night guest. Nagibin, Y.
Night is your friend. Ingalls, C. J.
Night man. McKinney, D. L.
Night my brother came home. Kaplan, R.
Night of disaster. MacLeish, R.
Night of panic. Kantor, M.
Night of terror. Foster, B.
Night of the Iguana. Williams, T.
Night of the two wakes. Curley, D.
Night on Octavia Street. Byers, J. M.
Night run to the West. Bates, H. E.
NIGHT SCHOOLS. See Evening and continuation schools
Night solo. Miller, E. M.
Night the men from Mars came. Polk, W. T.
Night the races were supposed to riot. Polk, W. T.
The night the stair creaked. Johnson, W. R.
Night walk. Blixen, K.
NIGHT WATCHMEN. See Watchmen
Night worker. Pritchett, V. S.
Nightcrawlers. Kennedy, R. C.
The nightingale. Anderson, H. C.
NIGHTINGALES
  Andersen, H. C. The nightingale
The nightmare. Cooke, D. C.
Nightmare blues. Herbert, F.
NIGHTMARES. See Dreams; Somnambulism
Nightsound. Budrys, A. J.
Niland, D'Arcy, 1920
  Away to moonlight
    World prize stories; 2d ser.
Nimrod, pseud. See Apperley, Charles James
Nine billion names of God. Clarke, A. C.
Nine friends.. Lederer, W. J. and Burdick, E. L.
Nine rosaries to St Stanislaus Kostika. Miller, E. M.
1959. Samuel, E. H.
1917. Tabib, M.
Ninth life. De La Roche, M.
Nitia. Reid, L.
No enemy. Kantor, M.
No fatted calf. West, A. C.
No game for children. Merritt, M.
No harm trying. Fitzgerald, F. S. K.

No loose ends. Coxe, G. H.
No man pursueth. Moore, W.
No mean city. Rhodes, E. M.
No medal for Mallory. Piesse, A. V.
No mistakes. O'Hara, J.
No more trouble for Jedwick. Paul, L.
No morning after. Clarke, A. C.
No, not like yesterday. Rice, C.
No place for girls. Polk, W. T.
No place for you, my love. Welty, E.
No road. Bentley, P. E.
No room at the Inn. Ferber, E.
No second coming. McCarthy, A. Q.
No sense of humor. Rosmond, B.
No sum too small. Hoyt, M.
No tea for the Memsahib. Cope, J.
No thoroughfare. Dickens, C.
No woman born. Moore, C. L.
NOBILITY. See Aristocracy
Noblesse oblige. Coleman, W. L.
Nobody bothers Gus. Budrys, A. J.
Nobody can beat Freidkin's meats. Kober, A.
Nobody knows what the stork will bring. Criswell, C.
Nobody's in town. Ferber, E.
Nobody's story. Dickens, C.
Nocturne. Berriault. G.
Noel candle. Moore, C. C.
Noncommissioned officer. Maupassant, G. de
NONCONFORMISTS. See Dissenters
Nonie. Kasson, H.
NONSENSE STORIES. See Humor
Noon wine. Porter, K. A.
Nor-Bibi's crime. Inber, V.
Nor dust corrupt. McConnell, J.
Nora. Soldati, M.
A Norman. Maupassant, G. de
Norman Allen. Farrell, J. T.
NORMANDY. See France, Provincial and rural—Normandy
Normandy joke. Maupassant, G. de
NORTH AFRICA. See Africa, North
NORTH AMERICAN INDIANS. See Indians of North America
NORTH CAROLINA

18th century

Key, A. Caroliny Trail

Folklore

  See Legends and folk tales—North Carolina

Roanoke Island

Rutledge, A. H. Lost colony
North of the corduroy. Gray, C.
NORTHWEST MOUNTED POLICE. See Canada. Royal Canadian Mounted Police

Norton, Alice Mary
Moustrap
    Best science-fiction stories and novels: 1955

Norton, Andre, pseud. See Norton, Alice Mary

NORWAY
Blixen, K. Babette's feast

NORWEGIANS IN THE UNITED STATES
Cather, W. S. Eric Hermannson's soul
Cather, W. S. On the divide
Lewis, S. Young Man Axelbrod

The **nose.** Gogol', N. V.

The **nose.** Pincherle, A.

Not a child any more. Schweitzer, G.

Not a lick of sense. Gardiner, D.

Not another word. Thurman, R. Y.

Not Isaac. West, A. C.

Not like in the movies. Logan, B. T.

Not like Tom. Van Doren, M.

Not liking to pass the road again. O'Brian, P.

Not to the victor. Rutledge, A. H.

Not with our fathers. Rothberg, A. A.

Not worthy of a Wentworth. Campbell, W. E. M.

NOTABLE PERSONS. See Celebrities

NOTARIES
Maupassant, G. de. Fair exchange
Maupassant, G. de. Queer night in Paris

NOTARY PUBLICS. See Notaries

Notes from the underground. Dostoevskiĭ, F. M.

Nothing ever happens. Fisher, D. F. C.

Notorious jumping frog of Calaveras County. Clemens, S. L.

Nourse, Alan Edward
Family resemblance
    Conklin, G. ed. Science-fiction adventures in mutation

NOVA SCOTIA
Bird, W. R. When a boy's a man

NOVELISTS. See Authors

November love. Gable, B. L.

November 2005: the luggage store. Bradbury, R.

November 2005: the off season. Bradbury, R.

November 2005: the watchers. Bradbury, R.

Novograd church. See Babel', I. E. Church at Novograd

Now hear the cattle. Llewellyn, R.

Now I lay me. Hemingway, E.

Now is the time. Schiller, M. B.

Now let us sleep. Davidson, A.

Now we know. O'Hara, J.

Number of things. Rhodes, E. M.

NUMBER SYMBOLISM. See Symbolism of numbers

The **numismatist.** Rhodes, E. M.

Nun and the sailor. Rogers, J. A.

NUNNERIES. See Convent life

Nunnery garden. MacMahon, B.

NUNS
Bonn, J. L. Mutiny of Sister Gervaise
Columcille, M. Reaction
Cook, B. G. Old English fishing
Coogan, J. F. Double skull, slow burn, and a ping
Doyle, M. Vicarious experience
Farrell, J. T. Bride of Christ
Farrell, J. T. Episode in a dentist's office
Hemingway, E. Gambler, the nun and the radio
Huxley, A. L. Nuns at luncheon
MacMahon, B. Nunnery garden
O'Faoláin, S. Mother Matilda's book
O'Faoláin, S. Teresa
Paul, L. Sin of Sister Louise
Rea, D. Piededifico
Rogers, J. A. Nun and the sailor
Thierry, M. P. The Sisters
    See also Convent life

Nuns at luncheon. Huxley, A. L.

The **nurse.** Pincherle, A.

NURSEMAIDS. See Servants—Nursemaids

Nursery rhyme. Beaumont, C.

NURSES AND NURSING
Anderson, E. Question of habit
Brown, T. K. Drink of water
Coleman, W. L. Nick and Letty, their love stories
Garrett, G. The witness
Hagedorn, H. Edith Cavell
Hale, N. Miss August
Heggen, T. The birthmark
Lardner, R. W. Zone of quiet
Maupassant, G. de. The devil
Pincherle, A. The nurse
Rinehart, M. R. The secret
Sommers, M. O. Haven't we been nice to you?

NURSING HOMES
Lofts, N. R. All that is necessary

NUTS
Clayton, J. B. Silence of the mountains

Nuts and reasons. Cohen, O. R.

Nye, Harriet L.
Jerry
    Oberfirst, R. ed. Anthology of best short-short stories v5

O

O. Henry, pseud. See Porter, William Sydney

O, lonely moon! MacMahon, B.

O youth and beauty! Cheever, J.

Oakes, Philip
Lion in the house
    Pudney, J. ed. Pick of today's short stories, 9

The **oar.** O'Flaherty, L.

O'Donovan, Michael—Continued

The pariah
  O'Donovan, M. Domestic relations
Peasants
  Davin, D. M. ed. English short stories
  of today, 2d ser.
  Jarrell, R. ed. Anchor book of stories
Pity
  O'Donovan, M. Domestic relations
Private property
  O'Donovan, M. Domestic relations
Repentance
  Gettman, R. A. and Harkness, B. eds.
  Book of stories
Salesman's romance
  O'Donovan, M. Domestic relations
Study of history
  O'Donovan, M. Domestic relations
That Ryan woman
  Saturday evening post (Periodical)
  Saturday evening post stories, 1957
Ugly duckling
  O'Donovan, M. Domestic relations
Uprooted
  Havighurst, W. ed. Masters of the mod-
  ern short story

Odor of chrysanthemums. Lawrence, D. H.

ODYSSEUS. See Ulysses

Odyssey of Old Specs. Annixter, P. pseud

The **Œdipus** complex. Pritchett, V. S.

Of course. Oliver, C.

Of Doctor Heraclius Gloss. Maupassant, G. de

Of hidden thoughts and of heaven. Blixen, K.

Of missing persons. Finney, J.

Of this time, of that place. Trilling, L.

Of those who came. Longdon, G.

O'Faoláin, Seán, 1900-

Admiring the scenery
  O'Faoláin, S. Finest stories of Seán
  O'Faoláin
Born genius
  O'Faoláin, S. Finest stories of Seán
  O'Faoláin
Broken world
  O'Faoláin, S. Finest stories of Seán
  O'Faoláin
Childybawn
  O'Faoláin, S. Finest stories of Seán
  O'Faoláin
The confessional
  O'Faoláin, S. Finest stories of Seán
  O'Faoláin
Discord
  O'Faoláin, S. Finest stories of Seán
  O'Faoláin
End of a good man
  O'Faoláin, S. Finest stories of Seán
  O'Faoláin
End of the record
  O'Faoláin, S. Finest stories of Seán
  O'Faoláin
An enduring friendship
  O'Faoláin, S. Finest stories of Seán
  O'Faoláin
Fugue
  O'Faoláin, S. Finest stories of Seán
  O'Faoláin

Fur coat
  O'Faoláin, S. Finest stories of Seán
  O'Faoláin
Judas touch
  O'Faoláin, S. Finest stories of Seán
  O'Faoláin
Lord and master
  O'Faoláin, S. Finest stories of Seán
  O'Faoláin
Lovers of the lake
  O'Faoláin, S. Finest stories of Seán
  O'Faoláin
Man who invented sin
  Hall, J. B. and Langland, J. T. eds.
  Short story
  Havighurst, W. ed. Masters of the mod-
  ern short story
  O'Faoláin, S. Finest stories of Seán
  O'Faoláin
Midsummer night madness
  O'Faoláin, S. Finest stories of Seán
  O'Faoláin
Mother Matilda's book
  O'Faoláin, S. Finest stories of Seán
  O'Faoláin
Old master
  O'Faoláin, S. Finest stories of Seán
  O'Faoláin
One true friend
  O'Faoláin, S. Finest stories of Seán
  O'Faoláin
The patriot
  O'Faoláin, S. Finest stories of Seán
  O'Faoláin
Persecution mania
  Garrity, D. A. ed. 44 Irish short stories
  O'Faoláin, S. Finest stories of Seán
  O'Faoláin
Silence of the valley
  O'Faoláin, S. Finest stories of Seán
  O'Faoláin
Sinners
  O'Faoláin, S. Finest stories of Seán
  O'Faoláin
Teresa
  Garrity, D. A. ed. 44 Irish short stories
  O'Faoláin, S. Finest stories of Seán
  O'Faoláin
The trout
  O'Donovan, M. ed. Modern Irish short
  stories
  O'Faoláin, S. Finest stories of Seán
  O'Faoláin
Unholy living and half dying
  O'Donovan, M. ed. Modern Irish short
  stories
  O'Faoláin, S. Finest stories of Seán
  O'Faoláin
Up the bare stairs
  O'Faoláin, S. Finest stories of Seán
  O'Faoláin

O'Farrell, William, 1904-

Girl on the beach
  Queen, E. pseud. ed. Ellery Queen's
  13th annual

OFFICE BOYS
  Pritchett, V. S. Chestnut tree
  Pritchett, V. S. It may never happen

OFFICE WORKERS. See Clerks

Officer Mulvaney and the hot buttered pig.
  Brooks, W.

Officers' club girl. Miller, E. M.

Ōgai, Mori, 1862-1922
Takasebune
McKinnon, R. N. ed. The heart is alone
Ogden, Florence (Sillers)
Ordeal by fire
Orr, E. and Hammett, E. A. eds. Delta
Decameron
Oh, brother! Schleyen, M.
Oh hymen honey moo. Piper, D.
Oh, once in my saddle. Lamson, D. A.
O'Hara, John, 1905-
Are we leaving tomorrow?
O'Hara, J. Selected short stories
Bread alone
O'Hara, J. Selected short stories
Cold house
O'Hara, J. Selected short stories
The decision
O'Hara, J. Selected short stories
Do you like it here?
O'Hara, J. Selected short stories
Doctor and Mrs Parsons
O'Hara, J. Selected short stories
Doctor's son
Baudin, M. ed. Contemporary short
stories v3
O'Hara, J. Selected short stories
Drawing room B
Lewis, J. D. ed. Great stories about
show business
Everything satisfactory
O'Hara, J. Selected short stories
Graven image
O'Hara, J. Selected short stories
Hotel kid
O'Hara, J. Selected short stories
I could have had a yacht
O'Hara, J. Selected short stories
Ideal man
O'Hara, J. Selected short stories
In the morning sun
O'Hara, J. Selected short stories
King of the desert
O'Hara, J. Selected short stories
Mrs Whitman
O'Hara, J. Selected short stories
The moccasins
O'Hara, J. Selected short stories
Next-to-last dance of the season
O'Hara, J. Selected short stories
No mistakes
O'Hara, J. Selected short stories
Now we know
O'Hara, J. Selected short stories
Other women's households
O'Hara, J. Selected short stories
Over the river and through the wood
O'Hara, J. Selected short stories
Pardner
O'Hara, J. Selected short stories
Phase of life
O'Hara, J. Selected short stories
Price's always open
O'Hara, J. Selected short stories
Public career of Mr Seymour Harrisburg
O'Hara, J. Selected short stories
Respectable place
O'Hara, J. Selected short stories
Secret meeting
O'Hara, J. Selected short stories

Summer's day
O'Hara, J. Selected short stories
Too young
O'Hara, J. Selected short stories
Walter T. Carriman
O'Hara, J. Selected short stories
War aims
O'Hara, J. Selected short stories
Where's the game?
Lewis, J. D. ed. Dealer's choice
O'Hara, J. Selected short stories
OHIO
Cincinnati
Lowry, R. J. C. Floodwater! Floodwater!
OIL. See Petroleum
Oil. Babel', I. E.
Oil. Levitt, L. I.
OIL WELLS. See Petroleum
OINTMENTS
Lofts, N. R. Father Francisco's ointment
O'Kelly, Seumas, 1881-1918
Michael and Mary
Garrity, D. A. ed. 44 Irish short stories
Nan Hogan's house
Garrity, D. A. ed. 44 Irish short stories
OKLAHOMA
19th century
Bailey, J. Run for the strip
Ol' Nick's wife. Dow, D.
Old acquaintance. Tolstoĭ, L. N. Graf
OLD AGE
Allen, S. The war
Angoff, C. Alto Bobbe
Babel', I. E. End of the old folk's home
Bahr, J. Old banker Evan
Bates, H. E. Queen of Spain fritillary
Beaumont, C. The customers
Berriault, G. Like a motherless child
Blackburn, T. W. Buckskin pensioner
Block, A. R. Man among men
Boyle, K. Keep your pity
Bradbury, R. Touched with fire
Cather, W. S. Neighbour Rosicky
Clark, W. Van T. Wind and the snow of
winter
Coates, R. M. The reward
Curley, D. House called Magnolia
Davis, H. L. Old man Isbell's wife
Divided horsecloth
Dreiser, T. Lost Phoebe
Ellin, S. Blessington Method
Enright, E. Moment before the rain
Enright, E. One for the collection
Epstein, S. Mr Isaacs
Evans, C. Be this her memorial
Ferber, E. Old Man Minick
Fisher, D. F. C. Old Man Warner
Fontaine, R. L. My mother's hands
Galsworthy, J. Ultima Thule
Hemingway, E. Clean, well-lighted place
Hemingway, E . Old man at the bridge
Jewett, S. O. Flight of Betsey Lane
Johns, V. P. Gentleman caller
Lampman, B. H. Blinker was a good dog
Lardner, R. W. Golden honeymoon
Lessing, D. M. The woman
Linklater, E. Kind Kitty
Lofts, N. R. Gift for a queen
Lofts, N. R. Good memory

Olgin, Joseph—*Continued*
Surprise attack
Olgin, J. Sports stories for boys
Two-play Kelton
Olgin, J. Sports stories for boys
Olive grove. See Maupassant, G. de. Olive orchard
Olive orchard. Maupassant, G. de
Oliver, Chad, 1928-
Artifact
Oliver, C. Another kind
Between the thunder and the sun
Magazine of fantasy and science fiction. Best from Fantasy and science fiction; 7th ser.
Didn't he ramble
Best science-fiction stories and novels; 9th ser.
Mother of necessity
Oliver, C. Another kind
Night
Oliver, C. Another kind
Of course
Best science-fiction stories and novels: 1955
Rite of passage
Oliver, C. Another kind
Scientific method
Oliver, C. Another kind
Star above it
Oliver, C. Another kind
Transformer
Oliver, C. Another kind
Oliver, Chad, 1928- and Beaumont, Charles, 1929-
Last word
Magazine of fantasy and science fiction. Best from Fantasy and science fiction; 5th ser.
Olsen, Tillie
Help her to believe
Stanford short stories, 1956
Same as: I stand here ironing
Hey sailor, what ship?
Miller, N. ed. New campus writing, no. 2
Stanford short stories, 1957
I stand here ironing
Best American short stories, 1957
Same as: Help her to believe
Olsen. Farrell, J. T.
Olson, Allen Dale, 1930-
Axel's adieu
Oberfirst, R. ed. Anthology of best short-short stories v5
O'Malley, Frank Ward
Shipping the claret to port
Saturday evening post (Periodical)
Saturday evening post Carnival of humor
Omar James. Farrell, J. T.
O'Meara at Troy. Marquis, D.
Omnibus of short stories. Farrell, J. T.
OMNIBUSES. See Motor buses
On a seder night. Heine, H.
On a spring evening. Maupassant, G. de
On account of a hat. Rabinowitz, S.
On cats. Maupassant, G. de
On Christmas Eve. Stökl, H. B.

On guard. Waugh, E.
On official business. Chekhov, A. P.
On Saturday afternoons. Kroner, J.
On stage. Schleyen, M.
On stony ground. Sansom, W.
On the beach. Hale, N.
On the bog. O'Brian, P.
On the divide. Cather, W. S.
On the elevator. Brennan, J. P.
On the hoof. Warner, A. S.
On the line. Swados, H.
On the mountainside. Roberts, E. M.
On the river. Maupassant, G. de.
On the threshold. Auerbach, E.
Once a lady. Wilson, A.
One afternoon, Adam. Calvino, I.
One arm. Williams, T.
One big error. Karner, E. F.
One coat of white. Smith, H. A.
One day in April. Block, A. R.
One-day land. Lesinš, K.
$1.98. Porges, A.
One evening. Maupassant, G. de
One-eyed poacher's revenge. Smith, E. W.
One-eyed wolf of Kaamas Fell. Wallenius, K. M.
One foot on the ground. Stillwell, G. F.
One for the book. Kober, A.
One for the collection. Enright, E.
One for the road. Swados, H.
One Friday morning. Hughes, L.
One interne. Fitzgerald, F. S. K.
One man's meat. Greene, V.
One moment of truth. Block, A. R.
One more mile to go. Smith, F. J.
One more river. Haycox, E.
One morning in June. Gallant, M.
One morning they'll hang him. Allingham, M.
One night. Kazuo, H.
One of the boys. Block, A. R.
One of the chosen. Calisher, H.
One of the family. O'Donovan, J.
One of the family. Yaffe, J.
One of us. Samuel, E. H.
One ordinary day, with peanuts. Jackson, S.
One phase of love. Maupassant, G. de
One star by night. Haycox, E.
One-tenth man. Gilbert, M. F.
$1,000 a week. Farrell, J. T.
One thousand miles up. Robinson, F. M.
One trip abroad. Fitzgerald, F. S. K.
One true friend. O'Faoláin, S.
One way street. Bixby, J.
One with Shakespeare. Foley, M.
O'Neill, A.
Survival
Pudney, J. ed. Pick of today's short stories, 9

O'Neill, James
Jake was a tomboy
Teen-age tales, bk 3
Onions in the garden. Burkett, B. S.
Only a miracle. Myers, W. L.
Only on rainy nights. Van Doren, M.
Only son. Farrell, J. T.
Only son, the mother, and Elijah the Prophet. Rabinowitz, S.
Only the dead ride proudly. Fox, N. A.
Only the trade winds know. Harrington, J.
O'Nolan, Brian, 1911-
Martyr's crown
Garrity, D. A. ed. 44 Irish short stories
ONTARIO. See Canada—Ontario
Open boat. Crane, S.
Open house. Beaumont, C.
Open season. Summers, J. L.
Open window. Munro, H. H.
Opened order. Aichinger, I.
OPERA SINGERS. See Musicians—Singers
Operation glazier. Day Lewis, C.
Operation octopus. Price, W. D.
Operation queen bee. O'Donovan, J.
OPERATIONS, SURGICAL. See Surgery
The **operator.** Enright, E.
OPIATES. See Narcotics
OPIUM HABIT
Clayton, J. B. Snowfall on Fourth Street
OPIUM TRADE
Smith, E. H. Justice and Juan Morales
Or else. Kuttner, H.
The **oracle.** Coates, R. M.
Oranges. Eidman, L.
ORATORIOS
Richards, A. E. Worthy is the lamb
Orchard, Vincent. See Welcome, J. jt. auth.
ORCHARDS
Granat, R. My apples
The **orchards.** Thomas, D.
Orchids and fishing togs. Henson, I.
Ordeal by fire. Ogden, F. S.
Ordeal of young Tuppy. Wodehouse, P. G.
The **orderly.** Maupassant, G. de
Orderly world of Mr Appleby. Ellin, S.
ORDERS, MONASTIC. See Monasticism and religious orders
OREGON
Davis, H. L. Old man Isbell's wife

Frontier and pioneer life
See Frontier and pioneer life—Oregon
OREGON TRAIL
Guthrie, A. B. The way West
ORGAN
West, J. Music on the Muscatatuck
ORGANISTS. See Musicians—Organists
The **Orient.** Maupassant, G. de
ORIGIN OF SPECIES. See Evolution
Original Sam. Angoff, C.
Ormond, Sophia. See Ormond, Sophie K.

Ormond, Sophie K.
All's fair
Oberfirst, R. ed. Anthology of best short-short stories v6
You're never too old
Oberfirst, R. ed. 1955 anthology of best original short-shorts
Orneriest three. Coburn, W.
O'Rourke, Frank, 1916-
Cool one
O'Rourke, F. Hard men
Crooked nail
O'Rourke, F. Hard men
Final payment
O'Rourke, F. Hard men
Grandpa's .45's
O'Rourke, F. Hard men
Home town
O'Rourke, F. Hard men
Point of justice
O'Rourke, F. Hard men
Reaction
O'Rourke, F. Hard men
Speak to me only with thine eyes
O'Rourke, F. Hard men
Stretch in time
O'Rourke, F. Hard men
Stronger medicine
O'Rourke, F. Hard men
Way of a trooper
O'Rourke, F. Hard men
The **orphan.** Maupassant, G. de
The **orphan.** Peretz, I. L.
ORPHANS
Bowen, E. Maria
Caldwell, E. Nannette
Enright, E. The Sardillion
Gallico, P. W. Never take no for an answer
O'Donovan, J. Little Scotch skirt
Peretz, I. L. The orphan
Rabinowitz, S. I'm lucky—I'm an orphan
Rawlings, M. K. Mother in Mannville
Ringwood, G. P. Little ghost
Simak, C. D. Contraption
Smith, E. H. Small side of Doroteo Arango
Orphans. O'Donovan, M.
Orr, Ellen
He found his fortune in the Delta
Orr, E. and Hammett, E. A. eds. Delta Decameron
Home again for Mr Muff
Orr, E. and Hammett, E. A. eds. Delta Decameron
Home for Consuela
New voices 2: American writing today
ORTHODOX EASTERN CHURCH, GREEK
Franko, I. I. The plague
ORTHODOX EASTERN CHURCH, RUSSIAN
Plimmer, D. Man in the black cloak
Ortiz's Mass. Lytle, A. N.
Osamu, Dazai. See Dazai, Osamu
Osborn, Millicent, 1910-
Spit
American vanguard, 1956

Osbourne, Lloyd, 1868-1947
  The renegade
    Stead, C. ed. Great stories of the South
    Sea Islands
Osgood, Laura, 1917-
  Birthday gift
    Oberfirst, R. ed. 1955 anthology of best
    original short-shorts
Oshidori. Hearn, L.
Osterman, Marjorie, 1917-
  First time
    American vanguard, 1956
  Fraulein
    New voices 2: American writing today
Ostroff, Anthony, 1923-
  La bataille des fleurs
    Best American short stories, 1958
The Ostrovskys. Angoff, C.
O'Sullivan-Barra, Jerem
  The password
    Hughes, R. ed. All manner of men
The other Alexander. Lyberaki, M.
Other Celia. Waldo, E. H.
Other inauguration. White, W. A. P.
Other man. Waldo, E. H.
The other Paris. Gallant, M.
Other people. Brackett, L.
The other side of the sky. Clarke, A. C.
Other two. Wharton, E. N. J.
Other women's households. O'Hara, J.
OTTERS
  Annixter, P. pseud. Keepers of the river
    dam
  Murphy, R. You've got to learn
Our best friend is an eagle. Mannix, J.
Our feathered friends. MacDonald, P.
Our friends the English. Maupassant, G. de
Our letters. Maupassant, G. de
Our very best people. Ferber, E.
Oursler, Will. See Oursler, William Charles
Oursler, William Charles, 1913-
  The shadow and the shadowed
    Mystery Writers of America, inc. Crime
    for two
Out of Chicago. Bahr, J.
Out of Nazareth. Faulkner, W.
Out of season. Gordimer, N.
Out of the darkness. Byrd, J. J.
Out of the sun. Clarke, A. C.
Outburst. Sansom, W.
The outcast. Nicholson, M.
The outcasts. Chute, B. J.
Outcasts of Poker Flat. Harte, B.
OUTDOOR LIFE
  Bird, W. R. When a boy's a man
  De Eds, J. And the moon rose on Yellow-
    hammer
    See also Camping
OUTER SPACE
      Exploration
  Clarke, A. C. Cosmic Casanova
  Clarke, A. C. The star
  Elam, R. M. First man into space
  St Clair, M. Prott

OUTER SPACE, VISITS TO OR FROM.
  See Interplanetary visitors; Inter-
  planetary voyages
Outgoing of the tide. Buchan, J. 1st baron
  Tweedsmuir
OUTLAWS
  Barker, S. O. Pup and the bad man
  Cameron, O. Civilized man
  Prebble, J. The regulator
  Rinehart, M. R. Cave on thunder cloud
  Welty, E. A still moment
    See also Brigands and robbers;
    Crime and criminals
Outpost of progress. Conrad, J.
Outside. Aldiss, B. W.
Outside and inside. Bennett, A.
Outside the cabinet-maker's. Fitzgerald,
  F. S. K.
Over here. Lowry, R. J. C.
Over the river and through the wood.
  O'Hara, J.
OVERLAND JOURNEYS
  La Farge, O. Old men's plans
OVERLAND JOURNEYS TO THE PA-
  CIFIC
  Ferber, E. Trees die at the top
OVERPRODUCTION
  Pohl, F. Midas plague
Overture. Neville, K.
Ovid
  Atalanta's race
    Rosenblum, M. ed. Stories from many
    lands
The owl. Gerchunoff, A.
Owl hoots twice. Rohmer, S. pseud
OWLS
  Brown, M. Snow owl
  Colette, S. G. Tawny owls
Owner of the pinto horse. Adams, A.
Ox and the ass at the manger. Supervielle, J.
OXEN
  Adams, A. Old Turk and the slicker
  Supervielle, J. Ox and the ass at the
  manger
    See also Cattle
The oyster. Godden, R.
Oyster-catcher. Gilbert, M. F.
OYSTERS
  Sullivan, F. The ugly mollusk

P

P. & O. Maugham, W. S.
P.C.X. 36. Beerbohm, Sir M.
PACIFISM. See Peace
Pacing goose. West, J.
PADRES. See Catholic priests
PADUA. See Italy—Padua
Pagano, Joe, 1906-
  Signor Santa
    Fremantle, A. J. ed. Christmas is here
Page from the Song of Songs. Rabino-
  witz, S.

PENNSYLVANIA

18th century
Allen, H. Boy turns turtle

Philadelphia
Madden, H. T. Date with a stranger

Penny is bitten by a rattlesnake. Rawlings, M. K.

PENOLOGY. See Punishment

PENSIONS (BOARDING HOUSES) See Boarding houses

Pentecost, Hugh, pseud. See Philips, Judson Pentecost

People in places. Hale, N.

The **people** vs. Abe Lathan: colored. Caldwell, E.

Pepicelli. Buechler, J.

PEPPERS
Street, J. H. Grains of paradise

Per far l'amore. Hartley, L. P.

Percheron. Sarver, L. J.

Peretz, Isaac Loeb, 1851-1915
All for a pinch of snuff
  Peretz, I. L. In this world and the next
Bass viol
  Peretz, I. L. In this world and the next
Beryl the tailor
  Peretz, I. L. In this world and the next
Buntcheh the Silent
  Peretz, I. L. In this world and the next
  Same as: Bontsha the Silent
The Cabalists
  Peretz, I. L. In this world and the next
Conversation on a hilltop
  Peretz, I. L. In this world and the next
Domestic idyll
  Peretz, I. L. In this world and the next
  Same as: Domestic peace
Domestic peace
  Kobler, F. ed. Her children call her blessed
  Same as: Domestic idyll
Eighth circle of Gehenna
  Peretz, I. L. In this world and the next
Eternal peace in the Land of Somewhere
  Peretz, I. L. In this world and the next
Four generations and four wills
  Peretz, I. L. In this world and the next
If not higher
  Peretz, I. L. In this world and the next
Journey in time
  Peretz, I. L. In this world and the next
The magician
  Peretz, I. L. In this world and the next
Marred holiday
  Peretz, I. L. In this world and the next
Marriage
  Peretz, I. L. In this world and the next
The messenger
  Peretz, I. L. In this world and the next
Miracles on the sea
  Peretz, I. L. In this world and the next
Morning in a basement
  Peretz, I. L. In this world and the next
Ne'ilah
  Peretz, I. L. In this world and the next
The orphan
  Peretz, I. L. In this world and the next

Pious cat
  Peretz, I. L. In this world and the next
Reb Noah and the Rabbi of Brest
  Peretz, I. L. In this world and the next
Reincarnation of a melody
  Peretz, I. L. In this world and the next
Seven good years
  Schwarz, L. W. ed. Feast of Leviathan
  Same as: Seven years of plenty
Seven years of plenty
  Peretz, I. L. In this world and the next
  Same as: Seven good years
Shtraimel
  Peretz, I. L. In this world and the next
Supreme sacrifice
  Peretz, I. L. In this world and the next
A teacher's tales
  Peretz, I. L. In this world and the next
Thou shalt not covet
  Peretz, I. L. In this world and the next
Three offerings
  Peretz, I. L. In this world and the next
Times of the Messiah
  Peretz, I. L. In this world and the next
The treasure
  Peretz, I. L. In this world and the next
Two deathbeds
  Peretz, I. L. In this world and the next
A woman's wrath
  Peretz, I. L. In this world and the next

Pérez de Ayala, Ramón, 1881-
Prometheus
  Flores, A. ed. Great Spanish stories

Perez Galdos, Benito, 1843-1920
Torquemada in the flames
  Flores, A. ed. Great Spanish stories

Perfect alibi. Cohen, O. R.

Perfect day. Block, A. R.

The **perfect** game. Pincherle, A.

Perfect marriage. Palme, I.

Perfect sucker. Charteris, L.

The **perfectionist.** Douglass, D. M.

Perfume spray. Strousse, F.

Peril from outer space. Elam, R. M.

Peril of the blue world. Abernathy, R.

Perils for trial. Harper, J.

Perils of certain English prisoners. Dickens, C.

Perkins, Frederick Beecher, 1828-1899
Devil-puzzlers
  Davenport, B. ed. Deals with the devil

Perl, Philip
Man in Israel
  Ribalow, H. U. ed. Treasury of American Jewish stories

Permission for Africa. Schiller, M. B.

Perra, Albert
Miss McGillicuddy
  Oberfirst, R. ed. Anthology of best short-short stories v6

Perret, Jacques, 1901-
The fly
  Lehmann, J. ed. Modern French stories

Perry, Jennings
Poker face
  Lewis, J. D. ed. Dealer's choice

PHOTOGRAPHS
Rosen, I. Time is, time was

PHOTOGRAPHY
Schleyen, M. And what's your hobby?
See also Photographers

PHOTOGRAPHY, JOURNALISTIC
Welch, D. Mr Digby's swindle sheet

Phyllis. Angoff, C.

PHYSICAL CULTURE. See Physical education and training

PHYSICAL EDUCATION AND TRAINING
Purdy, J. You may safely gaze

PHYSICIANS
Adams, A. Good for two drinks
Angoff, C. Leader of the community
Benét, S. V. Doc Mellhorn and the pearly gates
Bentley, P. E. No road
Blackwood, A. Psychical invasion
Blackwood, A. Smith: an episode in a lodginghouse
Blaustein, P. M. and Blaustein, A. P. eds. Doctor's choice; 16 stories
Boyle, K. White horses of Vienna
Brown, J. Rab and his friends
Buck, P. S. The enemy
Campbell, W. E. M. Bill's eyes
Campbell, W. E. M. The slate
Čapek, K. Giddiness
Chekhov, A. P. Two tragedies
Cobb, I. S. "Speaking of operations—"
Davis, M. Flip of a coin
Fitzgerald, F. S. K. One interne
Fox, N. A. Bannack doctor
Fox, N. A. Saddlebag sawbones
Fuchs, D. Twilight in Southern California
Gerchunoff, A. Miraculous doctor
Gorbatov, B. L. Man is born
Gordimer, N. Charmed lives
Graves, J. Green fly
Hawthorne, N. Rappaccini's daughter
Hecht, B. Miracle of the fifteen murderers
Horgan, P. Heart attack
James, H. Middle years
Kafka, F. Country doctor
Kornbluth, C. M. Little black bag
LaMar, N. Creole love song
Lardner, R. W. Zone of quiet
Lessing, D. M. Eye of God in paradise
Lochridge, B. H. Dr Borosky
Macken, W. The sailor
Macken, W. Tuesday's children
MacMahon, B. Candle is lighting
Marks, W. John's other practice
Marlett, M. B. G. Purring countess
Maugham, W. S. Lord Mountdrago
Maupassant, G. de. Affair of state
Maupassant, G. de. An artifice
Merritt, M. Till Gabriel blows his horn
Millar, M. The couple next door
O'Faoláin, S. Lovers of the lake
O'Hara, J. Doctor and Mrs Parsons
O'Hara, J. Doctor's son
O'Rourke, F. Speak to me only with thine eyes
Pritchett, V. S. Passing the ball
Stafford, J. The warlock
Strong, L. A. G. White cottage
Turgenev, I. S. District doctor
Unamuno y Jugo, M. de. Abel Sanchez

Unamuno y Jugo, M. de. Madness of Doctor Montarco
West, J. Horace Chooney, M. D.
Wharton, E. N. J. Angel at the grave
Williams, W. C. Jean Beicke
Williams, W. C. Use of force
Woollcott, A. Vanishing lady
Wright, R. What you don't know won't hurt you
Yellen, S. Saturn has the power
Zweig, S. Amok
See also Surgery; Women as physicians

PHYSICISTS
Balchin, N. God and the machine
Cooper, W. Ball of paper

PIANISTS. See Musicians—Pianists

The piano. Armel, C.

Picard, Jacob
The brother
Picard, J. The marked one, and twelve other stories
The call
Picard, J. The marked one, and twelve other stories
The darkest hour
Picard, J. The marked one, and twelve other stories
The fish
Picard, J. The marked one, and twelve other stories
The forest
Picard, J. The marked one, and twelve other stories
The fox
Picard, J. The marked one, and twelve other stories
Lottery ticket
Picard, J. The marked one, and twelve other stories
The marked one
Picard, J. The marked one, and twelve other stories
The Parnes is taught a lesson
Picard, J. The marked one, and twelve other stories
Raphael and Recha
Picard, J. The marked one, and twelve other stories
The sin
Picard, J. The marked one, and twelve other stories
Two mothers
Kobler, F. ed. Her children call her blessed
Picard, J. The marked one, and twelve other stories
The wooer
Picard, J. The marked one, and twelve other stories

Pickens, Lonnie, 1929-
Consolation prize
New voices 2: American writing today

PICKPOCKETS. See Crime and criminals

Pickthall, Marjorie Lowry Christie, 1883-1922
Worker in sandalwood
Nelson, G. E. ed. Cavalcade of the North
Swayze, B. ed. Short story magic

The **picnic**. Clegg, C.
The **picnic**. Gallant, M.
PICNICS
  Chute, B. J. Three in a stew
  Clegg, C. The picnic
  Gallant, M. The picnic
  Wilson, A. Et Dona Ferentes
Picture if you will. Taylor, R. L.
Picture-well. Aymé, M.
"The **picture** wouldn't fit in the stove."
    Bradshaw, G.
PICTURES
  Cather, W. S. Night at Greenway Court
  Epstein, S. Happy birthday
  Hirai, T. The traveler with the pasted **rag**
    picture
        See also Paintings
Pictures don't lie. MacLean, K.
Piece of bread. Patton, F. G.
Piece of cake. Creasey, J.
Piece of luck. Patton, F. G.
Piece of red calico. Stockton, F. R.
Piece of steak. London, J.
Piece of string. Maupassant, G. de
Piededifico. Rea, D.
Pierhead jump. Grablowsky, I.
Piesse, A. V.
  No medal for Mallory
    World prize stories; 2d ser.
PIETY. See Religion
The **pig**-bristle slugger. Graves, L.
Pig-fat and slick as weasels. Adams, A.
The **pigeon**. Allen, S.
PIGEONS
  Allen, S. The pigeon
  Carmer, C. L. Tale of the white dove
  Lessing, D. M. Flight
  O'Brian, P. Little death
  O'Faoláin, S. End of a good man
  Tekeyan, C. Wow!
PIGS
  Chesterton, G. K. Unobtrusive traffic of
    Captain Pierce
  Colette, S. G. Monsieur Rouzade's little
    sow
  Davis, W. F. Lady Luck and the guardian
    angel
  Linderman, F. B. Jake Hoover's pig
  MacMahon, B. Close to the clay
  Nourse, A. E. Family resemblance
  O'Flaherty, L. The blow
  Smith, E. H. Wake for El Gusano
Pilgrimage. Brophy, B.
PILGRIMAGES. See Pilgrims and pil-
    grimages
PILGRIMS AND PILGRIMAGES
  Brophy, B. Pilgrimage
  O'Faoláin, S. Lovers of the lake
  Tolstoi, L. N. Graf. Two old men
Pillar of fire. Wilde, P.
PILLORIES
  Haynes, D. K. The head
Pills of Lethe. King, R.
PILOTS, AIRPLANE. See Air pilots

PIMPS
  Kubly, H. Horseback
Pinch of salt. Sullivan, R.
Pincherle, Alberto, 1907-
  Agostino
    Hamalian, L. and Volpe, E. L. eds. **Ten**
      modern short novels
  Appetite
    Pincherle, A. Roman tales
  The baby
    Pincherle, A. Roman tales
  Back to the sea
    Pincherle, A. Bitter honeymoon, and
      other stories
  Bitter honeymoon
    Pincherle, A. Bitter honeymoon, and
      other stories
  The caretaker
    Pincherle, A. Roman tales
  The clown
    Pincherle, A. Roman tales
  Don't delve too deeply
    Pincherle, A. Roman tales
  English officer
    Pincherle, A. Bitter honeymoon, and
      other stories
  The fall
    Pincherle, A. Bitter honeymoon, and
      other stories
    Strachen, W. J. ed. Modern Italian
      stories
  The fanatic
    Pincherle, A. Roman tales
  The film test
    Pincherle, A. Roman tales
  Friendship
    Pincherle, A. Roman tales
  The girl from Ciociaria
    Pincherle, A. Roman tales
  The go-between
    Pincherle, A. Roman tales
  Hot weather jokes
    Pincherle, A. Roman tales
  I don't say no
    Pincherle, A. Roman tales
  The imbroglio
    Pincherle, A. Bitter honeymoon, and
      other stories
  Jewellery
    Pincherle, A. Roman tales
  The lorry-driver
    Pincherle, A. Roman tales
  Mario
    Pincherle, A. Roman tales
  The nose
    Pincherle, A. Roman tales
  The nurse
    Pincherle, A. Roman tales
  A pair of spectacles
    Pincherle, A. Roman tales
  The perfect game
    Pincherle, A. Roman tales
  Poor fish
    Pincherle, A. Roman tales
  Rain in May
    Pincherle, A. Roman tales
  Rapist and the fisherman
    Oberfirst, R. ed. Anthology of best
      short-short stories v6
  The ruin of humanity
    Pincherle, A. Roman tales

Pincherle, Alberto—*Continued*
Sick boy's winter
  Pincherle, A. Bitter honeymoon, and other stories
Silly old fool
  Pincherle, A. Roman tales
The strawberry mark
  Pincherle, A. Roman tales
Taboo
  Pincherle, A. Roman tales
The terror of Rome
  Pincherle, A. Roman tales
Tired courtesan
  Pincherle, A. Bitter honeymoon, and other stories
The treasure
  Pincherle, A. The treasure
Unfortunate lover
  Pincherle, A. Bitter honeymoon, and other stories
  Slonim, M. L. ed. Modern Italian short stories

Pinchot, Ann. See Pinchot, B. jt. auth.

Pinchot, Ben, and Pinchot, Ann
Two old for dolls
  Furman, A. L. ed. Everygirls romance stories

Pink. Parr, E.

PIONEER LIFE. See Frontier and pioneer life

Pioneers in Maine. Gould, J.

Pious cat. Peretz, I. L.

The pipe. Weatherby, K.

PIPE LINES
  Smith, E. W. Underground episode

Piper, David
Oh hymen honey moo
  Winter's tales, 1

Piper, H. Beam, 1904-
He walked around the horses
  Montgomery, R. B. ed. Best SF three
Police operation
  Norton, A. M. ed. Space police

Piping down the valleys wild. Brodkey, H.

Pip's first cricket match. Beith, J. H.

PIRACY. See Pirates

Pirandello, Luigi, 1867-1936
The bat
  Slonim, M. L. ed. Modern Italian short stories
Black kid
  Strachan, W. J. ed. Modern Italian stories
The cat, a goldfinch, and the stars
  Thurston, J. A. ed. Reading modern short stories
War
  Thurston, J. A. ed. Reading modern short stories

Pirate ghosts of Dismal Swamp. Carmer, C. L.

PIRATES
  Carmer, C. L. How ocean-born Mary came back from the dead
  Dickens, C. Perils of certain English prisoners
  Howard, R. E. and De Camp, L. S. Road of the eagles
  Masefield, J. Anty Bligh

Pirates aid decision. Morgan, A. V.

Pisa. See Italy—Pisa

Pitcher and the plutocrat. Wodehouse, P. G.

Pitfalls of love. Shenhar, Y.

Pitman, Sarah C.
Baby is born in Israel
  Kobler, F. ed. Her children call her blessed

Pittinger, Virginia
Next to godliness
  Seventeen (Periodical) Seventeen's stories

Pity. O'Donovan, M.

PIZARRO, FRANCISCO, 1475?-1538
  Lytle, A. N. Alchemy

The place and the time. Hale, N.

Place for lovers in the summertime. Kentfield, C.

A place in the heart. Bates, H. E.

Place of the throwing-stick. Bryning, F.

Placet is a crazy place. Brown, F.

PLAGUE
  Jenkins, W. F. Plague
  Poe, E. A. Masque of the Red Death

The plague. Franko, I. I.

Plague. Jenkins, W. F.

Plain and fancy. Van Doren, M.

Plain people of England. MacMahon, B.

The plan. Sulkin, S.

Plan now to attend. Purdy, J.

Plane down—hurricane area. Wylie, P.

Planet passage. Wollheim, D. A.

PLANETOIDS. See Planets, Minor

PLANETS. See names of individual planets, e.g. Mars; Venus; etc.

PLANETS, MINOR
  Oliver, C. Didn't he ramble

PLANTATION LIFE
  Conrad, J. Planter of Malata
  Curley, D. House called Magnolia
  Lytle, A. N. Jericho, Jericho, Jericho
  Lytle, A. N. Mr MacGregor
  Ritchie, L. A. da. C. Pleasure of their company

Planter of Malata. Conrad, J.

Plants and girls. Lessing, D. M.

PLATO
Death of Socrates
  Sterner, L. G. ed. Favorite short stories
      About
  Cook, B. G. Greek fishing

PLATONIC LOVE. See Love, Platonic

Play that got away. Saroyan, W.

The playground. Enright, E.

Playgrounds, parties, and the primordial molecule. Epstein, S.

PLAYING CARDS. See Cards

PLAYWRIGHTS. See Dramatists

Pleasure. Lessing, D. M.

Pleasure of their company. Ritchie, L. A. da C.

Plimmer, Denis
Man in the black cloak
This week magazine. This week's
Stories of mystery and suspense

Plomer, William Charles Franklyn, 1903-
Ever such a nice boy
Hudson, D. ed. Modern English short
stories; 2d ser.
Friend of her father's
Winter's tales, 2
Thy neighbour's creed
Gettman, R. A. and Harkness, B. eds.
Book of stories

Plow deep. Sampter, J. E.

Plowshare in heaven. Stuart, J.

PLUMBERS
Pincherle, A. Friendship

PLUMBING
Emerson, C. D. Running water

Plumtree, Catherine
Innuendo
Oberfirst, R. ed. Anthology of best
short-short stories v6

Plundered orchard. Gerchunoff, A.

Plunkett, James, 1920-
The damned
Plunkett, J. The trusting and the
maimed, and other Irish stories
Dublin Fusilier
Plunkett, J. The trusting and the
maimed, and other Irish stories
Eagles and the trumpets
O'Donovan, M. ed. Modern Irish short
stories
Plunkett, J. The trusting and the
maimed, and other Irish stories
Half-crown
Plunkett, J. The trusting and the
maimed, and other Irish stories
Janey Mary
Plunkett, J. The trusting and the
maimed, and other Irish stories
Mercy
Plunkett, J. The trusting and the
maimed, and other Irish stories
The trusting and the maimed
Plunkett, J. The trusting and the
maimed, and other Irish stories
Wearin' of the green
Plunkett, J. The trusting and the
maimed, and other Irish stories
The web
Plunkett, J. The trusting and the
maimed, and other Irish stories
Weep for our pride
Garrity, D. A. ed. 44 Irish short stories
Plunkett, J. The trusting and the
maimed, and other Irish stories

Plutarch's lives. Peattie, D. C. and Peattie,
L. R.

PNEUMONIA
Bates, H. E. Common denominator
Porter, W. S. Last leaf

The **poacher.** Hartley, F. P.

POACHERS. See Poaching

POACHING
Macken, W. The river
Munro, H. H. The interlopers
Smith, E. W. Courtship of Jeff Coongate
Smith, E. W. Rum over the dam
Walker, D. H. Summertime adventure

Pocock passes. Pritchett, V. S.

Pod in the barrier. Waldo, E. H.

Poe, Edgar Allan, 1809-1849
Casks of Amontillado
Jennings, F. G. and Calitri, C. J. eds.
Stories
Rosenblum, M. ed. Stories from many
lands
Sterner, L. G. ed. Favorite short stories
Descent into the Maelström
Hart, J. D. and Gohdes, C. L. eds.
America's literature
Swayze, B. ed. Short story magic
Fall of the House of Usher
Costain, T. B. and Beecroft, J. eds.
Stories to remember
Hart, J. D. and Gohdes, C. L. eds.
America's literature
McMaster, J. ed. Stories to remember
Gold bug
Sandrus, M. Y. ed. Famous mysteries
Masque of the Red Death
Hart, J. D. and Gohdes, C. L. eds.
America's literature
Locke, L. G.; Gibson, W. M. and Arms,
G. W. eds. Introduction to literature
Thorp, W. ed. Southern reader
Premature burial
Hall, J. B. and Langland, J. T. eds.
Short story
The purloined letter
Hart, J. D. and Gohdes, C. L. eds.
America's literature
Tell-tale heart
Hart, J. D. and Gohdes, C. L. eds.
America's literature

The **poet.** Gerchunoff, A.

The **poet.** Sandoz, M. Y.

The **poet.** Williams, T.

POETESSES. See Poets

POETRY
Curtis, M. Mission: romance!

POETS
Beerbohm, Sir M. Enoch Soames
Blixen, K. Converse at night in Copen-
hagen
Curley, D. Appointed hour
Dazai, O. Villon's wife
Farrell, J. T. Love story of our time
Jones, G. Night at Galon-Uchaf
Lardner, R. W. Maysville minstrell
Macauley, R. Chevigny man
Macauley, R. Guide to the Muniment
Room
Maugham, W. S. Colonel's lady
Mudrick, M. Professor and the poet
Nabokov, V. V. Forgotten poet
Sandoz, M. Y. The poet
Saroyan, W. Proud poet
Williams, T. Field of blue children
Williams, T. The poet

POGROMS. See Jews—Persecutions

Pohl, Frederik, 1919?-
Census takers
Magazine of fantasy and science fiction.
Best from Fantasy and science fiction;
6th ser.
The ghost-maker
Pohl, F. Alternating currents
Grandy devil
Pohl, F. Alternating currents

Pohl, Frederik—*Continued*
  Happy birthday, dear Jesus
    Pohl, F. Alternating currents
  Haunted corpse
    Galaxy science fiction magazine. Third
    Galaxy reader
  Let the ants try
    Pohl, F. Alternating currents
  The mapmakers
    Pohl, F. Alternating currents
  Midas plague
    Greenberg, M. ed. All about the future
  Pythias
    Pohl, F. Alternating currents
  Rafferty's reasons
    Pohl, F. Alternating currents
  Target one
    Pohl, F. Alternating currents
  Tunnel under the world
    Pohl, F. Alternating currents
  What to do until the analyst comes
    Pohl, F. Alternating currents
Point crazy. Olgin, J.
Point of honor. Beaumont, C.
Point of justice. O'Rourke, F.
Point of view. Allen, S.
POINTERS (DOGS)
  James, A. Something to talk with
  Prishvin, M. M. His first point
POISON PEN LETTERS. See Letters,
  Stories about
POISONING
  Canning, V. Mystery of Kela Ouai
    See also Poisons
POISONOUS PLANTS
  Hawthorne, N. Rappaccini's daughter
POISONS
  Creasey, J. Piece of cake
  Doyle, Sir A. C. Adventure of the devil's
    foot
  Eberhart, M. G. Deadly is the diamond
  Gilbert, M. F. After all these years
  Gilford, C. B. Bull in a china shop
  King, R. To remember you by
  MacDonald, J. D. Homicidal hiccup
  Malleson, L. B. Sequel to murder
  Robin, R. Mr Pruitt
  Sayers, D. L. Suspicion
  White, W. A. P. Crime must have a stop
POKER (GAME)
  Abdullah, A. Ambassador of poker
  Benchley, R. C. Ladies wild
  Broun, H. C. Jackpot
  Charteris, L. Mug's game
  Clemens, S. L. Professor's yarn
  Coates, R. M. Friendly game of cards
  Crane, S. Poker game
  Forester, C. S. Some kinds of bad luck
  Gardner, P. Cousin Willie is a card
  Le May, A. Ghost at his shoulder
  McLaughlin, R. J. Let's get rid of the
    ribbon clerks
  Maugham, W. S. Straight flush
  Newhouse, E. Poker game
  O'Hara, J. Where's the game?
  Perry, J. Poker face
  Reynolds, Q. J. Girl named Dora
  Thurber, J. Everything is wild
  Wilde, P. Pillar of fire
    See also Cards

Poker face. Perry, J.
Poker game. Crane, S.
Poker game. Newhouse, E.
POLAND
  Choynowski, P. Boarding house
  Dąbrowska, M. Father Philip
  Wierzyński, K. Patrol

1918-1939
  Babel', I. E. Afonka Bida
  Babel', I. E. Berestechko
  Babel', I. E. Brigade Commander
  Babel', I. E. The kiss
  Babel', I. E. Konkin's prisoner
  Babel', I. E. Squadron Commander Tru-
    nov
  Babel', I. E. Zamoste

1939-1945
  O'Sullivan-Barra, J. The password

Communism
  See Communism—Poland

POLAR BEARS. See Bears

POLAR REGIONS. See Antarctic regions;
  Arctic regions

POLES IN THE UNITED STATES
  Farrell, J. T. Saturday night in America
  O'Connor, F. Displaced person
  Sneider, V. J. Uncle Bosko
  Stegner, W. E. Field guide to the Western
    birds

POLICE
  Blish, J. Beep
  Clough, R. L. Bait
  Crossen, K. F. Closed door
  Hawkins, J. and Hawkins, W. Cop with-
    out a badge
  Hubbard, L. R. Tough old man
  Kuttner, H. Sub-standard sardines
  Longdon, G. Of those who came
  Norton, A. M. ed. Space police; 9 stories
  O'Hara, J. Respectable place
  Piper, H. B. Police operation
  Schmitz, J. H. Agent of Vega
  Sørensen, V. Murder case
  Sweeney, C. L. Decoy
  Williams, R. Pax Galactica
    See also Detectives; Mystery and
    detective stories

California
  Byrd, J. J. Reluctant cop

Hollywood
  Saroyan, W. Actress and the cop

Hungary
  Household, G. Roll out the barrel

Ireland
  Brooks, W. Officer Mulvaney and the
    hot buttered pig
  MacDonagh, D. "All the sweet butter-
    milk. . ."
  Macken, W. The river
  O'Donovan, M. Majesty of the law

London
  Rinehart, M. R. Tish marches on

PREHISTORIC MAN. See Man, Prehistoric

PREJUDICE, RACE. See Race problems

PREJUDICES AND ANTIPATHIES
Brown, F. Keep out
Payne, L. V. Prelude
Wilner, H. Passion for Silver's arm

Prelude. Payne, L. V.

Prelude. Smith, E. V.

Prelude to reunion. La Farge, O.

PREMATURE BURIAL. See Burial, Premature

Premature burial. Poe, E. A.

Premediated crime. Gombrowicz, W.

Prentice, Helen
Equinox
Stanford short stories, 1956

Prescott, John Brewster, 1919-
Ribbon for Ginger
Western Writers of America. Hound dogs and others

Presence of Grace. Powers, J. F.

Present for the boy. Swados, H.

Present from Joe. Russell, E. F.

Presents. See Gifts

The president calls. Zawieyski, J.

PRESS AGENTS. See Publicity

Preston, Betty Brown
Two Miss Koofers
Everygirls adventure stories

PRESUMPTION OF DEATH. See Death, Apparent

Pretty surprise. Tomlinson, N.

Prévost, Jean
The forge
Lehmann, J. ed. Modern French stories

Prévost, Marcel, 1862-1941
Solange, the wolf-girl
Lohan, R. ed. Christmas tales for reading aloud

Price, John Basye
Murder for fine art
Mystery Writers of America, inc. A choice of murders

Price, Reynolds
The anniversary
Winter's tales, 4

Price, Willard De Mille, 1887-
Operation octopus
Teen-age tales, bk 3

Price of the head. Russell. J.

Price-Parry. Jones, G.

Price's always open. O'Hara, J.

Prichard, Katharine Susannah, 1884-
Yoirimba
Stivens, D. comp. Coast to coast

PRIDE AND VANITY
Caldwell, E. Pride of Miss Stella Sibley
Cather, W. S. Count of Crow's Nest
Reid, L. Sir Pride
Sandoz, M. Y. Grandmama Gladys
Singer, I. B. The mirror

Pride of Miss Stella Sibley. Caldwell, E.

Pridgen, Tim, 1899-
Eighteen oak ties
Costain, T. B. and Beecroft, J. eds. More Stories to remember

The priest. Wulzen, A.

Priestess of Delphi. Warner, S. T.

PRIESTS, CATHOLIC. See Catholic priests

Prima belladonna. Ballard, J. G.

PRIMITIVE MAN. See Man, Primitive

Prince Roman. Conrad, J.

Prince who was a thief. Dreiser, T.

PRINCES
Conrad, J. Prince Roman

Princess and the wild ones. Mitchell, W. O.

Princess in the pecan tree. Sargent, E. N.

PRINCESSES
Street, J. L. Mr Bisbee's princess

Pringle, Murray T.
Karroo of the jungle
Teen-age tales, bk 4

Prishvin, Mikhail Mikhaĭlovich, 1873-1954
His first point
Loaf sugar, and other Soviet stories

The prison. Malamud, B.

PRISON ESCAPES. See Escapes

PRISON LABOR. See Convict labor

The prisoner. Avnieri, U.

The prisoner. Gunther, M.

Prisoner in the Caucasus. Tolstoĭ, L. N. Graf

The prisoners. Maupassant, G. de

PRISONERS, CONDEMNED
Andreev, L. N. Seven who were hanged

PRISONERS, POLITICAL
MacMahon, B. Kings asleep in the ground

PRISONERS, RELEASED. See Ex-convicts

PRISONERS AND PRISONS
Camus, A. The guest
Cather, W. S. Clemency of the court
Downey, H. The hobo
Franko, I. I. To the light!
McGuire, J. J. Queen's messenger
Maugham, W. S. Episode
Maugham, W. S. The kite
O'Flaherty, L. The tramp
Rice, C. Quiet day in the county jail
Silone, I. Along dusty roads and behind hedges
Van Doren, M. April fool
Woolrich, C. Guillotine
See also Prisoners of war; also names of wars with subdivision, Prisoners and prisons, e.g. World War, 1939-1945—Prisoners and prisons

Russia
Dostoevskii, F. M. The peasant Marey
Tolstoĭ, L. N. Graf. Long exile
Tolstoĭ, L. N. Graf. Prisoner in the Caucasus

United States
Capote, T. Diamond guitar

The promise. Steinbeck, J.

Promise for Elizabeth. Welch, H. L.

PROMISES
Camus, A. Growing stone
Smith, E. W. Specific gravity of Jeff
Coongate

Prongs. Strong, L. A. G.

Proof of the pudding. Porter, W. S.

PROPAGANDA, GERMAN
Nabokov, V. V. Conversation piece, 1945

Propagandist. Jenkins, W. F.

The propagandist. Whitehill, J.

PROPHECIES
Dumas, A. Man who lived four thousand years
Hawthorne, N. Great Stone Face

The prophet. Appet, N.

Proposal perilous. Hershman, M.

Prospect of the sea. Thomas, D.

PROSPECTORS
Clark, W. Van T. Wind and the snow of winter
London, J. All Gold Canyon
Palme, I. Water hole

PROSTITUTES
Algren, N. Beasts of the wild
Babel', I. E. Through the fanlight
Caldwell, E. Clementine
Capote, T. Breakfast at Tiffany's
Curley, D. The fugitive
Eastlake, W. Unhappy hunting grounds
Ferber, E. Woman who tried to be good
Jouve, P. J. In a certain house
Kerouac, J. Billowy trip in the world
Lessing, D. M. Road to the big city
Lowry, R. J. C. New York call girl
Lynds, D. Just once more
Maupassant, G. de. Ball of fat
Maupassant, G. de. Florentine
Maupassant, G. de. In port
Maupassant, G. de. Mademoiselle Fifi
Maupassant, G. de. Madame Tellier's establishment
Maupassant, G. de. Poor girl
Pincherle, A. Tired courtesan
Porter, K. A. Magic
Tuohy, F. Two private lives
Williams, T. Yellow bird
Wolfe, T. Face of the war
Wright, R. Big, black, good man

Protection. Sheckley, R.

PROTECTION OF GAME. See Game protection

Protestant Saint Francis. Newman, W. C.

Prott. St Clair, M.

Proud and virtuous. Betts, D.

Proud diggers. Turner, W. O.

The proud man. Macken, W.

Proud poet. Saroyan, W.

Proud possessor. Street, J. H.

Prove you love me. Masselink, B.

The proverb. Aymé, M.

PROVINCIAL AND RURAL LIFE. See names of countries, with phrase: Provincial and rural; e.g. England, Provincial and rural

Provost's tale. Cronin, A. J.

"Prrou." Colette, S. G.

PRUSSIAN SOLDIERS. See Soldiers, German

PSYCHIATRISTS
Clifton, M. Clerical error
Goldstein, C. H. Invisible barriers
Waldo, E. H. And now the news
Weigel, H. Changing mask

PSYCHIATRY
Waldo, E. H. Bulkhead

Psychic. Miner, L.

PSYCHIC PHENOMENA. See Supernatural phenomena

Psychical invasion. Blackwood, A.

PSYCHOANALYSIS. See Psychoanalysts

PSYCHOANALYSTS
Bloch, R. I do not love thee, Doctor Fell
Caper, K. Giddiness
Maugham, W. S. Lord Mountdrago
Russell, B. A. W. R. 3d earl. Psychoanalyst's nightmare
Waldo, E. H. Other man
White, E. B. Second tree from the corner
See also Psychiatrists

Psychoanalyst's nightmare. Russell, B. A. W. R. 3d earl

Psychological test. Hirai, T.

PSYCHOLOGICAL TESTS. See Mental tests

PSYCHOLOGISTS
Fonger, H. Lead me home

PSYCHOLOGY OF CHILDREN. See Children

PSYCHONEUROSES. See Neuroses

PUB (ENGLISH) See Hotels, taverns, etc.

PUBLIC-ADDRESS SYSTEM. See Loudspeakers

Public-address system. West, J.

Public auction. Ward, L. L.

Public career of Mr Seymour Harrisburg. O'Hara, J.

Public hating. Allen, S.

PUBLIC LANDS. See Homesteading

PUBLIC WELFARE
Bellow, S. Looking for Mr Green

PUBLICITY
Bloch, R. I do not love thee, Doctor Fell
Brier, H. M. Yogi's PR client
Lewis, S. Let's play king
O'Hara, J. Public career of Mr Seymour Harrisburg
See also Advertising

Publicity campaign. Clarke, A. C.

PUBLISHERS AND PUBLISHING
Kornbluth, C. M. Cosmic expense account
Wilson, A. More friend than lodger

PUERTO RICO
Combs, P. Man on the beach

PULLMAN PORTERS. See Railroads—Employees

PUMAS
Annixter, P. pseud. Deer slayer
Grey, Z. Don
Kelton, E. Yellow Devil
Niehuis, C. C. Hound music
Rutledge, A. H. Blood on the mountain laurels

PUMPING MACHINERY
Lederer, W. J. and Burdick, E. L. The ugly American and the ugly Sarkhanese

PUMPKINS
Alarcón, P. A. de. The stub-book—a rural story

PUNCH AND JUDY. See Puppets and puppet-plays

Punch bowl. Cullum, W.

PUNCTUALITY
Eisele, A. The vigil

PUNISHMENT
Alford, H. The shorn lamb
McComas, J. F. Shock treatment
Waldo, E. H. Shadow, shadow on the wall
See also Pillories

PUNS AND PUNNING
Asimov, I. Jokester

Pup and the bad man. Barker, S. O.

The **pupil**. James, H.

PUPPETS AND PUPPET-PLAYS
Fisher, D. F. C. "Vive Guignol!"
McCarthy, M. T. Unspoiled reaction

Purdy, James
Color of darkness
Purdy, J. Color of darkness
Cutting edge
Purdy, J. Color of darkness
Don't call me by my right name
New Directions in prose and poetry, 16
Purdy, J. Color of darkness
Eventide
Purdy, J. Color of darkness
Good woman
Purdy, J. Color of darkness
Man and wife
Purdy, J. Color of darkness
Plan now to attend
Purdy, J. Color of darkness
63: dream palace
Purdy, J. Color of darkness
Sound of talking
Purdy, J. Color of darkness
Why can't they tell you why?
Purdy, J. Color of darkness
You may safely gaze
Purdy, J. Color of darkness
You reach for your hat
Purdy, J. Color of darkness

Purdy, Kenneth W. 1914?-
Haunted hour
This week magazine. This week's Stories of mystery and suspense

Purification of Thelma Augenstern. Wolfson, V.

PURIM (FEAST OF ESTHER)
Rabinowitz, S. Two dead men

Purloined letter. Poe, E. A.

Purple Spad. Miller, E. M.

The **purpose** and the name. Allen, S.

Purring countess. Marlett, M. B. G.

The **pursuit**. Bacchelli, R.

PUSHKIN, ALEXANDER SERGEEVICH, 1799-1837
Paustovsky, K. Loaf sugar

Put them all together, they spell monster. Russell, R.

Putnam, Dorothy S.
Social event
Oberfirst, R. ed. 1955 anthology of best original short-shorts

Putter-to-sleep. Maupassant, G. de

Putting away of Uncle Quaggin. Kneale, N.

Puzzle for Poppy. Quentin, P. pseud

Pwll-yr-Onnen. Williams, D. J.

PYRAMIDS
Cather, W. S. Tale of the white pyramid

Pythias. Pohl, F.

Q

Q for quitclaim. Chute, B. J.

Quaker girl and the rocking ghost. Carmer, C. L.

QUAKERS. See Friends, Society of

Quality. Galsworthy, J.

The **quarrel.** Brodkey, H.

The **quarrel.** Ward, L. L.

QUARRELING
Rabinowitz, S. Tit for tat
Tolstoĭ, L. N. Graf. Little girls wiser than their elders
Tolstoĭ, L. N. Graf. Neglect a fire and it spreads

QUARRIES AND QUARRYING
Verga, G. Rosso Malpelo

Quarter-deck shell. Enright, E.

Quarternights near the salt licks. Adams, A.

Queen, Ellery, pseud.
Diamonds in paradise
Mystery Writers of America, inc. Crime for two
GI story
Best detective stories of the year—1955
Gettysburg bugle
Crime Writers Association, London. Planned departures
The inner circle
Mystery Writers of America, inc. A choice of murders
Kid stuff
Mystery Writers of America, inc. For love or money
Lamp of God
Haycraft, H. and Beecroft, J. eds. Treasury of great mysteries
Mad tea-party
Cooke, D. C. ed. My best murder story
Miracles do happen
Queen, E. pseud. ed. Ellery Queen's 13th annual
"My queer dean"
This week magazine. This week's Stories of mystery and suspense

Queen, Ellery, pseud.—*Continued*

Telltale bottle
Mystery Writers of America, inc. For tomorrow we die

Terror town
Best detective stories of the year (12th annual collection)

Queen Hortense. Maupassant, G. de

QUEEN OF SHEBA. See Sheba, Queen of

Queen of Sheba's nightmare. Russell, B. A. W. R. 3d earl

Queen of Spain fritillary. Bates, H. E.

Queen penicillin. Burns, J. H.

QUEENS (BOROUGH) See New York (City)—Queens

Queen's messenger. McGuire, J. J.

Queer heart. Bowen, E.

Queer night in Paris. Maupassant, G. de

Quentin, Patrick, pseud.

Death before breakfast
Mystery Writers of America, inc. Crime for two

Murder in the Alps
This week magazine. This week's Stories of mystery and suspense

Portrait of a murderer
Cooke, D. C. ed. My best murder story

Puzzle for Poppy
Haycraft, H. and Beecroft, J. eds. Treasury of great mysteries
Mystery Writers of America, inc. Big time mysteries

Quest. Farrell, J. T.

Quest buck. Triem, F.

Question and answer. Sansom, W.

Question of blood. Haycox, E.

Question of habit. Anderson, E.

Question of Latin. Maupassant, G. de

Quiet. Medici, R.

A **quiet** afternoon. Kubly, H.

Quiet chimneys. Eastlake, W.

Quiet day in the county jail. Rice, C.

Quiet man. Walsh, M.

Quiet post. Kalinovsky, G.

Quills. Roberts, Sir C. G. D.

QUILTS. See Coverlets

Quinn, Kevin

Molly on the shore
Hughes, R. ed. All manner of men

Quit zoomin' those hands through the air. Finney, J.

R

The **Rabbi.** Babel', I. E.

Rabbi Sharfman. Angoff, C.

RABBIS

Agnon, S. J. The minyan
Angoff, C. Rabbi Sharfman
Babel', I. E. The Rabbi
Bar-Joseph, J. Fettered Messiah

Ibn-Sahav, A. Moroccans at the Wailing Wall
Koteliansky, S. S. Salvation of a soul
Malamud, B. Magic barrel
Peretz, I. L. The Cabalists
Peretz, I. L. If not higher
Peretz, I. L. Reb Noah and the Rabbi of Brest
Rabinowitz, S. Tit for tat
Singer, I. B. Joy
Tabib, M. 1917
White, W. A. P. Balaam
See also Jews—Religion

Rabbi's son. Babel', I. E.

The **rabbit.** Maupassant, G. de

RABBITS

Harris, J. C. Mr Rabbit nibbles up the butter
Jacobson, D. Little pet
MacGrian, M. Myself and a rabbit
Zimmerman, M. Important wish

Rabinowitz, Shalom, 1859-1916

Clock that struck thirteen
Rabinowitz, S. Selected stories of Sholom Aleichem

Cnards
Rabinowitz, S. Selected stories of Sholom Aleichem

The convoy
Rabinowitz, S. Selected stories of Sholom Aleichem

Country Passover
Rabinowitz, S. Selected stories of Sholom Aleichem
Same as: Passover in a village

Daughter's grave
Rabinowitz, S. Selected stories of Sholom Aleichem

Day before Yom Kippur
Rabinowitz, S. Selected stories of Sholom Aleichem

Dead citron
Schwarz, L. W. ed. Feast of Leviathan

Dreyfus in Kasrilevka
Rabinowitz, S. Selected stories of Sholom Aleichem

Enchanted tailor
Rabinowitz, S. Selected stories of Sholom Aleichem

Eternal life
Rabinowitz, S. Selected stories of Sholom Aleichem

The fiddle
Rabinowitz, S. Selected stories of Sholom Aleichem

Hannukah money
Rabinowitz, S. Selected stories of Sholom Aleichem

Hodel
Rabinowitz, S. Selected stories of Sholom Aleichem

Home for Passover
Rabinowitz, S. Selected stories of Sholom Aleichem

I'm lucky—I'm an orphan
Rabinowitz, S. Selected stories of Sholom Aleichem

In haste
Rabinowitz, S. Selected stories of Sholom Aleichem

Rabinowitz, Shalom—*Continued*

The inheritors
Rabinowitz, S. Selected stories of Sholom Aleichem

Lottery ticket
Rabinowitz, S. Selected stories of Sholom Aleichem

Miracle of Hashono Rabo
Rabinowitz, S. Selected stories of Sholom Aleichem

Modern children
Rabinowitz, S. Selected stories of Sholom Aleichem
Same as: Children of today

On account of a hat
Rabinowitz, S. Selected stories of Sholom Aleichem

Only son, the mother, and Elijah the Prophet
Kobler, F. ed. Her children call her blessed

Page from the Song of Songs
Rabinowitz, S. Selected stories of Sholom Aleichem

The pair
Rabinowitz, S. Selected stories of Sholom Aleichem

Tevye wins a fortune
Rabinowitz, S. Selected stories of Sholom Aleichem

Three little heads
Rabinowitz, S. Selected stories of Sholom Aleichem

Tit for tat
Rabinowitz, S. Selected stories of Sholom Aleichem

Town of the little people
Rabinowitz, S. Selected stories of Sholom Aleichem

Two dead men
Rabinowitz, S. Selected stories of Sholom Aleichem

Yom Kippur scandal
Rabinowitz, S. Selected stories of Sholom Aleichem

You mustn't weep—it's Yom-Tev
Rabinowitz, S. Selected stories of Sholom Aleichem

RACCOON HUNTING. See Coon hunting

RACCOONS
Annixter, P. pseud. Odyssey of Old Specs
Montgomery, R. G. Voice of Jerome Kildee

Race around the sun. Elam, R. M.

Race at morning. Faulkner, W.

RACE PROBLEMS
Abdullah, M. K. Grandfather tiger
Balchin, N. Tinfield mascot
Boyle, K. Black boy
Brophy, B. Pilgrimage
Campbell, W. E. M. Happy Jack
Chute, B. J. Birthday gift
Conn, F. Coda
Enright, E. Quarter-deck shell
Gardner, C. Conflict
Gordimer, N. The smell of death and flowers
Gordimer, N. Which new era would that be?
Hughes, L. One Friday morning

Kubly, H. Halloween party
Lochridge, B. H. Will Davis
Millholland, R. Transformer on the line
Polk, W. T. Night the races were supposed to riot
Rosmond, B. No sense of humor
Ruhen, O. Village of phantom ships
Rutledge, A. H. Vanishing of Pegram
Yellen, S. The mystic presences
See also Prejudices and antipathies

RACE QUESTION. See subdivision Race question under names of countries: e.g. Australia—Race question

RACE RELATIONS
Ruhen, O. Brown Jonathan

Race with death. Miller, E. M.

RACES. See Automobile races; Bicycle racing; Horse racing; Running; Soap box derbies; Yacht races

RACKETEERS. See Gangsters

Rackety rax. Sayre, J.

Rackowe, Alec, 1900-
Four-minute mile
Stowe, A. comp. When boy dates girl

RADAR IN AERONAUTICS
Frank, P. Enemy bomber

Raddall, Thomas Head, 1903-
Man from Cap D'Amour
Schwed, P. and Wind, H. W. eds. Great stories from the world of sport
Resurrection
Nelson, G. E. ed. Cavalcade of the North

RADIATION POISONING. See Radioactivity

RADIO
Allen, S. Sunday morning shift
Cheever, J. Enormous radio

RADIO IN PROPAGANDA
Samuel, E. H. More coffee, Abdul

RADIO OPERATORS. See Radio

RADIO PROGRAMS
Campbell, W. E. M. Send in your answer

RADIO SCRIPTS
Shaw, I. Main currents of American thought

RADIOACTIVITY
Cooper, W. Ball of paper
Edwards, K. Counterspy
Elam, R. M. Peril from outer space

Rafferty's reasons. Pohl, F.

Ragtime Kid. Lederer, W. J. and Burdick, E. L.

Raid. Faulkner, W.

"Raidin' Maiden." Bahr, J.

RAILROAD ACCIDENTS. See Railroads—Accidents

RAILROAD MODELS. See Railroads—Models

RAILROAD STATIONS. See Railroads—Stations

Railroad to freedom. Swift, H. H.

RAILROAD TRAINS. See Railroads—Trains

RAILROAD TRAVEL. See Railroads—Travel

Rapunzel, Rapunzel, bind up your hair!
Lofts, N. R.
Rare ripe garden-seed. Harris, G. W.
The **rarer** thing. Garrett, G.
Raspevin, A. See Beliavsky, P. jt. auth.
RAT-CATCHING. See Rats
Rat trap. Whitehill, J.

Rathbone, Basil
Daydream
Oberfirst, R. ed. Anthology of best
short-short stories v6

Rathjen, Carl Henry
Runaway rig
Saturday evening post (Periodical) Sat-
urday evening post stories, 1957
RATIONING, CONSUMER
Roussakis, I. Loaf of bread
RATIONS. See Rationing, Consumer
RATS
Dickens, C. Devil and Mr Chips
Fournier, P. Gaston
Grahame, K. Dulce domum
Robinson, L. Among those present

Extermination
Fournier, P. Gaston

Rats. Alex, F.
The **rattlesnake.** Simms, W. G.
The **ravines.** Tolstoï, A. N. Graf
Raw land. Drago, H. S.

Rawlings, Charles A.
Young man on his own
Saturday evening post (Periodical) Sat-
urday evening post stories, 1955

Rawlings, Marjorie (Kinnan) 1896-
Cocks must crow
Rawlings, M. K. Marjorie Rawlings
reader
Gal young un
First-prize stories, 1919-1957
Rawlings, M. K. Marjorie Rawlings
reader
Jacob's ladder
Rawlings, M. K. Marjorie Rawlings
reader
Jessamine Springs
Rawlings, M. K. Marjorie Rawlings
reader
Jody finds the fawn
Rawlings, M. K. Marjorie Rawlings
reader
A mother in Mannville
Costain, T. B. and Beecroft, J. eds.
Stories to remember
Pelican's shadow
Rawlings, M. K. Marjorie Rawlings
reader
Penny is bitten by a rattlesnake
Rawlings, M. K. Marjorie Rawlings
reader
The shell
Rawlings, M. K. Marjorie Rawlings
reader

Raymund, Bernard
Last Christmas
Fremantle, A. J. ed. Christmas is here

Rea, Domenico, 1921-
Piededifico
Slonim, M. L. ed. Modern Italian short
stories
Reach for tomorrow. Clarke, A. C.
Reaction. Columcille, M.
Reaction. O'Rourke, F.
Reader of the "The World Almanac for
1944." Saroyan, W.
READING
Malamud, B. A summer's reading
Readville stars. Hale, N.
Ready, William B. 1914-
As it was and as it will be: a Christmas
tale
Hughes, R. ed. All manner of men
REAL ESTATE. See Real property
REAL ESTATE BUSINESS
Pincherle, A. The go-between
REAL PEOPLE. See names of individuals
REAL PROPERTY
Chute, B. J. The outcasts
Rosen, J. M. Fair game
Real thing. James, H.
Real Viennese schmalz. Schulberg, B. W.
Really good jazz piano. Yates, R.
Realpolitik. Wilson, A.
The **reaper** and the flowers. Stuart, J.
Rear window. Woolrich, C.
Rearward Dog. Saroyan, W.
Reasonable facsimile. Stafford, J.
Reasonable facsimile. Wester, J. B.
Reb Noah and the Rabbi of Brest. Peretz,
I. L.
Rebel horse. Kjelgaard, J. A.
The **Rebel** Trace. Hergesheimer, J.
Rebound man. Olgin, J.
RECEIVING STOLEN GOODS
Pincherle, A. The caretaker
RECLUSES
Enright, E. One for the collection
Sansom, W. The ballroom
Recollections of a billiard-marker. Tolstoï,
L. N. Graf
RECTORS. See Clergy
Recruiting station. Van Vogt, A. E.
Red. Maugham, W. S.
Red badge of courage. Crane, S.
Red Barbara. O'Flaherty, L.
Red chamber. Hirai, T.
Red coats galloping. Welcome, J.
Red diamond for Miss Detwiler. Miller,
E. M.
Red dress. Smith, E. H.
A **red-faced** chief who's just come offa the
Indian reservoir. Kober, A.
Red Hanrahan. Yeats, W. B.
Red-headed League. Doyle, Sir A. C.
Red ink dilemma. Allen, E. L.
Red King and the witch
Jarrell, R. ed. Anchor book of stories
Red Knight. Annixter, P. pseud.

Red necktie. Seid, R.

Red petticoat. MacMahon, B.

Red petticoat. O'Flaherty, L.

Red wine. Blochman, L. G.

Red wine. Fiene, D. M.

REDCAPS. See Railroads—Employees

Redeye. Williamson, H.

Redhead from New Orleans. Levin, R. J.

REDUCING (BODY WEIGHT CONTROL) See Corpulence

Reed, Louis, 1899-
    Banjo string
        Fenner, P. R. comp. Brother against brother

Reese, John Henry
    Frontier frenzy
        Meredith, S. ed. Bar 5

Reflection of Luanne. Holmes, M. R.

REFORM SCHOOLS. See Reformatories

REFORMATORIES
    Kantor, M. Unseen witness

REFORMERS
    Hawthorne, N. Earth's holocaust

Refugee. Clark, A. C.

REFUGEES
    Beigel, U. The mourners
    Bentley, P. E. "You see..."
    Boyle, K. This they took with them
    Burnet, D. Giant land
    Karp, D. B. Carmi
    Kristol, I. Adam and I
    Liang, C. Firecrackers
    Marshall, B. Brigadier smells a rat
    Nabokov, V. V. Assistant producer
    Nabokov, V. V. "That in Aleppo once..."
    Newhouse, E. The ambassador
    O'Connor, F. Displaced person
    Rowlands, L. "And what part of Europe do you come from?"
    Warner, S. T. Emil

REGENERATION
    Moore, C. L. No woman born

Regeneration of Thomas Larkin. Leroi, F. J.

Reginald Pomfret Skelton. Yellen, S.

Reginald's Christmas revel. Munro, H. H.

Regret. Maupassant, G. de

The regulator. Prebble, J.

The rehearsal. Borgese, E. M.

Reichenstein, Shlomo, 1900-1944
    Genesis
        Frank, M. Z. ed. Sound the great trumpet

Reid, Alexander
    The kitten
        Urquhart, F. ed. Scottish short stories

Reid, Lawrie
    Dehydrated romance
        Reid, L. My Lady Happiness, and other short stories
    Divorce
        Reid, L. My Lady Happiness, and other short stories
    Elnea
        Reid, L. My Lady Happiness, and other short stories

Granny Bapanira
    Reid, L. My Lady Happiness, and other short stories

Irony
    Reid, L. My Lady Happiness, and other short stories

A lifetime
    Reid, L. My Lady Happiness, and other short stories

Miss Glory
    Reid, L. My Lady Happiness, and other short stories

My Lady Happiness
    Reid, L. My Lady Happiness, and other short stories

Nitia
    Reid, L. My Lady Happiness, and other short stories

The old man
    Reid, L. My Lady Happiness, and other short stories

Sir Pride
    Reid, L. My Lady Happiness, and other short stories

Way life is
    Reid, L. My Lady Happiness, and other short stories

Reigate puzzle. Doyle, Sir A. C.

REINCARNATION
    Peretz, I. L. Thou shalt not covet
    Treat, L. Murder me twice

Reincarnation of a melody. Peretz, I. L.

REINDEER
    Wallenius, K. M. One-eyed wolf of Kaamas Fell

REJUVENATION
    Dumas, A. Man who lived four thousand years
    Hawthorne, N. Dr Heidegger's experiment

RELATIVES. See Family life; also specific relatives, e.g. Aunts; Brothers; etc.

The relic. Maupassant, G. de

RELIGION
    Ali, A. Before death
    Allen, S. The purpose and the name
    Angoff, C. Natalie and John
    Angoff, C. Reuben
    Burk, C. J. Trumpets in the morning
    Campbell, W. E. M. October Island
    Chekhov, A. P. The murder
    Connell, E. S. Color of the world
    Franko, I. I. The plague
    Kilcrin, I. Brad Halloran
    Pritchett, V. S. The saint
    Purdy, J. Plan now to attend
    Ruhen, O. Road to Heaven
    Russell, B. A. W. R. 3d earl. Faith and mountains
    Stuart, J. The devil and the television
    Stuart, J. Love in the spring

Religion comes to Pocatello. Melton, J.

RELIGIOUS BELIEF. See Faith

RELIGIOUS PILGRIMAGES. See Pilgrims and pilgrimages

Reluctant cop. Byrd, J. J.

Remarkable conversion of the Rev Thomas Ruddle. Roberts, M.

Rogers, John Allison
  Nun and the sailor
    New Directions in prose and poetry, 16
ROGERS, ROBERT, 1727-1795
  Roberts, K. L. Return of the Rangers
Roger's method. Maupassant, G. de
Rohmer, Sax, pseud.
  Mystery of the vanishing treasure
    This week magazine. This week's Sto-
      ries of mystery and suspense
  Owl hoots twice
    Cooke, D. C. ed. My best murder story
Roll of daughters. Aymé, M.
Roll out the barrel. Household, G.
Rollicking God. Johnson, N.
ROMAN CATHOLIC CHURCH. See
  Catholic Faith
Roman fever. Wharton, E. N. J.
Roman figures. Bates, H. E.
Roman holiday. Sansom, W.
Roman portrait. Rothberg, A. A.
Romance. Saroyan, W.
Romance in the roaring forties. Runyon, D.
Romance of Esther. Bible. Old Testament
ROMANS IN GREAT BRITAIN. See
  Great Britain—Antiquities, Roman
Romanticizing of Dr Fless. Cassill, R. V.
ROME
                30 B.C.-476 A.D.
  Jarnés, B. Saint Alexis
ROME (CITY) See Italy—Rome (City)
Roof in Manhattan. Lawrence, H.
Rookie cop. Chute, B. J.
Rookie of the year. Heuman, W.
Room at the Inn. Rainer, D.
Room no. 11. Maupassant, G. de
The roomer. Toney, R. B.
ROOMERS. See Boarding houses
ROOMING HOUSES. See Boarding
  houses
Rooney, Frank, 1913-
  Cyclists' raid
    McClennen, J. comp. Masters and mas-
      terpieces of the short story
Rope. Porter, K. A.
Rosalie Prudent. Maupassant, G. de
The rosary. Faulkner, W.
The rose. Bill, E. E.
Rose. Maupassant, G. de
Rose for Emily. Faulkner, W.
Rose of Sharon. Rutledge, A. H.
Rosegger, Peter, 1843-1918
  Carpenter's Christmas
    Fremantle, A. J. ed. Christmas is here
  When I fetched the fixin's fer Christmas
    dinner
    Lohan, R. ed. Christmas tales for read-
      ing aloud
Rosen, Isidore, 1917-
  Time is, time was
    New voices 2: American writing today
Rosen, J. M.
  Fair game
    Stivens, D. comp. Coast to coast

Rosenberg, Ethel (Clifford) 1915-
  Mrs Rivkin grapples with the drama
    Ribalow, H. U. ed. Treasury of Amer-
      ican Jewish stories
ROSES
  Dine, D. R. The fund
Roses. Dickinson, W. H.
Rosmond, Babette, 1917-
  No sense of humor
    Oberfirst, R. ed. Anthology of best
      short-short stories v5
Ross, Charlotte, and Ross, Dan
  Emergency call
    Mystery Writers of America, inc. Big
      time mysteries
Ross, Dan. See Ross, C. jt. auth.
Ross, Frances Dolores
  Especially twenty
    Oberfirst, R. ed. Anthology of best
      short-short stories v5
Ross, Leonard Q. pseud. See Rosten, Leo
  Calvin
Ross, Martin, pseud. See Martin, Violet
  Florence
Rosso Malpelo. Verga, G.
Rosten, Leo Calvin, 1908-
  Happy was the soldier!
    Saturday evening post (Periodical) Sat-
      urday evening post stories, 1956
  Mr Kaplan and the Magi
    Posselt, E. ed. A merry, merry Christ-
      mas book
  Mr K*A*P*L*A*N the magnificent
    Ribalow, H. U. ed. Treasury of Ameri-
      can Jewish stories
ROTARY INTERNATIONAL
  Kubly, H. The rallye of Rotary
Roth, Cecil, 1899-
  Tree of liberty
    Schwarz, L. W. ed. Feast of Leviathan
Roth, Joseph, 1894-
  Menuchim says mamma
    Kobler, J. ed. Her children call her
      blessed
Roth, Philip
  Contest for Aaron Gold
    Best American short stories, 1956
Rothberg, Abraham Allan, 1922-
  Not with our fathers
    Ribalow, H. U. ed. Treasury of Ameri-
      can Jewish stories
  Roman portrait
    New voices 2: American writing today
Rothschild's fiddle. Chekhov, A. P.
Rough turn. Millholland, R.
ROUMANIA. See Rumania
Round dozen. Maugham, W. S.
Round giant. Kentfield, C.
ROUND TABLE. See Arthur, King
Roussakis, Irene
  Cup with the pink forget-me-not
    New voices 2: American writing today
  Loaf of bread
    American vanguard, 1956
ROWING
  Winser, D. M. Boat race murder
    See also Boat racing

Rowland, Sidney
  Fixed fight
    Mystery Writers of America, inc. For love or money

Rowlands, Lesley
  "And what part of Europe do you come from?"
    Stivens, D. comp. Coast to coast

ROYAL CANADIAN MOUNTED PO-LICE. See Canada. Royal Canadian Mounted Police

ROYALTY. See Kings and rulers

RUBBER
  Blochman, L. G. Red wine

RUBBER PLANTATIONS. See Rubber

RUBIES
  Alvaro, C. The ruby
  Blochman, L. G. Dog that wouldn't talk

Rubin, Larry
  The heart is a lofty citadel
    Miller, N. ed. New campus writing, no. 2

The **ruby.** Alvaro, C.

Rudd, Hughes, 1921-
  Devil's Plain
    Stanford short stories, 1955
  A wry anecdote
    Stanford short stories, 1956

Rue de l'Évangile. Aymé, M.

RUGBY FOOTBALL
  Doyle, Sir A. C. Adventure of the missing three-quarter

RUGGER. See Rugby football

Ruhen, Olaf
  Beautiful pattern
    Ruhen, O. Land of Dahori
  Brown Jonathan
    Ruhen, O. Land of Dahori
  Dark of the moon
    Ruhen, O. Land of Dahori
  Guardians of Mobali
    Ruhen, O. Land of Dahori
  Head-hunters of Ianagl
    Ruhen, O. Land of Dahori
  The husbandmen
    Ruhen, O. Land of Dahori
  Road to heaven
    Ruhen, O. Land of Dahori
  Sergeant Pangae, detective
    Ruhen, O. Land of Dahori
  Sword of laughter
    Ruhen, O. Land of Dahori
  Village of phantom ships
    Ruhen, O. Land of Dahori
  Vision at the spring
    Ruhen, O. Land of Dahori
  Wisdom of Ragos
    Ruhen, O. Land of Dahori
  Woman Molak
    Ruhen, O. Land of Dahori
  Woman of Labu
    Ruhen, O. Land of Dahori

The **ruin** of humanity. Pincherle, A.

Rum over the dam. Smith, E. W.

RUM-RUNNING. See Liquor traffic

RUMANIA

  Peasants' Uprising, 1907
  Dumitriu, P. Family jewels

  1944-date
  Bogza, G. End of Jacob Onisia
  Cernescu, A. Daybreak meeting
  Sütö, A. Right man in the right place
  Zamfirescu, A. D. I. Popescu of the boundaries
    Bucharest
  Petrescu, C. They pay with their lives

Rumba Mosam. White, R.

Rummy affair of old Biffy. Wodehouse, P. G.

RUMOR
  Thurber, J. Day the dam broke

Run for the strip. Bailey, J.

Run, run away, brother. Smith, J. C.

Run sheep, run. Howland, R.

Run with the Sinnington. Allison, W.

The **runaway.** Farque, V.

Runaway bomber. Harvey, F. L.

Runaway honeymoon. La Farge, O.

Runaway rig. Rathjen, C. H.

RUNAWAYS (CHILDREN)
  Chute, B. J. The fiesta
  Hawkins, J. and Hawkins, W. Young and scared
  Waldo, E. H. Way home

Runbeck, Margaret Lee, 1905-1956
  The prom
    Teen-age tales, bk 4

RUNNERS. See Running

RUNNING
  Beachcroft, T. O. The half-mile
  Buckeridge, A. Jennings runs cross country
  Coxe, G. H. See how they run

Running water. Emerson, C. D.

Runyon, Damon, 1880-1946
  Blood pressure
    Baudin, M. ed. Contemporary short stories v2
  A call on the president
    Saturday evening post (Periodical) Saturday evening post Carnival of humor
  Dancing Dan's Christmas
    Lohan, R. ed. Christmas tales for reading aloud
    Posselt, E. ed. A merry, merry Christmas book
  Pick the winner
    Schwed, P. and Wind, R. W. eds. Great stories from the world of sport
  Romance in the roaring forties
    Lewis, J. D. ed. Great stories about show business
  Undertaker song
    Collier's (Periodical) Collier's Greatest sports stories

RURAL LIFE. See Farm life; Outdoor life

RURAL SCHOOLS. See School life

Ruskin, Stefanie, 1926-
  Four o'clock bell
    New voices 2: American writing today

Rynas, Stephen A.
Chain of command
Conklin, G. ed. Science-fiction adventures in mutation
Ryûnosuke, Akutagawa, 1892-1927
A clod of earth
McKinnon, R. N. ed. The heart is alone
Flatcar
McKinnon, R. N. ed. The heart is alone

S

S. A. Angoff, C.
S. S. Cow-Wheat. Babel', I. E.
SABBATH
Babel', I. E. Gedali
Babel', I. E. The Rabbi
Fineman, I. Elijah the Prophet
Gerchunoff, A. The siesta
Peretz, I. L. Marred holiday
Peretz, I. L. The treasure
Zangwill, I. Sabbath breaker
Sabbath breaker. Zangwill, I.
Sabbatical. Block, A. R.
SABOTAGE
Bennett, K. Death at attention
Gordon, A. Terror beneath the sea
Saccovanzetti. Curley, D.
Sacred and the profane. Sykes, C.
SACRIFICE
Peretz, I. L. Three offerings
The sacrifice. Dalal, N.
Sad and lonely one. Gerchunoff, A.
Sad fall. Wilson, A.
Saddlebag sawbones. Fox, N. A.
Sadness of Cruz. Smith, E. H.
Safety for the witness. De Meyer, J.
Saffron rug. Samuel, E. H.
Sagebrush champion. Drago, H. S.
SAIL BOATS. See Boats and boating
The sailor. Macken, W.
The sailor. Pritchett, V. S.
SAILING VESSELS
Bone, D. W. 'T' wind'ard!'
Conrad, J. The brute
Dingle, A. E. Bound for Rio Grande
Masefield, J. A memory
Roberts, M. Remarkable conversion of the Rev Thomas Ruddle
SAILORS. See Seamen
The saint. Allen, S.
The saint. Pritchett, V. S.
Saint Alexis. Jarnés, B.
Saint Bakeoven. Cross, E.
St Bride of the Isles. Sharp, W.
St Clair, Margaret
Age of prophecy
Conklin, G. ed. Science-fiction adventures in mutation
Prott
Montgomery, R. B. ed. Best SF
St Columba and the river. Dreiser, T.

Saint Emmanuel the Good, martyr. Unamuno y Jugo, M. de
St John, Mabel L.
Gate-leg table
Oberfirst, R. ed. 1955 anthology of best original short-shorts
St John, Orford
Diego Suarez story
World prize stories; 2d ser.
St Johns, Adela (Rogers)
First morning
Good housekeeping (Periodical) Editor's choice
Saint Manuel Bueno, martyr. Unamuno y Jugo, M. de
St Nicholas. See Santa Claus
Saint of the Old Seminary. Fisher, D. F. C.
ST PETERSBURG. See Florida—St Petersburg
Saint Simon, Louis de Rouvroy, duc de, 1675-1755
Death of Monseigneur
Jarrell, R. ed. Anchor book of stories
Saint Theodora. Jacobus de Voragine
SAINTS
Chavez, A. Bell that sang again
Chavez, A. Wake for Don Corsinio
Francis of Assisi, Saint. Little flowers of St Francis
Jarnés, B. Saint Alexis
Maupassant, G. de. Legend of Mont St-Michel
Unamuno y Jugo, M. de. Saint Emmanuel the Good, martyr
Unamuno y Jugo, M. de. Saint Manuel Bueno, martyr
Verga, G. War between saints
Williams, T. Chronicle of a demise
Saki, pseud. See Munro, Hector Hugh
Salcher, Peter
The octopus
Oberfirst, R. ed. Anthology of best short-short stories v5
A sale. Maupassant, G. de
Salesman's romance. O'Donovan, M.
SALESMEN AND SALESMANSHIP
Blake, L. J. Those green trousers
Campbell, W. E. M. Little wife
Coates, R. M. Hour after Westerly
Garrett, G. The lion hunter
Gollschewsky, E. A. Clear case of self-defence
Kober, A. Y'say ya not saddisfied
McCord, J. Somewhere out of nowhere
O'Connor, F. Good country people
Pincherle, A. Taboo
Powers, J. F. Blue Island
Powers, J. F. Devil was the joker
Sansom, W. On stony ground
Sansom, W. Outburst
Tekeyan, C. Mac loved Mr Kelly
Upson, W. H. I'm a natural-born salesman
SALESMEN, TRAVELING. See Commercial travelers
SALESWOMEN. See Salesmen and salesmanship
SALISH INDIANS
Johnson, D. M. Elk tooth dress

Sansom, William—Continued

The vertical ladder
Good housekeeping (Periodical) Editor's choice
Hudson, D. ed. Modern English short stories; 2d ser.

Visit to the dentist
Sansom, W. Among the dahlias, and other stories

What might it not have been
Sansom, W. Among the dahlias, and other stories

A white lie
Sansom, W. Contest of ladies

A woman seldom found
Sansom, W. Contest of ladies

SANTA CLAUS
Beerbohm, Sir M. P.C.X. 36
Bradford, R. How come Christmas?
Church, F. P. Is there a Santa Claus?
Chute, B. J. Vexation of Barney Hatch
Field, E. Mouse that didn't belive in Santa Claus
McLaverty, M. Father Christmas
Porter, H. E. The same old Christmas story

Santa Claus and the Tenth Avenue Kid. Cousins, M.

SANTA CRUZ. See California—Santa Cruz

SANTA FÉ. See New Mexico—Santa Fé

SANTA FÉ TRAIL
Athanas, V. Bridge crossing

Santha, Ferenc
Straw bliss
Juhasz, W. and Rothberg, A. A. eds. Flashes in the night

Santucci, Luigi, 1918-
Visions of Fra Gelsomino
Strachan, W. J. ed. Modern Italian stories

Sapper, pseud. See McNeile, Herman Cyril

SAPPHIRES
Sandoz, M. Y. Accessory

Sarah Brooke. Lochridge, B. H.

"**Sarah's** night." Fran, F. pseud.

SARATOGA SPRINGS. See New York (State)—Saratoga Springs

The **Sardillion.** Enright, E.

Sardinian fox. Deledda, G.

Sargent, E. N.
Awake and sing
New Directions in prose and poetry, 16
Princess in the pecan tree
New Directions 15

Saroyan, William, 1908-
Actress and the cop
Saturday evening post (Periodical) Saturday evening post stories, 1957
Aram Saeetyujkfog
Saroyan, W. Whole voyald, and other stories
Armenian writers
Saroyan, W. Whole voyald, and other stories
Bill McGee's brother
Saroyan, W. Whole voyald, and other stories

Daring young man on the flying trapeze
Baudin, M. ed. Contemporary short stories v 1
Fable IX
Laughton, C. ed. Tell me a story
Failure of friends
Saroyan, W. Whole voyald, and other stories
Home of the human race
Saroyan, W. Whole voyald, and other stories
Idea in the back of my brother's head
Saroyan, W. Whole voyald, and other stories
The inventor and the actress
Saroyan, W. Whole voyald, and other stories
Love of London
Saroyan, W. Whole voyald, and other stories
Mr Feeney's cheval
Oberfirst, R. ed. Anthology of best short-short stories v6
Palo
Saroyan, W. Whole voyald, and other stories
Paris and Philadelphia
Saroyan, W. Whole voyald, and other stories
Play that got away
Saroyan, W. Whole voyald, and other stories
Proud poet
Saroyan, W. Whole voyald, and other stories
Reader of "The World Almanac for 1944"
Saroyan, W. Whole voyald, and other stories
Rearward Dog
Saroyan, W. Whole voyald, and other stories
Rescue of the perishing
Saroyan, W. Whole voyald, and other stories
Return to the pomegranate trees
Saroyan, W. Whole voyald, and other stories
Romance
Jennings, F. G. and Calitri, C. J. eds. Stories
Sea and the small boy
Saroyan, W. Whole voyald, and other stories
Shepherd's daughter
Laughton, C. ed. Tell me a story
Sit down, won't you?
Saroyan, W. Whole voyald, and other stories
Sunday zeppelin
Laughton, C. ed. Tell me a story
Visitor in the piano warehouse
Saroyan, W. Whole voyald, and other stories
Whole voyald and heaven itself
Saroyan, W. Whole voyald, and other stories
Winter vineyard workers
Saroyan, W. Whole voyald, and other stories

Sartre, Jean Paul, 1905-
The wall
Hall, J. B. and Langland, J. T. eds. Short story
Lehmann, J. ed. Modern French stories

Sarver, Lizzie Johnston
Percheron
  Oberfirst, R. ed. 1955 anthology of best
  original short-shorts

Sashka the Christ. See Babel', I. E. Sandy
the Christ

Sassoon, Siegfried Lorraine, 1886-
The mister
  Welcome, J. and Orchard, V. eds. Best
  hunting stories

SATAN. See Devil

Satan and Sam Shay. Arthur, R.

SATIRE
Allen, S. The saint
Anderson, P. and Dickson, G. R. Adventure of the misplaced hound
Anderson, P. and Dickson, G. R. Don Jones
Anderson, P. and Dickson, G. R. Earthman's burden; 6 stories
Anderson, P. and Dickson, G. R. In Hoka Signo Vinces
Anderson, P. and Dickson, G. R. Sheriff of Canyon Gulch
Anderson, P. and Dickson, G. R. Tiddlywink warriors
Anderson, P. and Dickson, G. R. Yo ho Hoka!
Aymé, M. Legend of Poldevia
Aymé, M. State of grace
Bailey, J. Great stories of famous authors (Alphonse Vichysoisse)
Beaumont, C. Infernal bouillabaisse
Bradbury, R. Watchful poker chip of H. Matisse
Campbell, W. E. M. Send in your answer
Chesterton, G. K. Elusive companion of Parson White
Chesterton, G. K. Exclusive luxury of Enoch Oates
Chesterton, G. K. Improbable success of Mr Owen Hood
Chesterton, G. K. Tales of the Long Bow; 8 stories
Chesterton, G. K. Ultimate ultimatum of the League of the Long Bow
Chesterton, G. K. Unobtrusive traffic of Captain Pierce
Chesterton, G. K. Unprecedented architecture of Commander Blair
Chesterton, G.K. Unpresentable appearance of Colonel Crane
Chesterton, G. K. Unthinkable theory of Professor Green
Collier, J. Ah, the university
Collier, J. Devil, George, and Rosie
Collier, J. Lady on the grey
Collier, J. Thus I refute Beelzy
Dickens, C. Poor relation's story
Farrell, J. T. Little Johnny: A fable
Gyarfas, M. Louis Kossuth at Kisgomboc
Harte, B. Muck-a-Muck
Hawthorne, N. Earth's holocaust
Hay, J. Fabulous brew
Huxley, A. L. Happily ever after
Kersh, G. Murderer's eye
Lardner, R. W. Ex parte
MacDonald, J. D. Spectator sport
Mankowitz, W. Thirty-five minutes from nowhere
Miller, L. Available data on the Worp Reaction

Moore, G. Home sickness
Munro, H. H. The bag
Munro, H. H. Bertie's Christmas Eve
Munro, H. H. The interlopers
Munro, H. H. Open window
Munro, H. H. Schartz-Metterklume method
Munro, H. H. Story teller
Nathan, R. Digging the Weans
O'Flaherty, L. Fairy goose
O'Hara, J. Walter T. Carriman
Pérez de Ayala, R. Prometheus
Russell, B. A. W. R. 3rd earl. Dean Acheson's nightmare
Russell, B. A.W. R. 3d earl. Eisenhower's nightmare
Russell, B. A. W. R. 3d earl. Existentialist's nightmare
Russell, B. A. W. R. 3d earl. Faith and mountains
Russell, B. A. W. R. 3d earl. Mathematician's nightmare
Russell, B. A. W. R. 3d earl. Metaphysician's nightmare
Sullivan, F. The ugly mollusk
Thurber, J. Macbeth murder mystery
Waldo, E. H. Crime for Llewellyn
Wharton, E. N. J. Xingu
White, W. A. P. Nellthu
  See also Parodies

Satisfaction guaranteed. Asimov, I.

The satisfactory. Pritchett, V. S.

Saturday afternoon. Gibbons, S.

Saturday is a poor man's port. Weigel, H.

Saturday night. Adams, J.

Saturday night. Bahr, J.

Saturday night. Farrell, J. T.

Saturday night in America. Farrell, J. T.

Saturday night in Paris. Farrell, J. T.

Saturn has the power. Yellen, S.

Saul. Mason, M.

Saunders, Helen
The fifth season
  Oberfirst, R. ed. Anthology of best
  short-short stories v5

Savage, David
Killer in the club car
  Best detective stories of the year—1955
  This week magazine. The week's Stories of mystery and suspense

Savage, Les
Crow-bait caravan
  Western Writers of America. Hoof
  trails and wagon tracks
Traitor town
  Western Writers of America. Wild
  streets

SAVAGES
Camus, A. The renegade
Connell, R. E. The last of the flatfeet

Saved. Maupassant, G. de

Saved by the belle. Hall, A.

Say it! Say it! Wood, M.

Say it with flowers. Rice, C.

Sayers, Dorothy Leigh, 1893-
Bone of contention
  Haycraft, H. and Beecroft, J. eds.
  Treasury of great mysteries

SCIENCE FICTION—*Continued*

A **seed** as big as a hen's egg. Tolstoĭ, L. N.
Graf

Seed of McCoy. London, J.

Seeds. Anderson, S.

SEEING EYE DOGS
Christensen, B. My eyes no longer hear

Seekonk, the tale of a sea gull. Annixter, P.
pseud.

Seforim, Mendele Mocher, pseud. See
Abramowitz, Shalom Jacob

Seid, Ruth, 1913-
Red necktie
Ribalow, H. U. ed. Treasury of American Jewish stories

Seide, Michael, 1911-
Lady of my own
Kobler, F. ed. Her children call her blessed
Ribalow, H. U. ed. Treasury of American Jewish stories

Seidenberg, Ebe S.
Amelia
Stanford short stories, 1956

Seize the day. Bellow, S.

Selb, Kay
Mrs Baxter's butterfly
Furman, A. L. ed. Everygirls romance stories

SELF-CENTERED PEOPLE. See Egoism

SELF-CONTROL
Ruhen, O. Guardians of Mobali

SELF-SACRIFICE
Harte, E. Outcasts of Poker Flat
Peretz, I. L. Supreme sacrifice

Selfishness. Maupassant, G. de

SELLING. See Salesmen and salesmanship

Selma. Caldwell, E.

Semillante. Maupassant, G. de

Senator Sir. Lederer, W. J. and Burdick,
E. L.

SENATORS. See United States. Congress

Send in your answer. Campbell, W. E. M.

Sened, Alexander, and Sened Yonat
Bracha
Frank, M. Z. ed. Sound the great trumpet

Sened, Yonat. See Sened, Alexander, jt. auth.

Senior prom. Farrell, J. T.

Señor Pinedo. Gallant, M.

Sense from thought divide. Clifton, M.

Sense of destiny. Taper, B.

Sense of humour. Pritchett, V. S.

A **sense** of tribe. Wuest, S. M.

Sentiment. Maupassant, G. de

Sentimental education. Brodkey, H.

Sentimentality of William Tavener. Cather,
W. S.

September morn. Garrett, G.

September 2005: the Martian. Bradbury, R.

Sequel to murder. Malleson, L. B.

Serafina caper. Green, C.

SERAPHIM. See Angels

SERFDOM
Russia
Franko, I. I. Forests and pastures
Franko, I. I. Serf's bread
See also Peasant life—Russia

Serf's bread. Franko, I. I.

Sergeant Carmichael. Bates, H. E.

Sergeant Pangae, detective. Ruhen, O.

Sergeant Shmueli rides a donkey. Tabakai,
A.

SERGEANTS. See Soldiers, American

SERMONS
Verga, G. Donna Santa's sin

Serpent versus Donovan. MacCrae, A.

The **serpent** within us. McKinney, M.

SERPENTS. See Reptiles; Snakes

SERVANTS
Babel', I. E. Sin of Jesus
Blackwood, A. Strange adventures of a private secretary in New York
Chute, B. J. Miss Maggie Doons and the wicked city
Crews, S. P. Newspapers in heaven
Dickens, C. Mrs Lirriper's lodgings
Greene, G. Basement room
Huxley, A. L. Fard
Maupassant, G. de. Denis
Maupassant, G. de. Wooden shoes
Panzini, A. Mistress and the master speak
Pea, E. Moscardino
Samuel, E. H. Friend of the family
Steele, W. D. Bubbles
Warner, S. T. Shadwell
White, R. Devil of his own
See also Negroes as servants

Chauffeurs
Duke, M. Manuel at full moon
Lardner, R. W. Mr Frisbie
Pincherle, A. The film test
Sansom, W. Kindly
Yaffe, J. Mr Feldman

Cleaning women
Berriault, G. Houses of the city
Chute, B. J. Blue cup
Urquhart, F. Man about the house

Cooks
Blixen, K. Babette's feast
Cheever, J. Sorrows of gin
Day, C. Father and the cook
La Farge, O. La spécialité de M Duclos
Marby, T. D. Lula Borrow
Whitehill, J. Town is waiting

Hired girls
Conner, R. The witch
Suckow, R. Start in life

Hired men
Christie, K. Mrs Dixon's devil
Derleth, A. W. Whippoorwills in the hills
Jackson, J. H. Pastorale
Kasson, H. Nonie
Lofts, N. R. Happy Christmas
O'Connor, F. Greenleaf
Porter, K. A. Noon wine
Skuthorpe, L. Two plates at once
Stuart, J. The champions
Ward, L. L. Master and servant

SEX PROBLEMS—*Continued*

Pincherle, A. Back to the sea
Pincherle, A. Bitter honeymoon
Pincherle, A. Bitter honeymoon, and other stories; 8 stories
Pincherle, A. English officer
Pincherle, A. The fall
Pincherle, A. The imbroglio
Pincherle, A. Sick boy's winter
Pincherle, A. Tired courtesan
Pincherle, A. Unfortunate lover
Rosen, J. M. Fair game
Tuohy, F. Two private lives
West, A. C. Narcissus unto echo
West, A. C. Turning page

See also Marriage problems

SEXTONS

Dickens, C. Story of the goblins who stole a sexton
MacMahon, B. Cat and the cornfield
Maugham, W. S. The verger
Rabinowitz, S. Day before Yom Kippur

SEXUAL INSTINCT

Waldo, W. H. Never underestimate

Seymour, Marc

Theresa
Mystery Writers of America, inc. A choice of murders

Shaara, Michael

Grenville's planet
Montgomery, R. B. ed. Best SF three
2066: Election Day
Best science-fiction stories and novels; 9th ser.

Shades of yellow. Jordan, H. D.

The shadow. Dreiser, T.

The shadow and the shadowed. Oursler, W. C.

Shadow out of space. Lovecraft, H. P. and Derleth, A. W.

Shadow, shadow on the wall. Waldo, E. H.

Shadow show. Simak, C. D.

Shadows in the moonlight. Howard, R. E.

Shadows in Zamboula. Howard, R. E.

Shadows on the reef. Blackford, C. M.

Shadwell. Warner, S. T.

Shaggy lays off. Payne, S.

SHAKESPEARE, WILLIAM, 1564-1616

Asimov, I. Immortal bard
Blixen, K. Tempests
Irwin, I. H. Spring flight
Russell, B. A. W. R. 3d earl. Psychoanalyst's nightmare
Shaw, G. B. Dressing room secret
Thurber, J. Macbeth murder mystery

Shallit, Rebecca

Initiation fee
Ferris, H. J. comp. Girls, girls, girls

Sham. Seager, A.

Shami, Yitzhak, 1889-1949

Hamamah; a tale of the Arabian desert
Tehilla, and other Israeli tales

Shamir, Moshe, 1921-

First kiss
Tehilla, and other Israeli tales
He walked through the fields
Frank, M. Z. ed. Sound the great trumpet

SHANGHAIING

Dingle, A. E. Bound for Rio Grande
See also Impressment

Shapiro, Lionel, 1908-

Dieppe
Nelson, G. E. ed. Cavalcade of the North

SHARE CROPPERS. See Tenant farming

SHARKS

Ferguson, R. His lucky day
Whitehill, J. Young man with a spear

Sharp, William, 1855-1905

St Bride of the Isles
Fremantle, A. J. ed. Christmas is here

Sharp as the broken cup. Eckard, A. K.

Shaw, George Bernard, 1856-1950

Dressing room secret
Lewis, J. D. ed. Great stories about business
Miraculous revenge
Garrity, D. A. ed. 44 Irish short stories

Shaw, Irwin, 1913-

Act of faith
Fenton, C. A. ed. Best short stories of World War II
Ribalow, H. U. ed. Treasury of American Jewish stories
Age of reason
Shaw, I. Tip on a dead jockey, and other stories
Dry rock
McClennen, J. comp. Masters and masterpieces of the short story
Eighty-yard run
Schwed, P. and Wind, R. W. eds. Great stories from the world of sport
House of pain
Lewis, J. D. ed. Great stories about show business
In the French style
Shaw, I. Tip on a dead jockey, and other stories
The kiss at Croton Falls
Shaw, I. Tip on a dead jockey, and other stories
Main currents of American thought
Havighurst, W. ed. Masters of the modern short story
Havighurst, W. and others, eds. Selection
Peter Two
Shaw, I. Tip on a dead jockey, and other stories
Strawberry ice cream soda
Tibbets, A. B. ed. Youth, youth, youth
Sunny banks of the River Lethe
Shaw, I. Tip on a dead jockey, and other stories
Then we were three
Prize stories 1957: the O. Henry awards
Shaw, I. Tip on a dead jockey, and other stories
Tip on a dead jockey
Best American short stories, 1955
Shaw, I. Tip on a dead jockey, and other stories
Voyage out, voyage home
Shaw, I. Tip on a dead jockey, and other stories

SKEPTICISM
Blixen, K. Cardinal's third tale
Sandoz, M. Y. Suspicion

Sketch by MacNeil. Remington, F.

Ski high. Chute, B. J.

SKIING. See Skis and skiing

Skiing in a nutshell. Bird, D. M.

SKIN DIVING
King, R. Body in the rockpit

The **skipper** and el Capitan. Stockton, F. R.

Skirmish. Simak, C. D.

Skirmish on the head of the Arroyo Colorado. Adams, A.

SKIS AND SKIING
Bird, D. M. Skiing in a nutshell
Boyle, K. Diplomat's wife
Chute, B. J. Ski high
Coombs, C. I. Avalanche
Coombs, C. I. Winter sport
Mann, T. Snow world
Shaw, I. Voyage out, voyage home
Whitehill, J. The propagandist

Sklare, Rose Bernards, 1920-
Giant can weep
New voices 2: American writing today

Skool. Willans, G.

Skulking permit. Sheckley, R.

SKUNKS
Coombs, C. I. Frisbie—Santa's helper
Stuart, J. Wind blew east

Skuthorpe, Lance
Two plates at once
Stivens, D. comp. Coast to coast

The **sky** had fallen. Carlen, E. A.

The **slate.** Campbell, W. E. M.

Slater, Patrick
The wake
Nelson, G. E. ed. Cavalcade of the North

SLAUGHTERING AND SLAUGHTER-HOUSES
Fournier, P. House of blood
Vukelich, G. The scale room
West, A. C. Not Isaac

SLAVE TRADE
Davidson, A. Necessity of his condition

SLAVERY
Benét, S. V. Freedom's a hard-bought thing
Lytle, A. N. Mr MacGregor
Swift, H. H. Railroad to freedom

Slaying of the wolf. Shneur, Z.

SLED DOGS. See Sledge dogs

SLEDGE DOGS
Sullivan, A. Essence of a man

SLEEP, PROLONGED
Irving, W. Rip Van Winkle

SLEEP-WALKING. See Somnabulism

Sleeping Beauty. Bontempelli, M.

The **sleeping** beauty. Garrett, G.

SLEEPLESSNESS. See Insomnia

SLEIGHT OF HAND. See Conjuring

Slesar, Henry
Day of the execution
Best detective stories of the year (13th annual collection)

Trouble with Ruth
Best detective stories of the year (12th annual collection)
Victory parade
Oberfirst, R. ed. Anthology of best short-short stories v6

Slightly different story. Glaze, A.

Slime. Brennan, J. P.

Slope of the high mountain. O'Brian, P.

SLOT MACHINES. See Gambling

Slow boat to China. Hale, N.

Slow-motion crime. Sandoz, M. Y.

Slum cat. Seton, E. T.

Small assassin. Bradbury, R.

Small portion. Bates, H. E.

Small side of Doroteo Arango. Smith, E. H.

SMALL TOWN LIFE
Clemens, S. L. Man that corrupted Hadleyburg
Garland, H. Creamery man
Garland, H. God's ravens
Garland's H. "Good fellow's" wife
Kentfield, C. Bell of charity
MacLeish, R. Night of disaster
Upshaw, H. My brother's voice
See also Cities and towns; Peasant life; also names of countries with phrase: Provincial and rural, e.g. England, Provincial and rural

Small world of M-75. Clinton, E. M.

Smart guy. Jameson, C. G.

Smeddum. Mitchell, J. L.

The **smell** of death and flowers. Gordimer, N.

Smell of lilies. See Gellhorn, M. E. In sickness and in health

Smilanski, Moshe. See Smilansky, Moshe

Smilansky, Moshe, 1874-1953
Abdul Hadi's rifle
Schwarz, L. W. ed. Feast of Leviathan
Barhash
Tehilla, and other Israeli tales
Story of a love
Frank, M. Z. ed. Sound the great trumpet

The **smile.** Sansom, W.

Smith, Cordwainer
Game of Rat and Dragon
Best science-fiction stories and novels: 1956
Galaxy science fiction magazine. Third Galaxy reader
Montgomery, R. B. ed. Best SF three

Smith, Edgar Valentine, 1875-1953
Prelude
First-prize stories, 1919-1957

Smith, Edith Hutchins, 1914-
Conversation among friends
Smith, E. H. El Tigre!
The decision
Smith, E. H. El Tigre!
El Tigre!
Smith, E. H. El Tigre!
Four o'clock
Smith, E. H. El Tigre!
The gift
Smith, E. H. El Tigre!

Smith, Edith H.—*Continued*
Gomez
    Smith, E. H. El Tigre!
Justice and Juan Morales
    Smith, E. H. El Tigre!
Little brown ones
    Smith, E. H. El Tigre!
Manolo
    Smith, E. H. El Tigre!
Red dress
    Smith, E. H. El Tigre!
Repeat performance
    Smith, E. H. El Tigre!
Sadness of Cruz
    Smith, E. H. El Tigre!
Similar sauce
    Smith, E. H. El Tigre!
Small side of Doroteo Arango
    Smith, E. H. El Tigre!
Vaya con Dios
    Smith, E. H. El Tigre!
Wake for El Gusano
    Smith, E. H. El Tigre!

Smith, Edmund Ware, 1900-
An angler comes to life
    Smith, E. W. The one-eyed poacher and
    and the Maine woods
Axe on Slumber Lake
    Smith, E. W. The one-eyed poacher and
    and the Maine woods
Courtship of Jeff Coongate
    Smith, E. W. The one-eyed poacher and
    and the Maine woods
Decline and fall of a purist
    Smith, E. W. The one-eyed poacher and
    and the Maine woods
Escape to reality
    Smith, E. W. The one-eyed poacher and
    the Maine woods
Gates ajar
    Smith, E. W. The one-eyed poacher and
    the Maine woods
Jeff Coongate and the stolen crony
    Smith, E. W. The one-eyed poacher and
    the Maine woods
The long night
    Smith, E. W. The one-eyed poacher and
    the Maine woods
Men, women and wilderness
    Smith, E. W. The one-eyed poacher and
    the Maine woods
Most-remembered pools
    Smith, E. W. The one-eyed poacher and
    the Maine woods
One-eyed poacher's revenge
    Smith, E. W. The one-eyed poacher and
    the Maine woods
Rum over the dam
    Smith, E. W. The one-eyed poacher and
    the Maine woods
Short, happy death of Jeff Coongate
    Smith, E. W. The one-eyed poacher and
    the Maine woods
Specific gravity of Jeff Coongate
    Smith, E. W. The one-eyed poacher and
    the Maine woods
Underground episode
    Tibbets, A. B. ed. Youth, youth, youth
Woodsmoke from old cabins
    Smith, E. W. The one-eyed poacher and
    the Maine woods

Smith, Evelyn E. 1927-
Vilbar party
    Galaxy science fiction magazine. Third
    Galaxy reader
Smith, F. J.
One more mile to go
    Best detective stories of the year (12th
    annual collection)
Smith, Godfrey, 1926-
The girl
    Winter's tales, 2
Smith, Harry Allen, 1907-
One coat of white
    Burnett, W. ed. This is my best humor
Smith, Jean Rogers
Hyacinth from Limbo
    Smith, J. R. Hyacinth from Limbo, and
    other stories
Sweet beyond
    Smith, J. R. Hyacinth from Limbo, and
    other stories
To sleep and to wake
    Smith, J. R. Hyacinth from Limbo, and
    other stories
Smith, John Campbell, 1924-
Run, run away, brother
    Best American short stories, 1957
Smith, L. W. 1934-
Ace in the hole
    Oberfirst, R. ed. 1955 anthology of best
    original short-shorts
Smith, Shelley, pseud. See Bodington, Nancy
Smith: an episode in a lodginghouse. Black-
wood, A.

SMOKING
Beigel, U. The snapshots
Stout, R. Instead of evidence
Williams, T. Yellow bird

Smuggler's cove. Wylie, P.

SMUGGLING
Flanagan, T. Customs of the country
Gilbert, M. F. One-tenth man
Haliburton, T. C. Beating the smuggling
    game
Wylie, P. Smuggler's cove

Snafu murder. Palmer, S.

SNAILS
Andersen, H. C. Happy family

SNAKE CHARMERS
Crane, L. Dust and the serpent

Snake dance. Ford, C.

Snake doctor. Cobb, I. S.

SNAKES
Bierce, A. The man and the snake
Cobb, I. S. Snake doctor
Colette, S. G. The snakes
Cox, J. A. Dangerous cargo
Crane, L. Dust and the serpent
Doyle, Sir A. C. Adventure of the
    speckled band
Holmes, O. W. Elsie Venner arouses
    Master Bernard's suspicions
Jordan, D. S. Old Rattler and the King
    Snake
Kipling, R. "Rikki-tikki-tavi"
Peretz, I. L. Supreme sacrifice

SNAKES—*Continued*

Rawlings, M. K. Penny is bitten by a rattlesnake

Simms, W. G. The rattlesnake

Stuart, J. Old Ben

The **snakes.** Colette, S. G.

Snap shot. Gilbert, M. F.

The **snapshots.** Beigel, U.

SNEAKERS. See Boots and shoes

Sneakers. Bradbury, R.

Sneider, Vern J. 1916-
The box
Sneider, V. J. Long way from home, and other stories
Child of the regiment
Sneider, V. J. Long way from home, and other stories
Dumbest man in the Army
Sneider, V. J. Long way from home, and other stories
Even the leopard
Sneider, V. J. Long way from home, and other stories
Long way from home
Sneider, V. J. Long way from home, and other stories
Pail of oysters
Sneider, V. J. Long way from home, and other stories
Uncle Bosko
Sneider, V. J. Long way from home, and other stories
When winter comes
Sneider, V. J. Long way from home, and other stories

The **sniff.** Pritchett, V. S.

The **sniper.** O'Flaherty, L.

SNOBS AND SNOBISHNESS
Feng, M. Lady who was a beggar
Johnson, P. H. Death of a duchess
O'Hara, J. Summer's day

Snodgrass, Jean
To Dona—forever
Oberfirst, R. ed. Anthology of best short-short stories v6

SNOW
Aiken, C. P. Silent snow, secret snow
See also Avalanches

Snow angels. Kubly, H.

Snow on the sand. Watton, J. van H.

Snow owl. Brown, M.

SNOW STORMS
Brennan, J. P. Green parrot
Brennan, J. P. Mail for Juniper Hill
Chekhov, A. P. On official business
Hale, N. Snows of childhood
Harte, E. Outcasts of Poker Flat
Peretz, I. L. The messenger
Roberts, K. Two storms
Tolstoï, L. N. Graf. Lost on the steppe
Voronov, N. The cashier
Whitehill, J. Town is waiting

Snow world. Mann, T.

Snowball man and Holy Writ. Berg, L.

Snowfall on Fourth Street. Clayton, J. B.

Snows of childhood. Hale, N.

SNOWSLIDES. See Avalanches

SNOWSTORMS. See Snow storms

Snulbug. White, W. A. P.

"**So** early in the morning, O!" MacMahon, B.

So good for the boys. Waugh, E.

So help me. Algren, N.

So pale, so cold, so fair. Brackett, L.

'**So** we'll drink. . .' Kemp, P. K.

SOAP BOX DERBIES
Olgin, J. Soap box derby

Soap box derby. Olgin, J.

Sobol, Donald J. 1924-
Two-timers
Teen-age tales, bk 4

Social call. Gerchunoff, A.

SOCIAL CHANGE
Oliver, C. Mother of necessity

SOCIAL CLASSES
Block, A. R. Father image
Campbell, W. E. M. Not worthy of a Wentworth
Hale, N. New order
OHara, J. Price's always open
Zamfirescu, A. D. I. Popescu of the boundaries
See also Class distinction; Social status

Social event. Putnam, D. S.

SOCIAL PROBLEMS
Abdullah, M. K. Grandfather tiger
Farrell, J. T. Little Johnny: a fable
Gardner, C. Conflict
Hawthorne, N. Earth's holocaust

SOCIAL SECRETARIES. See Secretaries

SOCIAL SERVICE
Hale, N. Readville stars

SOCIAL STATUS
Babel', I. E. In the basement
Feng, M. Lady who was a beggar
Hale, N. How would you like to be born
O'Hara, J. Graven image
O'Hara, J. King of the desert
Scott, J. D. Favourite author
See also Class distinction; Social classes

SOCIAL WORKERS
Farrell, J. T. Little Johnny: a fable
Stegner, W. E. Pop goes the alley cat

SOCIALISM
Chesterton, G. K. Unprecedented architecture of Commander Blair
Plomer, W. C. F. Friend of her father's

SOCIETY OF JESUS. See Jesuits

Sock finish. Bloch, R.

SOCRATES
Plato. Death of Socrates

SODA FOUNTAIN WORKERS
Yellen, S. The glass jaw

Soft step of the Shawnee. Clayton, J. B.

SOFTBALL
Evans, E. Diamond dilemma

Solange, the wolf-girl. Prévost, M.

Soldati, Mario, 1906-
Nora
Slonim, M. ed. Modern Italian short stories

A soldier. Katai, T.
Soldier-poet in a Northern prison. Lanier, S.
SOLDIERS
Aichinger, K. Opened order
Drury, W. P. Concerning a treaty with
  France
Fournier, P. The horses
Haupt, Z. Girl with her heels set on half
  moons
Lesinš, K. The leavetaking
MacLeish, R. Night of disaster

American
Bahr, J. Irrepressible sergeant
Balchin, N. Tinfield mascot
Boyle, K. Canals of Mars
Boyle, K. Loneliest man in the U.S. Army
Campbell, W. E. M. Company K
Chavez, A. Colonel and the santo
Connell, V. Riviera affair
Crane, S. Red badge of courage
Downey, H. The hunters
Gallant, M. The picnic
Garrett, G. How the last war ended
Hawkins, J. and Hawkins, W. Young and
  scared
Innerst, I. Brother's ring
Jones, J. Thirty-year man
Kubly, H. A quiet afternoon
Litwak, L. Making of a clerk
Lowry, R. J. C. The bambino
Lowry, R. J. C. Over here
Macauley, R. End of pity
Macauley, R. The mind is its own place
Macauley, R. Nest of gentlefolk
Macauley, R. Thin voice
McLaughlin, R. Short wait between trains
Mailer, N. K. Paper house
Murphy, D. Camp in the meadow
Patton, F. G. Little obvious
Polk, W. T. Croix de cuisine
Rosten, L. C. Happy was the soldier!
Shaw, I. Act of faith
Truax, L. Man alone
Yates, R. Jody rolled the bones
  See also Veterans

Arab
Dubonnet, R. Arab officer

Austrian
Mann, T. A gleam

British
Amis, K. My enemy's enemy
Balchin, N. Gentle counsels
Bates, H. E. A place in the heart
Cary, J. Umaru
Dickens, C. Seven poor travellers
Downey, H. The hunters
Ewing, J. H. G. Peace egg
Household, G. Drug for the Major
Household, G. The idealist
Mead, H. Soldier's farewell
Pincherle, A. English officer
Shaw, I. Walking wounded
Shaw, I. Wedding of a friend
Sutherland, H. As Joe said

Chinese
Sneider, V. J. Pail of oysters

English
See Soldiers, British

French
Fisher, D. F. C. In the eye of the storm
Household, G. The case of Valentin Le-
  cormier
Maupassant, G. de. Bed no. 29
Maupassant, G. de. Colonel's ideas
Maupassant, G. de. Epiphany

Furloughs
Fisher, D. F. C. In the eye of the storm
Garrett, G. Don't take no for an answer
Lowry, R. J. C. Layover in El Paso
Montague, M. P. England to America
Tabakai, A. Sergeant Shmueli rides a
  donkey

German
Lesinš, K. The dove
Maupassant, G. de. Mademoiselle Fifi
Maupassant, G. de. The prisoners
Maupassant, G. de. Walter Schnaffs' ad-
  venture

Irish
O'Donovan, M. Private property
O'Faoláin, S. Fugue
O'Faoláin, S. Midsummer night madness
O'Faoláin, S. The patriot
O'Flaherty, L. Mountain tavern
Plunkett, J. Dublin Fusilier

Italian
Hofmannsthal, H. H. Edler von. Tale of
  the cavalry
Verga, G. Buddies

Japanese
Katai, T. A soldier

Korean
Sneider, V. J. When winter comes

Negroes
See Negroes as soldiers

Prussian
See Soldiers, German

Russian
Babel', I. E. After the battle
Babel', I. E. Death of Dolgushov
Babel', I. E. Italian sunshine
Babel', I. E. My first goose
Babel', I. E. Salt
Babel', I. E. The widow
Kay, T. Captain Luba and the white dress
Lesinš, K. The dove

Welsh
Lewis, A. They came

SOLDIERS, DISABLED. See Cripples
SOLDIERS, MISSING. See War—Casual-
ties
Soldier's farewell. Mead, H.
SOLDIERS' MONUMENTS. See War
  memorials
Solitude. Maupassant, G. de
SOLOMON, KING OF ISRAEL
Allen, A. The judgment
Russell, B. A. W. R. 3d earl. Queen of
  Sheba's nightmare
Solomon, Barbara Probst
A day in Toledo
  Miller, N. ed. New campus writing, no. 2

Solomon primitive. Hammett, E. A.

Soman, Florence Jane
  Sweet eighteen
    Teen-age tales, bk 4

Some are so lucky. Garner, H.

Some day I'll find you. Hale, N.

Some demon's mistress. Bayley, J.

Some kinds of bad luck. Forester, C. S.

Some like them cold. Lardner, R. W.

Some people are just plumb crazy. Kober, A.

Some with a flattering word. McGerr, P.

Somebody's luggage. Dickens, C.

Someday. Asimov, I.

**Somerville, Edith Anna Œnone, 1861-1949,
    and Martin, Violet Florence, 1862-1915**
  Lisheen races, second-hand
    O'Donovan, M. ed. Modern Irish short
      stories
    Schwed, P. and Wind, H. W. eds. Great
      stories from the world of sport
  A misdeal
    Schwed, P. and Wind, H. W. eds. Great
      stories from the world of sport
  The Whiteboys
    Welcome, J. and Orchard, V. eds. Best
      hunting stories

Something about my father. Angoff, C.

Something borrowed—something blue. Block,
  A. R.

Something different. Mackenzie, O. C.

Something for nothing. Sheckley, R.

Something in a boat. Fallon, P.

Something in a cloud. Finney, J.

Something in common. Finkelstein, B.

Something in wood. Derleth, A. W.

Something like love. Howland, R.

Something old—something new. Block, A. R.

Something special. Murdoch, I.

Something to talk with. James, A.

Somewhere out of nowhere. McCord, J.

Sommers, Marion Oliver, 1915-
  Haven't we been nice to you?
    American vanguard, 1956

SOMNAMBULISM
  Hirai, T. Two crippled men

Son he'd never met. Shenton, E.

Son of a bishop. Babcock, H.

Son of liberty. Pessin, D.

Son of the Celestial: a character. Cather,
  W. S.

Sonata of autumn. Valle-Inclán, R. del

The **song.** Babel', I. E.

The **song.** Downey, H.

Song at twilight. Gibbs, W.

Song of songs. Gerchunoff, A.

Song of the barrow. West, A. C.

Song of yesterday. Stettner, S.

SONG WRITERS. See Musicians—Composers

SONGS
  Babel', I. E. The song
  Faulkner, W. The rosary

Fontenay, C. L. Silk and the song
Maupassant, G. de. Accursed bread
Peretz, I. L. Reincarnation of a melody

Songs of the distant earth. Clarke, A. C.

Sonny's blues. ·Baldwin, J.

SONS. See Fathers and sons; Mothers and
  sons

Soquots. Caldwell, E.

SORCERY. See Magic; Witchcraft

Sorel. Farrell, J. T.

Sørensen, Villi, 1929-
  Child's play
    Sørensen, V. Tiger in the kitchen, and
      other strange stories
  The concert
    Sørensen, V. Tiger in the kitchen, and
      other strange stories
  Murder case
    Sørensen, V. Tiger in the kitchen, and
      other strange stories
  Strange tree
    Sørensen, V. Tiger in the kitchen, and
      other strange stories
  The tigers
    Sørensen, V. Tiger in the kitchen, and
      other strange stories
  Two legends
    Sørensen, V. Tiger in the kitchen, and
      other strange stories
  Two twins
    Sørensen, V. Tiger in the kitchen, and
      other strange stories

Sørensen, Villy. See Sørensen, Villi

SORORITIES. See Greek letter societies

Sorrow-Acre. Blixen, K.

Sorrows of gin. Cheever, J.

SOTO, HERNANDO DE, 1500?-1542
  Lytle, A. N. Alchemy

The **soul.** O'Brian, P.

Soul-machine. Elliott, W. Y.

Souls belated. Wharton, E. N. J.

Sound effects. Allen, M. P.

Sound of talking. Purdy, J.

Sound of the bell. MacMahon, B.

Sound that God heard. Clayton, J. B.

The **source.** Porter, K. A.

THE SOUTH. See Southern States

SOUTH AFRICA. See Africa, South

SOUTH AMERICA
  Household, G. Six legs are welcome

SOUTH CAROLINA

Charleston
Steele, W. D. Can't cross Jordan by myself

Farm life
See Farm life—South Carolina

Folklore
See Legends and folk tales—South
Carolina

Sullivan's Island
Poe, E. A. Gold bug

SOUTH DAKOTA
Garland, H. Among the corn-rows

Farm life
See Farm life—South Dakota
SOUTH SEA ISLANDS
Hodgson, W. H. Island of the Ud
London, J. Seed of McCoy
Maugham, W. S. Red
Michener, J. S. Boar's tooth
Phillpotts, E. King of Kanga
Russell, J. Price of the head
Stacpoole, H. de V. Problem of the sea
Stead, C. ed. Great stories of the South Sea Islands; 9 stories
Southern accent. Allen, S.

SOUTHERN DIALECT. See Dialect stories—Southern
SOUTHERN STATES
Curley, D. House called Magnolia
Curley, D. A. Spring
Faulkner, W. The bear
Faulkner, W. Rose for Emily
Faulkner, W. Uncle Willy
Gordon, C. Old Red
Hale, N. New order
O'Connor, F. Artificial nigger
O'Connor, F. Circle in the fire
O'Connor, F. Displaced person
O'Connor, F. Good country people
O'Connor, F. A good man is hard to find, and other stories; 10 stories
O'Connor, F. Late encounter with the enemy
O'Connor, F. The life you save may be your own
O'Connor, F. The river
O'Connor, F. Temple of the Holy Ghost
Patton, F. G. Let it rest
Porter, K. A. Old mortality
Porter, K. A. Old order; 10 stories
See also names of individual Southern states
Farm life
See Farm life—Southern States
SOUTHERNERS. See Southern States
Souvenir of Hammam Meskoutine. Sandoz, M. Y.
SPACE AND TIME
Moore, W. No man pursueth
See also Time
SPACE FLIGHT. See Interplanetary voyages; also Space flight to specific planets, e.g., Space flight to the moon; etc.
SPACE FLIGHT TO PLUTO
Elam, R. M. Expedition Pluto
SPACE FLIGHT TO THE MOON
Asimov, I. Ideas die hard
Clarke, A. C. Venture to the moon
Harris, A. W. The unique conception
SPACE FLIGHT TO VENUS
Elam, R. M. Space steward
Miller, E. M. Red diamond for Miss Detwiler
SPACE SHIPS
Clarke, A. C. Refugee
Clarke, A. C. This earth of majesty
Elam, R. M. Race around the sun

Gunn, J. E. Cave of night
Pohl, F. The mapmakers
Sheckley, R. Hands off
Russell, E. F. Present from Joe
Simak, C. D. Target generation
Waldo, E. H. Medusa
See also Interplanetary voyages; Rocket ships
SPACE STATIONS
Clarke, A. C. The other side of the sky
Elam, R. M. Ghost ship of space
Elam, R. M. Mercy flight to Luna
Robinson, F. M. One thousand miles up
Space steward. Elam, R. M.
SPACE TRAVEL. See Interplanetary voyages
SPACEMEN. See Air pilots
SPAIN
Alarcón, P. A. de. The stub-book—a rural story
16th century
Ayala, F. The bewitched
17th century
Irving, W. Legend of the Moor's legacy
18th Century
Alarcón, P. A. de. Three-cornered hat
19th century
Alas, L. Doña Berta
Valle-Inclán, R. del. Sonata of autumn
20th century
Connell, E. S. Walls of Ávila
Gallant, M. Señor Pinedo
Hemingway, E. Capital of the world
Solomon, B. P. A day in Toledo
20th century—Civil War, 1936-1939
Sartre, J. P. The wall
Andalusia
Duke, M. Manuel at full moon
Folklore
See Legends and folk tales—Spain
Granada
Irving, W. Legend of the Moor's legacy
Madrid
Perez Galdos, B. Torquemada in the flames
Pritchett, V. S. Evils of Spain
Seville
Bécquer, G. A. Master Pérez the organist
SPANIARDS IN CALIFORNIA
Gulick, G. C. "Conquest"
Kuttner, H. Near miss
SPANIARDS IN FRANCE
O'Brian, P. Nicolas
SPANIARDS IN IRELAND
O'Flaherty, L. Post office
SPANIARDS IN NEW MEXICO
Chavez, A. Ardent commandant
Chavez, A. Bell that sang again
SPANISH-AMERICAN WAR, 1898. See United States—19th century—War of 1898

Starbride. See White, W. A. P. Star bride

Stardust. Hewitt, J.

Stark, Irwin, 1912-
Shock treatment
Ribalow, H. U. ed. Treasury of American Jewish stories

Starrett, Vincent, 1886-
Eleventh juror
Cooke, D. C. ed. My best murder story

The stars in their courses. Thomason, J. W.

Start in life. Suckow, R.

STARVATION
Saroyan, W. Daring young man on the flying trapeze

State of grace. Aymé, M.

State of grace. Brodkey, H.

State of well-being. White, R.

STATIONS, RAILROAD. See Railroads—Stations

STATUE OF LIBERTY, NEW YORK
Woolrich, C. The corpse in the Statue of Liberty

STATUES
Criswell, C. Goddess of Mercy
Hale, N. Object of virtue
Taper, B. Sense of destiny

STATUS, SOCIAL. See Social status

Staudy, Agnes
Little Miss Big Shot
Oberfirst, R. ed. Anthology of best short-short stories v6

Stay away from my mother. Whitehill, J.

STEALING. See Shoplifting; Theft; Thieves

STEAMBOATS
Beldon, A. A. Road to the shore

Stedman, S.
Stroke of a master
Stivens, D. comp. Coast to coast

STEEL INDUSTRY. See Iron and steel industry

Steele, Max, 1922-
Ah love! Ah me!
Stowe, A. comp. When boy dates girl
Wanton troopers
Prize stories, 1955: the O. Henry awards

Steele, Wilbur Daniel, 1886-
Bubbles
First-prize stories, 1919-1957
Blue Murder
Baudin, M. ed. Contemporary short stories v2
Can't cross Jordan by myself
First-prize stories, 1919-1957

STEEPLECHASING. See Horse racing

STEERS. See Cattle

Steffens, Lincoln, 1866-1936
Miserable merry Christmas
Lohan, R. ed. Christmas tales for reading aloud

Stegner, Wallace Earle, 1909-
Blue-winged teal
First-prize stories, 1919-1957
Stegner, W. E. City of the living, and other stories

City of the living
Prize stories, 1955: the O. Henry awards
Stegner, W. E. City of the living, and other stories

The colt
Schaefer, J. W. ed. Out West

Field guide to the Western birds
New short novels, 2
Stegner, W. E. City of the living, and other stories

Impasse
Stegner, W. E. City of the living, and other stories

Maiden in a tower
Best American short stories, 1955
Stegner, W. E. City of the living, and other stories

Pop goes the alley cat
Stegner, W. E. City of the living, and other stories

The traveler.
Stegner, W. E. City of the living, and other stories

View from the balcony
Gettman, R. A. and Harkness, B. eds. Book of stories

The volunteer
Stegner, W. E. City of the living, and other stories

Women on the wall
Fenton, C. A. ed. Best short stories of World War II

Stein, Aaron Marc, 1906-
This was Willi's day
Best detective stories of the year (12th annual collection)

Steinbeck, John, 1902-
Affair at 7, rue de M—
Prize stories, 1956: the O. Henry awards

The chrysanthemums
McClennen, J. comp. Masters and masterpieces of the short story

Flight
Havinghurst, W. ed. Masters of the modern short story
McClennen, J. comp. Masters and masterpieces of the short story

The gift
Sterner, L. G. ed. Favorite short stories

Leader of the people
Baudin, M. ed. Contemporary short stories v2
McClennen, J. comp. Masters and masterpieces of the short story
Short, R. W. and Sewall, R. B. eds. Short stories for study
Thurston, J. A. ed. Reading modern short stories

Molly Morgan
Jennings, F. G. and Calitri, C. J. eds. Stories

The promise
McClennen, J. comp. Masters and masterpieces of the short story

Steiner, George, 1929-
Deeps of the sea
Prize stories, 1958: the O. Henry awards

STENOGRAPHERS
Parker, D. R. Standard of living
See also Secretaries

STEPFATHERS
Babel', I. E. Sandy the Christ
Criswell, C. The hobby
Stephen Skarridge's Christmas. Stockton,
    F. R.
Stephens, James, 1882-1950
    Coming of Pan
        Laughton, C. ed. Tell me a story
    A rhinoceros, some ladies and a horse
        Garrity, D. A. ed. 44 Irish short stories
        O'Donovan, M. ed. Modern Irish short
          stories
    Schoolfellows
        Garrity, D. A. ed. 44 Irish short stories
Stephenson, Carl, 1886-
    Leiningen versus the ants
        McMaster, J. ed. Stories to remember
        Swayze, B. ed. Short story magic
STEPMOTHERS
Bailey, B. and Walworth, D. He loved
    me truly
Criswell, C. Crying through the lock
Gordimer, N. My first two women
Schweitzer, G. Not a child anymore
Stettner, Stella, 1923-
    Song of yesterday
        New voices 2: American writing today
STEVEDORES. See Longshoremen
Stevenson, Robert Louis, 1850-1894
    Bottle imp
        Sandrus, M. Y. ed. Famous mysteries
    Espiritio Santo
        Swayze, B. ed. Short story magic
    Isle of Voices
        Stead, C. ed. Great stories of the South
          Sea Islands
    Markheim
        Havighurst, W. and others, eds. Selec-
          tion
    Sire de Malétroit's door
        Costain, T. B. and Beecroft, J. eds.
          Stories to remember
        Langford, W. F. ed. Book of better
          stories
        Sterner, L. G. ed. Favorite short stories
    Strange case of Dr Jekyll and Mr Hyde
        Sandrus, M. Y. ed. Famous mysteries
    Suicide Club
        Costain, T. B. and Beecroft, J. eds.
          More Stories to remember
        Same as: Story of the young man with
          the cream tarts
Stewart, John Innes Mackintosh, 1906-
    Bear's box
        Stewart, J. I. M. Appleby talks again
    Dangerfield's diary
        Stewart, J. I. M. Appleby talks again
    Enigma Jones
        Stewart, J. I. M. Appleby talks again
    The exile
        Stewart, J. I. M. Appleby talks again
    False colours
        Stewart, J. I. M. Appleby talks again
    Four seasons
        Stewart, J. I. M. Appleby talks again
    Grey's ghost
        Stewart, J. I. M. Appleby talks again
    Here is the news
        Stewart, J. I. M. Appleby talks again
    Heritage portrait
        Stewart, J. I. M. Appleby talks again

    Lombard books
        Stewart, J. I. M. Appleby talks again
    Matter of goblins
        Stewart, J. I. M. Appleby talks again
    Mouse-trap
        Stewart, J. I. M. Appleby talks again
    Murder on the 7.16
        Stewart, J. I. M. Appleby talks again
    The reprisal
        Stewart, J. I. M. Appleby talks again
    The ribbon
        Stewart, J. I. M. Appleby talks again
    Tom, Dick and Harry
        Stewart, J. I. M. Appleby talks again
    A very odd case
        Stewart, J. I. M. Appleby talks again
    Was he Morton?
        Stewart, J. I. M. Appleby talks again
Stewed beans. Austin. M. A. Van N.
Sticky Pierce, diplomat. Rhodes, E. M.
Stifter, Adalbert, 1805-1868
    Rock crystal
        Lohan, R. ed. Christmas tales for read-
          ing aloud
Stiles, Bert, 1920?-1944
    Leipzig
        Fenton, C. A. ed. Best short stories of
          World War II
A **still** moment. Welty, E.
Stillman, William James, 1787-1849
    Billy and Hans
        Skelton, P. ed. Animals all
Stillwell, Glen F.
    One foot on the ground
        Furman, A. L. ed. Teen-age humorous
          stories
The **sting** of the lance. Carousso, G.
Stinkpot. Verga, G.
Stock, George A. 1897-
    Busting out all over
        Oberfirst, R. ed. Anthology of best
          short-short stories v6
STOCK-YARDS
Ferber, E. Blue blood
STOCKHOLM. See Sweden—Stockholm
STOCKS
De Camp, L. S. and Pratt, F. Caveat
    emptor
Stockton, Frank Richard, 1834-1902
    Asaph
        Stockton, F. R. Best short stories
    Christmas wreck
        Lohan, R. ed. Christmas tales for read-
          ing aloud
    Discourager of hesitancy
        Swayze, B. ed. Short story magic
    "His wife's deceased sister"
        Stockton, F. R. Best short stories
    The lady, or the tiger?
        McMaster, J. ed. Stories to remember
        Stockton, F. R. Best short stories
        Swayze, B. ed. Short story magic
    Old Pipes and the dryad
        Stockton, F. R. Best short stories
    "The philosophy of relative existences"
        Stockton, F. R. Best short stories
    Piece of red calico
        Stockton, F. R. Best short stories

Sullivan, Frank—*Continued*
Jukes family
Burnett, W. ed. This is my best humor
Trip to Hollywood
Lewis, J. D. ed. Great stories about show business
The ugly mollusk
Saturday evening post (Periodical) Saturday evening post Carnival of humor
Sullivan, Richard, 1908-
Pinch of salt
Hughes, R. ed. All manner of men
SULLIVAN'S ISLAND. See South Carolina—Sullivan's Island
The sum of tiny things. Lederer, W. J. and Burdick, E. L.
SUMMER CAMPS. See Camps, Summer
Summer day. Stafford, J.
Summer in Salandar. Bates, H. E.
Summer in the air. Bradbury, R.
Summer night. Bowen, E.
Summer of the insistent voices. Clayton, J. B.
Summer of truth. Payne, L. V.
SUMMER RESORTS
Bates, H. E. Across the bay
Gibbs, W. Song at twilight
Mann, T. Mario and the magician
Maugham, W. S. Round dozen
Morton, C. W. Away from it all
O'Hara, J. Next-to-last dance of the season
O'Hara, J. Price's always open
Whitehill, J. Stay away from my mother
Summer serenade. Robert, J.
Summer shower. Clemons, W.
Summer sun. Ivins, A.
SUMMER THEATER. See Theater and stage life
SUMMER VACATIONS. See Vacations
Summers, Hollis, 1916-
Black and white and gray
New voices 2: American writing today
Summers, James L. 1910-
Open season
Stowe, A. comp. When boy dates girl
Summer's day. O'Hara, J.
A summer's long dream. Hale, N.
A summer's reading. Malamud, B.
Summertime adventure. Walker, D. H.
SUN
Clarke, A. C. Out of the sun
Sun. Grandamy, I.
Sun and shadow. Bradbury, R.
Sunday afternoon hanging. Stuart, J.
Sunday afternoon. Sunny. MacMahon, B.
Sunday ice cream. Clayton, J. B.
Sunday in April. Farrell, J. T.
Sunday morning. Block, A. R.
Sunday morning shift. Allen, S.
Sunday punch. Keir, R. H.
SUNDAY SCHOOLS
Campbell, W. E. M. Miss Daisy
Saroyan, W. Sunday zeppelin

Sunday zeppelin. Saroyan, W.
Sunna
Love is humbug
World prize stories; 2d ser.
Sunny banks of the River Lethe. Shaw, I.
Sunset. Faulkner, W.
Sunwall, Betty, 1925-
Things changed
Prize stories 1957: the O. Henry awards
Supercharged harmony. Millholland, R.
SUPERNATURAL PHENOMENA
Adams, A. Cat in the jacal
Aymé, M. The walker-through-walls
Blackwood, A. Haunted island
Blackwood, A. Man whom the trees loved
Blackwood, A. The willows
Brennan, J. P. Green parrot
Brennan, J. P. Slime
Buchan, J. 1st baron Tweedsmuir. Outgoing of the tide
Chopelas, J. The conjuror
Del Rey, L. Dead ringer
Finney, J. Behind the news
Finney, J. Cousin Len's wonderful adjective celler
Finney, J. I'm scared
Forster, E. M. Celestial omnibus
Henderson, Z. Pottage
Janvier, I. Thing
Kentfield, C. The angel and the sailor
Lovecraft, H. P. and Derleth, A. W. Gable window
Lovecraft, H. P. and Derleth, A. W. The survivor
Lovecraft, H. P. and Derleth, A. W. Wentworth's day
Lucas, E. V. Face on the wall
Maupassant, G. de. The Englishman
Maupassant, G. de. The horla
Mitchison, N. M. H. In the family
Simak, C. D. Worrywart
Stevenson, R. L. Isle of Voices
Waldo, E. H. Blabbermouth
Wharton, E. N. J. Kerfol
See also Ghosts; Witchcraft
SUPERSTITION
Balchin, N. Mrs Sludge
Cobb, I. S. Snake doctor
Gerchunoff, A. The owl
Holmes, O. W. Elsie Venner arouses Master Bernard's suspicions
LaMar, N. Creole love song
MacMahon, B. Close to the clay
Supervielle, Jules, 1884-
Ox and the ass at the manger
Fremantle, A. J. ed. Christmas is here
Rape of Europa
Lehmann, J. ed. Modern French stories
Supply man. Polk, W. T.
Supreme sacrifice. Peretz, I. L.
SURGEONS. See Physicians
SURGERY
Benét, S. V. End to dreams
Blassingame, W. Horse that saved a million lives
Brown, J. Rab and his friends
Cobb, I. S. "Speaking of operations—"
Fitzgerald, F. S. K. One interne
O'Brian, P. Minor operation

SURNAMES. See Names, Personal

A surprise. Maupassant, G. de

Surprise attack. Olgin, J.

SURPRISE ENDINGS
Brennan, J. P. The hunt
Jackson, S. One ordinary day, with peanuts
Ross, F. D. Especially twenty

Surprise visit. Leach, F. H.

The surrogate. Whitehill, J.

Surtees, Robert Smith, 1803-1864
Kennel and the stud
Welcome, J. and Orchard, V. eds. Best hunting stories

SURVIVAL (AFTER AIRPLANE ACCIDENTS, SHIPWRECKS, ETC.)
Connell, E. S. Yellow raft
Harper, J. Perils for trial
London, J. Love of life
Robinson Crusoe of the polar regions
Wallenius, K. M. Merciless and merciful sea

Survival. O'Neill, A.

The survivor. Lovecraft, H. P. and Derleth, A. W.

Susana and the shepherd. Craven, M.

Susanna at the beach. Gold, H.

Susie Q. Butler, M.

SUSPICION. See Skepticism

Suspicion. Lamptey, J.

Suspicion. Sandoz, M. Y.

Suspicion. Sayers, D. L.

Suter, John F.
Thousand mile shot
Mystery Writers of America, inc. Big time mysteries

Sutherland, Herbert, 1917-
As Joe said
Pudney, J. ed. Pick of today's short stories, 9

Sütö, András, 1927-
Right man in the right place
Short stories

Svevo, Italo, pseud. See Schmitz, Ettore

Swados, Harvey, 1920-
Back in the saddle again
Swados, H. On the line
Day the singer fell
Swados, H. On the line
Fawn, with a bit of green
Swados, H. On the line
Herman's day
Best American short sotries, 1955
Joe, the Vanishing American
Best American short stories, 1958
Swados, H. On the line
Just one of the boys
Swados, H. On the line
On the line
Swados, H. On the line
One for the road
Swados, H. On the line
Present for the boy
Swados, H. On the line

Swami of Northbank. Blochman, L. G.

SWAMIS. See India—Religion

SWAMPS
Brennan, J. P. Slime
Rutledge, A. H. Demon of the ocean

SWANS
Annixter, P. pseud. Trumpeter of the air lines
Carmer, C. L. Whooper swan of Olivebridge
O'Flaherty, L. Wild swan
Sullivan, A. Circuit of the wild swan

SWEARING
Green, H. G. Boy with the big tongue

Swede. Hughes, V. J.

SWEDEN

18th century
Lagerlöf, S. O. L. General's ring

Stockholm
Farrell, J. T. Dangerous woman

SWEDES IN ENGLAND
Wilson, A. Et Dona Ferentes

SWEDES IN THE UNITED STATES
Farrell, J. T. Olsen
West, J. Little collar for the monkey

Sweeney, C. L.
Decoy
Mystery Writers of America, inc. For love or money

SWEEPSTAKES. See Gambling

Sweet beyond. Smith, J. R.

Sweet eighteen. Soman, F. J.

Sweet red wine. Balick, S. G.

Swenson, dispatcher. Miller, R. D.

Swift, Hildegarde (Hoyt)
Railroad to freedom
Fenner, P. R. ed. Heroes, heroes, heroes

SWIMMING
Gold, H. Susanna at the beach
Hall, A. Breathe, Coach, breathe!
Lavrenev, B. A. Last swimming event
Lessing, D. M. Through the tunnel
Macauley, R. The invaders
Maugham, W. S. Friend in need
Olgin, J. Right event
Seager, A. Fifty and eight
    See also Aquatic sports; Diving

SWINDLERS AND SWINDLING
Balchin, N. Patience
Charteris, L. Bunco artists
Cozzens, J. G. Clerical error
Dickens, C. Sam Weller makes his bow
Greene, G. When Greek meets Greek
Macken, W. Gaeglers and the wild geese
Maupassant, G. de. The donkey
Pincherle, A. The imbroglio
Porter, W. S. Jeff Peters as a personal magnet
Zamonski, S. W. Pay-off

SWINDLING. See Swindlers and swindling

SWINE. See Pigs

SWING MUSIC. See Jazz music

SWISS ALPS. See Alps, Swiss

Swiss interlude. Curtis, M.

SWITCHBOARD OPERATORS. See Telephone workers

SWITZERLAND
Wain, J. Discipline

Lucerne
Tolstoĭ, L. N. Graf. Lucerne

Sword in the stone. Malory, Sir T.

Sword of laughter. Ruhen, O.

SWORDS
MacDonald, J. D. There hangs death!
Malory, Sir T. Sword in the stone

Sybilla. Manners, M.

Sykes, Christopher, 1907-
Sacred and the profane
Hudson, D. ed. Modern English short
stories; 2d ser.

Sylvania is dead. Stuart, J.

Sylvester, William
Death of Francisco
World prize stories; 2d ser.

Symbiosis. Jenkins, W. F.

SYMBOLISM OF NUMBERS
Huxley, A. L. Eupompus gave splendour
to art by numbers

Symons, Julian, 1912-
Eight minutes to kill
Crime Writers Association, London.
Planned departures

SYMPATHY
Garland, H. Day's pleasure

SYMPHONY CONCERTS. See Concerts

SYNAGOGUES
Angoff, C. The Ostrovskys

SYPHILIS. See Venereal diseases

SYRIA
Household, G. The case of Valentin
Lecormier

Szabó, Pál
Mother's tears in the Bukk Mountains
Juhasz, W. and Rothberg, A. A. ed.
Flashes in the night

T

'T' wind'ard!' Bone, D. W.

Taaffe, Michael. See Maguire, R. A.

Tabakai, Aryeh
Sergeant Shmueli rides a donkey
Schwarz. L. W. ed. Feast of Leviathan

Taber, Gladys (Bagg) 1899-
Just a little havoc
Teen-age tales, bk 3

TABERNACLES, FEAST OF. See Suk-
koth

**Tabib, Mordecai, 1910-
1917**
Frank, M. Z. ed. Sound the great trumpet

Taboo. Pincherle, A.

Tact. Beer, T.

Taffrail, pseud. See Dorling, Henry Taprell

Tail-gunner over Europe. Falstein, L.

Tailor and the wolves. Lesinš, K.

TAILOR SHOPS. See Tailors

TAILORS
Angoff, C. Original Sam
Buck, P. S. The frill
Peretz, I. L. Beryl the tailor
Rabinowitz, S. Enchanted tailor

TAIWAN. See Formosa

Takasebune. Ōgai, M.

Take a deep breath. Thorne, R.

Take care of our little Nell. Coleman, W. L.

Take pity. Malamud, B.

Talbot, Laura
Maundesly J. Chandler
Winter's tales, 3

Tale about prosperity. Franko, I. I.

Tale for a deaf ear. Enright, E.

Tale for the soldiers' little ones. Colette,
S. G.

Tale of my aunt Jenepher's wooing. Byrne,
D.

Tale of negative gravity. Stockton, F. R.

Tale of the cavalry. Hofmannsthal, H. H.
Edler von

Tale of the 672nd night. Hofmannsthal, H.
H. Edler von

Tale of the white dove. Carmer, C. L.

Tale of the white pyramid. Cather, W. S.

Tale of two mules. Zemach, S.

TALES. See Fables; Legends and folk tales

Tales of demons and dervishes. Bin Gorion,
M. J.

Tales of two old gentlemen. Blixen, K.

TALISMANS. See Charms

The talking dog. Germann, R. F.

Tall as the stars. Lambert, J.

TALL STORIES. See Improbable stories

TALL TALES. See Improbable stories

Talleyrand Penrod. Tarkington, B.

Tallow ball. See Maupassant, G. de. Ball of
fat

Tamási, Áron, 1897-
Flashes in the night
Juhasz, W. and Rothberg, A. A. eds.
Flashes in the night
Old man December
Juhasz, W. and Rothberg, A. A. eds.
Flashes in the night

Tangle hold. Wallace, F. L.

Taper, Bernard, 1918-
Inge
Stanford short stories, 1954
Sense of denstiny
Stanford short stories, 1955

TARDINESS
Eisele, A. The vigil

Target generation. Simak, C. D.

Target one. Pohl, F .

Tarkington, Booth, 1869-1946
Mary Smith
Costain, T. B. and Beecroft, J. eds.
More Stories to remember
Miss Rennsdale accepts
Nash, O. comp. I couldn't help laughing

Terriss, Tom
Bravest of the bulls
Teen-age tales, bk 3

Terror beneath the sea. Gordon, A.

The **terror** of Rome. Pincherle, A.

Terror town. Queen, E. pseud.

Terry Bindle. Whitehill, J.

The **test.** Matheson, R.

Test jump. Harvey, F. L.

TEST PILOTS. See Air pilots

Testimony after death. Van Doren, M.

TESTS, MENTAL. See Examinations; Mental tests

Tevye wins a fortune. Rabinowitz, S.

TEXAS
Clemons, W. Dark roots of the rose
Porter, K. A. The grave

20th century
Merritt, M. Till Gabriel blows his horn

Farm life
See Farm life—Texas

Ranch life
See Ranch life—Texas

TEXAS RANGERS
Adams, A. Buffaloed by a bear
Adams, A. Comanche fight in the Tallow Cache Hills
Adams, A. In a spur of the county
Adams, A. Judge Bean in court
Adams, A. Little paseo over into Mexico
Adams, A. El Lobo's sweetheart
Adams, A. Skirmish on the head of the Arroyo Colorado

TEXTILE INDUSTRY AND FABRICS
Bentley, P. E. Love and money
Bentley, P. E. No road

THAILAND
Bangkok
Harvey, F. L. Murder in the sky

Thanks very much, but no thank you. Whitehill, J.

THANKSGIVING DAY
Person, W. T. "Look back and be thankful"
Queen, E. pseud. Telltale bottle

That evening sun. Faulkner, W.

That Greek dog. Kantor, M.

"**That** in Aleppo once. . ." Nabokov, V. V.

That last buckskin. Goehring, D.

That marriage bed of Procrustes. Curley, D.

That New York woman. Woolrich, C.

That old jive. Spencer, J. L.

That pig of a Morin. Maupassant, G. de.

That Ryan woman. O'Donovan, M.

That tree. Porter, K. A.

That's marriage. Ferber, E.

Thaw. Hankins, J. W.

THEATER AND STAGE LIFE
Bemelmans, L. Dear General, what a surprise!
Davis, R. H. Her first appearance
Hellinger, M. Encouragement

Marsh, N. I can find my way out
Rosenberg, E. C. Mrs Rivkin grapples with the drama
See also Actors; Actresses; Moving picture actors and actresses

THEATERS. See Theater and stage life

THEATRICAL AGENTS. See Agents, Theatrical

THEATRICAL PRODUCERS
Cobb, I. S. Silent partner
Farrell, J. T. Mr Gremmer
Lardner, R. W. Day with Conrad Green
Pirandello, L. The bat
Tekeyan, C. Growing pains on Broadway

THEATRICALS, AMATEUR. See Amateur theatricals

The **Theban** warriors. Coleman, W. L.

THEFT
Antonov, S. The destroyer
Carter, B. Thief of diamonds
Cheever, J. Housebreaker of Shady Hill
Coates, R. M. Rendezvous
Enright, E. The operator
Gerchunoff, A. Silver candlestick
Guilloux, L. Man's name
Holder, W. Face next door
Jameson, C. G. Smart guy
Kantor, M. Grave grass quivers
Keir, R. H. Sunday punch
Macken, W. Duck soup
MacMahon, B. Red petticoat
Maupassant, G. de. Who knows?
O'Donovan, M. Peasants
O'Donovan, M. Private property
Runyon, D. Dancing Dan's Christmas
Stafford, J. Bad characters
Stewart, J. I. M. Bear's box
Stewart, J. I. M. The exile
See also Thieves

Theft. Porter, K. A.

Their name is Macaroni. Boyle, K.

Thelma. Angoff, C.

Then we were three. Shaw, I.

THEODORA, SAINT, OF ALEXANDRIA
Jacobus de Voragine. Saint Theodora

Theodore, Roy
The Greek
Stivens, D. comp. Coast to coast

THERAPEUTICS, SUGGESTIVE
Waldo, E. H. Other man

There are smiles. Lardner, R. W.

There hangs death! MacDonald, J. D.

There is a tide. Finney, J.

There isn't time now. Gregutt, H. C.

There was a bigger one. Murphy, R.

There was an old woman. Bradbury, R.

There's my horse's track. Adams, A.

THÉRÈSA, SAINT, 1873-1897
Sandoz, M. Y. The visitation

Theresa. Seymour, M.

THÉRÈSE DE LISIEUX. See Thérèsa, Saint

Theseus. Gide, A. P. G.

They ain't the men they used to be. Farrell, J. T.

They bite. White, W. A. P.

They brought their women. Ferber, E.

They came. Lewis, A.

They don't know what time it is. Farrell, J. T.

They grind exceeding small. Williams, B. A.

They pay with their lives. Petrescu, C.

They weren't going to die. Boyle, K.

Thick on the bay, La Farge, O.

Thicker than water. Gallico, P. W.

Thief by choice. Foster, B.

Thief in time. Sheckley, R.

Thief of diamonds. Carter, B.

Thierry, Marie-Paule
The Sisters
World prize stories; 2d ser.

THIEVES
Brown, W. Anonymous fame
Cecchi, E. Visitors
Chaucer, G. Pardoner's tale
Dostoevskiĭ, F. M. The honest thief
Doyle, Sir A. C. Adventure of the six Napoleons
Duvernois, H. Clothes make the man
Gold, H. Burglars and the boy
Hardy, T. Thieves who couldn't help sneezing
Malamud, B. The prison
Maupassant, G. de. Lucky burglar
Maupassant, G. de. The rabbit
Moretti, U. He should never have become a painter
Pincherle, A. The nose
Rabinowitz, S. Yom Kippur scandal
Rea, D. Piededifico
Sandoz, M. Y. Suspicion
Sansom, W. Face at the window
Staudy, A. Little Miss Big Shot
Whitehill, J. Rat trap
See also Theft

Thieves who couldn't help sneezing. Hardy, T.

Thin voice. Macauley, R.

Thing. Janvier, I.

Things as they are. Pritchett, V. S.

Things changed. Sunwall, B.

Things remembered. Haycox, E.

THINKING MACHINES. See Automata

The third A.D.C. Simonov, K. M.

Third honeymoon. Knight, R.

The third level. Finney, J.

Third partner. Philipson, M. H.

Third view on the Reichenbach. Bates, H. E.

Thirty-five minutes from nowhere. Mankowitz, W.

Thirty-year man. Jones, J.

THIRTY YEARS' WAR, 1618-1648
Lernet-Holenia, A. M. Three wise men of Totenleben

This boy, Jim Stephens. Block, A. R.

This cockpit my grave. Miller, E. M.

This earth of majesty. Clarke, A. C.

This heavy load. Campbell, W. E. M.

This indolence of mine. Schmitz, E.

This is where we are. Moretti, U.

This miracle. Brunton, A.

This old house. Walko, A.

This one's on me. Russell, E. F.

This they took with them. Boyle, K.

This town and Salamanca. Seager, A.

This was Willi's day. Stein, A. M.

This will do nicely. Flanagan, T.

Tho' the pleasant life is dancing round. Bodington, N.

Thomas, Agnes W.
Mighty moustache
Oberfirst, R. ed. 1955 anthology of best original short-shorts

Thomas, Calvin, 1929-
The repatriate
Stanford short stories, 1957

Thomas, Dylan, 1914-1953
Adventure from a work in progress
Thomas, D. Adventures in the skin trade, and other stories
Adventures in the skin trade
Thomas, D. Adventures in the skin trade, and other stories
After the fair
Thomas, D. Adventures in the skin trade, and other stories
Burning baby
Thomas, D. Adventures in the skin trade, and other stories
The dress
Thomas, D. Adventures in the skin trade, and other stories
The enemies
Jones, G. ed. Welsh short stories
Thomas, D. Adventures in the skin trade, and other stories
The followers
Thomas, D. Adventures in the skin trade, and other stories
Holy Six
Thomas, D. Adventures in the skin trade, and other stories
Horse's ha
Thomas, D. Adventures in the skin trade, and other stories
Just like little dogs
Laughton, C. ed. Tell me a story
The lemon
Thomas, D. Adventures in the skin trade, and other stories
Map of love
Thomas, D. Adventures in the skin trade, and other stories
Mouse and the woman
Thomas, D. Adventures in the skin trade, and other stories
The orchards
Thomas, D. Adventures in the skin trade, and other stories
The peaches
Thurston, J. A. ed. Reading modern short stories
Prospect of the sea
Thomas, D. Adventures in the skin trade, and other stories
School for witches
Thomas, D. Adventures in the skin trade, and other stories

Thurber, James—*Continued*
More alarms at night
Nash, O. comp. I couldn't help laughing
Secret life of Walter Mitty
Laughton, C. ed. Tell me a story
Locke, L. G.; Gibson, W. M. and Arms, G. W. eds. Introduction to literature
You could look it up
Saturday evening post (Periodical) Saturday evening post Carnival of humor
Schwed, P. and Wind, H. W. eds. Great stories from the world of sport
Thurman, Richard Young, 1921-
Credit line
Prize stories 1957: the O. Henry awards
Not another word
Best American short stories, 1958
Thursday date. Borland, H. and Borland, B.
Thus I refute Beelzy. Collier, J.
Thy need. Thomas, G.
Thy neighbour's creed. Plomer, W. C. F.
Ti Jacques. Lucas, W. F.
TIBET
Ewarts, H. G. Horse for the colonel

20th century
Hilton, J. Lost horizon
Ticket to death. Hunter, E.
Ticket to Tranai. Sheckley, R.
The **tide.** O'Flaherty, L.
Tieck, Johann Ludwig, 1773-1853
Fair Eckbert
Jarrell, R. ed. Anchor book of stories
The **tiger.** Buechner, F.
Tiger hound. Annixter, P. pseud.
Tiger in the night. Lipsky, E.
Tiger was a lady. Edell, H.
TIGERS
Annixter, P. pseud. Tiger hound
Coombs, C. I. Cat man
Edell, H. Tiger was a lady
Ferry, J. Fashionable tiger
Kjelgaard, J. A. Tiger's heart
Marshall, E. Heart of Little Shikara
Miller, E. M. Left-handed Texan
Sørensen, V. The tigers
The **tigers.** Sørensen, V.
Tiger's heart. Kjelgaard, J. A.
El **Tigre!** Smith, E. H.
Tikhonov, Nikolaï Semenovich, 1896-
A cavalcade
Loaf sugar, and other Soviet stories
Till death us do part. Gellhorn, M. E.
Till Gabriel blows his horn. Merritt, M.
Tillotson Banquet. Huxley, A. L.
TIME
Asimov, I. Immortal bard
Bradbury, R. August 2002: night meeting
Clarke, A. C. All the time in the world
Finney, J. Quit zoomin' those hands through the air
Finney, J. Second chance
Finney, J. There is a tide

Finney, J. The third level
Johnson, P. H. Death of a duchess
Wells, H. G. New accelerator
    See also Space and time; Time, Travels in
TIME, TRAVELS IN
Asimov, I. A loint of paw
Bester, A. Hobson's choice
Bradbury, R. Fox and the forest
Jackson, S. Bulletin
Logan, B. T. Time is out of the whiskey glass
Lovecraft, H. P. and Derleth, A. W. The ancestor
Oliver, C. Star above it
Peretz, I. L. Journey in time
Pohl, F. Target one
Reynolds, M. Compounded interest
White, W. A. P. Snulbug
    See also Time
Time and ebb. Nabokov, V. V.
Time for smiles. Hoffman, I. B.
Time for waiting. Welch, H. L.
Time in the round. Leiber, F.
Time is out of the whiskey glass. Logan, B. T.
Time is, time was. Rosen, I.
TIME MACHINES
Asimov, I. Dead past
Cogswell, T. R. Impact with the devil
DeFord, M. A. Time trammel
Finney, J. Such interesting neighbors
Oliver, C. and Beaumont, C. Last word
Sheckley, R. Thief in time
Van Vogt, A. E. Recruiting station
White, W. A. P. Elsewhen
Time of learning. West, J.
Time trammel. DeFord, M. A.
TIME TRAVEL. See Time, Travels in
Time's arrow. Clarke, A. C.
Times of the Messiah. Peretz, I. L.
Tinfield mascot. Balchin, N.
Tinker of Tamlacht. MacManus, S.
TINKERS
MacMahon, B. Broken lyre
MacMahon, B. Cat and the cornfield
O'Flaherty, L. The tent
    See also Gipsies
Tiny and the monster. Waldo, E. H.
Tip on a dead jockey. Shaw, I.
Tired courtesan. Pincherle, A.
Tish does her bit. Rinehart, M. R.
Tish goes to jail. Rinehart, M. R.
Tish marches on. Rinehart, M. R.
Tish plays the game. Rinehart, M. R.
Tit for tat. Rabinowitz, S.
To ask the hard question is easy. Curley, D.
To be a cowboy. Wyckoff, J.
To Dona—forever. Snodgrass, J.
To Margaret. Morrison, J.
To remember you by. King, R.
To see once more. Criswell, C.
To sleep and to wake. Smith, J. R.
To the chaparral. Caldwell, E.

Tolstoĭ, Lev N. Graf—*Continued*
　Story of Yemilyan and the empty drum
　　Tolstoĭ, L. N. Graf. Tolstoy's Tales of
　　courage and conflict
　Three deaths
　　Tolstoĭ, L. N. Graf. Tolstoy's Tales of
　　courage and conflict
　Three hermits
　　Jarrell, R. ed. Anchor book of stories
　　Laughton, C. ed. Tell me a story
　　Tolstoĭ, L. N. Graf. Tolstoy's Tales of
　　courage and conflict
　Two brothers and gold
　　Tolstoĭ, L. N. Graf. Tolstoy's Tales of
　　courage and conflict
　Two old men
　　Tolstoĭ, L. N. Graf. Tolstoy's Tales of
　　courage and conflict
　Vronsky's steeplechase
　　Schwed, P. and Wind, H. W. eds. Great
　　stories from the world of sport
　Walk in the light while there is light
　　Tolstoĭ, L. N. Graf. Tolstoy's Tales of
　　courage and conflict
　What men live by
　　Tolstoĭ, L. N. Graf. Tolstoy's Tales of
　　courage and conflict
　Where love is, there God is also
　　Tolstoĭ, L. N. Graf. Tolstoy's Tales of
　　courage and conflict
　Wood-cutting expedition
　　Tolstoĭ, L. N. Graf. Tolstoy's Tales of
　　courage and conflict
Tolstoy, Alexei. See Tolstoĭ, Alekseĭ Niko-
　laevich, Graf
Tolstoy, Leo. See Tolstoĭ, Lev Nikolaevĭch,
　Graf
Tolstoy, Leo N. count. See Tolstoĭ, Lev
　Nikolaevĭch, Graf
Tolvanen, Eero
　Paper plague
　　World prize stories; 2d ser.
Tom a' Tuddlams. Baring-Gould, S.
Tom-cat. Colette, S. G.
Tom, Dick and Harry. Stewart, J. I. M.
Tom Ivory, the cat. Roberts, M. C.
Tom Outland's story. Cather, W. S.
Tom Tiddler's ground. Dickens, C.
Tom Wolfe's my name. West, J.
Tom won't forget Jan. Tekeyan, C.
The tomb. Maupassant, G. de
Tombari, Fabio, 1899-
　Miracle at Frusaglia
　　Strachan, W. J. ed. Modern Italian
　　stories
Tomboy. Schweitzer, G.
Tomkins, Calvin
　Weird sisters
　　Seventeen　　(Periodical)　　Seventeen's
　　stories
Tomlinson, Henry Major, 1873-1958
　Heart's desire
　　Kemp, P. K. ed. Hundred years of sea
　　stories
Tomlinson, Norma, 1926-
　Pretty surprise
　　Stanford short stories, 1957

Tommy Gallagher's crusade. Farrell, J. T.
Tommy, the unsentimental. Cather, W. S.
Tomorrow afternoon. Ward, L. L.
Toney, Ruth B.
　The roomer
　　Oberfirst. R. ed. Anthology of best
　　short-short stories v5
Too early spring. Benét, S. V.
Too late to love. Carpenter, W. W.
Too much man. Mankowitz, W.
Too old for dolls. Pinchot, B. and Pinchot,
　A.
Too young. O'Hara, J.
The tool. Harvey, W. F.
TOOTH. See Teeth
The tooth. Jackson, S.
TOOTHPICKS
　Boyle, K. Major engagement in Paris
Topelius, Zachris. See Topelius, Zakarias
Topelius, Zakarias, 1818-1898
　Christmas with the goblins
　　Fremantle. A. J. ed. Christmas is here
Torn invitation. Katkov, N.
Torquemada in the flames. Perez Galdos, B.
Total stranger. Cozzens, J. G.
TOTALITARIANISM
　Benét, S. V. Judgment in the mountains
The touch. O'Flaherty, L.
Touch of Arab. Breckenfeld, V. G.
Touch of greatness. La Farge, O.
Touch of strange. Waldo, E. H.
Touch of tenderness. Case, V.
Touch of the sun. Sansom, W.
Touch of your hand. Waldo, E. H.
Touchdown play. Temple, W. H.
Touched with fire. Bradbury, R.
Tough old man. Hubbard, L. R.
TOURIST CAMPS, HOSTELS, ETC.
　Shore, W. Cow on the roof
TOURIST TRADE
　Liberman, M. M. Big Buick to the pyra-
　mids
　Weston, C. G. Four annas
TOURISTS. See Tourist trade
TOURNAMENTS
　Wylie, P. Danger at Coral Key
TOWBOATS. See Tugboats
Towers, Frances, 1885-1948
　Little willow
　　Hudson, D. ed. Modern English short
　　stories; 2d ser.
Towery, James G.
　Double surprise
　　Oberfirst, R. ed. 1955 anthology of best
　　original short-shorts
The town. Lochridge, B. H.
Town is waiting. Whitehill, J.
Town of the little people. Rabinowitz, S.
TOWNS. See Cities and towns
TOWNS, GHOST. See Ghost towns
Towry, Peter, pseud. See Piper, David
Towser the terrific. Goehring, D.

Trease, Geoffrey, 1909-
  Military glory
    Buckeridge, A. comp. In and out of
    school
Treason. Babel', I. E.
The treasure. Maugham, W. S.
The treasure. Peretz, I. L.
The treasure. Pincherle, A.
Treasure cruise. Wylie, P.
Treasure game. Bates, H. E.
Treasure hunt. Household, G.
Treasure hunt. Wallace, E.
TREASURE HUNTS. See Treasure-trove
TREASURE-TROVE
  Annixter, P. pseud. Flounder, flounder
    in the sea
  Blackford, C. M. Shadows on the reef
  Cottrell, D. W. Mysterious box
  Elam, R. M. Ghost ship of space
  Howard, R. E. and De Camp, L. S.
    Blood-stained god
  O'Brian, P. Happy despatch
  Peretz, I. L. The treasure
  Pincherle, A. The treasure
  Poe, E. A. Gold bug
  Stevenson, R. L. Espirito Santo
  Wylie, P. Treasure cruise
Treat, Lawrence, 1903-
  Homicide expert
    Mystery Writers of America, inc. Crime
    for two
  Justice magnifique
    Mystery Writers of America, inc. A
    choice of murders
  Murder me twice
    Mystery Writers of America, inc. For
    love or money
The tree. Thomas, D.
Tree of heaven. Enright, E.
Tree of liberty. Roth, C.
TREES
  Blackwood, A. Man whom the trees loved
  Blackwood, A. The willows
  Bradbury, R. December 2001: the green
    morning
  Enright, E. Tree of heaven
  Sørensen, V. Strange tree
    See also Apple trees; Christmas
    trees
Trees die at the top. Ferber, E.
The trellis. Connell, E. S.
Tremendous adventures of Major Brown.
  Chesterton, G. K.
Tremp. Samuel, E. H.
TRIALS
  Benét, S. V. Devil and Daniel Webster
  Duranty, W. The parrot
  Harte, B. Colonel Starbottle for the plain-
    tiff
  Harte, B. Tennessee's partner
  Johnson, W. R. The night the stair
    creaked
  La Farge, O. La spécialité de M Duclos
  Levin, R. J. Redhead from New Orleans
  Masur, H. Q. $2,000,000 defense
  Maupassant, G. de. The assassin
  Maupassant, G. de. Hippolyte's claim

Maupassant. G. de. The hole
Maupassant, G. de. In the courtroom
Maupassant, G. de. Rosalie Prudent
Maupassant, G. de. A sale
Polk, W. T. According to the law and the
  evidence
Porges, A. Guilty as charged
Reid, L. Dehydrated romance
Simak, C. D. How-2
Starrett, V. Eleventh juror
Train, A C. The bloodhound
Wells, R W. The day all traffic stopped
Woolrich, C. That New York woman

Ireland
Cross, E. Jury case
TRIBES AND TRIBAL SYSTEM
  Ruhen, O. Guardians of Mobali
  Ruhen, O. Head-hunters of Iangl
TRICKERY. See Hoaxes
Tricks in all trades. Applegate, F. G.
TRICYCLES. See Bicycles and tricycles
TRICYCLING. See Cycling
Triem, Frank
  Guest buck
    Teen-age tales, bk 3
Trifonov, Yury
  Fedor Kuzmich of the conservatoire
    Loaf sugar, and other Soviet stories
Trigg, Pearl E.
  Second chance
    Oberfirst, R. ed. Anthology of best
    short-short stories v6
Trilling, Lionel, 1905-
  Of this time, of that place
    Thurston, J. A. ed. Reading modern
    short stories
Tring, A. Stephen
  Grammar v. modern
    Buckeridge, A. comp. In and out of
    school
Trio for three gentle voices. Brodkey, H.
Trip to Hollywood. Sullivan, F.
Trip to Paris. Barker, D.
Triumph of night. Wharton, E. N. J.
Triumph of Willie Collins. Farrell, J. T.
Trojan horse. Blassingame, W.
TROJAN WAR
  Blassingame, W. Trojan horse
  Marquis, D. O'Meara at Troy
Trojan women. Maxwell, W.
Trollope, Anthony, 1815-1882
  Nappie's grey horse
    Welcome, J. and Orchard, V. eds. Best
    hunting stories
TROMBONE PLAYERS. See Musicians—
  Trombone players
Troops of lovely children. Barrett, B. L.
The trophy. Burnett, J.
TROPICS
  Ritchie, L. A. da C. Pleasure of their
    company
Trotter's sack of salt. Adams, A.
Trouble man. Rhodes, E. M.
Trouble of Marcie Flint. Cheever, J.
Trouble with captains. Byrd, J. J.

Trouble with Ruth. Slesar, H.

Trouble with the natives. Clarke, A. C.

Trouble with traders. Gulick, G. C.

Troubled summer. Cundiff, L.

The trout. O'Faoláin, S.

Truax, Lee
Man alone
Stanford Short stories, 1958

TRUCK DRIVERS
Bates, H. E. Night run to the West
Pincherle, A. The lorry-driver
Rathjen, C. H. Runaway rig

True story. Maupassant, G. de

True story. Thomas, D.

TRUMPET
Clayton, J. B. Last blast of the trumpet

Trumpet man. Cundiff, L.

Trumpeter of the air lanes. Annixter, P. pseud.

Trumpeter swan. Enright, E.

TRUMPETER SWANS. See Swans

TRUMPETERS. See Musicians—Trumpeters

Trumpets in the morning. Burk, C. J.

Trust and betrayal. Adams, A.

The trusting and the maimed. Plunkett, J.

TRUTH
Macauley, R. Windfall

Truth about Pyecraft. Wells, H. G.

TRUTHFULNESS AND FALSEHOOD .
Abernathy, R. Grandma's lie soap
Elliott, W. Y. Soul-machine
Farrell, J. T. Sport of kings
Samson, W. A white lie

Truxell, Leland Ellis. See Rhine, Richard

Truxton against Greyhound. Blassingame, W.

Try it my way. Nebel, F.

Tubb, E. C.
Last day of summer
Merril, J. ed. S-F: ['56]

TUBERCULOSIS
Angoff, C. Goldie Tabak
Riichi, Y. Spring came on a horse-drawn cart
Sandoz, M. Y. Leaning rock
Verga, G. Consolation
West, J. Home-coming
West, J. Mr Cornelius, I love you
Williams, T. Angel in the alcove

Tuesday's children. Macken, W.

Tugboat Annie quotes the law. Raine, N. R.

TUGBOATS
Conrad, J. Falk: a reminiscence
Raine, N. R. Tugboat Annie quotes the law

TUMBLING
Olgin, J. Full twists
See also Acrobats and acrobatism

TUNA FISH
Wylie, P. Danger at Coral Key

The tunesmith. Biggle, L.

Tunis, John Roberts, 1889-
Mother of a champion
Schwed, P. and Wind, H. W. eds. Great stories from the world of sport

Tunnel at the frontier. O'Brian, P.

Tunnel under the world. Pohl, F.

TUNNELS AND TUNNELING
Dreiser, T. St Columba and the river

Tuohy, Frank, 1925-
Admiral and the nuns
Winter's tales, 3
Two private lives
Winter's tales, 1

Tuong, Ho Huu
Margouillat who chose its destiny
World prize stories; 2d ser.

A turban. Kuncewiczowa, M. S.

Turbulence at the lake. Brenner, A. E.

Turgenev, Ivan Sergeevich, 1818-1883
Byezhin Prairie
Jarrell, R. ed. Anchor book of stories
Same as: Byezhin Meadow

District doctor
Thurston, J. A. ed. Reading modern short stories

TURKEY
Muldur, N. Friday is a lucky day

Istanbul
Sandoz, M. Y. In the cemetery at Scutari

TURKISH BATHS. See Baths, Turkish

TURKS IN AFRICA
Maupassant, G. de. Mohammed Fripouli

TURKS IN THE UNITED STATES
Harvey, F. L. Flame-out

Turn about. Faulkner, W.

Turnabout. See Faulkner, W. Turn about

Turner, Robert
Killers die young
Meredith, S. ed. Bar 6
11 o'clock bulletin
Mystery Writers of America, inc. A choice of murders

Turner, William Oliver
Proud diggers
Western Writers of America. Wild streets

Turning page. West, A. C.

TURTLES
Block, A. R. Perfect day
Carr, A. F. Black beach
Combs, P. Man on the beach
Wilson, E. Man who shot snapping turtles

The tussle. Van Doren, M.

TUTORS
Aichinger, I. Private tutor
James, H. The pupil

The tuxedoes. Weidman, J.

Twain, Mark, pseud. See Clemens, Samuel Langhorne

12 flights up. Chandler, D.

Twenty below, at the end of a lane. Molloy, R. B.

Twiddlywink warriors. Anderson, P. and Dickson, G. R.

Twilight in extremadura. Chacel, R.

Twilight in southern California. Fuchs, D.

Twilight over Jerusalem. Kessary, O.

Twink. Waldo, E. H.

VACCINATION
Moscardelli, N. Face of destiny

A **vagabond.** Maupassant, G. de

VAGABONDS. See Tramps

VAGRANTS. See Tramps

Vain beauty. See Maupassant, G. de. Useless beauty

VALETS. See Servants—Valets

Valiant woman. Powers, J. F.

Valle-Inclán, Ramón del, 1870-1936
Sonata of autumn
Flores, A. ed. Great Spanish stories

VAMPIRES
Bradbury, R. Homecoming
Bradbury, R. Man upstairs
Bradbury, R. Skeleton
Greene, V. One man's meat

Vance, Jack, pseud. See Kuttner, Henry

VANDALISM. See Malicious mischief

Van Doren, Mark, 1894-
Abide with me
Van Doren, M. Home with Hazel, and other stories
April fool
Van Doren, M. Home with Hazel, and other stories
The ballad singer
Van Doren, M. Home with Hazel, and other stories
The diary
Van Doren, M. Home with Hazel, and other stories
Home with Hazel
Van Doren, M. Home with Hazel, and other stories
I got a friend
Best American short stories, 1955
Van Doren, M. Home with Hazel, and other stories
If Lizzie tells
Van Doren, M. Home with Hazel, and other stories
If only
Van Doren, M. Home with Hazel, and other stories
The little house
Van Doren, M. Home with Hazel, and other stories
Madam X and Madam Y
Van Doren, M. Home with Hazel, and other stories
Man who made people mad
Queen, E. pseud. ed. Ellery Queen's awards: 10th ser.
Van Doren, M. Home with Hazel, and other stories
Miss Hew
Van Doren, M. Home with Hazel, and other stories
My son, my son
Van Doren, M. Home with Hazel, and other stories
Not like Tom
Van Doren, M. Home with Hazel, and other stories
Only on rainy nights
Queen, E. pseud. ed. Ellery Queen's awards: 11th ser.

The pasture
Van Doren, M. Home with Hazel, and other stories
Plain and fancy
Van Doren, M. Home with Hazel, and other stories
Testimony after death
Van Doren, M. Home with Hazel, and other stories
The tussle
Van Doren, M. Home with Hazel, and other stories
The uncertain glory
Van Doren, M. Home with Hazel, and other stories
Wild justice
Van Doren, M. Home with Hazel, and other stories

Van Druten, John, 1901-1957
Gavin
Good housekeeping (Periodical) Editor's choice

Vanishing American. Beaumont, C.

Vanishing lady. Woollcott, A.

Vanishing of Pegram. Rutledge, A. H.

VANITY. See Pride and vanity

Van Loan, Charles Emmett, 1876-1919
Last chance
Schwed, P. and Wind, H. W. eds. Great stories from the world of sport

Van Scoyk, Bob, 1928?-
Home from camp
Best American short stories, 1958

Van Vechten, Carl, 1880-
Feathers
Mason, P. O. and Mason, J. eds. Favorite cat stories of Pamela and James Mason
My cat
Skelton, P. ed. Animals all

Van Vogt, Alfred Elton, 1912-
Dormant
Montgomery, R. B. ed. Best SF
Recruiting station
Conklin, G. ed. Strange adventures in science fiction

Varsbergs, Maija
The fall
Orr, E. and Hammet, E. A. eds. Delta Decameron

VASES
Samuel, E. H. Filigree vase

Vaughan, Aled, 1920-
White dove
Jones, G. ed. Welsh short stories

Vaya con Dios. Smith, E. H.

VEGETABLE TRADE
Saroyan, W. Play that got away

The **vegetarian.** Samuel, E. H.

VEGETARIANS
Huxley, A. L. The Ciaxtons
Samuel, E. H. The vegetarian

Veiled island. McDowell, E.

VEILS
Hawthorne, N. Minister's black veil

VENDETTA. See Feuds

VENEREAL DISEASES
Babel', I. E. Sandy the Christ
Burns, J. H. Queen penicillin

VENGEANCE. See Revenge

Vengeance of Padre Arroyo. Atherton, G. F. H.

Vengeance trail. Stone, N. B.

VENICE. See Italy—Venice

Venice. Sansom, W.

Venture to the moon. Clarke, A. C.

VENUS (PLANET)
Bradbury, R. All summer in a day
McDowell, W. Veiled island
Wallace, F. L. Tangle hold

VENUSIANS
Waldo, E. H. Special aptitude

Verdad
Good-tempered fellow
World prize stories; 2d ser.

Verga, Giovanni, 1840-1922
Buddies
Verga, G. She-wolf, and other stories
Cavalleria rusticana
Verga, G. She-wolf, and other stories
Consolation
Verga, G. She-wolf, and other stories
Donna Santa's sin
Verga, G. She-wolf, and other stories
Gramigna's mistress
Verga, G. She-wolf, and other stories
Ieli
Verga, G. She-wolf, and other stories
Last day
Verga, G. She-wolf, and other stories
La Lupa
Jarrell, R. ed. Anchor book of stories
Slonim, M. L. ed. Modern Italian short
stories
Mark X
Verga, G. She-wolf, and other stories
Nanni Volpe
Verga, G. She-wolf, and other stories
Rosso Malpelo
Verga, G. She-wolf, and other stories
She-wolf
Verga, G. She-wolf, and other stories
Stinkpot
Verga, G. She-wolf, and other stories
Temptation
Verga, G. She-wolf, and other stories
War between saints
Verga, G. She-wolf, and other stories

The verger. Maugham, W. S.

VERGERS. See Sextons

Vergilian vespers. Yellen, S.

Vergine con bambino. Lofts, N. R.

VERMONT
Fisher, D. F. C. Flint and fire
Jackson, J. H. Winter Sunday

18th century
Fisher, D. F. C. Ann Story

Country life
See Country life—Vermont

Frontier and pioneer life
See Frontier and pioneer life—Vermont

Verna. Gallico, P. W.

Vertical ladder. Sansom, W.

Very odd case. Stewart, J. I. M.

Very shy gentleman. Wodehouse, P. G.

Vessel of wrath. Maugham, W. S.

The **vest.** Thomas, D.

Vestal, Stanley, 1887-
Warpath
Western Writers of America. Hoof
trails and wagon tracks

The **veteran.** Crane, S.

VETERANS (CIVIL WAR)
Benét, S. V. The die-hard
Crane, S. The veteran
Danielson, R. E. Corporal Hardy
Frazee, S. Payroll of the dead
Garland, H. Return of a private
Mitchell, M. E. For the honor of the company
O'Connor, F. Late encounter with the enemy
Van Doren, M. My son, my son

VETERANS (EUROPEAN WAR, 1914-1918)
Ferber, E. Long distance
Hemingway, E. In another country
Miller, E. M. Pay and the uniform

VETERANS (KOREAN WAR, 1950-1953)
Bowen, R. O. Matter of price
Burnet, D. Giant land
Forrestier, M. Gifts to my people
Joseph, G. Return of a warrior
Kubly, H. The merry dance

VETERANS (REVOLUTION)
Fisher, D. F. C. Old soldier

VETERANS (WORLD WAR, 1939-1945)
Chandler, D. 12 flights up
Cohen, O. R. Always trust a cop
Glanville, B. The hero
La Farge, O. Bright faces
Lee, R. J. Moth and the star
Rothberg, A. A. Not with our fathers
Wilson, S. School days

VETERANS, DISABLED. See Cripples

Vexation of Barney Hatch. Chute, B. J.

Vexations of A. J. Wentworth, B.A. Ellis, H. F.

Vicarious experience. Doyle, M.

VICARS. See Clergy

Vick Shore and the good of the game. Caldwell, E.

Vickers, Roy
Murder in the cowshed
Crime Writers Association, London.
Planned departures

Vicki. Caldwell, E.

The **victim.** Maupassant, G. de

Victim of a lust. Barrett, B. L.

Victims. O'Donovan, J.

Victoria at night. Beigel, U.

The **victory.** Schwartz, M.

Victory parade. Slesar, H.

Vidal, Gore, 1925-
Erlinda and Mr Coffin
Vidal, G. A thirsty evil
Ladies in the library
Vidal, G. A thirsty evil
Moment of green laurel
Vidal, G. A thirsty evil

Vrettos, Theodore, 1918-
My name is Legion
Oberfirst, R. ed. 1955 anthology of best original short-shorts
Vronsky's steeplechase. Tolstoi, L. N. Graf
Vukelich, George, 1927-
The scale room
Best American short stories, 1955

W

The **Wabbler.** Jenkins, W. F.
Waddington, Patrick
Street that got mislaid
Nelson, G. E. ed. Cavalcade of the North
Wade, Bob, 1920- and Miller, Bill, 1920-
Bad time of day
Queen, E. pseud. ed. Ellery Queen's awards: 11th ser.
Invitation to an accident
Queen, E. pseud. ed. Ellery Queen's awards: 10th ser.
Women in his life
Queen, E. pseud. ed. Ellery Queen's 13th annual
WAGERS
Allen, S. The sidewalk
Chekhov, A. P. The bet
Chesterton, G. K. Improbable success of Mr Owen Hood
Chesterton, G. K. Unpresentable appearance of Colonel Crane
Clemens, S. L. Celebrated jumping frog of Calaveras County
Fiore, A. C. Faith
Macken, W. Hurling match
McMullen, J. A. Sampson and the blue "Delilahs"
Maugham, W. S. Mr Know-All
O'Rourke, F. Stronger medicine
Rhodes, E. M. The numismatist
Street, J. H. Grains of paradise
Wagon-tongue north. Foreman, L. L.
WAGON TRAINS
Athanas, V. Bridge crossing
Case, V. Lost wagons
Gulick, G. C. Fire-water fiasco
Gulick, G. C. Squaw fever
Guthrie, A. B. The way West
Stone, N. B. Vengeance trail
WAGONS. See Carriages and carts
Wagstaff pearls. Eberhart, M. G.
The **waifs.** Faulkner, W.
Wain, John, 1925-
Discipline
Winter's tales, 2
Waiter, a bock! Maupassant, G. de
WAITERS. See Servants—Waiters
The **waiting.** Agee, J.
Waiting thing inside. Waldo, E. H. and Ward, D.
WAITRESSES. See Servants—Waitresses
The **wake.** Annunzio, G. d'
The **wake.** Slater, P.

Wake for Don Corsinio. Chavez, A.
Wake for El Gusano. Smith, E. H.
WAKEFULNESS. See Insomnia
WAKES. See Funeral rites and ceremonies
Waldo, Edward Hamilton, 1918-
Affair with a green monkey
Waldo, E. H. Touch of strange
And now the news
Magazine of fantasy and science fiction. Best from Fantasy and science fiction; 6th ser.
". . .and my fear is great. . ."
Waldo, E. H. Way home
Blabbermouth
Waldo, E. H. Caviar
Bright segment
Waldo, E. H. Caviar
Bulkhead
Merril, J. ed. S-F: ['56]
Waldo, E. H. Way home
Crime for Llewellyn
Waldo, E. H. Touch of strange
Ghost of a chance
Waldo, E. H. Caviar
Girl had guts
Waldo, E. H. Touch of strange
Granny won't knit
Galaxy science fiction magazine. Five Galaxy short novels
Greenberg, M. ed. All about the future
The hurkle is a happy beast
Waldo, E. H. Way home
Hurricane trio
Waldo, E. H. Way home
It opens the sky
Waldo, E. H. Touch of strange
Love of heaven
Conklin, G. ed. Science-fiction adventures in mutation
Medusa
Waldo, E. H. Caviar
Mewhu's jet
Waldo, E. H. Way home
Microcosmic god
Waldo, E. H. Caviar
Minority report
Waldo, E. H. Way home
Mr Costello, hero
Waldo, E. H. Touch of strange
Never underestimate
Conklin, G. ed. Strange adventures in science fiction
Other Celia
Waldo, E. H. Touch of strange
Other man
Merril, J. ed. SF: '57
Pod in the barrier
Waldo, E. H. Touch of strange
Prodigy
Waldo, E. H. Caviar
Shadow, shadow on the wall
Waldo, E. H. Caviar
Special aptitude
Waldo, E. H. Way home
Thunder and roses
Waldo, E. H. Way home
Tiny and the monster
Waldo, E. H. Way home
Touch of strange
Waldo, E. H. Touch of strange
Touch of your hand
Waldo, E. H. Touch of strange

Waldo, Edward H.—*Continued*
Twink
    Waldo, E. H. Caviar
Unite and conquer
    Waldo, E. H. Way home
Way home
    Waldo, E. H. Way home
When you're smiling
    Montgomery, R. B. ed. Best SF two
Waldo, Edward Hamilton, 1918- and Ward, Don
Waiting thing inside
    Queen, E. pseud. ed. Ellery Queen's awards: 11th ser.
WALES
Griffith, W. Ifan Owen and the grey rider
Hughes, J. G. Master of the golden game
Jones, G. Night at Galon-Uchaf
Jones, G. Price-Parry
Jones, G. What Pantathro
Machen, A. Shining pyramid
Manley-Tucker, A. Wanted—a miracle
O'Brian, P. Slope of the high mountain
Roberts, K. Two storms
Thomas, D. The peaches
Thomas, G. Thy need

Farm life
See Farm life—Wales

Walk-away kid. Bachrach, S. F.
Walk in the dark. Clarke, A. C.
Walk in the light while there is light. Tolstoĭ, L. N. Graf
Walk in the moon shadows. Stuart, J.
Walker, David Harry, 1911-
Summertime adventure
    Saturday evening post (Periodical) Saturday evening post stories, 1955
Walker, Mary
Mrs Confedrington
    Oberfirst, R. ed. Anthology of best short-short stories v6
The **walker**. O'Brian, P.
The **walker**-through-walls. Aymé, M.
WALKING
Rinehart, M. R. Cave on Thunder Cloud
Sansom, W. Country walk
    See also Hitchhikers
Walking, running people. Kapelner, A.
Walking woman. Austin, M. A. Van N.
Walking wounded. Shaw, I.
Walko, Ann, 1908-
This old house
    Oberfirst, R. ed. 1955 anthology of best original short-shorts
The **wall**. Karlen, A.
The **wall**. Sartre, J. P.
Wall of darkness. Clarke, A. C.
Wallace, Edgar, 1875-1932
Treasure hunt
    Haycraft, H. and Beecroft, J. eds. Treasury of great mysteries
Wallace, F. L.
Driving lesson
    Queen, E. pseud. ed. Ellery Queen's awards: 12th ser.

End as a world
    Galaxy science fiction magazine. Third Galaxy reader
Impossible voyage home
    Conklin, G. ed. Science-fiction adventures in mutation
Tangle hold
    Galaxy science fiction magazine. Five Galaxy short novels
Wallant, Edward L. 1926-
I held back my hand
    New voices 2: American writing today
Wallenius, Kurt Martti, 1893-
Bare land
    Wallenius, K. M. Men from the sea
Illep and the whale
    Wallenius, K. M. Men from the sea
Merciless and merciful sea
    Wallenius, K. M. Men from the sea
One-eyed wolf of Kaamas Fell
    Wallenius, K. M. Men from the sea
Waller, Leslie
Restless ones
    Teen-age tales, bk 3
WALLS
Bradbury, R. The golden kite, the silver wind
Walls of Ávila. Connell, E. S.
Walnut bed. Morton, C.
Walnut trees. Akin, V.
Walpole, Sir Hugh, 1885-1941
Silver mask
    Costain, T. B. and Beecroft, J. eds. More Stories to remember
Walsh, Maurice, 1879-
Come back, my love
    Garrity, D. A. ed. 44 Irish short stories
Quiet man
    Jennings, F. G. and Calitri, C. J. eds. Stories
Walsh, Thomas, 1908-
Cop on the prowl
    Queen, E. pseud. ed. Ellery Queen's 13th annual
I killed John Harrington
    Mystery Writers of America, inc. For love or money
Name for baby
    Mystery Writers of America, inc. Crime for two
Walter, Eugene
I love you batty sisters
    Prize stories 1957: the O. Henry awards
Walter Schnaffs' adventure. Maupassant, G. de
Walter T. Carriman. O'Hara, J.
WALTON, IZAAK, 1593-1683
Cook, B. G. We get set for a long jump
The **wanderer**. Hasas, H.
The **wanderers**. Lewis, A.
The **wandering** Nephite. Carmer, C. L.
A **wand'ring** minstrel, I. Gordimer, N.
Wanted—a miracle. Manley-Tucker, A.
Wanted: one hideous secretary. Moretti, U.
Wanton troopers. Steele, M.

WAR

Aichinger, I. Opened order
Barbudo, A. S. In the trenches
Crane, S. Upturned face
Lesiņš, K. The dove
Lesiņš, K. The leavetaking
Russell, B. A. W. R. 3d earl. Dr Southport Vulpes's nightmare
Stockton, F. R. The skipper and el Capitan
Verga, G. Buddies
Wierzyński, K. Patrol

Casualties

Bowen, R. O. Matter of price
Brown, T. K. Drink of water
Crane, S. An episode of war
Huxley, A. L. Happily ever after
Rothberg, A. A. Roman portrait

The **war.** Allen, S.

War. Pirandello, L.

War aims. O'Hara, J.

War between saints. Verga, G.

WAR CASUALTIES. See War—Casualties

WAR CORRESPONDENTS. See Journalists

WAR MEMORIALS

Campbell, W. E. M. Memorial to the slain

WAR USE OF ANIMALS. See Animals, War use of

WAR USE OF DOGS. See Dogs, War use of

WAR VETERANS. See Veterans

Ward, Don. See Waldo, E. H. jt. auth.

Ward, Leo Lewis, 1898-1953
After cornhusking
    Ward, L. L. Men in the field
Balaam in Burrville
    Ward, L. L. Men in the field
Bicycle built for two
    Ward, L. L. Men in the field
Black-purple in the corn
    Ward, L. L. Men in the field
Cutting dock
    Ward, L. L. Men in the field
Drought
    Ward, L. L. Men in the field
Master and servant
    Ward, L. L. Men in the field
New-fangled machinery
    Ward, L. L. Men in the field
Possession
    Ward, L. L. Men in the field
Public auction
    Ward, L. L. Men in the field
The quarrel
    Ward, L. L. Men in the field
The rain
    Ward, L. L. Men in the field
Rust in the wheat
    Ward, L. L. Men in the field
Threshing ring
    Ward, L. L. Men in the field
Tobe Snow
    Ward, L. L. Men in the field
Tomorrow afternoon
    Ward, L. L. Men in the field
Where daddy was looking
    Ward, L. L. Men in the field
Winter wheat
    Ward, L. L. Men in the field

Ware, Edmund, pseud. See Smith, Edmund Ware

Ware, Leon
Commissar in Connecticut
    Saturday evening post (Periodical)
    Saturday evening post stories, 1955

WAREHOUSES

Saroyan, W. Visitor in the piano warehouse

WARFARE. See War

The **warlock.** Stafford, J.

Warm day in November. Clayton, J. B.

Warm matzos. Halper, A.

Warmhearted polar bear. Murphy, R.

Warned by Satan. Davis, M.

Warner, Ann Spence
On the hoof
    Everygirls horse stories

Warner, Sylvia Townsend, 1893-
Absalom, my son
    Warner, S. T. Winter in the air, and other stories
At a monkey's breast
    Warner, S. T. Winter in the air, and other stories
At the Trafalgar Bakery
    Warner, S. T. Winter in the air, and other stories
Children's grandmother
    Warner, S. T. Winter in the air, and other stories
Emil
    Warner, S. T. Winter in the air, and other stories
Evan
    Warner, S. T. Winter in the air, and other stories
Funeral at Clovie
    Warner, S. T. Winter in the air, and other stories
Hee-haw!
    Warner, S. T. Winter in the air, and other stories
Idenborough
    Warner, S. T. Winter in the air, and other stories
Kitchen knife
    Warner, S. T. Winter in the air, and other stories
Passing weakness
    Warner, S. T. Winter in the air, and other stories
Priestess of Delphi
    Warner, S. T. Winter in the air, and other stories
The reredos
    Warner, S. T. Winter in the air, and other stories
Second visit
    Warner, S. T. Winter in the air, and other stories
Shadwell
    Warner, S. T. Winter in the air, and other stories
Uncle Blair
    Warner, S. T. Winter in the air, and other stories

WEBSTER, DANIEL, 1782-1852
Benét, S. V. Devil and Daniel Webster
The wedding. O'Flaherty, L.
WEDDING ANNIVERSARIES
Forde, M. Washboard blues
Suckow, R. Golden wedding
Wedding day. Boyle, K.
Wedding eve. MacMahon, B.
Wedding for four. Schuman, S.
Wedding gift. Foote, J. T.
Wedding journey. Alvaro, C.
Wedding night. Maupassant, G. de
Wedding of a friend. Shaw, I.
Wedding picture. Robertson, G. M.
Wedding ring. Toland, S.
WEDDING TRIPS. See Honeymoons;
Marriage
WEDDINGS
Babel', I. E. The King
Beigel, U. World without a sun
Block, A. R. Something borrowed—some-
thing blue
Boyle, K. Wedding day
Chavez, A. Lean years
Gerchunoff, A. Camacho's wedding feast
Mackenzie, O. C. Something different
Maupassant, G. de. Accursed bread
Reynolds, Q. J. The bride looked sad
Runyon, D. Romance in the roaring forties
Schuman, S. Wedding for four
Shaw, I. Wedding of a friend
Ward, L. L. Bicycle built for two
Wharton, E. N. J. Last asset
See also Elopements; Marriage

Ireland
O'Flaherty, L. The wedding
Wednesday for Bradley. Parker, K. A.
Wee bit crude. Brown, I.
Wee nip. Gaitens, E.
Weed, Alberta
Matter of months
Oberfirst, R. ed. 1955 anthology of best
original short-shorts
WEEDS
Auerbach, E. Wild growth
A week in Turenevo. Tolstoĭ, A. N. Graf
Weep for our pride. Plunkett, J.
Weep no more, my lady! Fox, N. A.
Weep not for me. Fay, W.
Weep not for them. Dowdey, C.
Weidman, Jerome, 1913-
The kinnehórrah
Ribalow, H. U. ed. Treasury of Amer-
ican Jewish stories
The tuxedos
Baudin, M. ed. Contemporary short
stories v2
Weigel, Henrietta
Changing mask
New voices 2: American writing today
Saturday is a poor man's port
Best American short stories, 1957
WEIGHT CONTROL. See Corpulence

Weinberg, Edith
Bigger than life
Stanford Short stories, 1958
Weird sisters. Tomkins, C.
Weiss, Peter, 1916-
Document I
New directions 15
Welch, Douglass, 1906-
Mr Digby and the talking dog
Saturday evening post (Periodical)
Saturday evening post Carnival of
humor
Mr Digby's swindle sheet
Saturday evening post (Periodical)
Saturday evening post stories, 1954
Welch, Helen Laurie
Promise for Elizabeth
Seventeen (Periodical) Stories from
Seventeen
Time for waiting
Oberfirst, R. ed. Anthology of best
short-short stories v5
Welcome, John
Red coats galloping
Welcome, J. and Orchard, V. eds. Best
hunting stories
WELDING
Curley, D. The ship
Millholland, R. Temperamental jailbird
WELLINGTON, ARTHUR WELLES-
LEY, 1ST DUKE OF, 1769-1852
Blassingame, W. Copenhagen and the
Iron Duke
Wellman, Manly Wade, 1905-
Little black train
Magazine of fantasy and science fiction.
Best from Fantasy and science fiction;
4th ser.
Mayor calls his family
Queen, E. pseud. ed. Ellery Queen's
awards: 12th ser.
Wells, Herbert George, 1886-1946
Inexperienced ghost
Laughton, C. ed. Tell me a story
Ridler, A. B. comp. Best ghost stories
New accelerator
Laughton, C. ed. Tell me a story
Story of the late Mr Elvesham
Costain, T. B. and Beecroft, J. eds.
Stories to remember
Truth about Pyecraft
Laughton, C. ed. Tell me a story
Wells, Kenneth McNeill, 1905-
We hire a witch
Nelson, G. E. ed. Cavalcade of the
North
Wells, Mary
The coverlid
Fenner, P. R. comp. Brother against
brother
Wells, Robert W.
The day all traffic stopped
Saturday evening post (Periodical)
Saturday evening post stories, 1956
WELLS
Aymé, M. Picture-well
Barash, A. Hai's well
Wells, K. M. We hire a witch
WELSH FARM LIFE. See Farm life—
Wales

WELSH IN IRELAND
O'Brian, P. Drawing of the Curranwood badgers

Welty, Eudora, 1909-
Bride of the Innisfallen
  Welty, E. Bride of the Innisfallen, and other stories
The burning
  Welty, E. Bride of the Innisfallen, and other stories
Circe
  Welty, E. Bride of the Innisfallen, and other stories
Going to Naples
  Best American short stories, 1955
  Welty, E. Bride of the Innisfallen, and other stories
Kin
  Welty, E. Bride of the Innisfallen, and other stories
Ladies in spring
  Welty, E. Bride of the Innisfallen, and other stories
Lily Daw and the three ladies
  Thorp, W. ed. Southern reader
Livvie
  Havighurst, W. ed. Masters of the modern short story
Livvie is back
  First-prize stories, 1919-1957
A memory
  Thurston, J. A. ed. Reading modern short stories
No place for you, my love
  Welty, E. Bride of the Innisfallen, and other stories
Petrified man
  McClennen, J. comp. Masters and masterpieces of the short story
  Thurston, J. A. ed. Reading modern short stories
Shower of gold
  Hall, J. B. and Langland, J. T. eds. Short story
A still moment
  Gettman, R. A. and Harkness, B. eds. Book of stories
Why I live at the P. O.
  Locke, L. G.; Gibson, W. M. and Arms, G. W. eds. Introduction to literature
Wide net
  First-prize stories, 1919-1957
The winds
  Havighurst, W. and others, eds. Selection
Worn path
  Laughton, C. ed. Tell me a story
  McClennen, J. comp. Masters and masterpieces of the short story
  McMaster, J. ed. Stories to remember

The wendigo. Blackwood, A.

Wenter, Josef
His last adventure
  Skelton, P. ed. Animals all

Wentworth's day. Lovecraft, H. P. and Derleth, A. W.

We're all guests. Clay, G. R.

West, Anthony C. 1910-
The monocrats
  West, A. C. River's end, and other stories

Narcissus unto echo
  West, A. C. River's end, and other stories
No fatted calf
  West, A. C. River's end, and other stories
Not Isaac
  Oberfirst, R. ed. Anthology of best short-short stories, v6
  West, A. C. River's end, and other stories
River's end
  West, A. C. River's end, and other stories
Song of the barrow
  West, A. C. River's end, and other stories
Turning page
  West, A. C. River's end, and other stories
Upper room
  West, A. C. River's end, and other stories

West, Jessamyn
Battle of the suits
  West, J. Love, death, and the ladies' drill team
Breach of promise
  West, J. Love, death, and the ladies' drill team
First day finish
  Baudin, M. ed. Contemporary short stories v3
Foot-shaped shoes
  West, J. Love, death, and the ladies' drill team
Home-coming
  West, J. Love, death, and the ladies' drill team
Horace Chooney, M. D.
  West, J. Love, death, and the ladies' drill team
Learn to say good-by
  West, J. Love, death, and the ladies' drill team
The lesson
  Tibbets, A. B. ed. Youth, youth, youth
The linden trees
  West, J. Love, death, and the ladies' drill team
Little collar for the monkey
  West, J. Love, death, and the ladies' drill team
Love, death, and the ladies' drill team
  West, J. Love, death, and the ladies' drill team
Mr Cornelius, I love you
  Havighurst, W. ed. Masters of the modern short story
Music on the Muscatatuck
  Costain, T. B. and Beecroft, J. eds. Stories to remember
Mysteries of life in an orderly manner
  West, J. Love, death, and the ladies' drill team
Pacing goose
  Costain, T. B. and Beecroft, J. eds. Stories to remember
Public-address system
  West, J. Love, death, and the ladies' drill team

WESTERN STORIES—*Continued*

MacDonald, D. B. The last notch
Meredith, S. ed. Bar 5; 11 stories
Meredith, S. ed. Bar 6; 11 stories
Meyers, B. Devil Dust
Montgomery, R. G. King of the mesa
Montgomery, R. G. Voice of Jerome Kildee
Mowery, W. B. Corporal Nat
O'Rourke, F. Cool one
O'Rourke, F. Crooked nail
O'Rourke, F. Final payment
O'Rourke, F. Grandpa's .45's
O'Rourke, F. Hard men; 11 stories
O'Rourke, F. Home town
O'Rourke, F. Point of justice
O'Rourke, F. Reaction
O'Rourke, F. Speak to me only with thine eyes
O'Rourke, F. Stretch in time
O'Rourke, F. Stronger medicine
O'Rourke, F. Way of a trooper
Patten, L. B. Big Black and the bully
Payne, S. Black outlaw
Payne, S. Shaggy lays off
Prebble, J. The regulator
Reese, J. H. Frontier frenzy
Rhodes, E. M. Aforesaid Bates
Rhodes, E. M. Barred door
Rhodes, E. M. Beyond the desert
Rhodes, E. M. Bird in the bush
Rhodes, E. M. Cheerful land
Rhodes, E. M. Enchanted valley
Rhodes, E. M. Fool's heart
Rhodes, E. M. Long shift
Rhodes, E. M. Loved I not honor more
Rhodes, E. M. No mean city
Rhodes, E. M. Number of things
Rhodes, E. M. The numismatist
Rhodes, E. M. Rhodes reader; 13 stories
Rhodes, E. M. Sticky Pierce, diplomat
Rhodes, E. M. Trouble man
Richter, C. Early marriage
Richter, C. Sea of grass
Russell, C. M. Dog eater
Sandoz, M. Miss Morissa
Sandoz, M. Y. Girl in the Humbert
Savage, L. Crow-bait caravan
Savage, L. Traitor town
Schaefer, J. W. Three days for revenge
Searles, L. J. Death deals this hand
Spears, R. S. The nester and the unclothed lady
Stone, N. B. Vengeance trail
Thompson, T. Lynch mob at Cimarron Crossing
Thompson, T. Trail's end in Tombstone
Turner, R. Killers die young
Turner, W. O. Proud diggers
Vestal, S. Warpath
Waldo, E. H. and Ward, D. Waiting thing inside
Western Writers of America. Branded West; 14 stories
Western Writers of America. Hoof trails and wagon tracks; 15 stories
Western Writers of America. Wild horse roundup; 14 stories
Western Writers of America. Wild streets; 12 stories
Wister, O. At the sign of the Last Chance
Wormser, R. The hunter

> *See also* Cattle drives; Cowboys; Ranch life; Wagon trains; The West

Weston, Christine (Goutiere) 1904-
Four annas
Best American short stories, 1956

Wet day. Lavin, M.

WHALES
Doyle, A. C. Lover of the Coral Glades
Wallenius, K. M. Illep and the whale
Wyndham, L. Affectionate whale

WHALING
Melville, H. Moby Dick's last fight
> *See also* Sea stories

Wharton, Edith Newbold (Jones) 1862-1937
After Holbein
Wharton, E. N. J. Best short stories of Edith Wharton
Angel at the grave
Wharton, E. N. J. Best short stories of Edith Wharton
Autres temps
Wharton, E. N. J. Best short stories of Edith Wharton
Bunner Sisters
Wharton, E. N. J. Best short stories of Edith Wharton
Kerfol
Costain, T. B. and Beecroft, J. eds. Stories to remember
Last asset
Wharton, E. N. J. Best short stories of Edith Wharton
Other two
Wharton, E. N. J. Best short stories of Edith Wharton
Pomegranate seed
Wharton, E. N. J. Best short stories of Edith Wharton
Roman fever
Gettman, R. A. and Harkness, B. eds. Book of stories
Wharton, E. N. J. Best short stories of Edith Wharton
Souls belated
Wharton, E. N. J. Best short stories of Edith Wharton
Triumph of night
Ridler, A. B. comp. Best ghost stories
Xingu
Baudin, M. ed. Contemporary short stories v 1
Wharton, E. N. J. Best short stories of Edith Wharton

What a thing, to keep a wolf in a cage! Calisher, H.

What about Susanna? Worthington, R.

What Christmas is as we grow older. Dickens, C.

What every boy should know. Maxwell, W.

What it takes. Leyson, B. W.

What men live by. Tolstoĭ, L. N. Graf

What might it not have been. Sansom, W.

What son tells everything? Block, L.

What the old man does is always right. Andersen, H. C.

What to do until the analyst comes. Pohl, F.

What would you do if you were president? Lederer, W. J. and Burdick, E. L.

What would you have done? Armstrong, C.

What you don't know won't hurt you. Wright, R.

What you hear from 'em? Taylor, P. H.

What's a girl supposed to do—sit aroun' and twill her thumbs? Kober, A.

What's the purpose of the bayonet? Garrett, G.

WHEAT
  Babel', I. E. S. S. Cow-Wheat
  Ward, L. L. Rust in the wheat

WHEELWRIGHTS
  Prévost, J. The forge

When a boy's a man. Bird, W. R.

When grandfather flew to the moon. Malpass, E. L.

When Greek meets Greek. Greene, G.

When I fetched the fixin's fer Christmas dinner. Rosegger, P.

When old age shall this generation waste. Cassill, R. V.

When the bough breaks. Enright, E.

When the cloud burst. Samuel, E. H.

When winter comes. Sneider, V. J.

When you're smiling. Waldo, E. H.

Where angels fear to tread. Palmer, S.

Where are your guns? Fast, H. M.

Where daddy was looking. Ward, L. L.

Where love is, there God is also. Tolstoĭ, L. N. Graf

Where there is nothing, there is God. Yeats, W. B.

Where's Francesca? Moretti, U.

Where's the game? O'Hara, J.

Wherever you may be. Gunn, J. E.

Which new era would that be? Gordimer, N.

WHIMSICAL STORIES. See Fantasies

Whipping boy. Block, A. R.

WHIPPOORWILLS
  Derleth, A. W. Whippoorwills in the hills

Whippoorwills in the hills. Derleth, A. W.

WHIRLPOOLS
  Poe, E. A. Descent into the Maelström

WHISKEY
  Adams, A. In a spur of the county
  Smith, E. W. Gates ajar

WHISKY. See Whiskey

White, Elwyn Brooks, 1899-
  Decline of sport
    Schwed, P. and Wind, H. W. eds. Great stories from the world of sport
  Second tree from corner
    Baudin, M. ed. Contemporary short stories v3

White, James
  The conspirators
    Conklin, G. ed. Science-fiction adventures in mutation

White, Robin, 1930?-
  Devil of his own
    Stanford Short stories, 1958
  First voice
    Prize stories, 1958: the O. Henry awards

House of many rooms
  Best American short stories, 1958
Rumba Mosam
  Seventeen (Periodical) Seventeen's stories
State of well-being
  Stanford Short stories, 1958

White, Stewart Edward, 1873-1946
  Honk-honk breed
    Schaefer, J. W. ed. Out West
  Long rifle
    Costain, T. B. and Beecroft, J. eds. Stories to remember

White, William Anthony Parker, 1911-
  Anomaly of the empty man
    White, W. A. P. Far and away
  Balaam
    Healy, R. J. ed. 9 tales of time and space
    White, W. A. P. Far and away
  Crime must have a stop
    Mystery Writers of America, inc. For tomorrow we die
  Elsewhen
    White, W. A. P. Far and away
  The first
    White, W. A. P. Far and away
  Like Count Palmieri
    Crime Writers Association, London. Planned departures
  A matter of scholarship
    Mystery Writers of America, inc. A choice of murders
  Mystery for Christmas
    Mystery Writers of America, inc. Crime for two
  Nellthu
    Davenport, B. ed. Deals with the devil
  Other inauguration
    White, W. A. P. Far and away
  Review copy
    White, W. A. P. Far and away
  Secret of the house
    White, W. A. P. Far and away
  Snulbug
    White, W. A. P. Far and away
  Sriberdegibit
    White, W. A. P. Far and away
  Star bride
    White, W. A. P. Far and away
    Same as: Starbride
  They bite
    White, W. A. P. Far and away

White against winter dawn. Clayton, J. B.

White army. Dresser, D.

White as snow. Boyle, K.

White blackbird. MacMahon, B.

White boat. Alexander, S.

White circle. Clayton, J. B.

White cottage. Strong, L. A. G.

White dove. Vaughan, A.

White Fang. London, J.

White feather. Aldrich, T. B.

The **white** goddess and the mealie question. Gordimer, N.

White horses of Vienna. Boyle, K.

A **white** lie. Sansom, W.

White man. Lofts, N. R.

WHITE MOUNTAINS
Hawthorne, N. Great Stone Face

White musky. Young, S.

White mustang. McCourt, E. A.

White night. Dostoevskiĭ, F. M.

The white ribbons of the curling surf. Rey, M.

WHITE RUSSIANS IN FOREIGN COUNTRIES
Nabokov, V. V. Assistant producer

White shawl. Robb, E. C.

White water. Johnson, W. R.

White wolf. Maupassant, G. de

The Whiteboys. Somerville, E. A. O. and Martin, V. F.

Whitehill, Joseph, 1927-
Able Baker
Prize stories, 1956: the O. Henry awards
Whitehill, J. Able Baker, and others
The academicians
Whitehill, J. Able Baker, and others
Cymbal makers
Whitehill, J. Able Baker, and others
Day of the last rock fight
Whitehill, J. Able Baker, and others
The propagandist
Whitehill, J. Able Baker, and others
Rat trap
Whitehill, J. Able Baker, and others
Stay away from my mother
Queen, E. pseud. ed. Ellery Queen's awards: 10th ser.
The surrogate
Whitehill, J. Able Baker, and others
Terry Bindle
Whitehill, J. Able Baker, and others
Thanks very much, but no thank you
Whitehill, J. Able Baker, and others
Town is waiting
Queen, E. pseud. ed. Ellery Queen's awards: 12th ser.
Young man with a spear
Whitehill, J. Able Baker, and others

Who dealt? Lardner, R. W.

Who knows? Maupassant, G. de

The whole audience woulda bust right out laughin'. Kober, A.

Whole voyald and heaven itself. Saroyan, W.

Whole world in his hands. Griffin, J. H.

Whoopee for the new deal! Farrell, J. T.

Whooper swan of Olivebridge. Carmer, C. L.

Why can't they tell you why? Purdy, J.

Why I live at the P. O. Welty, E.

Why rustlers never win. Felsen, G.

Why the Chisholm Trail forks. Adams, A.

Wicked story. Shaw, I.

Wide net. Welty, E.

The widow. Babel', I. E.

WIDOWERS
Block, A. R. Blind journey
Campbell, W. E. M. The slate
Carr, A. H. Z. Black kitten
Chavez, A. Wake for Don Corsinio

Chute, B. J. Escape
Chute, B. J. The legacy
Hale, N. The place and the time
Lowry, R. J. C. Long for this world
MacMahon, B. O' lonely moon!
Maupassant, G. de. Little one
Muldur, N. Friday is a lucky day
Pritchett, V. S. The scapegoat
Purdy, J. Color of darkness

WIDOWS
Blakiston, N. Mrs Webster
Campbell, W. E. M. Willow fields
Chavez, A. Ardent commandant
Criswell, C. Wreath for the living
Dickinson, W. H. Roses
Ferber, E. Molly Brandeis takes hold
Ferber, E. Sudden sixties
Franko, I. I. Les's widow's household
Hale, N. People in places
Kober, A. It'll be too late then. You just wait and see!
Lavin, M. Story of the widow's son
Malamud, B. Take pity
Merritt, M. No game for children
Nagai, T. In a small art gallery
O'Kelly, S. Nan Hogan's house
Peretz, I. L. Conversation on a hilltop
Peyton, A. H. The last laugh
Purdy, J. You reach for your hat
Rao, R. Akkayya
Singmaster, E. The battleground
Spark, M. Bang-bang you're dead
Stafford, J. In the zoo
Ward, L. L. Tomorrow afternoon
Warner, S. T. Children's grandmother
Wharton, E. N. J. Roman fever

Wierzyński, Kazimierz, 1894-
Patrol
Ordon, E. ed. 10 contemporary Polish stories

Wife killer. Singer, I. B.

Wife's confession. Maupassant, G. de

Wiggin, Kate Douglas (Smith) 1856-1923
Birds' Christmas carol
Lohan, R. ed. Christmas tales for reading aloud

Wilbur in the amusement park. Rhine, R.

WILD ANIMALS. See Animals

WILD CATS. See Lynx; Pumas

Wild duck's nest. McLaverty, M.

WILD FLOWERS. See Flowers

Wild goat's kid. O'Flaherty, L.

Wild growth. Auerbach, E.

Wild justice. Van Doren, M.

Wild leather. Fox, N. A.

Wild swan. O'Flaherty, L.

The wild wood. Clingerman, M.

WILDCATS. See Lynx; Pumas

Wilde, Oscar, 1854-1900
Canterville ghost
Ridler, A. B. comp. Best ghost stories
Happy Prince
Garrity, D. A. ed. 44 Irish short stories
Swayze, B. ed. Short story magic

Wilde, Percival, 1887-
Pillar of fire
Costain, T. B. and Beecroft, J. eds. Stories to remember

WITCHCRAFT—*Continued*

Lovecraft, H. P. and Derleth, A. W. Peabody heritage

MacMahon, B. Close to the clay

Ruhen, O. Dark of the moon

Ruhen, O. Woman of Labu

Sheckley, R. The accountant

Thomas, D. School for witches

WITCHES. See Witchcraft

Witches. Gerchunoff, A.

With intent to steal. Blackwood, A.

With old man Makhno. Babel', I. E.

With the aid of the One Above. Suhl, Y.

Within the law. Cunningham, J. M.

The **witness.** Garrett, G.

The **witness.** Lessing, D. M.

The **witness.** Porter, K. A.

Witwer, Harry Charles, 1890-

Leather pushers
Collier's (Periodical) Collier's Greatest sports stories

WIVES. See Husband and wife

Wodehouse, Pelham Grenville, 1881-

Artistic career of Corky
Wodehouse, P. G. Selected stories

The aunt and the sluggard
Saturday evening post (Periodical) Saturday evening post Carnival of humor
Wodehouse, P. G. Selected stories

Bertie changes his mind
Wodehouse, P. G. Selected stories

Clicking of Cuthbert
Schwed, P. and Wind, R. W. eds. Great stories from the world of sport

Clustering round young Bingo
Wodehouse, P. G. Selected stories

Episode of the dog McIntosh
Wodehouse, P. G. Selected stories

Heart of a goof
Schwed, P. and Wind, H. W. eds. Great stories from the world of sport

Jeeves and the impending doom
Wodehouse, P. G. Selected stories

Jeeves and the kid Clementina
Wodehouse, P. G. Selected stories

Jeeves and the old school chum
Wodehouse, P. G. Selected stories

Jeeves and the song of songs
Wodehouse, P. G. Selected stories

Jeeves and the unbidden guest
Wodehouse, P. G. Selected stories

Jeeves and the yuletide spirit
Wodehouse, P. G. Selected stories

Jeeves takes charge
Wodehouse, P. G. Selected stories

Love that purifies
Wodehouse, P. G. Selected stories

Mainly about shoes
Buckeridge, A. comp. In and out of school

Ordeal of young Tuppy
Wodehouse, P. G. Selected stories

Pitcher and the plutocrat
Collier's (Periodical) Collier's Greatest sport stories

Rummy affair of old Biffy
Wodehouse, P. G. Selected stories

Uncle Fred Flits
Nash, O. comp. I couldn't help laughing

Very shy gentleman
Great dog stories

Wohl, Sam

The bride
Ridalow, H. U. ed. Treasury of American Jewish stories

Wolfe, Thomas, 1900-1938

Alone
Laughton, C. ed. Tell me a story

Dark in the forest, strange as time
McClennen, J. comp. Masters and masterpieces of the short story

Death the proud brother
Hart, J. D. and Gohdes, C. L. eds. America's literature

Face of the war
Thorp, W. ed. Southern reader

Paper route
Laughton, C. ed. Tell me a story

Wolfert, Ira, 1908-

Indomitable blue
Prize stories, 1955: the O. Henry awards

Wolfson, Victor

Purification of Thelma Augenstern
Ridalow, H. U. ed. Treasury of American Jewish stories

Wollheim, Donald A.

Planet passage
Gallant, J. ed. Stories of scientific imagination

WOLVERINES

Annixter, P. pseud. Blasted pine

Annixter, P. pseud. Devil of the woods

Annixter, P. pseud. Injun devil

James, A. Something to talk with

WOLVES

Annixter, P. pseud. Injun Devil

Francis of Assisi, Saint. Little flowers of St Francis

Kipling, Y. Mowgli's brothers

Lesinš, K. Tailor and the wolves

McCall, E. Wolves cornered us

Prévost, M. Solange, the wolf-girl

Sandoz, M. Y. In the cemetary at Scutari

Shneur, Z. Slaying of the wolf

Wallenius, K. M. One-eyed wolf of Kaamas Fell

Wolves cornered us. McCall, E.

WOMAN

Balchin, N. Three ladies

Hale, N. Mocha cakes

Employment

Millholland, R. Rough turn

Relation to other women

Glaspell, S. Jury of her peers

Household, G. Salute

O'Hara, J. Other women's households

Purdy, J. Good woman

Welty, E. The winds

Rights of women

Farrell, J. T. Dangerous woman

Inber, V. Nor-Bibi's crime

Karbovskaya, V. Bondage

Sütő, A. Right man in the right place

Social and moral questions

Maugham, W. S. Rain

Wouk, Herman, 1915-
Herbie solves a mystery
Schwarz, L. W. ed. Feast of Leviathan
Wounded cormorant. O'Flaherty, L.
WOUNDED IN BATTLE. See War—
Casualties
Wow! Tekeyan, C.
Wraith on Cedar Street. Carmer, C. L.
WRATH. See Anger
Wray, Joy
Doublecross
Oberfirst, R. ed. Anthology of best
short-short stories v6
Wreath for the living. Criswell, C.
The **wreck.** Maupassant, G. de
Wreck of the Golden Mary. Dickens, C.
Wrecked houses; the big thing. Rilke, R. M.
WRECKS, RAILROAD. See Railroads—
Accidents
WRESTLING
Colette, S. G. Circus wrestlers
Kersh, G. Ali the Terrible Turk
Shenton, E. Son he'd never met
Wright, Gilbert
Madman's chain
Saturday evening post (Periodical)
Saturday evening post stories, 1955
Wright, Judith
Colour of death
Stivens, D. comp. Coast to coast
Wright, Richard, 1908-
Big, black, good man
Best American short stories, 1958
What you don't know won't hurt you
Blaustein, P. M. and Blaustein, A. P.
eds. Doctors' choice
Wright, Sydney Fowler, 1874-
Better choice
Conklin, G. ed. Science-fiction adven-
tures in mutation
Writ of divorcement. Lewisohn, L.
WRITERS. See Authors
WRITING
Doyle, Sir A. C. Reigate puzzle
WRITING, AUTOMATIC
Stewart, J. I. M. Grey's ghost
A **wry** anecdote. Rudd, H.
WU PAO-AN
Feng, M. Journey of the corpse
Feng, M. Story of Wu Pao-an
Wuest, Sarellen M.
A sense of tribe
Miller, N. ed. New campus writing, no. 2
Wulzen, Ann, 1934-
The priest
Stanford short stories, 1957
Wyckoff, James, 1918-
To be a cowboy
New voices 2: American writing today
Wylie, Ida Alexa Ross, 1885-
Crack-up at curtain time
This week magazine. This week's Sto-
ries of mystery and suspense
Wylie, Philip, 1902-
Affair of the ardent amazon
Wylie, P. Treasure cruise and other
Crunch and Des stories

The answer
Jennings, F. G. and Calitri, C. J. eds.
Stories
Saturday evening post (Periodical)
Saturday evening post stories, 1955
Danger at Coral Key
Wylie, P. Treasure cruise and other
Crunch and Des stories
Light tackle
Schwed, P. and Wind, H. W. eds. Great
stories from the world of sport
Man who loved a joke
Wylie, P. Treasure cruise and other
Crunch and Des stories
Plane down—hurricane area
Wylie, P. Treasure cruise and other
Crunch and Des stories
Smuggler's cove
Wylie, P. Treasure cruise and other
Crunch and Des stories
Treasure cruise
Wylie, P. Treasure cruise and other
Crunch and Des stories
Wyndham, John, pseud. See Harris, John
Beynon
Wyndham, Lee, 1912-
Affectionate whale
Teen-age tales, bk 4
WYOMING
Gardner, E. S. Flight into disaster
Ranch life
See Ranch life—Wyoming

X

Xi effect. Richardson, R. S.
Xingu. Wharton, E. N. J.

Y

Yaari, Yehuda, 1900-
Shepherd and his dog
Tehilla, and other Israeli tales
Three-fold covenant
Frank, M. Z. ed. Sound the great
trumpet
Schwarz, L. W. ed. Feast of Leviathan
YACHTS AND YACHTING
Ball, D. B. C. Sea decides
Yaffe, James, 1927-
Mr Feldman
Ribalow, H. U. ed. Treasury of Amer-
ican Jewish stories
Mom makes a wish
Queen, E. pseud. ed. Ellery Queen's
awards: 10th ser.
Mom sheds a tear
Best detective stories of the year—1955
One of the family
Queen, E. pseud. ed. Ellery Queen's
awards: 11th ser.

Yates, Richard, 1926-
  Best of everything
    Prize stories, 1956: the O. Henry awards
    Short story, 1
  Fun with a stranger
    Short story, 1
  Jody rolled the bones
    Short story, 1
  Really good jazz piano
    Short story, 1
Year I had the colds. Hale, N.
Yeats, William Butler, 1865-1939
  Red Hanrahan
    Garrity, D. A. ed. 44 Irish short stories
  Where there is nothing, there is God
    Garrity, D. A. ed. 44 Irish short stories
Yechiel's Sabbath mother. Asch, S.
Yellen, Samuel, 1906-
  And there are things for tears
    Yellen, S. The passionate shepherd
  Four sides of a triangle
    Yellen, S. The passionate shepherd
  The glass jaw
    Yellen, S. The passionate shepherd
  The mystic presences
    Yellen, S. The passionate shepherd
  The passionate shepherd
    Yellen, S. The passionate shepherd
  Reginald Pomfret Skelton
    Best American short stories, 1956
    Yellen, S. The passionate shepherd
  Saturn has the power
    Yellen, S. The passionate shepherd
  Stoneville Pike
    Yellen, S. The passionate shepherd
  Vergilian vespers
    Yellen, S. The passionate shepherd
  Your children will burn
    Yellen, S. The passionate shepherd
Yellow bird. Williams, T.
Yellow Devil. Kelton, E.
YELLOW FEVER
  Drury, W. P. Concerning a treaty with
    France
  Floherty, J. J. Yellow terror
Yellow raft. Connell, E. S.
Yellow terror. Floherty, J. J.
YELLOWSTONE NATIONAL PARK
  Rinehart, M. R. The dipper
Yellowstone Park. McCarthy, M. T.
YEMENITES
  Tabib, M. 1917
Yerby, Frank Garvin, 1916-
  Health card
    Fenton, C. A. ed. Best short stories of
    World War II
Yesterday's love. Farrell, J. T.
Yezierska, Anzia, 1885-
  Hunger
    Ribalow, H. U. ed. Treasury of Ameri-
    can Jewish stories
Yisgadal. Klein, J. M.
Yo ho and two bottles of rum. Faulkner, W.
Yo ho Hoka! Anderson, P. and Dickson,
  G. R.
Yoder, Robert McAyeal, 1907-
  Merry Christmas in ten pieces
    Posselt, E. ed. A merry, merry Christ-
    mas book

Yogi's PR client. Brier, H. M.
Yoirimba. Prichard, K. S.
YOM KIPPUR
  Brinig, M. Day of Atonement
  Peretz, I. L. Miracles on the sea
  Peretz, I. L. Ne'ilah
  Rabinowitz, S. Yom Kippur scandal
Yom Kippur scandal. Rabinowitz, S.
Yorck, Ruth L. 1909-
  Big bird-watcher
    New Directions in prose and poetry, 16
Yore. Nemerov, H.
YORKSHIRE. See England, Provincial
  and rural—Yorkshire
YORKSHIRE DIALECT. See Dialect sto-
  ries—English—Yorkshire
You bet your life. Palmer, S.
You can't be a little girl all your life. Ellin,
  S.
You can't run away. Chesson, R.
You can't trust a man. Nielsen, H.
You could look it up. Thurber, J.
You created us. Godwin, T.
You know Willie. Cogswell, T. R.
You make your own life. Pritchett, V. S.
You may safely gaze. Purdy, J.
You mustn't weep—it's Yom-Tev. Rabino-
  witz, S.
You reach for your hat. Purdy, J.
"You see. . ." Bentley, P. E.
You were too trusting, Captain. Babel',
  I. E.
You'll be late for supper. Criswell, C.
Young, Robert Flint
  Goddess in granite
    Magazine of fantasy and science fiction.
    Best from Fantasy and science fic-
    tion; 7th ser.
  Jungle doctor
    Best science-fiction stories and novels:
    1956
Young, Scott
  White musky
    Nelson, G. E. ed. Cavalcade of the
    North
Young and scared. Hawkins, J. and Haw-
  kins, W.
The young and the brave Marmur, J.
Young Archimedes. Huxley, A. L.
Young artist. Farrell, J. T.
Young convicts. Farrell, J. T.
Young girl. Mansfield, K.
Young Goodman Brown. Hawthorne, N.
Young Man Axelbrod. Lewis, S.
Young man on his own. Rawlings, C. A.
Young man who flew past. Averchenko,
  A. T.
Young man with a spear. Whitehill, J.
Young patriot. Dutourd, J.
Young Turk. Macken, W.
Young warrior. La Farge, O.
Your body is a jewel box. Boyle, K.
Your children will burn. Yellen, S.
Your obituary, well written. Aiken, C. P.

You're another. Knight, D.

You're never too old. Ormond, S. K.

You're not the type. Ferber, E.

YOUTH
Baker, L. N. Maybe next week
Bates, H. E. Queen of Spain fritillary
Beigel, U. Mirror days
Beigel, U. Poor in spirit
Beigel, U. Victoria at night
Bennett, K. Death at attention
Brodkey, H. Laurie dressing
Brodkey, H. The quarrel
Brodkey, H. Sentimental education
Brown, J. The way I feel
Brunton, A. This miracle
Clayton, J. B. Summer of the insistent voices
Cundiff, L. Troubled summer
Enright, E. Tree of heaven
Finney, J. Something in a cloud
Fitzgerald, F. S. K. Forging ahead
Foley, M. One with Shakespeare
Folinsbee, J. P. Final question
Gallant, M. One morning in June
Guldager, C. Dollar a kiss
Hall, M. Height of love
Henson, I. Orchids and fishing togs
Howland, R. Something like love
Huxley, A. L. Hubert and Minnie
Leigh, J. The adventurers: a reminiscence
Lessing, D. M. Words he said
Lowry, R. J. C. Marie
Miller, R. M. The gavel
Nabokov, V. V. Lance
O'Donovan, J. Big Bertha
O'Hara, J. The moccasins
O'Hara, J. Too young
Payne, L. V. Prelude
Saroyan, W. Paris and Philadelphia
Shaw, I. Then we were three
Shrubb, P. Rites of spring
Tarkington, B. Mary Smith
Welch, H. L. Time for waiting
White, R. State of well-being
Williams, T. Field of blue children
Williams, T. Important thing
Wolfe, T. Alone
  See also Adolescence; Boys; Girls

YOUTH, ETERNAL. See Rejuvenation

Youth. Conrad, J.

You've got to learn. Murphy, R.

Y'say ya not saddisfied. Kober, A.

YUKON TERRITORY
London, J. All Gold Canyon
London, J. Call of the wild
London, J. Love of life
London, J. White Fang

YUM KIPPUR. See Yom Kippur

Yvette. Maupassant, G. de

Z

Zabara, Joseph Ibn. See Joseph Zabara

Zahatopolk. Russell, B. A. W. R. 3d earl

Zakhar Berkut. Franko, I. I.

Zamfirescu, A. D.
  I. Popescu of the boundaries
  Short stories

Zamonski, Stanley W.
  Battle of Grunwald
    Bronfeld, S. ed. Treasury of new short fiction
  Pay-off
    Oberfirst, R. ed. 1955 anthology of best original short-shorts

Zamoste. Babel', I. E.

Zangwill, Israel, 1864-1926
  Prodigal son
    Schwarz, L. W. ed. Feast of Leviathan
  Sabbath breaker
    Kobler, F. ed. Her children call her blessed

Zara, Louis, 1910-
  Resurgam
    Ribalow, H. U. ed. Treasury of American Jewish stories

Zawieyski, Jerzy, 1902-
  The president calls
    Ordon, E. ed. 10 contemporary Polish stories

Zeal. Powers, J. F.

Zealots of Cranston Tech. Oldham, A.

ZEBRAS
  Hoys, D. King Dron

Zeffirino. Baldini, A.

Zeke Hammertight. Stuart, J.

Zelda. Oberfirst, R.

Zemach, Shlomo, 1886-
  Tale of two mules
    Schwarz, L. W. ed. Feast of Leviathan

Zenner trophy. Vidal, G.

Zero hour. Bradbury, R.

Ziller, Eugene
  Journey to Brentwood
    Stanford short stories, 1956

Zimmerman, Margie, 1915-
  Important wish
    Oberfirst, R. ed. Anthology of best short-short stories v5

ZIONISM
  Household, G. Children's crusade

Zipper trouble. Hedgecock, L. J.

ZIPPERS. See Fastenings

Zistel, Ezra
  Biography
    Mason, P. O. and Mason, J. eds. Favorite cat stories of Pamela and James Mason

Zone of quiet. Lardner, R. W.

Zoological garden. Colette, S. G.

ZOOLOGICAL GARDENS
  Daley, J. B. The man who liked lions
  Sansom, W. Among the dahlias

ZOOS. See Zoological gardens

Zweig, Stefan, 1881-1942
  Amok
    Blaustein, P. M. and Blaustein, A. P. eds. Doctors' choice

PART II

List of Collections Indexed

An author and title list of collections indexed, with their various editions.

Blackwood, Algernon, 1869-1951
In the realm of terror; 8 haunting tales. Pantheon Bks. 1957 312p

Blassingame, Wyatt, 1909-
His kingdom for a horse; with pictures by Sergei Korolkoff. Watts, F. 1957 179p illus

Blaustein, Albert P. 1921-   See Blaustein, P. M. jt. ed.

Blaustein, Phyllis M. 1926- and Blaustein, Albert P. 1921-
(eds.) Doctors' choice; sixteen stories about doctors and medicine selected by famous physicians. With an introduction by Walter C. Alvarez. Funk, W. 1957 310p

Blixen, Karen, 1885-
Anecdotes of destiny [by] Isak Dinesen [pseud]. Random House 1958 244p

Last tales [by] Isak Dinesen [pseud]. Random House 1957 341p

Block, Anita Rowe
Love is a four letter word. Doubleday 1958 261p

Blue Chip Haggerty. Millholland, R.

Blue cup, and other stories. Chute, B. J.

Blue river. Lochridge, B. H.

Bodington, Nancy, 1912-
Rachel weeping; a triptych, by Shelley Smith [pseud]. Harper 1957 213p

Book of better stories. Langford, W. F. ed.

Book of stories. Gettman, R. A. and Harkness, B. eds.

Boucher, Anthony, pseud.   See White, William Anthony Parker

Bound man, and other stories. Aichinger, I.

Boyle, Kay, 1903-
Thirty stories. New Directions 1957 362p

Bradbury, Ray, 1920-
Martian chronicles. Prefatory note by Clifton Fadiman. Doubleday 1958 222p

October country. Illus. by Joe Mugnaini. Ballantine 1955 306p illus

Branded West. Western Writers of America

Brennan, Joseph Payne, 1918-
Nine horrors and a dream. Arkham House 1958 120p

Bride of the Innisfallen, and other stories. Welty, E.

The brides of Solomon, and other stories. Household, G.

Brodkey, Harold
First love and other sorrows. Dial Press 1957 223p

Bronfeld, Stewart
(ed.) Treasury of new short fiction. Nat. Pub. Co. 1955 191p

Brother against brother. Fenner, P. R. comp.

Buckeridge, Anthony
(comp.) In and out of school; stories chosen by Anthony Buckeridge. Faber 1958 250p

Burdick, Eugene L. 1918-   See Lederer, W. J. jt. auth.

Burnett, David
(ed.) Best American short stories, 1958. See Best American short stories, 1958

Burnett, Whit, 1899-
(ed.) This is my best humor. Dial Press 1955 552p illus
Analyzed for short stories only

Byrd, Jerome J.
Three flights up, seven down; stories of high and low adventure. Tuttle 1958 205p

C

Caldwell, Erskine, 1903
Certain women. Little 1957 249p

Erskine Caldwell's Gulf coast stories. Little 1956 248p

Calitri, Charles J.   See Jennings, F. G. jt. ed.

Campbell, William Edward March, 1894-1954
William March omnibus; with an introduction by Alistair Cooke. Rinehart 1956 397p
Analyzed for short stories only

Camus, Albert, 1913-1960
Exile and the kingdom; tr. from the French by Justin O'Brien. Knopf 1958 213p

Canfield, Dorothy.   See Fisher, Dorothea Frances (Canfield)

Capote, Truman, 1924-
Breakfast at Tiffany's; a short novel and three stories. Random House 1958 179p

Carmer, Carl Lamson, 1893-
The screaming ghost, and other stories, collected and told by Carl Carmer. Illus. by Irv Docktor. Knopf 1956 146p illus

Carnival of humor, Saturday evening post. Saturday evening post (Periodical)

Carroll, Gordon
(ed.) Saturday evening post (Periodical) The Post Reader of Civil War stories

Cather, Willa Sibert, 1873-1947
Early stories of Willa Cather; selected and with commentary by Mildred R. Bennett. Dodd 1957 275p

Ellin, Stanley, 1917?-
Mystery stories. Simon & Schuster 1956 237p

Empress's ring. Hale, N.

End of pity, and other stories. Macauley, R.

Engle, Paul, 1908-
(ed.) Prize stories, 1955-1958: the O. Henry awards. See Prize stories, 1955-1958: the O. Henry awards

English short stories of today, 2d ser. Davin, D. M. ed.

Enright, Elizabeth, 1909-
Moment before the rain. Harcourt 1955 253p

Everygirls adventure stories; by Adele De Leeuw, and others; illus. by Richard W. Burhans. Lantern Press 1955 222p illus (Everygirls lib)

Everygirls horse stories, by Marion Holland, and others. Illus. by Richard W. Burhans. Lantern Press 1956 223p illus (Everygirls lib)

Everygirls romance stories. Furman, A. L. ed.

Everygirls sports stories. Furman, A. L. ed.

Exile and the kingdom. Camus, A.

F

Fallen angel, and other stories. Polk, W. T.

Famous mysteries. Sandrus, M. Y. ed.

Fantastic memories. Sandoz, M. Y.

Far and away. White, W. A. P.

Farrell, James Thomas, 1904-
Dangerou woman, and other stories. Vanguard 1957 160p
French girls are vicious, and other stories. Vanguard 1955 177p
Omnibus of short stories. Vanguard 1956 3v in 1
Contents: $1,000 a week; To whom it may concern; Life adventurous; separately indexed in main volume
Analyzed for short stories only

Faulkner, William, 1897-
Big woods; decorations by Edward Shenton. Random House 1955 198p illus
New Orleans sketches. Introduction by Carvel Collins. Rutgers Univ. Press 1958 223p

Favorite cat stories of Pamela and James Mason. Mason, P. O. and Mason, J. eds.

Favorite short stories. Sterner, L. G. ed.

Feast of Leviathan. Schwarz, L. W. ed.

Fêng, Mêng-lung, 1574?-1645
Stories from a Ming collection; translations of Chinese short stories published in the 17th century, by Cyril Birch. Bodley Head 1958 205p illus (UNESCO Collection of representative works: Chinese ser)

Fenner, Phyllis Reid, 1899-
(comp.) Brother against brother; stories of the War between the States; illus. by William R. Lohse. Morrow 1957 192p illus
Analyzed for short stories only
(ed.) Heroes, heroes, heroes; stories of rescue, courage and endurance; illus. by Bill Lohse. Watts, F. 1956 246p illus (Terrific triple title ser)

Fenton, Charles A.
(ed.) Best short stories of World War II; an American anthology. Viking 1957 428p

Ferber, Edna, 1887-
One basket; thirty-one short stories. Doubleday 1957 581p

Ferris, Helen Josephine, 1890-
(comp.) Girls, girls, girls; stories of love, courage, and the quest for happiness. Watts, F. 1956 241p (Terrific triple title ser)

Fifteen by three; R. V. Cassill, Herbert Gold [and] James B. Hall. New Directions 1957 248p (New Directions paperbk)

Finest stories of Sean O'Faolain. O'Faoláin, S.

Finney, Jack, 1912?-
The third level. Rinehart 1957 256p

First love and other sorrows. Brodkey, H.

First-prize stories, 1919-1957; from the O. Henry Memorial Awards; introduction by Harry Hansen. Hanover House 1957 552p

Fisher, Dorothea Frances (Canfield) 1879-1958
Harvest of stories; from a half century of writing, by Dorothy Canfield. Harcourt 1956 352p

Fitzgerald, Francis Scott Key, 1896-1940
Afternoon of an author; a selection of uncollected stories and essays. With an introduction and notes by Arthur Mizener. Scribner 1958 [c1957] 226p
Analyzed for short stories only

Five Galaxy short novels. Galaxy science fiction magazine

Five stories. Cather, W. S.

Flashes in the night. Juhasz, W. and Rothberg, A. A. eds.

Humphreville, Frances T. 1909-
(ed.) In other days; 15 stories; prepared under the direction of Betty Russell; designed and illus. by Catherine Hinkle. Scott 1956 252p illus map

Hundred years of sea stories. Kemp, P. K. ed.

The hunger, and other stories. Beaumont, C.

Hunting horn, and other dog stories. Annixter, P. pseud.

Huxley, Aldous Leonard, 1894-
Collected short stories. Harper 1957 397p

Hyacinth from Limbo, and other stories. Smith, J. R.

I

I couldn't help laughing. Nash, O. comp.

I don't want to shoot an elephant. Babcock, H.

In and out of school. Buckeridge, A. comp.

In other days. Humphreville, F. T. ed.

In this world and the next. Peretz, I. L.

Innes, Michael, pseud. See Stewart, John Innes Mackintosh

Introduction to literature. Locke, L. G.; Gibson, W. M. and Arms, G. W. eds.

Ivens, Bryna
(ed.) Seventeen (Periodical) Stories from Seventeen

J

James, Henry, 1843-1916
Selected short stories; ed. with an introduction by Quentin Anderson. Rev. ed. Rinehart 1957 xxiv, 357p (Rinehart eds)
Earlier edition indexed in main catalog

Jarrell, Randall, 1914-
(ed.) Anchor book of stories; selected and with an introduction. Doubleday 1958 330p (Doubleday Anchor bks)
Analyzed for short stories only

Japanese tales of mystery and imagination. Hirai, T.

Jennings, Frank G. and Calitri, Charles J.
(eds.) Stories. Harcourt 1957 394p
Analyzed for short stories only

Jet. Harvey, F. L.

Jewish Gauchos of the Pampas. Gerchunoff, A.

Johnston, R. T. 1913-
Century of a lifetime; illus. by the author. St Martins 1956 150p illus

Jones, Gwyn, 1907-
(ed.) Welsh short stories; selected and with an introduction. Oxford 1956 330p (World's classics)

Juhasz, William, and Rothberg, Abraham Alan, 1922-
(eds.) Flashes in the night; a collection of stories from contemporary Hungary; under the auspices of the East Europe Institute. Random House 1958 87p

K

Kemp, Peter Kemp
(ed.) Hundred years of sea stories; from Melville to Hemingway. British Bk. Service 1955 287p

Kentfield, Calvin, 1924-
The angel and the sailor; a novella and nine stories. McGraw 1957 217p

King of the mountain. Garrett, G.

King, Rufus, 1893-
Malice in wonderland. Doubleday 1958 187p

Kjelgaard, James Arthur, 1910-1959
(ed.) Western Writers of America. Hound dogs and others
(ed.) Western Writers of America. Wild horse roundup

Kjelgaard, Jim. See Kjelgaard, James Arthur

Kober, Arthur, 1900-
Oooh, what you said! Illus. by Frederick E. Banbery. Simon & Schuster 1958 184p illus

Kobler, Franz, 1882-
(ed.) Her children call her blessed; a portrait of the Jewish mother. Ed. with introduction and notes. Daye 1955 392p illus
Analyzed for short stories only

Kubly, Herbert, 1915-
Varieties of love. Simon & Schuster 1958 305p

L

La Farge, Oliver, 1901-
Pause in the desert; a collection of short stories. Houghton 1957 235p

Malamud, Bernard, 1914-
Magic barrel. Farrar, Straus 1958 214p

Malice in wonderland. King, R.

Mankowitz, Wolf, 1924-
Mendelman fire, and other stories. Little 1957 191p

March, William, pseud. See Campbell, William Edward March

Marjorie Rawlings reader. Rawlings, M. K.

The marked one, and twelve other stories. Picard, J.

Marlett, Melba Balmat (Grimes) 1909-
Frightened ones. Doubleday 1956 206p

Martian chronicles. Bradbury, R.

Martin, Hansford
(ed.) Prize stories, 1955-1956: the O. Henry awards. See Prize stories, 1955-1956: the O. Henry awards

Mask of Cthulhu. Derleth, A. W.

Mason, Pamela (Ostrer) 1915- and Mason, James, 1909-
(eds.) Favorite cat stories of Pamela and James Mason; illus. by Gladys Emerson Cook. Messner 1956 158p illus

Mason, James, 1909- See Mason, P. O. jt. ed.

Masters and masterpieces of the short story. McClennen, J. comp.

Masters of the modern short story. Havighurst, W. ed.

Maugham, William Somerset, 1874-
Best short stories; selected, and with an introduction, by John Beecroft. Modern Lib. 1957 489p

Maupassant, Guy de, 1850-1893
Complete short stories of Guy de Maupassant. Introduction by Artine Artinian. Hanover House 1955 1339p

Mayes, Herbert Raymond, 1900-
(ed.) Good housekeeping (Periodical) Editor's choice

Meany, Thomas William, 1903-
(ed.) Colliers (Periodical) Collier's Greatest sports stories

Meany, Tom. See Meany, Thomas William

Men from the sea. Wallenius, K. M.

Men in the field. Ward, L. L.

Mendelman fire, and other stories. Mankowitz, W.

Meredith, Scott, 1923-
(ed.) Bar 5; roundup of best Western stories; selected and with introductions by Scott Meredith. Dutton 1956 190p

(ed.) Bar 6; roundup of best Western stories; selected and with introductions by Scott Meredith. Dutton 1957 189p

Merril, Judith, 1923-
(ed.) S-F ['56] the year's greatest science-fiction and fantasy; with an introduction by Orson Welles. Gnome Press 1956 342p

(ed.) SF: '57; the years greatest science fiction and fantasy. Gnome Press 1957 320p

(ed.) SF: '58; the year's greatest science fiction and fantasy. Gnome Press 1958 255p
Analyzed for short stories only

A merry, merry Christmas book. Posselt, E. ed.

Miller, Ed Mack, 1921-
Tales of a fliers faith. Doubleday 1958 215p

Miller, Nolan, 1912-
(ed.) New campus writing, no. 2; ed. by Nolan Miller, assisted by Judson Jerome. Putnam 1957 277p
Analyzed for short stories only

Millholland, Ray, 1892?-1956
Blue Chip Haggerty; the collected stories. Morrow 1956 256p

Modern English short stories; 2d ser. Hudson, D. ed.

Modern French stories. Lehmann, J. ed.

Modern Irish short stories. O'Donovan, M. ed.

Modern Italian short stories. Slonim, M. L. ed.

Modern Italian stories. Strachan, W. J. ed.

Moment before the rain. Enright, E.

Montgomery, Robert Bruce, 1921-
(ed.) Best SF [one]-three; science fiction stories. Ed. with an introduction by Edmund Crispin [pseud]. Faber 1955-1958 3v

Moravia, Alberto, pseud. See Pincherle, Alberto

More Stories to remember. Costain, T. B. and Beecroft, J. eds.

Moretti, Ugo
Artists in Rome; tr. from the Italian by William Weaver. Macmillan (N Y) 1958 197p

Morison, Walter
(tr.) Babel', I. E. Collected stories

Morton, Frederic
(ed.) American vanguard, 1956. See American vanguard, 1956

My best murder story. Cooke, D. C. ed.

My Lady Happiness, and other short stories. Reid, L.

Mystery stories. Ellin, S.

Mystery Writers of America, inc.
  Big time mysteries, by members of the Mystery Writers of America, ed. by Brett Halliday [pseud]. Dodd 1958 242p

  A choice of murders; 23 stories by members of the Mystery Writers of America; ed. by Dorothy Salisbury Davis. Scribner 1958 312p

  Crime for two, by members of the Mystery Writers of America; ed. by Frances and Richard Lockridge. Lippincott 1955 256p

  For love or money; the 1957 anthology of The Mystery Writers of America; selected by Dorothy Gardiner. Doubleday 1957 233p

  For tomorrow we die, by members of the Mystery Writers of America; ed. and with an introduction by Rex Stout. MacDonald & Co. 1958 256p

N

N.Y. is all ours! and other stories. Tekeyan, C.

Nabokov, Vladimir Vladimirovich, 1899-
  Nabokov's dozen; a collection of thirteen stories. Doubleday 1958 214p

Nabokov's dozen. Nabokov, V. V.

Nash, Ogden, 1902-
  (comp.) I couldn't help laughing; stories selected and introduced by Ogden Nash. Lippincott 1957 231p
    Analyzed for short stories only

Nelson, George Edmondson, 1902-
  (ed.) Cavalcade of the North; an entertaining collection of distinguished writing by Canadian authors with an introduction by Thomas B. Costain. Doubleday 1958 640p
    Analyzed for short stories only

New campus writing, no. 2. Miller, N. ed.

New Directions in prose and poetry, 16. New Directions 1957 264p
    Analyzed for short stories only

New directions 15; an anthology of new directions in prose and poetry. International issue. New Directions 1955 328p illus
    Analyzed for short stories only

New Orleans sketches. Faulkner, W.

New short novels, 2; by Norman Mailer [and others]. Ballantine 1956 147p

New voices 2: American writing today; ed. by Don M. Wolfe. Hendricks House 1955 481p
    Analyzed for short stories only

New York call girl. Lowry, R. J. C.

Nightmares of eminent persons, and other stories. Russell, B. A. W. R. 3d earl

Nine horrors and a dream. Brennan, J. P.

9 tales of space and time. Healy, R. J. ed.

1955 anthology of best original short-shorts. Oberfirst, R. ed.

Nobody knows what the stork will bring, and other stories. Criswell, C.

Norton, Alice Mary
  (ed.) Space police; ed. with an introduction and notes by Andre Norton [pseud]. World Pub. 1956 255p

Norton, Andre, pseud. See Norton, Alice Mary

A **novel,** a novella and four stories. Lytle, A. N.

O

Oberfirst, Robert
  (ed.) Anthology of best short-short stories, v5. Introduction by Robert Fontaine; guest short-short, by Steve Allen. Fell 1957 281p
    Partially analyzed

  (ed.) Anthology of best short-short stories, v6. Introduction by Pat Frank; foreword by Arthur Gordon; guest short-short by Basil Rathbone. Fell 1958 375p

  (ed.) 1955 anthology of best original short-shorts; with a guest introduction by Duane Decker. Oberfirst Publications 1955 232p

O'Brian, Patrick, 1914-
  The walker, and other stories. Harcourt 1955 244p

O'Connor, Flannery, 1924?-
  A good man is hard to find, and other stories. Harcourt 1955 251p

O'Connor, Frank, pseud. See O'Donovan, Michael

October country. Bradbury, R.

O'Donovan, Joan
  Dangerous worlds; stories and tales. Morrow 1958 190p

Sandoz, Maurice Yves, 1892-
Fantastic memories. Doubleday 1957 146p

Sandrus, Mary Yost
(ed.) Famous mysteries; illus. by Don Merrick. Scott 1955 298p illus.

Sansom, William, 1912-
Among the dahlias, and other stories. Hogarth 1957 213p
Contest of ladies. Reynal & Co. 1956 255p
Touch of the sun. Reynal & Co. 1958 249p

Saroyan, William, 1908-
Whole voyald, and other stories. Little 1956 243p

Saturday evening post (Periodical)
Post Reader of Civil War stories; ed. by Gordon Carroll; with an introduction by E. B. Long. Illus. by Ray Houlihan. Doubleday 1958 331p illus
Saturday evening post Carnival of humor; ed. by Robert M. Yoder. Prentice-Hall 1958 362p illus
    Analyzed for short stories only
Saturday evening post stories, 1954-1957. Random House 1954-1957 4v

Saturday evening post stories. Saturday evening post (Periodical)

Schaefer, Jack Warner, 1907-
(ed.) Out West; an anthology of stories. Houghton 1955 331p

Schleyen, Milton
Stories for today's youth; illus. by Isabel Schleyen. Globe Bk. 1958 217p illus

Schwarz, Leo Walder, 1906-
(ed.) Feast of Leviathan; tales of adventure, faith and love from Jewish literature. Rinehart 1956 365p

Schwed, Peter, and Wind, Herbert Warren, 1918-
(eds.) Great stories from the world of sport. Simon & Schuster 1958 3v

Science-fiction adventures in mutation. Conklin, G. ed.

Scottish short stories. Urquhart, F. ed.

Scowcroft, Richard, 1916-
(ed.) Stanford short stories, 1954-1957. See Stanford short stories, 1954-1957

The screaming ghost, and other stories. Carmer, C. L.

Sieze the day. Bellow, S.

Selected short stories. James, H.

Selected short stories. O'Hara, J.

Selected stories. Wodehouse, P. G.

Selected stories of Sholom Aleichem. Rabinowitz, S.

Selection. Havighurst, W. and others, eds.

7 by Colette. Colette, S. G.

Seventeen (Periodical)
Seventeen's stories; stories from Seventeen magazine; selected and ed. by Babette Rosmond. Lippincott 1958 253p
Stories from Seventeen; selected by Bryna Ivens. Lippincott 1955 214p

Seventeen's stories. Seventeen (Periodical)

Sewall, Richard Benson. See Short, R. W. jt. ed.

Shaw, Irwin, 1913-
Tip on a dead jockey, and other stories. Random House 1957 242p

She-wolf, and other stories. Verga, G.

Sheckley, Robert, 1928-
Citizen in space. Ballantine 1955 200p

Ship's company. Coleman, W. L.

Sholom, Aleichem, pseud. See Rabinowitz, Shalom

Short, Raymond Wright, 1903- and Sewall, Richard Benson
(eds.) Short stories for study; an anthology. 3d ed. Holt 1956 618p
    Earlier editions indexed in main catalog and in the 1950-1954 supplement

Short stories; v 1 by Geo Bogza [and others]. "The Book" Pub. House 1955 204p (Rumanian contemporary authors)

Short stories for study. Short, R. W. and Sewall, R. B. eds.

Short story. Hall, J. B. and Langland, J. T. eds.

Short story, 1; The best of everything, stories by Richard Yates; The houses of the city, stories by Gina Berriault; The family tree, stories by B. L. Barrett; Come to the fair, stories by Seymour Epstein. Scribner 1958 304p

Short story magic. Swayze, B. ed.

Simak, Clifford Donald, 1904-
Strangers in the universe; science-fiction stories. Simon & Schuster 1956 371p

Singer, Isaac Bashevis, 1904-
Gimpel the fool, and other stories. Noonday 1957 205p

Six feet of the country. Gordimer, N.

Skelton, Peter
(ed.) Animals all; stories selected by Peter Skelton. Foreword by "Elephant Bill." Day 1956 [c1955] 253p illus

    & Schuster 1954 429p

Slonim, Mark L'vovich
(ed.) Modern Italian short stories, ed. by Marc Slonim. Simon

Smith, Edith Hutchins, 1914–
 El Tigre! Mexican short stories;
 illus. by Elizabeth Toth Spencer. Blair, J.F. 1956 178p illus

Smith, Edmund Ware, 1900–
 The one-eyed poacher and the
 Maine woods; with an introduction by Bernard DeVoto. Fell
 1955 269p

Smith, Jean Rogers
 Hyacinth from Limbo, and other
 stories. Philosophical Lib. 1958
 59p

Smith, Shelley, pseud. See Bodington, Nancy

Sneider, Vern J. 1916–
 Long way from home, and other
 stories. Putnam 1956 256p

Something about my father, and
 other people. Angoff, C.

Sørensen, Villi, 1929–
 Tiger in the kitchen, and other
 strange stories, by Villy Sørensen; tr. from the Danish by
 Maureen Neiiendam. With an
 introduction by Angus Wilson.
 Abelard-Schuman 1957 204p

Sørensen, Villy. See Sørensen, Villi

Sound the great trumpet. Frank,
 M. Z. ed.

Southern reader. Thorp, W. ed.

Space police. Norton, A. M. ed.

Sports stories for boys. Olgin, J.

Stanford short stories, 1954. Ed. by
 Wallace Stegner and Richard
 Scowcroft. Stories by Jean
 Byers [and others]. Stanford
 Univ. Press 1954 173p

Stanford short stories, 1955. Ed. by
 Wallace Stegner and Richard
 Scowcroft. Stories by Mary
 Fassett Hunt [and others].
 Stanford Univ. Press 1955 167p

Stanford short stories, 1956. Ed. by
 Wallace Stegner and Richard
 Scowcroft. Stories by Ebe S.
 Seidenberg [and others]. Stan-
 ford Univ. Press 1956 149p

Stanford short stories, 1957; ed. by
 Wallace Stegner [and] Richard
 Scowcroft; foreword by Mal-
 colm Cowley. Stanford Univ.
 Press 1957 145p

Stanford short stories, 1958, ed. by
 Wallace Stegner [and] Richard
 Scowcroft. Stories by Peter
 Shrubb [and others]. Stanford
 Univ. Press 1958 170p

Stead, Christina, 1902–
 (ed.) Great stories of the South
 Sea Islands. Saunders, S.J.R.
 1956 223p

Stegner, Wallace Earle, 1909–
 City of the living, and other stories. Houghton 1956 206p
 (ed.) Stanford short stories, 1954–
 1958. See Stanford short stories, 1954-1958

Sterner, Lewis George, 1894–
 (ed.) Favorite short stories; selected and ed. by Lewis G.
 Sterner. Globe Bk. 1958 512p
 illus

Stewart, John Innes Mackintosh,
 1906–
 Appleby talks again, by Michael
 Innes [pseud]. Dodd 1957 [c1956]
 189p

Stivens, Dallas, 1911–
 (comp.) Coast to coast; Aus-
 tralian stories, 1957-1958; illus.
 by Jennifer Murray. Angus 1958
 217p illus

Stockton, Frank Richard, 1834-1902
 Best short stories. Scribner 1957
 128p

Stories [by] Jean Stafford [and
 others]. Farrar, Straus 1956
 309p

Stories. Jennings, F. G. and Calitri,
 C. J. eds.

Stories for today's youth. Schleyen,
 M.

Stories from a Ming collection.
 Feng, M.

Stories from many lands. Rosenblum, M. ed.

Stories of Liam O'Flaherty. O'Flaherty, L.

Stories of mystery and suspense,
 This week's. This week magazine

Stories of scientific imagination.
 Gallant, J. ed.

Stories to remember. Costain, T. B.
 and Beecroft, J. eds.

Stories to remember. McMaster, J.
 ed.

Stout, Rex, 1886–
 (ed.) Mystery Writers of America, inc. For tomorrow we die

Stowe, Aurelia
 (comp.) When boy dates girl;
 boy-girl stories for the teens.
 Random House 1956 215p

Strachan, Walter John, 1903–
 (ed.) Modern Italian stories. Philosophical Lib. 1956 [c1955] 304p

Strang, Ruth May, 1895–
 (ed.) Teen-age tales, bk 3 and
 bk 6. See Teen-age tales, bk 3
 and bk 6

Strange adventures in science fiction. Conklin, G. ed.

Strangers in the universe. Simak,
 C. D.

Strangers were there. Clayton, J. B.

Stuart, Jesse, 1907–
 Plowshare in heaven; stories.
 McGraw 1958 273p illus

Sturgeon, Theodore, pseud. See
 Waldo, Edward Hamilton

Summer in Salandar. Bates, H. E.

The survivor, and others. Lovecraft,
 H. P. and Derleth, A. W.

Swados, Harvey, 1920-
On the line. Little 1957 233p

Swayze, Beulah
(ed.) Short story magic; a collection of short stories for grades IX and X; ed. with notes and questions. Ryerson Press 1955 184p

T

Tales of a flier's faith. Miller, E. M.

Tales of Conan. Howard, R. E. and De Camp, L. S.

Tales of courage and conflict, Tolstoy's. Tolstoĭ, L. N. Graf

Tales of the East and West. Conrad, J.

Tales of the Long Bow. Chesterton, G. K.

Teen-age humorous stories. Furman, A. L. ed.

Teen-age super science stories. Elam, R. M.

Teen-age tales, bks 3-6. Heath 1956-1958 4v illus
Volumes 1 and 2 indexed in 1950-1954 supplement under editors: R. M. Strang and R. M. Roberts
Analyzed for short stories only

Tehilla, and other Israeli tales [by] S. J. Agnon [and others]. Tr. by I. M. Laska [and others]. Abelard-Schuman 1956 271p (Ram's horn bks)

Tekeyan, Charles
N. Y. is all ours! and other stories. Beekman 1956 136p

Tell me a story. Laughton, C. ed.

10 contemporary Polish stories. Ordon, E. ed.

Ten modern short novels. Hamalian, L. and Volpe, E. L. eds.

Thanks to the Saint. Charteris, L.

That marriage bed of Procrustes, and other stories. Curley, D.

Their guns were fast. Drago, H. S.

Third Galaxy reader. Galaxy science fiction magazine

The **third** level. Finney, J.

A **thirsty** evil. Vidal, G.

Thirty stories. Boyle, K.

This is my best humor. Burnett, W. ed.

This week magazine
This week's Stories of mystery and suspense; ed. with a preface, notes and an essay, How to write the mystery and suspense story, by Stewart Beach. Introduction by Alfred Hitchcock. Random House 1957 330p

This week's Stories of mystery and suspense. This week magazine

Thomas, Dylan, 1914-1953
Adventures in the skin trade, and other stories. New Directions 1955 275p
Analyzed for short stories only

Thorp, Willard, 1899-
(ed.) Southern reader. Knopf 1955 xxi, 760p illus
Analyzed for short stories only

Three flights up, seven down. Byrd, J. J.

Thurston, Jarvis A.
(ed.) Reading modern short stories. Scott 1955 720p

Tibbets, Albert B.
(ed.) Youth, youth, youth; stories of · challenge, confidence and comradeship; selected by Albert B. Tibbets. Watts, F. 1955 246p

Tiger in the kitchen, and other strange stories. Sørensen, V.

El **Tigre!** Smith, E. H.

Tip on a dead jockey, and other stories. Shaw, I.

Tolstoĭ, Alekseĭ Nikolaevich, Graf, 1882-1945
A week in Turenevo, and other stories, by Alexei Tolstoy; introduction by George Reavey. Grove 1958 (Evergreen bks) 187p

Tolstoĭ, Lev Nikolaevĭch, Graf, 1828-1910
Tolstoy's Tales of courage and conflict, by Count Leo N. Tolstoy; ed. with an introduction by Charles Neider. Hanover House 1958 574p

Tolstoy, Alexei. See Tolstoĭ, Alekseĭ Nikolaevich, Graf

Tolstoy, Leo N. count. See Tolstoĭ, Lev Nikolaevĭch, Graf

Touch of strange. Waldo, E. H.

Touch of the sun. Sansom, W.

Treasure cruise, and other Crunch and Des stories. Wylie, P.

Treasury of American Jewish stories. Ribalow, H. U. ed.

Treasury of great mysteries. Haycraft, H. and Beecroft, J. eds.

Treasury of new short fiction. Bronfeld, S. ed.

Treasury of Sherlock Holmes. Doyle, Sir A. C.

Treasury of snake lore. Aymar, B. ed.

The **trusting** and the maimed, and other Irish stories. Plunkett, J.

Truth is stranger than fishin'. Cook, B. G.

Two by two. Gellhorn, M. E.

U

The **ugly** American. Lederer, W. J. and Burdick, E. L.

Unamuno y Jugo, Miguel de, 1864-1936
Abel Sanchez, and other stories; tr. and with an introduction by Anthony Kerrigan. Gateway eds. distributed by Regnery 1956 216p

Urquhart, Fred, 1912-
(ed.) Scottish short stories. ₁3d rev. ed₁ Faber 1957 246p

V

Valiant ones. Fox, N. A.

Van Doren, Mark, 1894-
Home with Hazel, and other stories. Harcourt 1957 248p

Varieties of love. Kubly, H.

Verga, Giovanni, 1840-1922
She-wolf, and other stories. Tr. with an introduction by Giovanni Cecchetti. Univ. of Calif. Press 1958 197p illus

Victoria at night, and other stories. Beigel, U.

Vidal, Gore, 1925-
A thirsty evil; seven short stories. Zero Press 1956 154p

Violence. Woolrich, C.

Volpe, Edmond Louis, 1922- See Hamalian, L. jt. ed.

W

Waldo, Edward Hamilton, 1918-
Caviar, by Theodore Sturgeon ₁pseud₁. Ballantine 1955 167p

Touch of strange, by Theodore Sturgeon ₁pseud₁. Doubleday 1958 262p

Way home, by Theodore Sturgeon ₁pseud₁; stories of science fiction and fantasy; selected and with an introduction by Groff Conklin. Funk 1955 333p

The **walker,** and other stories. O'Brian, P.

Wallenius, Kurt Martti, 1893-
Men from the sea. Tr. from the Finnish by Alan Blair; with an introduction by Vilhjalmur Stefansson. Oxford 1955 268p illus

Ward, Don
(ed.) Western Writers of America. Branded West

(ed.) Western Writers of America. Hoof trails and wagon tracks

Ward, Leo Lewis, 1898-1953
Men in the field; eighteen short stories; with a foreword by John T. Frederick. Univ. of Notre Dame Press 1955 248p

Warner, Sylvia Townsend, 1893-
Winter in the air, and other stories. Viking 1956 ₁c1955₁ 249p

Way home. Waldo, E. H.

A **week** in Turenevo, and other stories. Tolstoĭ, A. N. Graf

Welcome, John, and Orchard, Vincent
(eds.) Best hunting stories. Faber 1954 320p

Welsh short stories. Jones, G. ed.

Welty, Eudora, 1909-
Bride of the Innisfallen, and other stories. Harcourt 1955 207p

West, Anthony C. 1910-
River's end, and other stories. McDowell, Obolensky 1958 204p

West, Jessamyn
Love, death, and the ladies' drill team. Harcourt 1955 248p

Western Writers of America
Branded West; a Western Writers of America anthology; ed. by Don Ward. Houghton 1956 242p

Hoof trails and wagon tracks. Stories of the Western trails by members of Western Writers of America; ed. with an introduction by Don Ward. Dodd 1957 298p

Hound dogs and others; a collection of stories by members of Western Writers of America; ed. by Jim Kjelgaard; illus. by Paul Brown. Dodd 1958 245p illus

Wild horse roundup; a collection of stories by members of Western Writers of America; ed. by Jim Kjelgaard; illus. by Paul Brown. Dodd 1957 275p illus

Wild streets; tales of the frontier towns by members of the Western Writers of America; ed. with an introduction by Don Ward. Doubleday 1958 285p
Analyzed for short stories only

Wharton, Edith Newbold (Jones) 1862-1937
Best short stories of Edith Wharton; ed. with an introduction by Wayne Andrews. Scribner 1958 292p

When boy dates girl. Stowe, A. comp.

White, William Anthony Parker, 1911-
Far and away; eleven fantasy and science-fiction stories, by Anthony Boucher ₁pseud₁. Ballantine 1955 166p

Directory of Publishers

Abelard-Schuman. Abelard-Schuman, Ltd, Publishers, 6 W 57th St, N.Y. 19

Advent. Advent Publishers, 3508 N Sheffield Av, Chicago 13

Angus. Angus & Robertson, 89 Castlereagh St, Sydney, N.S.W.

Arkham House, Sauk City, Wis.

Ballantine. Ballantine Books, Inc, 101 5th Av, N.Y. 3

Barnes, A.S. A. S. Barnes & Company, Inc, 11 E 36th St, N.Y. 16

Batchworth. Batchworth Press, Ltd, Spring Pl, London, N.W. 5

Beacon Press, Inc, 25 Beacon St, Boston 8

Beekman, 17 E 48th St, N.Y. 17

Blackie & Son, Ltd, 17 Stanhope St, Glasgow, C, 4

Blair, J. F. John F. Blair, Publisher, 404 First National Bank Bldg, Winston-Salem, N.C.

Bobbs. The Bobbs-Merrill Company, Inc, 1720 E 38th St, Indianapolis 6

Bodley Head. The Bodley Head, John Lane, Ltd, 10 Earlham St, London, W.C. 2

"The Book" Pub. House. "The Book" Publishing House, Bucharest, Rumania

British Bk. Service. British Book Service, Ltd, Kingswood House, 1068 Broadview Av, Toronto 6

Cambridge Pub. Co. Cambridge Publishing Company, 315 E 69th St, N.Y. 21

Chilton Co. Chilton Company, Book Division, 56th & Chesnut Sts, Philadelphia 39

Copp. The Copp Clark Company, Ltd, 495-517 Wellington St, W, Toronto 2B

Coward-McCann, Inc, 210 Madison Av, N.Y. 16

Criterion Bks. Criterion Books, Inc, 6 W 57th St, N.Y. 19

Crowell. Thomas Y. Crowell Company, 432 Park Av, S, N.Y. 16

Day. John Day Company, Inc, 210 Madison Av, N.Y. 16

Daye. Stephen Daye Press, Inc. See Ungar

Devin-Adair. The Devin-Adair Company, Publishers, 23 E 26th St, N.Y. 10

Dial Press, inc, 461 Park Av, S, N.Y. 16

Dodd. Dodd, Mead & Company, Inc, 432 Park Av, S, N.Y. 16

Doubleday. Doubleday & Company, Inc, 575 Madison Av, N.Y. 22

Dryden. See Holt

Dutton. E. P. Dutton & Company, Inc, 300 Park Av, S, N.Y. 10

Faber. Faber & Faber, Ltd, 24 Russell Sq, London, W.C. 1

Farrar, Straus. Farrar, Straus & Cudahy, Inc, 101 5th Av, N.Y. 3

Fell. Frederick Fell, Inc, 386 4th Av, N.Y. 16

Funk. Funk & Wagnalls Company, 153 E 24th St, N.Y. 10

Globe Bk. Globe Book Company, Inc, 175 5th Av, N.Y. 10

Gnome Press, Inc, Box 161, Hicksville, N.Y.

Grayson. Grayson & Grayson, Ltd, 16 Maddox St, London, W. 1

Greenberg. See Chilton Co.

Grosset. Grosset & Dunlap, Inc, 1107 Broadway, N.Y. 10

Grove. Grove Press, 64 University Pl, N.Y. 3

Hanover House. See Doubleday

Harcourt. Harcourt, Brace and Company, 750 3d Av, N.Y. 17

Harper. Harper & Brothers, 49 E 33d St, N.Y. 16

Harvey House. Harvey House, Publishers, 5 S Buckhout St, Irvington-on-Hudson, N.Y.

Heath. D. C. Heath & Company, 285 Columbus Av, Boston 16

Hendricks House. Hendricks House, Inc, Publishers, 103 Park Av, N.Y. 7

Hill & Wang. Hill and Wang, Inc, Publishers, 104 5th Av, N.Y. 11

Hodder. Hodder & Stoughton, Ltd, St Paul's House, 20 Warwick St, London, E.C. 4

Hogarth. Hogarth Press, Ltd, 40-42 William IV St, London, W.C. 2

Hokuseido. The Hokuseido Press, 12, 3-Chome Nishikicho, Kanda, Chiyoda-Ku, Tokyo

Holt. Holt, Rinehart & Winston, Inc, 383 Madison, Av, N.Y. 17

Houghton. Houghton Mifflin Company, 2 Park St, Boston 7

Jewish Pub. Jewish Publication Society of American, 222 N 15th St, Philadelphia 2

Kenedy. P. J. Kenedy & Sons, 12 Barclay St, N.Y. 8

Knopf. Alfred A. Knopf, Inc, 501 Madison Av, N.Y. 22

Lantern Press (N Y). Lantern Press, Inc, 257 4th Av, N.Y. 10

Lawrence. Lawrence & Wishart, Ltd, 81 Chancery Lane, London, W.C. 2

Liberal Arts. Liberal Arts Press, Inc, 153 W 72d St, N.Y. 23

Lippincott. J. B. Lippincott Company, E. Washington Sq, Philadelphia 5

Little. Little, Brown & Company, 34 Beacon St, Boston 6

Longmans (Toronto) Longmans, Green & Company, 20 Cranfield Rd, Toronto 16

MacDonald & Company, Ltd, 16 Maddox St, London, W. 1

McDowell, Obolensky. See Obolensky

McGraw. McGraw-Hill Book Company, Inc, 330 W 42d St, N.Y. 36

Macmillan (N Y) The Macmillan Company, Publishers, 60 5th Av, N.Y. 11

Merlin. Merlin Press, Inc, 250 W 57th St, N.Y. 19

Messner. Julian Messner, Inc, Publishers, 8 W 40th St, N.Y. 18

Modern Lib. Modern Library, Inc, 457 Madison Av, N.Y. 22

Morrow. William Morrow & Company, Inc, Publishers, 425 Park Av, S, N.Y. 16

Nat. Pub. Co. National Publishing Company, 15 W 44th St, N.Y. 36

Naylor. The Naylor Company, 918 N St Mary's St, San Antonio 6, Tex.

New Directions, Norfolk, Conn.

Noonday. The Noonday Press, 101 5th Av, N.Y. 3

Norton. W. W. Norton & Company, Inc, Publishers, 55 5th Av, N.Y. 3

Oberfirst Publications, Box 539 Ocean City, N.J.

Obolensky. Ivan Obolensky, Inc, 219 E 61st, N.Y. 21

Odhams. Odhams Press, Ltd, Book Department, 24 Henrietta St, London, W.C. 2

Orr, E. E. Orr, Box 82, Shelby, Miss.

Oxford. Oxford University Press, 16-00 Pollitt Drive, Fair Lawn, N.J.

Oxford Bk. Co. Oxford Book Company, Inc, 71 5th Av, N.Y. 3

Pantheon Bks. Pantheon Books, Inc, 333 6th Av, N.Y. 14

Philosophical Lib. Philosophical Library, Inc, 15 E 40th St, N.Y. 16

Prentice-Hall, Inc, Route 9W, Englewood Cliffs, N.J.

Putnam. G. P. Putnam's Sons, Inc, 210 Madison Av, N.Y. 16

Random House, Inc, 33 W 60th St, N.Y. 23

Regnery. Henry Regnery Company, Publishers, 64 E Jackson Blvd, Chicago 4

Reynal & Co. Reynal & Company, Inc, 221 E 49th St, N.Y. 17

Rinehart. See Holt

Rutgers Univ. Press. Rutgers University Press, 30 College Av, New Brunswick, N.J.

Ryerson Press, 299 Queen St, W, Toronto 2B

St Martins. St Martin's Press, Inc, 175 5th Av, N.Y. 10

Saunders, S.J.R. S. J. Reginald Saunders & Company, Ltd, 266 King St, W, Toronto 2B

Scribner. Charles Scribner's Sons, 597-599 5th Av, N.Y. 17

Scott. Scott, Foresman & Company, Educational Publishers, 433 E Erie St, Chicago 11

Sheed. Sheed & Ward Inc, 64 University Pl, N.Y. 3

Simon & Schuster. Simon and Schuster, Inc, Publishers, 630 5th Av, N.Y. 20

Stanford Univ. Press. Stanford University Press, Stanford, Calif.

Trempealeau Press, 109 South St, Baltimore 2

Tuttle. Charles E. Tuttle Company, 28-30 S Main St, Rutland, Vt.

Ukrainska Knyha, 1162 Dundas St, W, Toronto

Ungar. Frederick Ungar Publishing Company, 131 E 23d St, N.Y. 10

Univ. of Calif. Press. University of California Press, Berkeley 4, Calif.

Univ. of Minn. Press. University of Minnesota Press, 2037 University Av, S.E, Minneapolis 14

Univ. of Notre Dame Press. University of Notre Dame Press, Notre Dame, Ind.

Univ. of Okla. Press. University of Oklahoma Press, Faculty Exchange, Norman, Okla.

Univ. of Tex. Press. University of Texas Press, 2211 Red River St, Austin 12, Tex.

Vanguard. The Vanguard Press, 424 Madison Av, N.Y. 17

Viking. The Viking Press, Inc, Publishers, 625 Madison Av, N.Y. 22

Vintage. Vintage Books, Inc, 501 Madison Av, N.Y. 22

Watts, F. Franklin Watts, Inc, 575 Lexington Av, N.Y. 22

Wayne State Univ. Press. Wayne State University Press, 4841 Cass Av, Detroit 2

Whittier Bks. Whittier Books, Inc, 31 Union Sq, N.Y. 3

World Pub. The World Publishing Company, 2231 W 110th St, Cleveland 2

Yoseloff. Thomas Yoseloff, Inc, Publisher, 11 E 36th St, N.Y. 16

Zero Press. Out of business